Java EE Development with Eclipse

Second Edition

AF764162

Develop, debug, test, and troubleshoot Java EE 7 applications rapidly with Eclipse

Ram Kulkarni

[PACKT] PUBLISHING open source
community experience distilled

BIRMINGHAM - MUMBAI

Java EE Development with Eclipse

Second Edition

First published: December 2012

Second edition: September 2015

Production reference: 1240915

Published by Packt Publishing Ltd.
Livery Place
35 Livery Street
Birmingham B3 2PB, UK.

ISBN 978-1-78528-534-9

www.packtpub.com

Credits

Author
Ram Kulkarni

Reviewers
Aristides Villarreal Bravo
Jeff Maury
Phil Wilkins

Commissioning Editor
Neil Alexander

Acquisition Editor
Kevin Colaco

Content Development Editor
Nikhil Potdukhe

Technical Editor
Tanmayee Patil

Copy Editors
Tani Kothari
Kausambhi Majumdar
Alpha Singh

Project Coordinator
Izzat Contractor

Proofreader
Safis Editing

Indexer
Tejal Soni

Production Coordinator
Manu Joseph

Cover Work
Manu Joseph

About the Author

Ram Kulkarni has more than two decades of experience in developing software. He has architected and developed many enterprise web applications, client-server and desktop applications, application servers, IDE, and mobile applications. Also, he is the author of *Eclipse 4 RCP Development How-to* published by Packt Publishing. He blogs at `ramkulkarni.com`.

I would like to thank Kevin Colaco and Nikhil Potdukhe of Packt Publishing for giving me the opportunity to write this book and helping me decide the content and format.

Writing this book has been a long process, and it would not have been possible without the support and patience of my family.

I would like to thank my parents, my wife, Vandana, and son, Akash, for their continuous love and support. This book is dedicated to Vandana and Akash.

About the Reviewers

Aristides Villarreal Bravo is a Java developer and a member of the NetBeans Dream Team and Java User Groups leaders. He lives in Panamá.

He has organized and participated in various national as well as international conferences and seminars related to Java, JavaEE, NetBeans, NetBeans Platform, free software, and mobile devices. He has been a writer of tutorials and blogs on Java, NetBeans, and web developers.

He has participated in several interviews on sites such as NetBeans, NetBeans DZone, and javaHispano. Also, he has been a developer of plugins for NetBeans. He has written technical reviews of many books on PrimeFaces, that includes *Primefaces BluePrints, Packt Publising*.

He is also the CEO of Javscaz Software Developers.

I would like to dedicate this to Oris in the sky.

Jeff Maury is currently working as the technical lead of the Java team at SysperTec Communication, a French ISV that offers mainframe integration tools.

Prior to SysperTec Communication, in 1996, he was a cofounder of a French ISV called SCORT, a precursor to the application server concept that offered J2EE-based integration tools.

He started his career in 1988 at Marben Products, a French integration company that specialized in telecommunication protocols. At Marben Products, he started as a software developer and left as an X.400 team technical lead and Internet division strategist.

I would like to dedicate my work to Jean-Pierre ANSART, my mentor, and thank my wife, Julia, for her patience, and my three sons, Robinson, Paul, and Ugo.

Phil Wilkins has spent over 25 years in the software industry working for both multinationals and software startups. He started out as a developer and worked his way up through technical and developmental leadership roles, primarily in Java-based environments. Currently, he is working as an enterprise technical architect in the IT group of a global optical healthcare manufacturer and retailer using Oracle middleware, cloud, and Red Hat JBoss technologies.

Outside his work commitments, he has contributed his technical capabilities to supporting others in a wide range of activities that include developing community websites, providing input and support to people authoring books, developing software ideas and businesses, and reviewing a range of technical books for Packt and other publishers. Also, he is a blogger and a participant in the Oracle middleware community.

When not immersed in work and technology, he spends his downtime pursuing his passion for music and with his wife and two boys.

I'd like to take this opportunity to thank my wife, Catherine, and our two sons, Christopher and Aaron, for their tolerance for the innumerable hours that I've spent in front of a computer contributing to activities for both my employer and other IT-related activities that I've supported over the years.

www.PacktPub.com

Support files, eBooks, discount offers, and more

For support files and downloads related to your book, please visit www.PacktPub.com.

Did you know that Packt offers eBook versions of every book published, with PDF and ePub files available? You can upgrade to the eBook version at www.PacktPub.com and as a print book customer, you are entitled to a discount on the eBook copy. Get in touch with us at service@packtpub.com for more details.

At www.PacktPub.com, you can also read a collection of free technical articles, sign up for a range of free newsletters and receive exclusive discounts and offers on Packt books and eBooks.

PACKTLIB™

https://www2.packtpub.com/books/subscription/packtlib

Do you need instant solutions to your IT questions? PacktLib is Packt's online digital book library. Here, you can search, access, and read Packt's entire library of books.

Why subscribe?

- Fully searchable across every book published by Packt
- Copy and paste, print, and bookmark content
- On demand and accessible via a web browser

Free access for Packt account holders

If you have an account with Packt at www.PacktPub.com, you can use this to access PacktLib today and view 9 entirely free books. Simply use your login credentials for immediate access.

Table of Contents

Preface

Java 2 Enterprise Edition (J2EE) has been used to develop enterprise applications for many years. It provides a standard technique to implement the many aspects of an enterprise application, such as handling web requests, accessing database, connecting to other enterprise systems, and implementing web services. Over the years, it has evolved and made enterprise application development easier than before. Its name has changed as well, from J2EE to JEE, after the J2EE version 1.4. Currently, it is in version 7.

Eclipse is a popular Integrated Development Environment (IDE) for developing Java applications. It has a version specific to the JEE development too, which makes it faster to write code and easier to deploy JEE applications on a server. It provides excellent debugging and unit testing support. Eclipse has a modular architecture, and many plugins are available today to extend its functionality for performing many different tasks.

This book provides you with all the information that you will need to use Eclipse to develop, deploy, debug, and test JEE applications. The focus of this book is to provide you with practical examples of how to develop applications using JEE and Eclipse. The scope of this book is not limited to JEE technologies, but covers other technologies used in the different phases of application development as well, such as source control, unit testing, and profiling.

JEE is a collection of many technologies and specifications. Some of the technologies are so vast that separate books will have to be written on them and many have been already written. This book takes the approach of providing you with a brief introduction to each technology in JEE and provides links for detailed information. Then it moves on to develop sample applications using specific technologies under discussion and explains the finer aspects of the technologies in the context of the sample applications.

This book could be useful to you if you are new to JEE and want to get started with developing JEE applications quickly. You will also find this book useful if you are familiar with JEE but looking for hands-on approach to use some of the technologies in JEE.

What this book covers

Chapter 1, Introducing JEE and Eclipse, explains in brief the different technologies in JEE and where they fit in a typical multitier JEE application. This chapter describes installing Eclipse JEE, Tomcat, GlassFish, and MySQL, which are used to develop sample applications in the later chapters.

Chapter 2, Creating a Simple JEE Web Application, describes the development of web applications using JSP, Servlet, JSTL, and JSF. It also explains how to use Maven for project management.

Chapter 3, Source Control Management in Eclipse, explains how to use the SVN and Git plugins of Eclipse for source code management.

Chapter 4, Creating a JEE Database Application, explains the creation of database applications using JDBC and JPA. You will learn how to execute SQL statements directly using JDBC, map Java classes to database tables, and set relationships between classes using the JPA and database connection pool.

Chapter 5, Unit Testing, describes how to write and run unit tests for Java applications, mock external dependencies in unit tests, and calculate the code coverage.

Chapter 6, Debugging a JEE Application, shows the techniques used to debug JEE applications and covers the debugging support of Eclipse.

Chapter 7, Creating JEE Applications with EJB, describes the use of EJBs to code business logic in the JEE applications. Also, it explains how to connect to remote EJBs using JNDI and inject EJBs into container-managed beans.

Chapter 8, Creating Web Applications with Spring MVC, describes the creation of web applications using Spring MVC and how some of the JEE technologies can be used in a Spring MVC application.

Chapter 9, Creating Web Services, explains the creation of SOAP-based and RESTful web services in JEE applications. You will learn how to consume these web services from JEE applications as well.

Chapter 10, Asynchronous Programming with JMS, shows explains how to write applications to process messages asynchronously. It describes how to program queues and topics of messaging systems using JMS and MDBs.

Chapter 11, Java CPU Profiling and Memory Tracking, describes the techniques for profiling CPU and memory in Java applications to find performance bottlenecks.

What you need for this book

You will need JDK 1.7 or later, Eclipse JEE 4.4 or later, Tomcat 7 or later, GlassFish Server 4 or later, and MySQL Community Server 5.6 or later.

Who this book is for

If you are a Java developer who has little or no experience in JEE application development, or you have an experience in JEE technology but are looking for tips to simplify and accelerate your development process, then this book is for you.

Conventions

In this book, you will find a number of text styles that distinguish between different kinds of information. Here are some examples of these styles and an explanation of their meaning.

Code words in text, database table names, folder names, filenames, file extensions, pathnames, dummy URLs, user input, and Twitter handles are shown as follows: "We can include other contexts through the use of the `include` directive."

A block of code is set as follows:

```
<body>
  <h2>Login:</h2>
  <form method="post">
    User Name: <input type="text" name="userName"><br>
    Password: <input type="password" name="password"><br>
    <button type="submit" name="submit">Submit</button>
    <button type="reset">Reset</button>
  </form>
</body>
```

When we wish to draw your attention to a particular part of a code block, the relevant lines or items are set in bold:

```
try {
  Thread.sleep(5000);
} catch (InterruptedException e) {}
```

Any command-line input or output is written as follows:

```
>catalina.bat jpda start
```

New terms and **important words** are shown in bold. Words that you see on the screen, for example, in menus or dialog boxes, appear in the text like this: "To set a breakpoint for an exception, select **Run | Java Breakpoint Exception** and select the `Exception` class from the list."

> Warnings or important notes appear in a box like this.

> Tips and tricks appear like this.

Reader feedback

Feedback from our readers is always welcome. Let us know what you think about this book—what you liked or disliked. Reader feedback is important for us as it helps us develop titles that you will really get the most out of.

To send us general feedback, simply e-mail `feedback@packtpub.com`, and mention the book's title in the subject of your message.

If there is a topic that you have expertise in and you are interested in either writing or contributing to a book, see our author guide at `www.packtpub.com/authors`.

Customer support

Now that you are the proud owner of a Packt book, we have a number of things to help you to get the most from your purchase.

Downloading the example code

You can download the example code files from your account at http://www.packtpub.com for all the Packt Publishing books you have purchased. If you purchased this book elsewhere, you can visit http://www.packtpub.com/support and register to have the files e-mailed directly to you.

Errata

Although we have taken every care to ensure the accuracy of our content, mistakes do happen. If you find a mistake in one of our books—maybe a mistake in the text or the code—we would be grateful if you could report this to us. By doing so, you can save other readers from frustration and help us improve subsequent versions of this book. If you find any errata, please report them by visiting http://www.packtpub.com/submit-errata, selecting your book, clicking on the **Errata Submission Form** link, and entering the details of your errata. Once your errata are verified, your submission will be accepted and the errata will be uploaded to our website or added to any list of existing errata under the Errata section of that title.

To view the previously submitted errata, go to https://www.packtpub.com/books/content/support and enter the name of the book in the search field. The required information will appear under the **Errata** section.

Piracy

Piracy of copyrighted material on the Internet is an ongoing problem across all media. At Packt, we take the protection of our copyright and licenses very seriously. If you come across any illegal copies of our works in any form on the Internet, please provide us with the location address or website name immediately so that we can pursue a remedy.

Please contact us at copyright@packtpub.com with a link to the suspected pirated material.

We appreciate your help in protecting our authors and our ability to bring you valuable content.

Questions

If you have a problem with any aspect of this book, you can contact us at questions@packtpub.com, and we will do our best to address the problem.

1

Introducing JEE and Eclipse

Java Enterprise Edition (JEE, which was earlier called J2EE) has been around for many years now. It is a very robust platform for developing enterprise applications. J2EE was first released in 1999, but underwent major changes in version 5, in 2006. Since version 5, it has been renamed **Java Enterprise Edition** (**JEE**). Recent versions of JEE has made developing a multi-tier distributed application a lot easier. J2EE had focused on core services and had left the tasks that made application development easier to external frameworks, for example, MVC and persistent frameworks. But JEE has brought many of these frameworks in the core services. Along with the support for annotations, these services simplify application development to a large extent.

Any runtime technology is not good without great development tools. **Integrated Development Environment** (**IDE**) plays a major part in developing applications faster, and Eclipse provides just that for JEE. Not only do you get a good editing support in Eclipse, but you also get support for build, unit testing, version control, and many other tasks important in different phases of software application development.

The goal of this book is to show how you can efficiently develop JEE application using Eclipse by using many of its features during different phases of the application development. But first, the following is a brief introduction to JEE and Eclipse.

Java Enterprise Edition (JEE)

JEE is a collection of many different specifications intended to perform specific tasks. These specifications are defined by the Java Community Process (`https://www.jcp.org`) program. Currently, JEE is in version 7. However, different specifications of JEE are at their own different versions.

JEE specifications can be broadly classified in the following groups:

- Presentation layer
- Business layer
- Enterprise integration layer

Note that JEE specification does not necessarily classify APIs in such broad groups, but such classification could help in better understanding the purpose of the different standards and APIs in JEE. Before we see APIs in each of these categories, let's understand a typical JEE web application flow where each of these layers fits in.

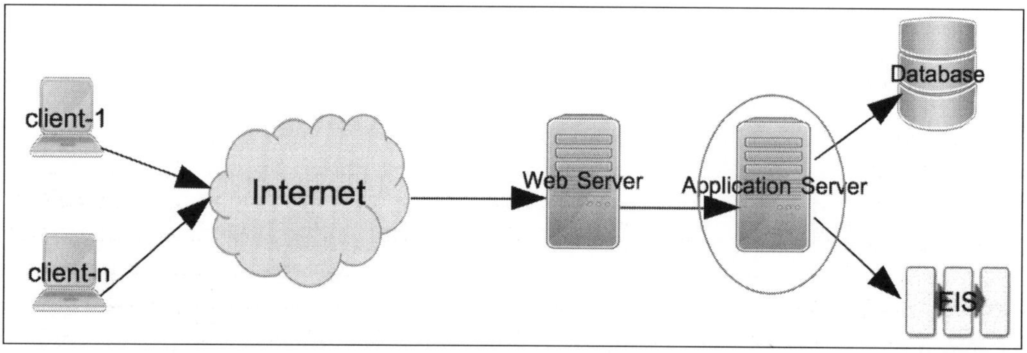

Figure 1.1 A typical JEE web application flow

Requests start from client. Client can be any application requesting services from a remote application – for example, it could be a browser or a desktop application. The request is first received by Web Server at the destination. Examples of Web Servers are Apache Web Server, IIS, Nginx, and so on. If it is a request for static content, then it is served by the web server(s). However, dynamic request typically requires an Application Server to process it. JEE servers are such Application Servers that handle the dynamic requests. Most JEE specification APIs execute in the application server. Examples of JEE application servers are WebLogic, WebSphere, GlassFish, JBoss, and so on.

Most non-trivial JEE applications access external systems such as database or **Enterprise Integration Server (EIS)** for data and process it. Response is returned from the application server to the web server and then to the clients.

The following is the brief description of each of the JEE specifications in different layers of applications that we saw previously. We will see how to use these APIs in more detail in subsequent chapters. However, note that the following is not the exhaustive list of all the specifications in JEE. We will see the most commonly used specifications here. For the exhaustive list, please visit `http://www.oracle.com/technetwork/java/javaee/tech/index.html`.

The presentation layer

JEE specifications or technologies in this group receive the request from web server and send back the response, typically, in an HTML format. However, it is also possible to return only the data from the presentation layer, for example, in **JavaScript Object Notation (JSON)** or **eXtensible Markup Language (XML)** format, which could be consumed by AJAX (Asynchronous JavaScript and XML) calls to update only part of the page, instead of rendering the entire HTML page. Classes in the presentation layer are mostly executed in a Web Container - it is a part of the application server that handles web requests. Tomcat is an example of a popular Web Container.

Now, we will take a look at some of the specifications in this group.

Java Servlet

Java servlets are server side modules, typically used to process a request and send back response in the web applications. Servlets are useful for handling requests that do not generate large HTML markup responses. They are typically used as controllers in MVC (Model View Controller) frameworks, for forwarding/redirecting requests or for generating non-HTML responses, such as PDFs. To generate an HTML response from Servlet, you need to embed the HTML code (as Java String) in the Java code. Therefore, it is not the most convenient option for generating large HTML response. JEE 7 contains Servlet API 3.1.

Java Server Pages

Like Servlets, JSPs are also server side modules used to process the web requests. JSPs (Java Server Pages) are great for handling requests that generate large HTML markup responses. In JSP pages, Java code or JSP tags can be mixed with other HTML code, such as HTML tags, JavaScript, and CSS. Since Java code is embedded in the larger HTML code, it is easier (than Servlet) to generate an HTML response from the JSP pages. JSP specification 2.3 is included in JEE 7.

Java Server Faces

Java Server Faces makes creating user interface on the server side modular by incorporating the MVC design pattern in its implementation. It also provides easy to use tags for common user interface controls that can save states across multiple request-response exchanges between the client and server. For example, if you have a page that posts form data from a browser, you can have JSF save that data in a Java Bean so that it can be used subsequently in the response to the same or different request. JSF also makes it easier to handle UI events on the server side and specify page navigation in an application.

You write the **Java Server Faces** (**JSF**) code in JSP, using custom JSP tags created for JSF. Java Server Faces API 2.2 is part of JEE 7.

The business layer

The business layer is where you typically write code to handle the business logic of your application. The request to this layer could come from the presentation layer, directly from the client application, or from the middle layer consisting of, but not limited to, web services. Classes in this layer are executed in the application container part of JEE Server. GlassFish and WebSphere are examples of web container plus application container.

Let us take a tour of some of the specifications in this group.

Enterprise Java Beans

Enterprise Java Beans (**EJBs**) are the Java classes where you can write your business logic. Though it is not a strict requirement to use EJBs to write business logic, they do provide many of the services that are essential in enterprise applications. These services are security, transaction management, component lookup, object pooling, and so on. You can have EJBs distributed across multiple servers and let the application container (also called EJB container) take care of component look up (searching component) and component pooling (useful for scalability). This can improve scalability of the application.

EJBs are of two types:

- **Session beans**: Session beans are called directly by clients or middle tier objects
- **Message driven beans**: Message driven beans are called in response to **Java Messaging Service** (**JSM**) events

JMS and message driven beans can be used for handling asynchronous requests. In a typical asynchronous request processing scenario, the client puts a request in a messaging queue or a topic and does not wait for immediate response. Server application gets the request message, either directly using JMS APIs or by using MDB. It processes the request and may put response in a different queue or topic to which the client would listen and get the response.

Java EE 7 contains EJB specification 3.2 and JMS specification 2.0.

The enterprise integration layer

APIs in this layer are used for interacting with external (to JEE application) systems in Enterprise. Most applications would need to access database, and APIs to access it fall in this group.

Java Database Connectivity (JDBC)

JDBC is a specification to access relational database in a common and consistent way. Using JDBC you can execute SQL statements and get results on different databases using common APIs. Database specific driver sits between the JDBC call and the database, which translates JDBC calls to database vendor specific API calls. JDBC can be used in both the Presentation and Business layers directly, but it is recommended to separate the database calls from both UI and the business code. Typically, this is done by creating **Data Access Objects** (**DAO**) which encapsulate logic to access the database.

JEE 7 contains JDBC specification 4.0.

The Java Persistent API (JPA)

One of the problems of using JDBC APIs directly is that you have to constantly map the data between Java Objects and the data in columns of rows in relational database. Frameworks such as Hibernate and Spring have made this process simpler by using a concept known as **Object Relationship Mapping** (**ORM**). ORM is incorporated in JEE in the form of **Java Persistent API** (**JPA**). JPA gives you the flexibility to map the objects to the tables in relational database and execute the queries with or without using **Structured Query Language** (**SQL**). Though when used in the content of JPA, query language is called Java Persistence Query Language. JPA specification 2.1 is a part of JEE.

Java Connector Architecture (JCA)

JCA APIs can be used in JEE applications for communicating with Enterprise Integration Systems, such as SAP, Salesforce, and so on. Just like you have database drivers to broker communication between JDBC APIs and relational database, you have JCA adapters between JCA calls and EIS. Most EIS applications now provide REST APIs, which are lightweight and easy to use, so REST could replace JCA in some cases. However, if you use JCA, you get transaction and pooling support from JEE application server.

Web services

Web services are remote application components that expose self-contained APIs. Broadly, web services can be classified based on the following two standards:

- **Simple Object Access Protocol** (**SOAP**)
- **Representational State Transfer** (**REST**)

Web services can play a major role in integrating disparate applications, because they are standard based and platform independent.

JEE provides many specifications to simplify development and consumption of both types of web services, for example, JAX-WS (Java API for XML - web services) and JAX-RS (Java API for RESTful web services).

The preceding are just some of the specifications that are part of JEE. There are many other independent specifications, such as web services, and many enabling specifications, such as dependency injection and concurrency utilities, that we will see in subsequent chapters.

Eclipse IDE

As mentioned earlier, a good IDE is essential for better productivity while coding. Eclipse is one such IDE, which has great editor features and many integration points with JEE technologies. The primary purpose of this book is to show you how to develop JEE applications using Eclipse. So following is a quick introduction to Eclipse, if you are not already familiar with it.

Eclipse is an open source IDE for developing applications in many different programming languages. It is quite popular for developing many different types of Java applications. Its architecture is pluggable – there is a core IDE and many different plugins can be added to it. In fact, support for many languages is added as Eclipse plugins, including support for Java.

Along with editor support, Eclipse has plugins to interact with many of the external systems used during development. For example, source control systems such as SVN and Git, build tools such as Apache Ant and Maven, file explorer for remote systems using FTP, managing servers such as Tomcat and GlassFish, database explorer, memory and CPU profiler, and so on. We will see many of these features in the subsequent chapters.

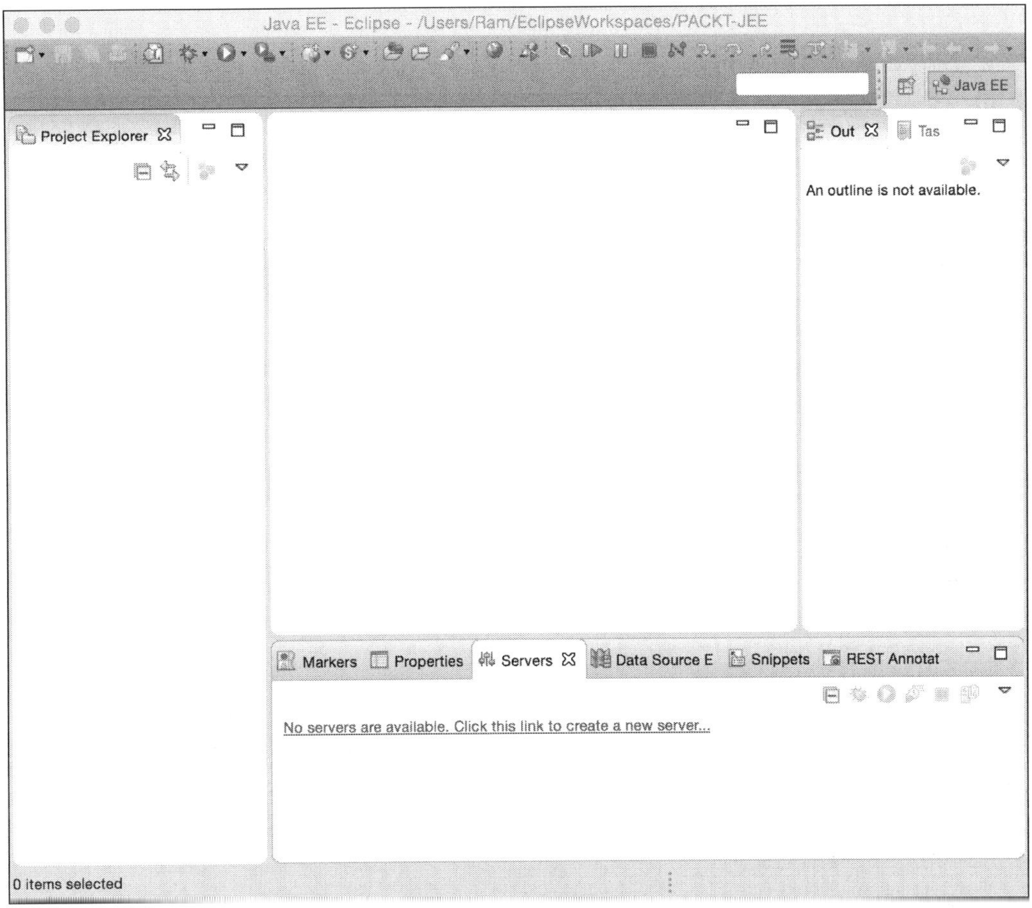

Figure 1.2 Default Eclipse View

Figure 1.2 shows the default view of Eclipse for JEE application development. When working with Eclipse, it is good to understand the following terms used in the context of Eclipse.

Workspace

The Eclipse workspace is a collection of projects, settings, and preferences. Workspace is a folder where Eclipse stores this information. You must create a workspace to use Eclipse. You can create multiple workspaces, but at a time only one can be opened by one running instance of Eclipse. However, you can launch multiple instances of Eclipse with different workspaces.

Plugin

Eclipse has pluggable architecture. Many of the features of Eclipse are implemented as plugins, for example, editor plugins for Java and many other languages, plugins for SVN and Git, and many others. Default installation of Eclipse comes with many built-in plugins and you can add more plugins for the features you want later.

Editors and views

Most windows in Eclipse can be classified either as editor or views. Editor is something where you can change the information displayed in it. View just displays the information and does not allow you to change it. An example of an editor is the Java editor where you write a code. An example of view is the outline view that displays the hierarchical structure of the code you are editing (in case of Java editor, it shows classes in a file, and methods in them).

To see all views in a given Eclipse installation, open the **Window** | **Show View** | **Other** menu.

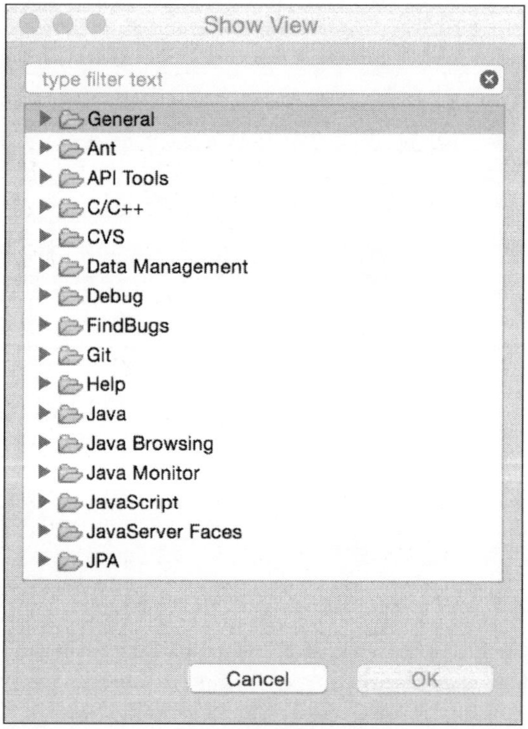

Figure 1.3 Show all Eclipse Views

Perspective

Perspective is a collection of editors and views, and how they are laid out or arranged in the main Eclipse window. At different stages of development, you need different views to be displayed. For example, when you are editing a code, you need to see the **Project Explorer** and **Task** views, but when you are debugging an application, you don't need those views, but instead want to see the variables and breakpoints view. So, the editing perspective displays, among other views and editor, the **Project Explorer** and **Task** view and the Debug perspective displays views and editors relevant to the debugging activities. You can change the default perspectives to suit your purpose, though.

Eclipse preferences

The Eclipse preferences window is where you customize many features of plugins/features. Preferences are available from the **Window** menu in Windows and Linux installation of Eclipse, and from Eclipse menu in Mac installation of Eclipse.

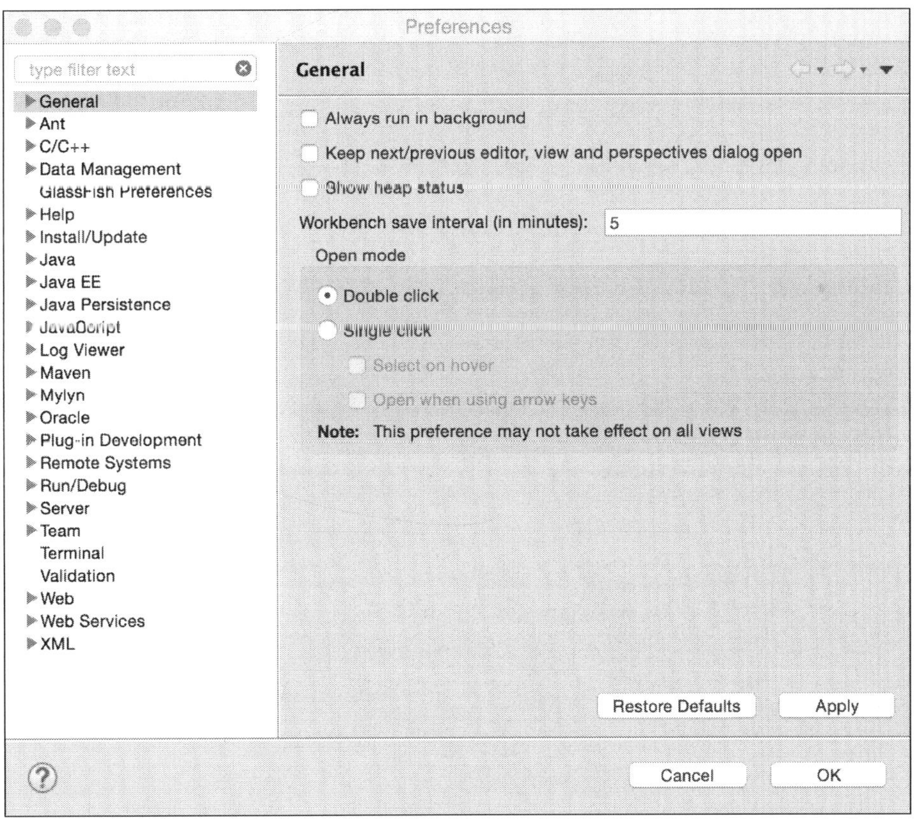

Figure 1.4 Eclipse Preferences

Installing products

In the subsequent chapters, we will see how to develop JEE applications using different APIs in Eclipse. But the applications are going to need a JEE application server and a database. We are going to use Tomcat web container for the initial few chapters and then use GlassFish JEE application server. We are going to use MySQL database. We are going to need these products for most of the applications that we are going to develop. So the following sections describe how to install and configure Eclipse, Tomcat, GlassFish, and MySQL.

Installing Eclipse (Version 4.4)

You can download Eclipse from `https://eclipse.org/downloads/`. You will see many different packages for Eclipse. Make sure you install the **Eclipse IDE for Java EE Developers** package. Select an appropriate package based on your OS and JVM architecture (32 or 64 bit). You may want to run the command java -version to know if the JVM is 32-bit or 64-bit.

Unzip the downloaded zip file and then run the Eclipse application (you need to install JDK before you run Eclipse). The first time you run Eclipse, you will be asked to specify a workspace. Create a new folder in your file system and select that as the initial workspace folder. If you intend to use the same folder for workspace on every launch of Eclipse, then check the **Use this as the default and do not ask again** check box.

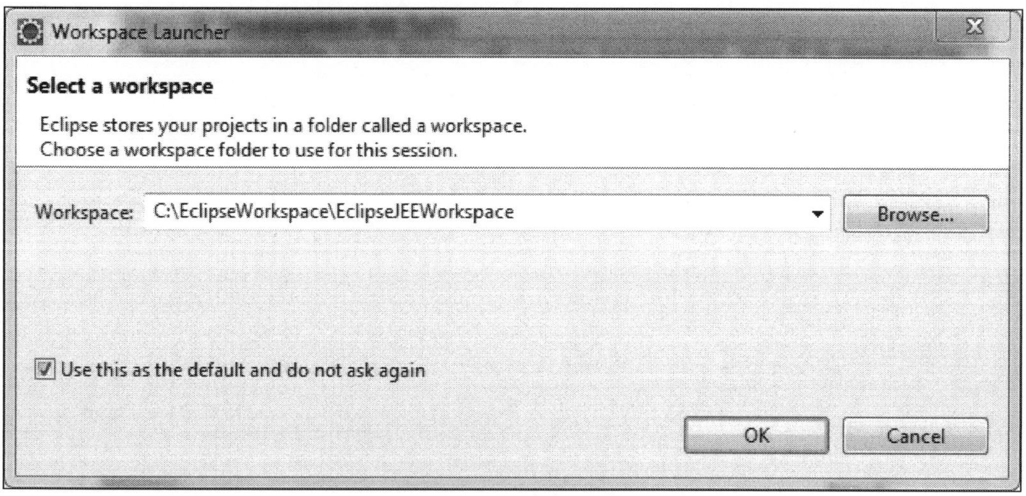

Figure 1.5 Select Eclipse Workspace

You will then see default Java EE perspective of Eclipse as shown in Figure 1.2.

Installing Tomcat

Tomcat is a Web Container. It supports APIs in the presentation layer described earlier. In addition, it supports JDBC and JPA also. It is easy to use and configure, and could be a good option if you do not want to use EJBs.

Download Tomcat from `http://tomcat.apache.org/`. At the time of writing, the latest version of Tomcat available was 8. Download the zip file and unzip in a folder. Set the `JAVA_HOME` environment variable to point to the folder where JDK is installed (the folder path should be the JDK folder, which has `bin` as one of the sub folders). Then run `startup.bat` at the Command Prompt on Windows and `startup.sh` in a Terminal window on Mac and Linux, to start the Tomcat server. If there are no errors, then you should see the message `Server startup in --ms` or `Tomcat started`.

Default Tomcat installation is configured to use port `8080`. If you want to change the port, open `server.xml` under the `conf` folder and look for connector declaration like:

```
<Connector port="8080" protocol="HTTP/1.1"
               connectionTimeout="20000"
               redirectPort="8443" />
```

Change the port value to any port number you want, though in this book we will be using the default `port 8080`. Before we open the default page of Tomcat, we will add a user for administration of the Tomcat server. Open `tomcat-users.xml` under the `conf` folder in any text editor. At the end of the file you will see commented example of how to add users. Add the following configuration before closure of the `</tomcat-users>` tag:

```
<role rolename="manager-gui"/>
<user username="admin" password="admin" roles="manager-gui"/>
```

Here we are adding a user `admin`, with password also as `admin`, to a role called `'manager-gui'`. This role has access to web pages for managing an application in Tomcat. This and other security roles are defined in `web.xml` of the `manager` application. You can find it at `webapps/manager/WEB-INF/web.xml`. For more information for managing Tomcat server, see `http://tomcat.apache.org/tomcat-8.0-doc/manager-howto.html`.

After making the preceding changes, open a web browser and browse to `http://localhost:8080` (modify port number if you have changed the default port as described previously). You will see the following default Tomcat page:

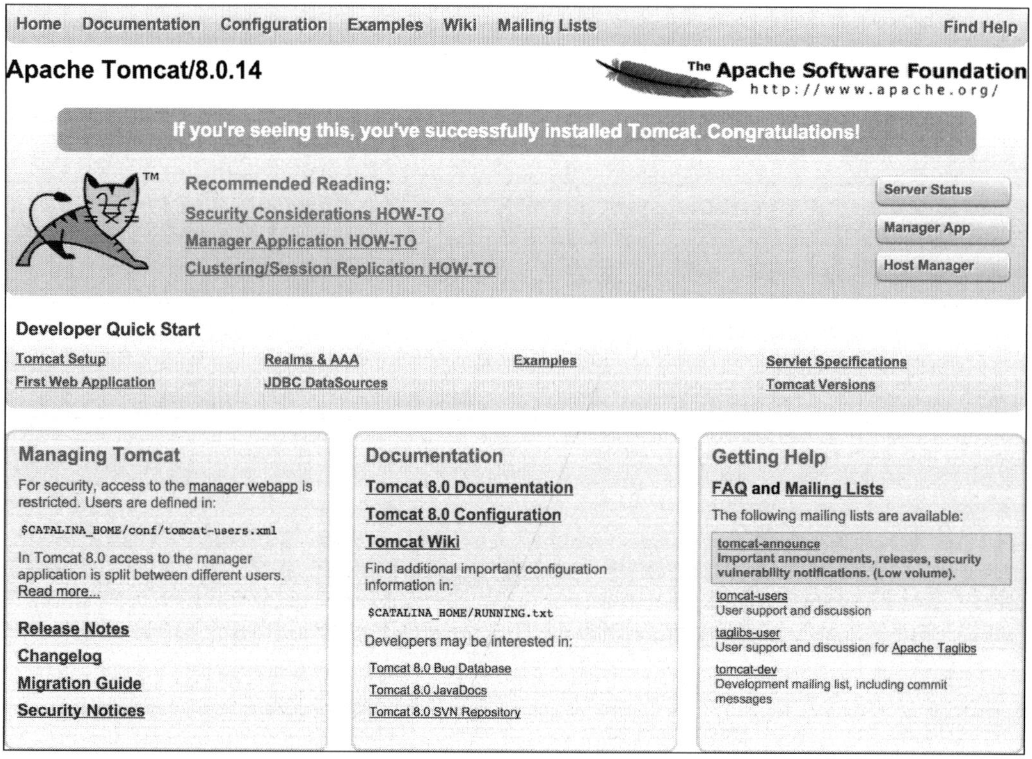

Figure 1.6 The default Tomcat web application

Click on the **Manager App** button on the right. You will be asked for the user name and password. Enter the user name and password you configured in `tomcat-users.xml` for `manager-gui`, as described earlier. After you are successfully logged in, you will see the **Tomcat Web Application Manager** page, as shown in the following image. You can see the applications deployed in Tomcat in this page. You can also deploy your applications from this page.

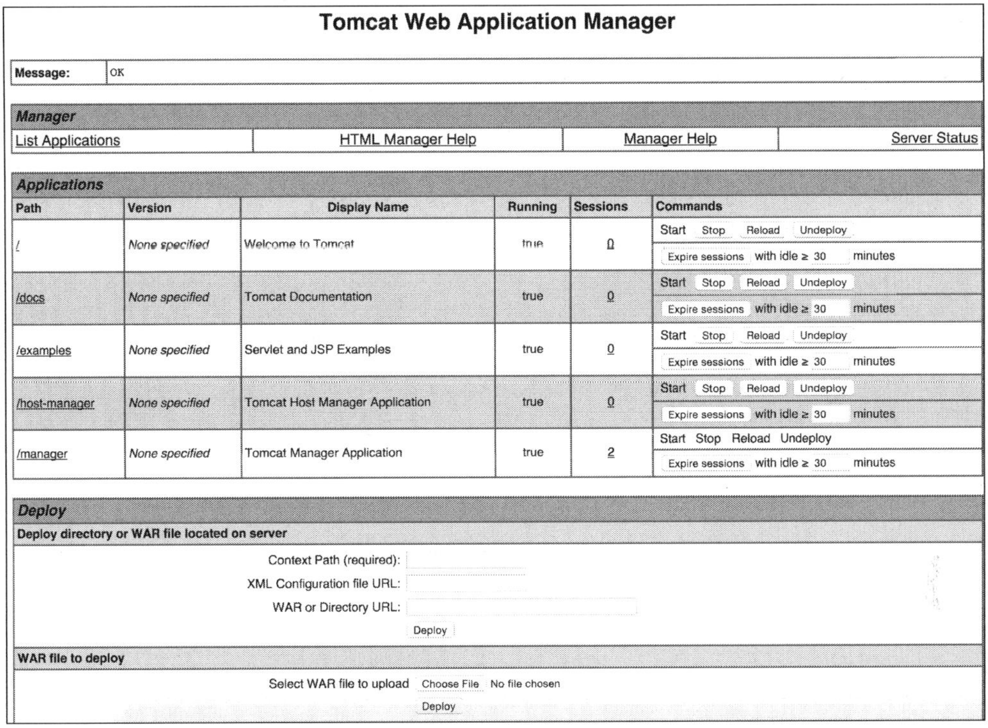

Figure 1.7 Tomcat Web Application Manager

To stop the Tomcat server, press *Ctrl*/COMMAND + *C* or run shutdown script in the bin folder.

Installing the GlassFish server

Download GlassFish from `https://glassfish.java.net/download.html`. GlassFish comes in two flavors: Web Profile and Full Platform. Web Profile is like Tomcat, which does not include EJB support. So download Full Platform. See `https://glassfish.java.net/webprofileORfullplatform31x.html` for comparison of Web Profile and Full Platform.

Unzip the downloaded file in a folder. Default port of GlassFish server is also `8080`. If you want to change that, open `glassfish/domains/domain1/config/domain.xml` in a text editor (you could open it in Eclipse too, using the **File** | **Open File** menu option) and look for `8080`. You should see it in one of the `<network-listener>`. Change the port if you want to (which may be the case if some other application is already using that port).

To start the server, run the `startserv` script (`.bat` or `.sh` depending on the OS you use). Once the server has started, open a web browser and browse to `http://localhost:8080`. You should see a page like the following screenshot:

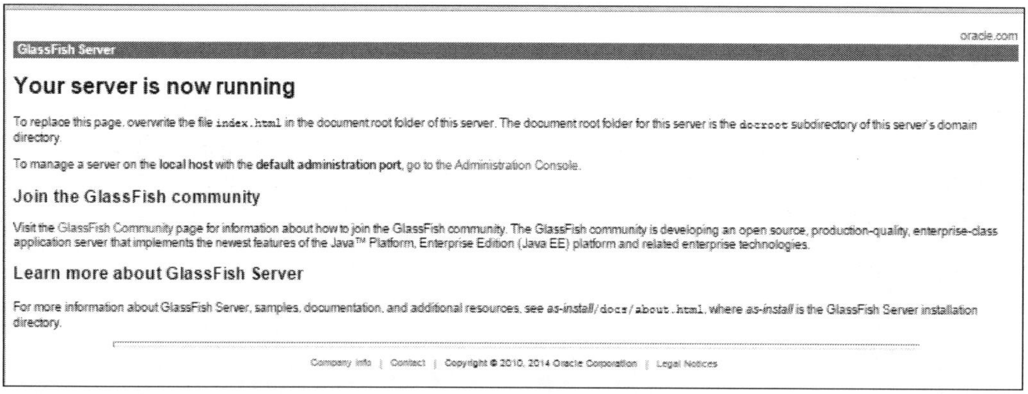

Figure 1.8 The default GlassFish web application

This page is located at `glassfish/domains/domain1/docroot/index.html`. Click on the **go to the Administration Console** link in the preceding page to open GlassFish administrator. For details on administrating GlassFish server, see `https://glassfish.java.net/docs/4.0/administration-guide.pdf`.

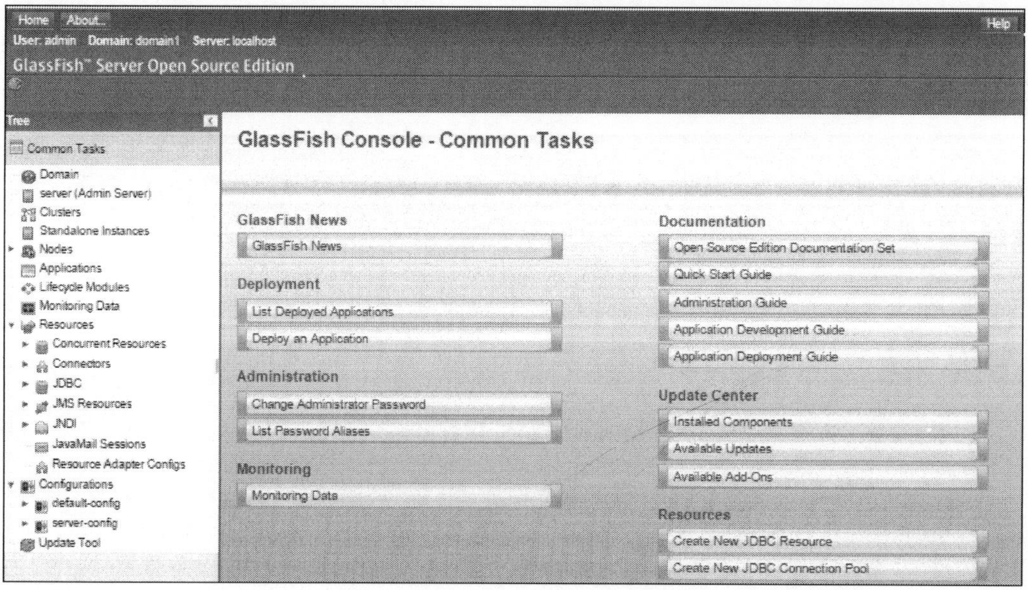

Figure 1.9 The GlassFish administrator

To stop the GlassFish server, run the `stopserv` script in the `glassfish/bin` folder.

Installing MySQL

We will be using MySQL database for many of the examples in this book. Following sections describe how to install and configure MySQL for different platforms.

Installing MySQL on Windows

Download MySQL Community Server from `http://dev.mysql.com/downloads/mysql/`. You can either download the web installer or the all in one installer. The web installer would download only those components that you have selected. Following instructions show the download options using the web installer.

Web installer first downloads a small application, and when you run that, it gives you options to select components that you want to install.

We would like to install MySQL Workbench too, which is a client application to manage MySQL Server. As of writing this chapter, MySQL Workbench required Visual C++ 2013 Runtime for Windows installation. If you don't have it already installed, you can download it from `http://www.microsoft.com/en-in/download/details.aspx?id=40784`.

1. Select the **Custom** option and click on **Next**.

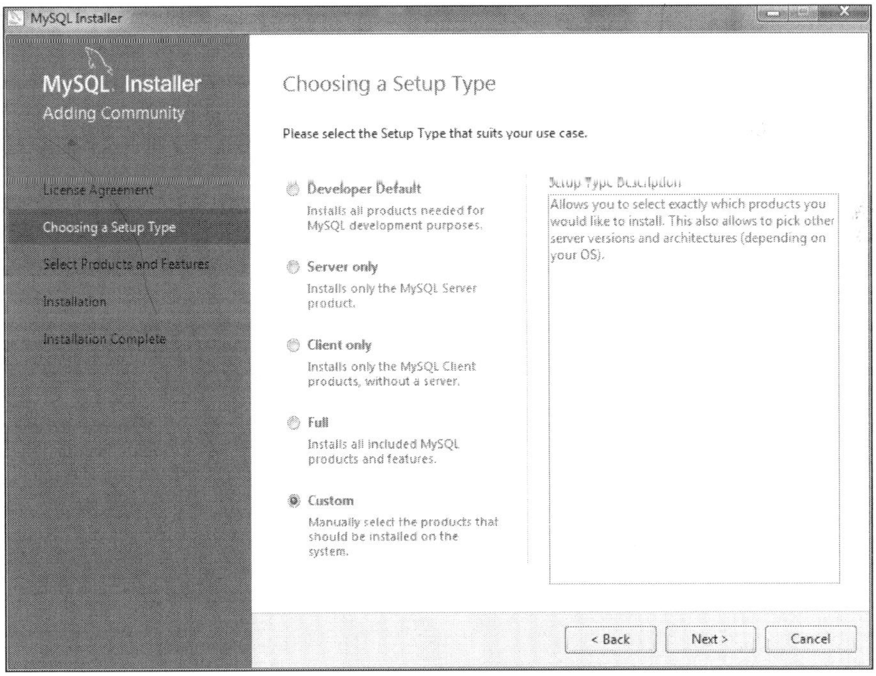

Figure 1.10 MySQL Installer for Windows

2. Select **MySQL Server** and **MySQL** Workbench products and complete the installation. During the installation of Server, you will be asked to set the `root` password and given the option to add more users. It is always a good idea to add user other than root for applications to use.

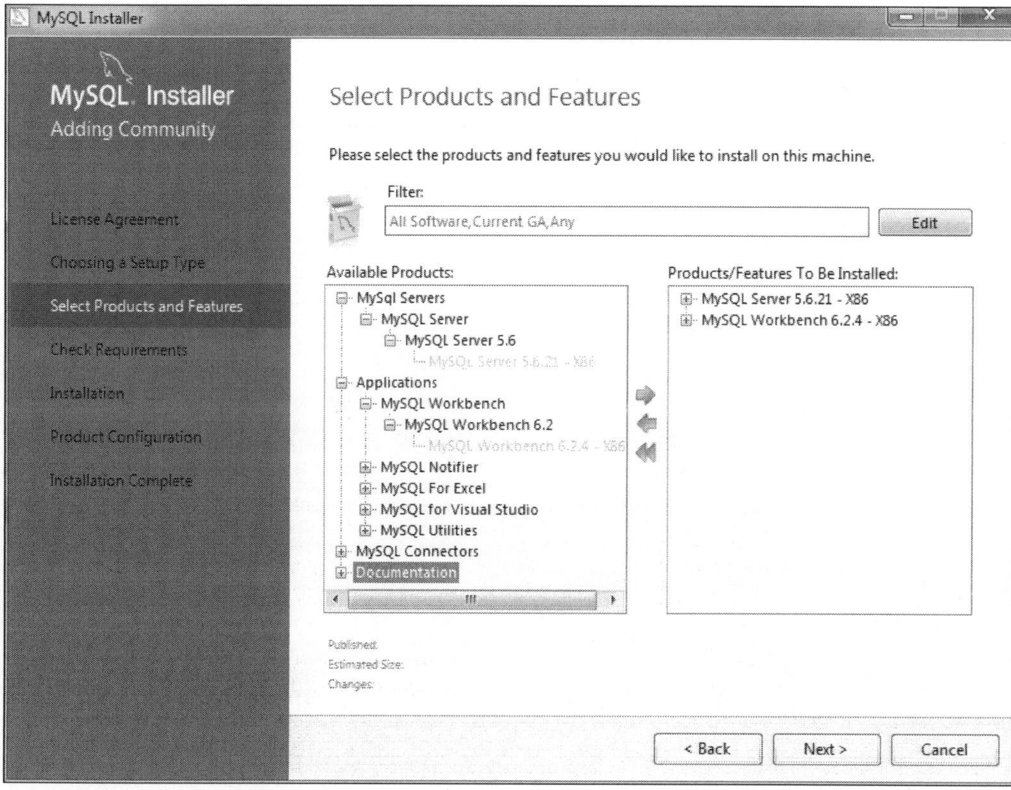

Figure 1.11 Select MySQL Products and Features to Install

3. Make sure you select All Hosts when adding a user so that you are able to access MySQL database from any remote machine that has network access to the machine where MySQL is installed.

Figure 1.12 Add MySQL User

4. Run MySQL Workbench after installation. You will find that the default connection to the local MySQL instance is already created for you.

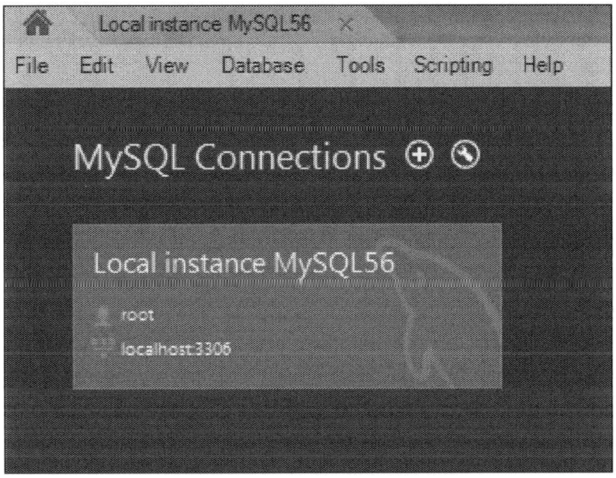

Figure 1.13 MySQL Workbench Connections

5. Click on the local connection and you will be asked to enter the `root` password. Enter the `root` password that you typed during the installation of MySQL server. MySQL Workbench opens and displays the default test schema.

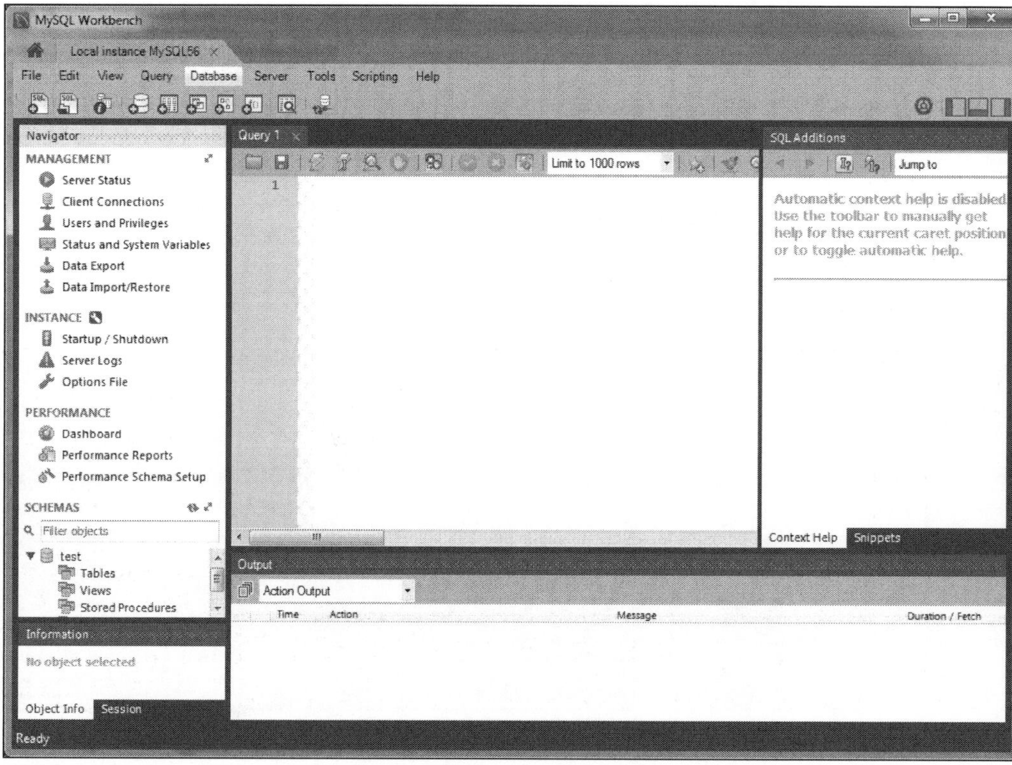

Figure 1.14 My SQL Workbench

Installing MySQL on Mac OS X

OS X versions before 10.7 had MySQL server installed by default. See `http://dev.mysql.com/doc/mysql-macosx-excerpt/5.7/en/macosx-installation-server.html` to know which version of MySQL was installed for different versions of OS X. If you are using OS X 10.7 or later, then you will have to download and install MySQL Community Server from `http://dev.mysql.com/downloads/mysql/`.

There are many different ways to install MySQL on OS X. See `http://dev.mysql.com/doc/refman/5.7/en/osx-installation.html` for installation instruction for OS X. Note that users on OS X should have administrator privileges to install the MySQL server.

Once you install the server, you can start it either from the Command Prompt or from the system preferences.

1. To start it from the Command Prompt, execute the following command in **Terminal**:

   ```
   sudo /usr/local/mysql/support-files/mysql.server start
   ```

2. To start it from **System Preferences**, open the preferences and click the **MySQL** icon.

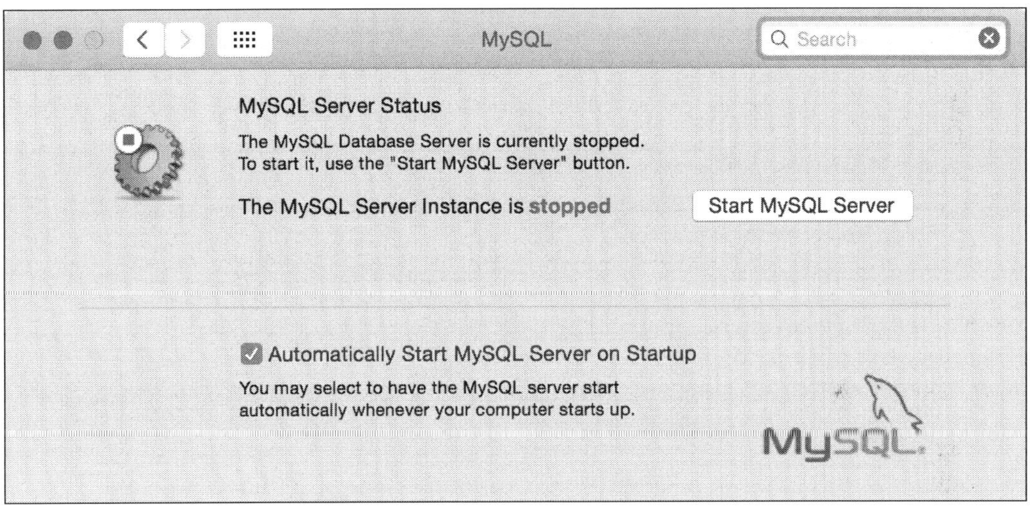

Figure 1.15 MySQL System Preferences - OSX

3. Click the **Start MySQL Server** button.
4. Next, download MySQL Workbench for OSX from `http://dev.mysql.com/downloads/workbench/`.

Installing MySQL on Linux

There are many different ways to install MySQL on Linux. Refer to `https://dev.mysql.com/doc/refman/5.7/en/linux-installation.html` for details.

Creating MySQL users

You can create MySQL user either from the Command Prompt or by using MySQL Workbench.

1. To execute SQL and other commands from the Command Prompt, open **Terminal** and type the following:

   ```
   mysql -u root -p <root_password>
   ```

2. Once logged in successfully, you will see the `mysql` Command Prompt:

   ```
   mysql>
   ```

3. To create a user, first select the `mysql` database.

   ```
   mysql>user mysql;
   Database changed
   mysql>insert into user (host, user, password, select_priv, insert_
   priv, update_priv)
               values ('%', 'user1', password('usper1_
   pass'),'Y','Y','Y');
   ```

The preceding command will create a user named `'user1'` with password 'user1_pass' having privileges to insert, update, and select. And because we have specified host as `'%'`, this user can access the server from any host.

If you prefer a graphical user interface to manage the users, then run MySQL Workbench, connect to the local MySQL server (see *Figure 1.13 MySQL Workbench Connections*), and click on **Users and Privileges** under the **Management** section.

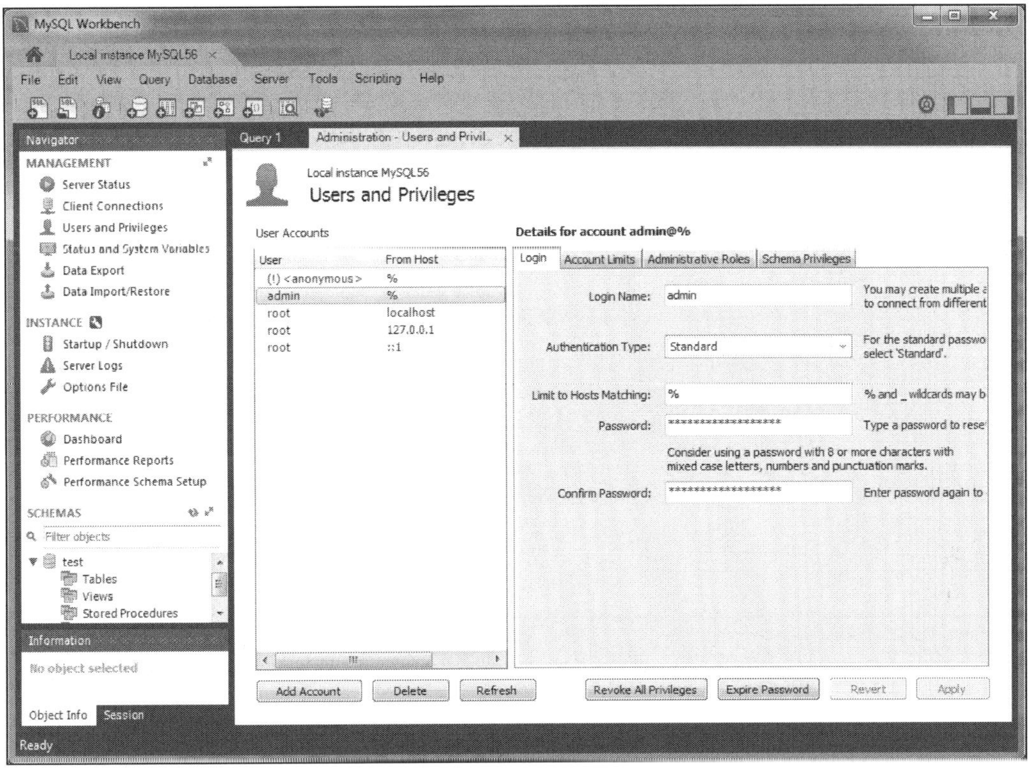

Figure 1.16 Creating a user in MySQL Workbench

Having installed all the above products, you should be in a position to start developing JEE applications. We may need a few additional software, but we will see how to install and configure them at appropriate time.

Summary

In this chapter, we had a brief introduction to different JEE APIs for the presentation layer, business layer, and Enterprise integration layer. We learnt some of the important terminologies in Eclipse IDE. We then learned how to install Eclipse, Tomcat, GlassFish, MySQL, and MySQL Workbench. We are going to use these products in this book to develop JEE applications.

In the next chapter, we will configure the JEE server and database in Eclipse, and create a simple application using Servlet, JSP, and Java Server Faces.

We will also see how to crate JEE Web Applications using Servlet, JSP, and JSF. Along with that, we will learn how to use Maven to build and package the JEE applications.

2
Creating a Simple JEE Web Application

The previous chapter gave you a brief introduction to JEE and Eclipse. You also learned how to install the Eclipse JEE package and install and configure Tomcat. Tomcat is a servlet container and is easy to use and configure. Therefore, many developers use it to run JEE web applications on local machines.

In this chapter, we will see how to configure Tomcat in Eclipse and develop and deploy web applications. The advantage of configuring Tomcat in Eclipse is that you can easily start and stop the server from Eclipse, and deploy a JEE project right from within Eclipse to Tomcat.

Configuring Tomcat in Eclipse

Follow these steps for configuring the Tomcat server in Eclipse:

1. In the Java EE view of Eclipse, you will find the **Servers** tab at the bottom. Since no server is added yet, you will see a link in the **Servers** tab - **No servers are available. Click this link to create a new server....**

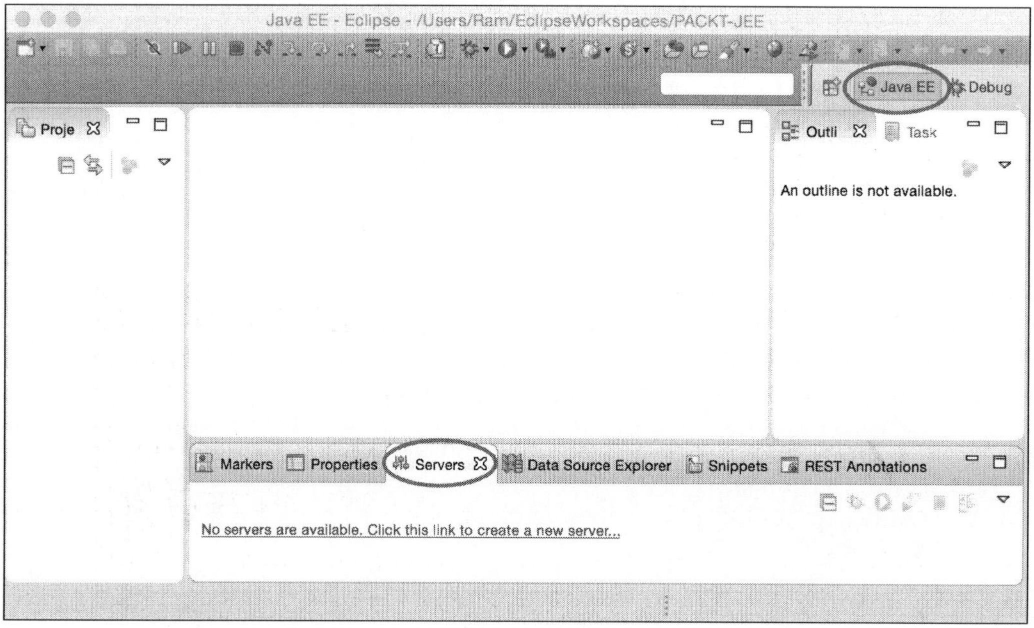

Figure 2.1 The Servers tab in Eclipse JEE

2. Click the link in the **Servers** tab.

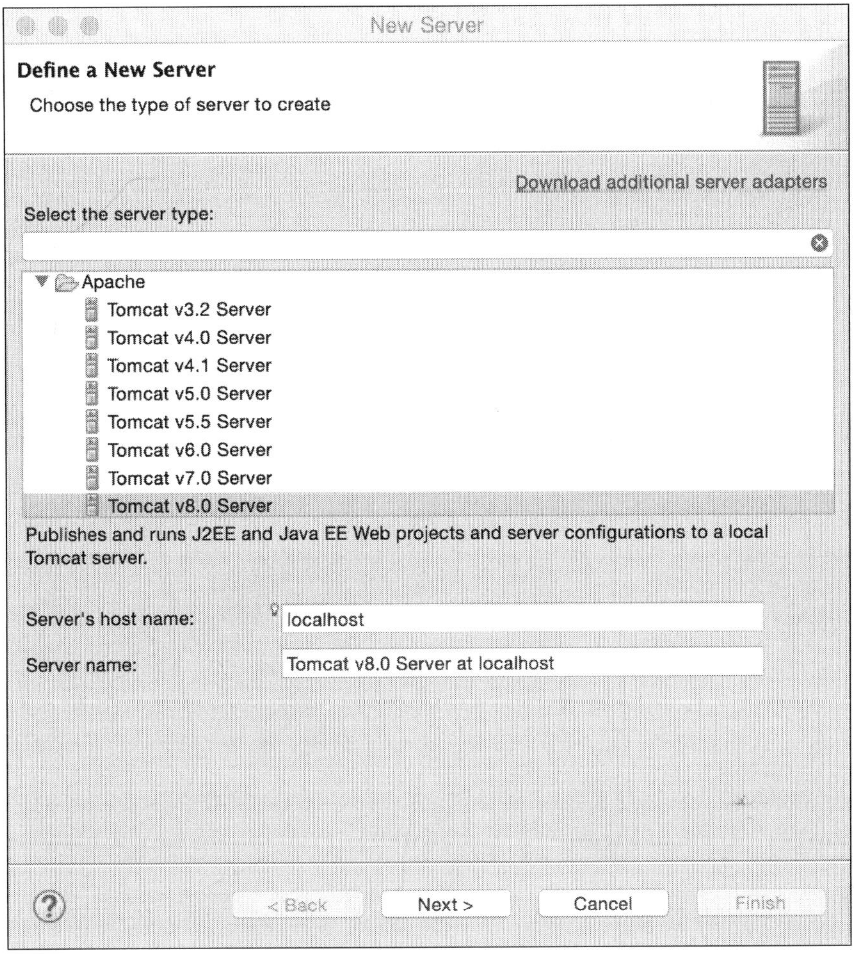

Figure 2.2 New Server wizard. Select server

3. Expand the **Apache** group and select the Tomcat version that you have already installed. If Eclipse and the Tomcat server are on the same machine, then leave **Server's host name** as `localhost`. Otherwise, enter the hostname or IP address of the Tomcat server. Click **Next**.

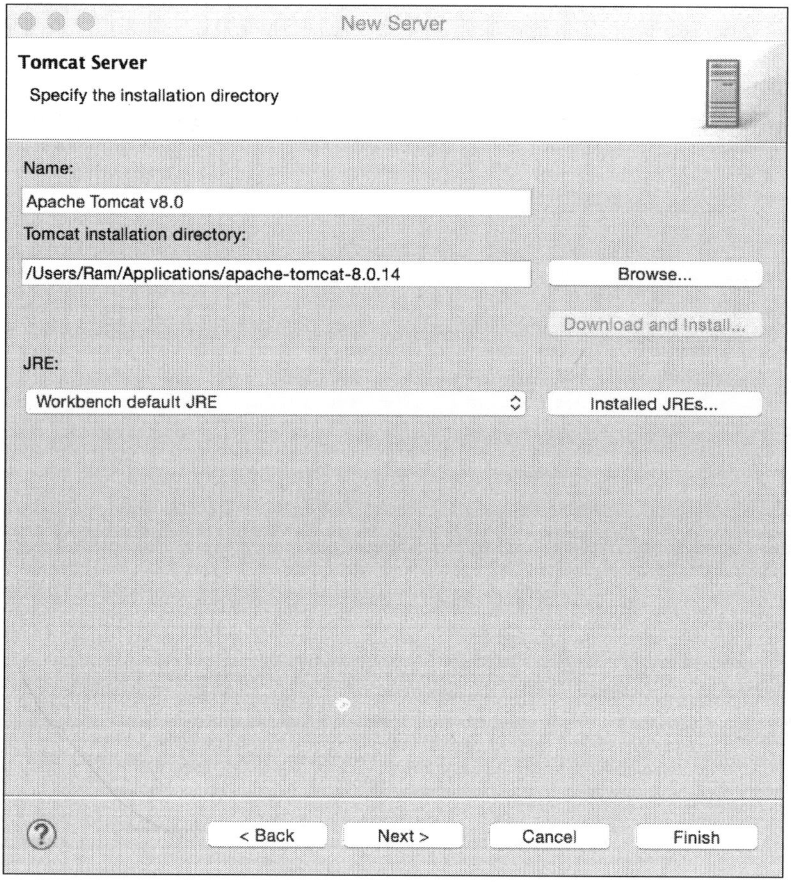

Figure 2.3 New Server wizard. Configure the Tomcat folder

4. Click the **Browse...** button and select the folder where Tomcat is installed.
5. Click **Next** till you complete the wizard. At the end of it, you will see the Tomcat server added to the **Servers** view. If Tomcat is not already started, you will see the status as stopped.
6. To start the server, right-click on the server and select the **Start** menu option. You can also start the server by clicking the start button in the toolbar of the **Servers** view.

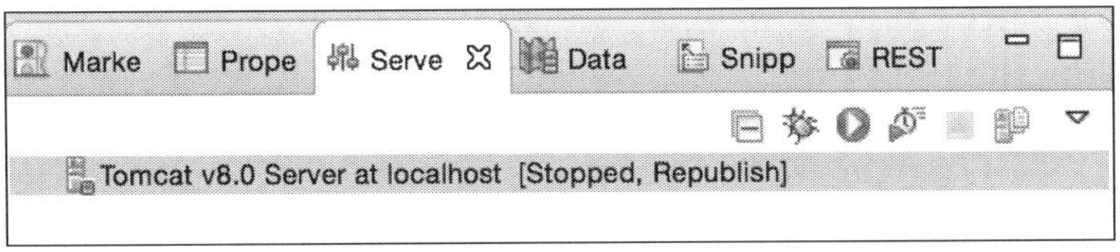

Figure 2.4 The Tomcat server added to the Servers view

Once the server is started successfully, you will see the status changed to `Started`. If you click on the **Console** tab, you will see console messages that the Tomcat server output during startup.

If you expand the **Servers** group in the **Project Explorer** view, you will find the Tomcat server that you just added. Expand the Tomcat server node to view the Tomcat configuration files. This gives you an easy way to edit the Tomcat configuration; you don't have to go look for the configuration files in the file system. Double-click `server.xml` to open it in the XML editor. You get a **Design** view as well as a **Source** view (two tabs at the bottom of the editor). We saw how to change the default port of Tomcat in the last chapter. You can easily change that in the Eclipse editor by opening `server.xml` and going to the **Connector** node. If you need to search the text, you can switch to the **Source** tab (at the bottom of the editor) and perform a search operation.

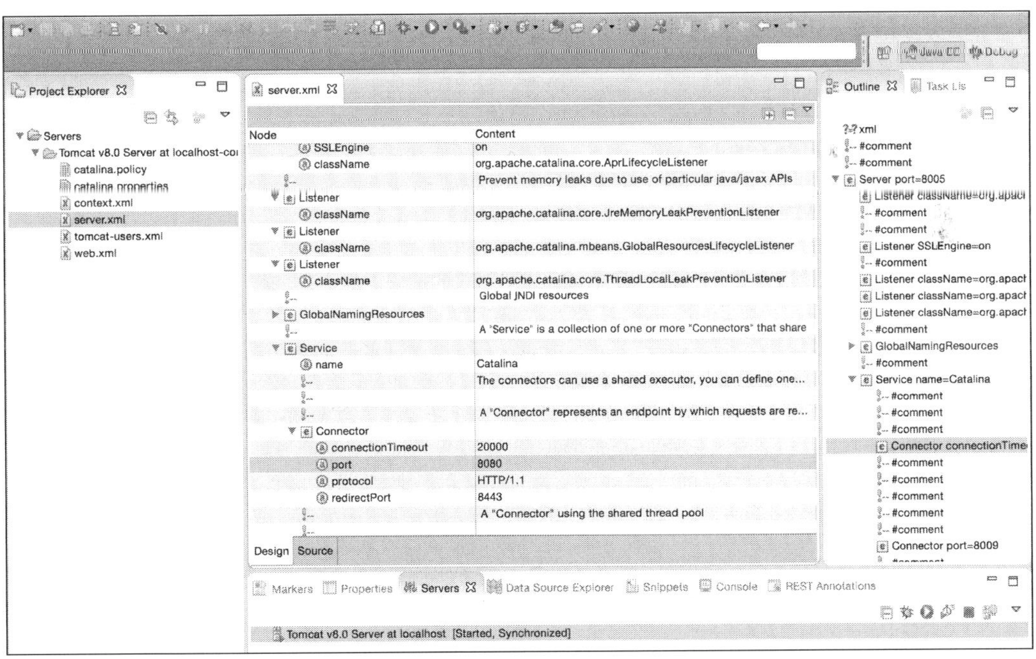

Figure 2.5 Open server.xml

You can also easily edit `tomcat-users.xml` to add/edit Tomcat users. Recall that we added a Tomcat user in *Chapter 1, Introducing JEE and Eclipse*, to administer the Tomcat server.

By default, Eclipse does not change anything in the Tomcat Installation folder when you add the server in Eclipse. Instead, it creates a folder in the workspace and copies the Tomcat configuration files to this folder. Applications to deploy on Tomcat are also copied and published from this folder. This is good during development when you do not want to modify the Tomcat settings and any application deployed in the Tomcat server. However, if you want to use the Tomcat installation folder, then you need to modify the server settings in Eclipse. Double-click the server in the **Servers** view to open it in the editor.

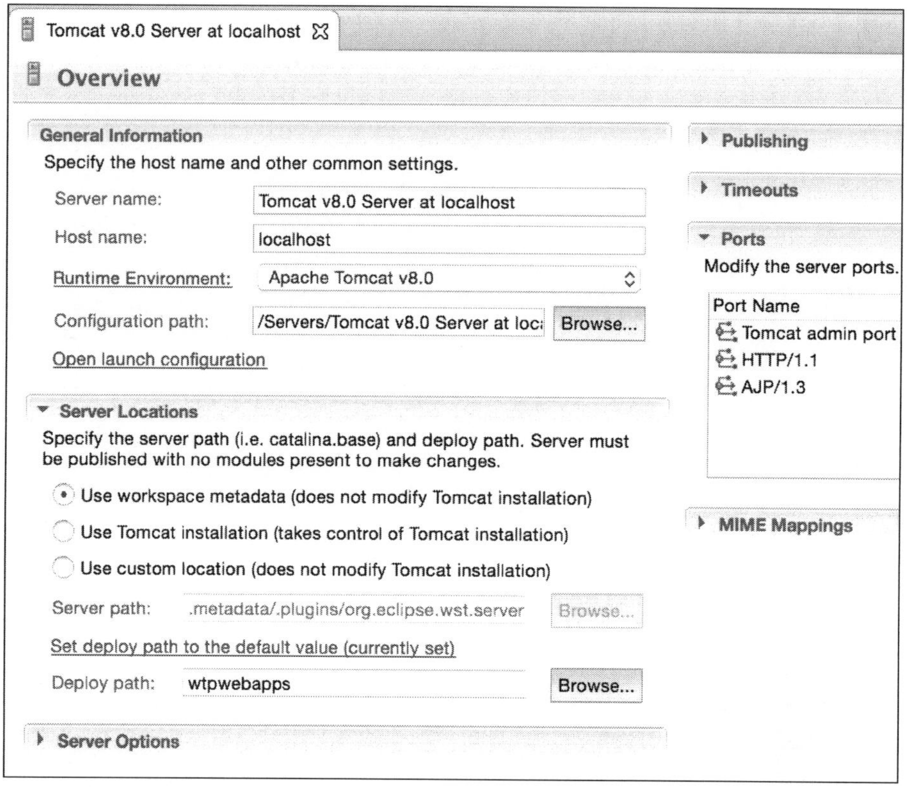

Figure 2.6 Tomcat settings

See options under **Server Locations**. Select the second option, the **Use Tomcat installation** option, if you want to use the Tomcat installation folders for configuration and for publishing applications from within Eclipse.

Java Server Pages

We will start with a project to create a simple JSP. We will create a login JSP that submits data to it and validates the user.

Creating a dynamic web project

To create a dynamic web project, we will perform the following steps:

1. Select the **File** | **New** | **Other** menu. This opens the selection wizard. At the top of the wizard, you will find a textbox with a cross icon on the extreme right side.
2. Type `web` in the textbox. This is the filter box. Many wizards and views in Eclipse have such a filter textbox that makes finding items very easy.

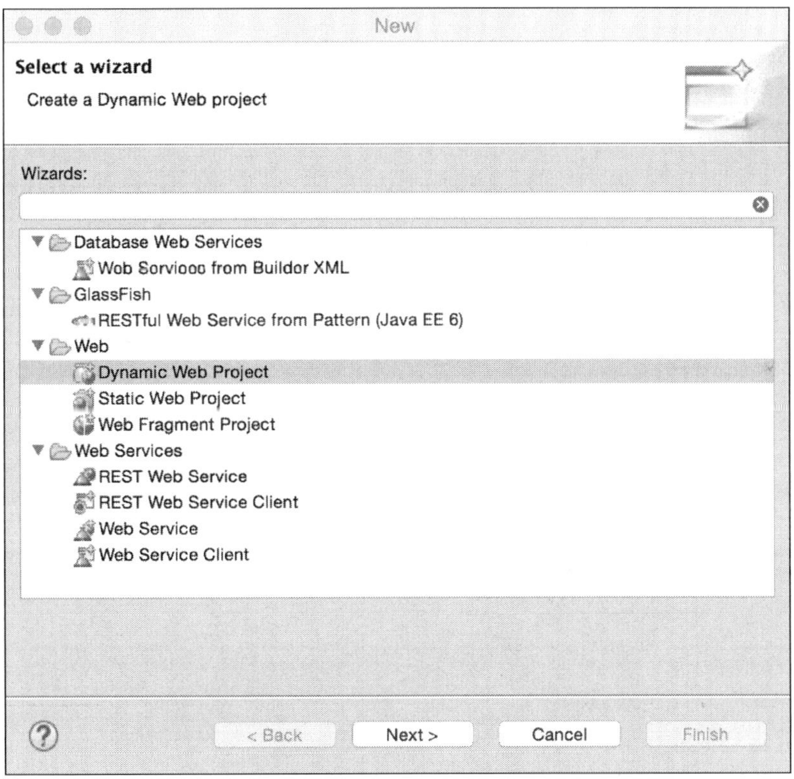

Figure 2.7 New selection wizard

3. Select **Dynamic Web Project** and click **Next** to open the **Dynamic Web Project** wizard. Enter a project name, for example, `LoginSampleWebApp`. Note that the **Dynamic web module version** field in this page lists the Servlet API version numbers. Select version 3.0 or greater. Click **Next**.

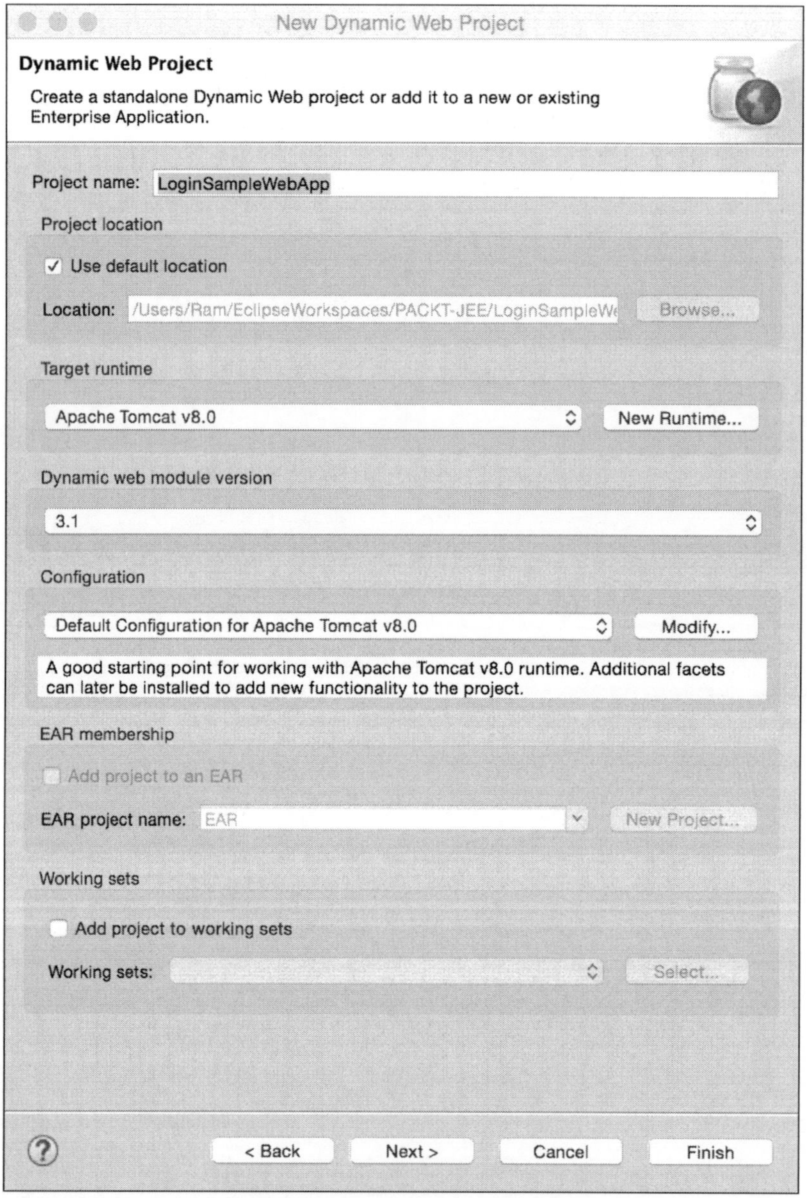

Figure 2.8 Dynamic web project wizard

4. Click **Next** in the following pages and click **Finish** on the last page to create the `LoginSimpleWebApp` project. This project is also added to **Project Explorer**.

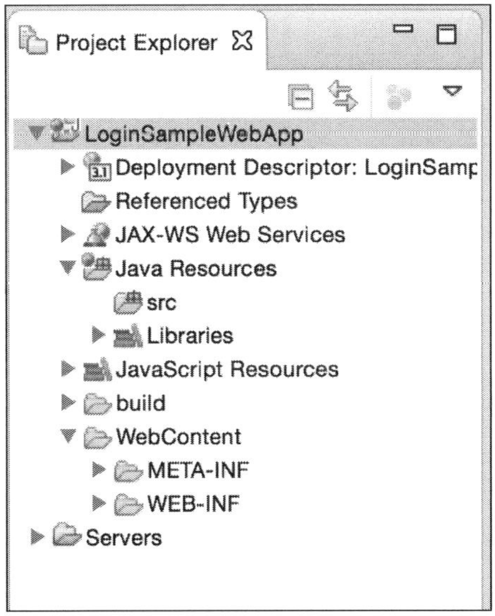

Figure 2.9 New web project

Java source files go in the `src` folder under **Java Resources**. Web resources such as the HTML, JS, and CSS files go in the `WebContent` folder.

We will first create the JSP for login.

> To keep the page simple, in the first JSP, we will not follow many of the best practices. We will have the UI code mixed with the application business code. Such design is not recommended in production applications but could be useful for quick prototyping. We will see how to write a better JSP code with a clear separation of the UI and the business logic later in the chapter.

Creating JSP

The following are the steps for creating a JSP:

1. Right-click on the `WebContent` folder and select **New | JSP File**. Name it `index.jsp`. The file will open in the editor with a split view. The top part shows the design view, and the bottom part shows the code. If the file is not opened in the split editor, right-click on `index.jsp` in the **Project Explorer** and select **Open With | Web Page Editor**.

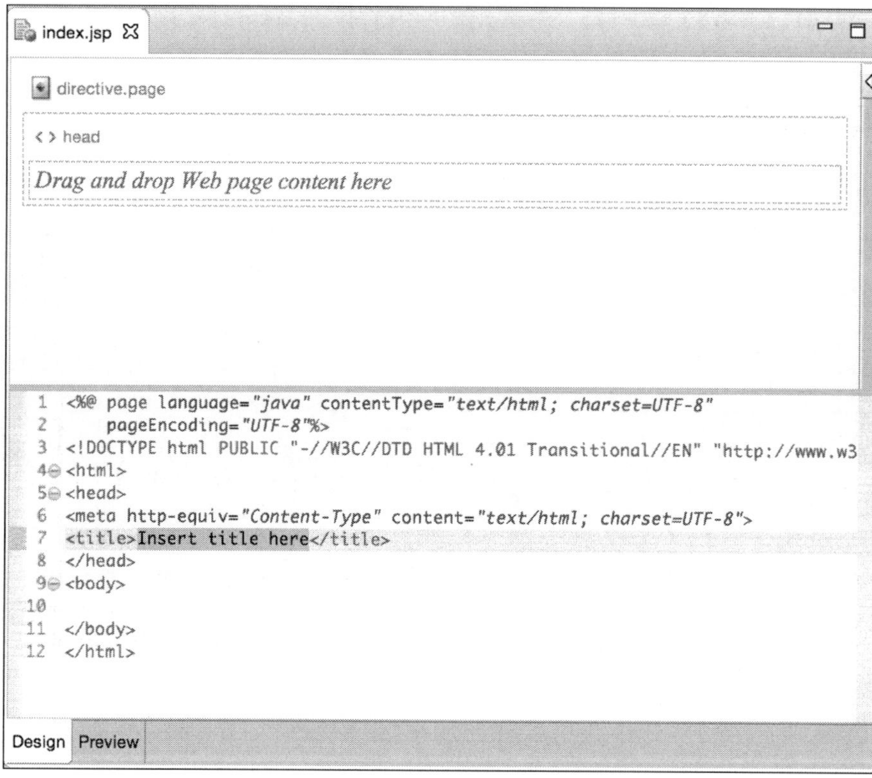

Figure 2.10 The JSP editor

2. If you do not like the split view and want to see either the full design view or the full code view, then use the toolbar button at the top right, as shown in the following screenshot:

Figure 2.11 The JSP editor display buttons

3. Change the title from `Insert title here` to `Login`.
4. Let's see how Eclipse provides code assistance for HTML tags. Note that input fields must be in a `Form` tag. We will add a `form` tag later. Inside the `body` tag, type the `User Name:` label. Then, type <. If you wait for a moment, Eclipse pops up a code assist window showing options for all the valid HTML tags. You can also invoke code assist manually.
5. Place a caret just after < and press *Ctrl* + *Space*.

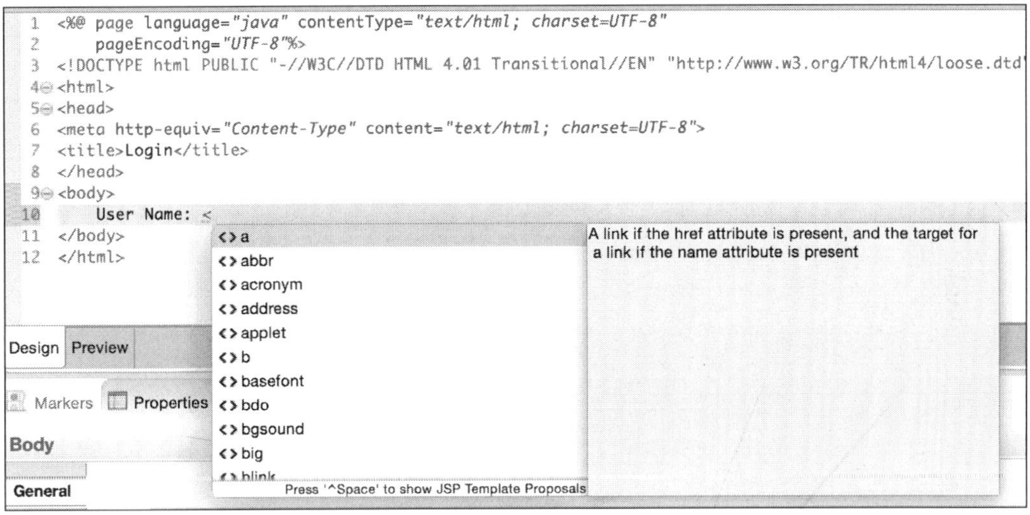

Figure 2.12 HTML code assist in JSP

Code assist works on partial text too; for example, if you invoke code assist after text `<i`, you will see a list of HTML tags starting with `i` (`i`, `iframe`, `img`, `input`, and so on). You can also use code assist for tag attributes and attribute values.

For now, we want to insert the `input` field for username.

6. Therefore, select `input` from the code assist proposals, or type it.

7. After the `input` element is inserted, move the caret inside the closing > and invoke code assist again (*Ctrl*/*Command* + *Space*). You will see a list of proposals for the attributes of the `input` tag.

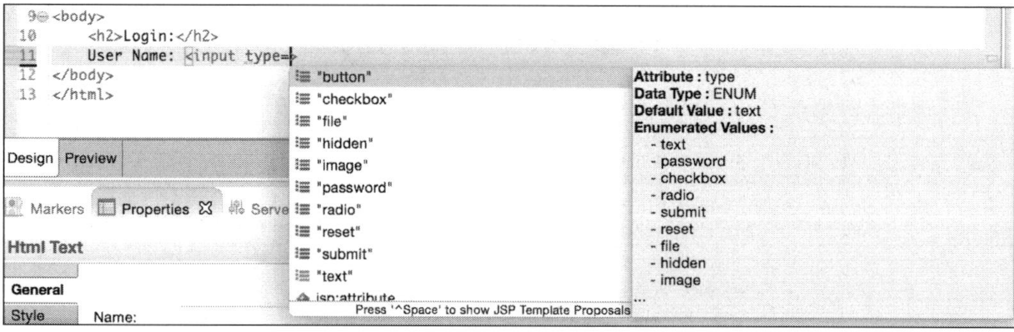

Figure 2.13 Code assist for the tag attribute value

8. Type the following code to create a login form:

```
<body>
  <h2>Login:</h2>
  <form method="post">
    User Name: <input type="text" name="userName"><br>
    Password: <input type="password" name="password"><br>
    <button type="submit" name="submit">Submit</button>
    <button type="reset">Reset</button>
  </form>
</body>
```

> **Downloading the example code**
>
> You can download the example code files from your account at `http://www.packtpub.com` for all the Packt Publishing books that you have purchased. If you purchased this book elsewhere, you can visit `http://www.packtpub.com/support` and register to have the files e-mailed directly to you.

If you are using the split editor (design and source pages), you can see the login form rendered in the design view. If you want to see how the page would look in a web browser, click the **Preview** tab at the bottom of the editor. You will see that the web page is displayed in the browser view inside the editor. Therefore, you don't need to move out of Eclipse to test your web pages.

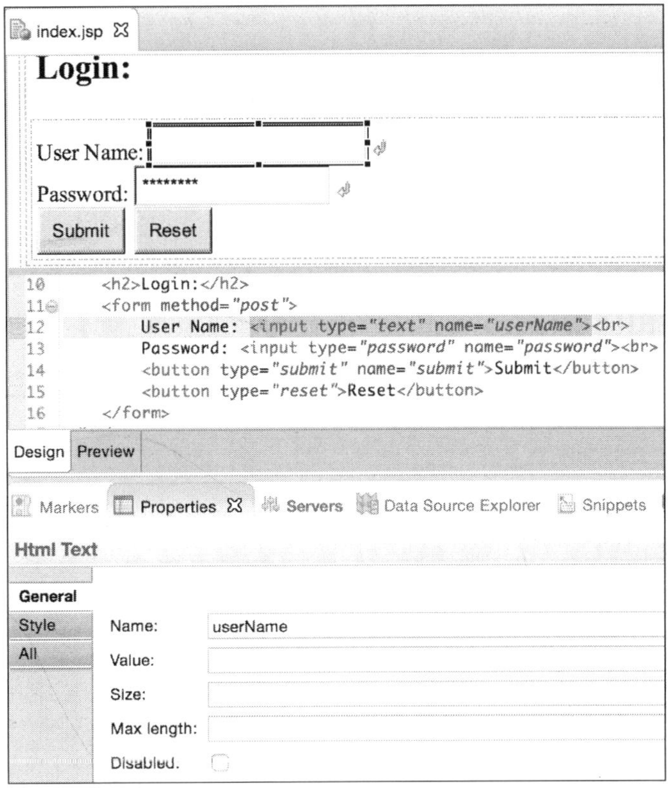

Figure 2.14 Design and Source views

If you click on any user interface control in the design view, you will see its properties in the **Properties** view (see the previous screenshot). You can edit properties, such as the **Name** and **Value** of the selected element. Click on the **Style** tab of the **Properties** window to edit the CSS style of the element.

> We have not specified the `action` attribute in the previous form. This attribute specifies a URL to which the form data is to be posted when the user clicks the **Submit** button. If this attribute is not specified, then the request or the form data would be submitted to the same page; in this case, the form data would be submitted to `index.jsp`. We will now write the code to handle form data.

As mentioned in *Chapter 1, Introducing JEE and Eclipse*, you can write the Java code and the client-side code (HTML, CSS, and JavaScript) in the same JSP. It is not considered a good practice to mix the Java code with the HTML code, but we will do that anyway for this example to keep the code simple. Later in the book, we will see how to make our code modular.

Java code is written in JSP between `<%` and `%>`; such Java code blocks in JSP are called **scriplets**. You can also set page-level attributes in JSP. They are called **page directives** and are included between `<%@` and `%>`. The JSP that we created already has a page directive to set the content type of the page. The content type tells the browser the type of the response (in this case, `html/text`) returned by the server. On the basis of the content type, the browser displays the appropriate response.

```
<%@ page language="java" contentType="text/html; charset=UTF-8"
    pageEncoding="UTF-8"%>
```

In JSP, you have access to a number of objects to help you process and generate a response, as described in the following table:

Object	**Response**
`Request`	`HTTPServletRequest` (`http://docs.oracle.com/javaee/7/api/javax/servlet/http/HttpServletRequest.html`). Use it to get request parameters and other request-related data.
`response`	`HtpServletResponse` (`http://docs.oracle.com/javaee/7/api/javax/servlet/http/HttpServletResponse.html`). Use it to send a response.
`Out`	`JSPWriter` (`http://docs.oracle.com/javaee/7/api/javax/servlet/jsp/JspWriter.html`). Use this to generate a text response.
`session`	`HTTPSession` (`http://docs.oracle.com/javaee/7/api/javax/servlet/http/HttpSession.html`). Use this to get/put objects in a session.
`Application`	`ServletContext` (`http://docs.oracle.com/javaee/7/api/javax/servlet/ServletContext.html`). Use this to get/put objects shared in the sample application.

In this example, we are going to make use of the `request` and `out` objects. We will first check whether the form is submitted by the `POST` method. Then, we will get the values of username and password. If the credentials are valid (in this example, we are going to hardcode the username and the password as `admin`), we will print a welcome message.

```
<%
  String errMsg = null;
  //first check whether the form was submitted
  if ("POST".equalsIgnoreCase(request.getMethod()) &&
  request.getParameter("submit") != null)
  {
    //form was submitted
    String userName = request.getParameter("userName");
    String password = request.getParameter("password");
    if ("admin".equalsIgnoreCase(userName) &&
    "admin".equalsIgnoreCase(password))
    {
      //valid user
      System.out.println("Welcome admin !");
    }
    else
    {
      //invalid user. Set error message
      errMsg = "Invalid user id or password. Please try again";
    }
  }
%>
```

We use two built-in objects in the preceding code - `request` and `out`. We first check whether the form was submitted - `"POST".equalsIgnoreCase(request.getMethod()`. Then, we check whether the submit button was used to post the form - `request.getParameter("submit") != null`.

We then get the username and the password by calling the `request.getParameter` method. To keep the code simple, we compare them with the hardcoded values. In a real application, you would most probably validate credentials against a database or some naming and folder service. If the credentials are valid, we print a message by using the `out` (`JSPWriter`) object. If the credentials are not valid, we set an error message. We will print the error message just before the login form:

```
<h2>Login:</h2>
  <!-- Check error message. If it is set, then display it -->
```

```
<%if (errMsg != null) { %>
  <span style="color: red;"><%=;"><%=;"><%=errMsg %></span>
<%} %>
<form method="post">
...
</form>
```

Here, we start another Java code block by using `<%%>`. If the error message is not null, we display it by using the `span` tag. Notice how the value of the error message is printed - `<%=errMsg %>`. This is the shortcut for `<%out.print(errMsg);%>`. Also, notice that the curly brace that started in one Java code block is completed in a separate Java code block. Between these two code blocks, you can add any HTML code and it will be included in the response only if the conditional expression in the if statement is evaluated to true.

Here is the complete code:

```
<%@ page language="java" contentType="text/html; charset=UTF-8"
    pageEncoding="UTF-8"%>
<!DOCTYPE html PUBLIC "-//W3C//DTD HTML 4.01 Transitional//EN"
"http://www.w3.org/TR/html4/loose.dtd">
<html>
<head>
<meta http-equiv="Content-Type" content="text/html;
charset=UTF-8">
<title>Login</title>
</head>
<%
  String errMsg = null;
  //first check whether the form was submitted
  if ("POST".equalsIgnoreCase(request.getMethod()) &&
  request.getParameter("submit") != null)
  {
    //form was submitted
    String userName = request.getParameter("userName");
    String password = request.getParameter("password");
    if ("admin".equalsIgnoreCase(userName) &&
    "admin".equalsIgnoreCase(password))
    {
      //valid user
      out.println("Welcome admin !");
```

```
        return;
      }
      else
      {
        //invalid user. Set error message
        errMsg = "Invalid user id or password. Please try again";
      }
    }
%>
<body>
  <h2>Login:</h2>
  <!-- Check error message. If it is set, then display it -->
  <%if (errMsg != null) { %>
    <span style="color: red;"><%out.print(errMsg); %></span>
  <%} %>
  <form method="post">
    User Name: <input type="text" name="userName"><br>
    Password: <input type="password" name="password"><br>
    <button type="submit" name="submit">Submit</button>
    <button type="reset">Reset</button>
  </form>
</body>
</html>
```

Running JSP in Tomcat

To run this page in a web browser, you will need to deploy the application in a Servlet container. We have already seen how to configure Tomcat in Eclipse. Make sure that Tomcat is running by checking its status in the **Servers** view of Eclipse.

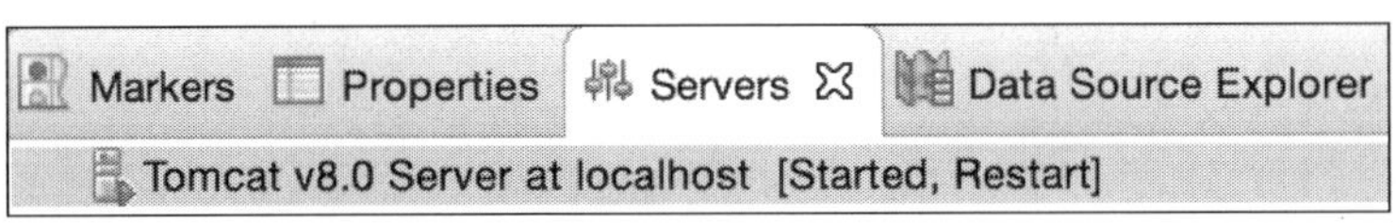

Figure 2.15 Tomcat started in the Servers view

There are two ways to add a project to a configured server so that the application can be run on this server:

- Right-click on the server in the **Servers** view and select the **Add and Remove** option. Select your project from the list on the left (**Available Resources**), and click **Add** to move it to the **Configured** list. Click **Finish**.

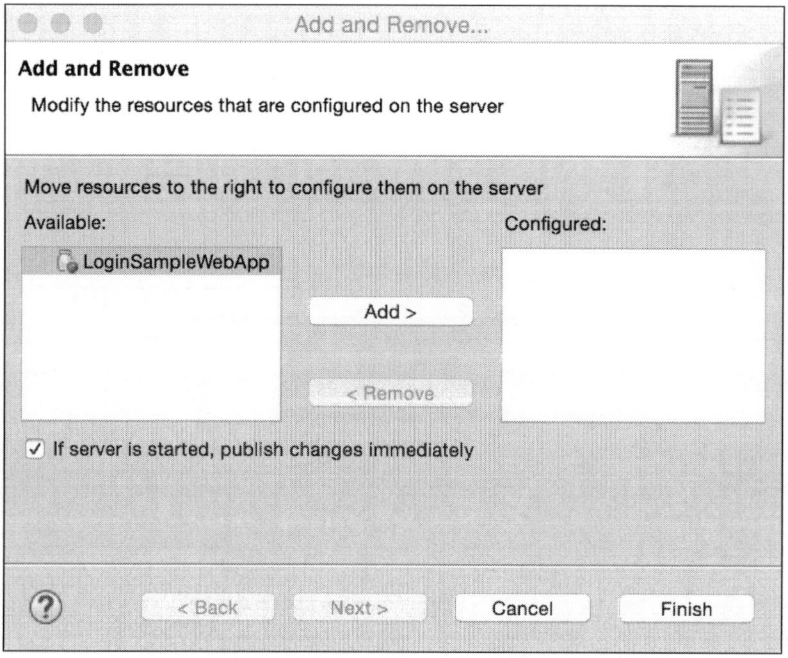

Figure 2.16 Add a project to the server

- The other method to add a project to the server is to right-click on the project in the **Project Explorer** and select **Properties**. This opens the **Project Properties** dialog box. Click on **Server** in the list, and select the server on which you want to deploy this project. Click **OK** or **Apply**.

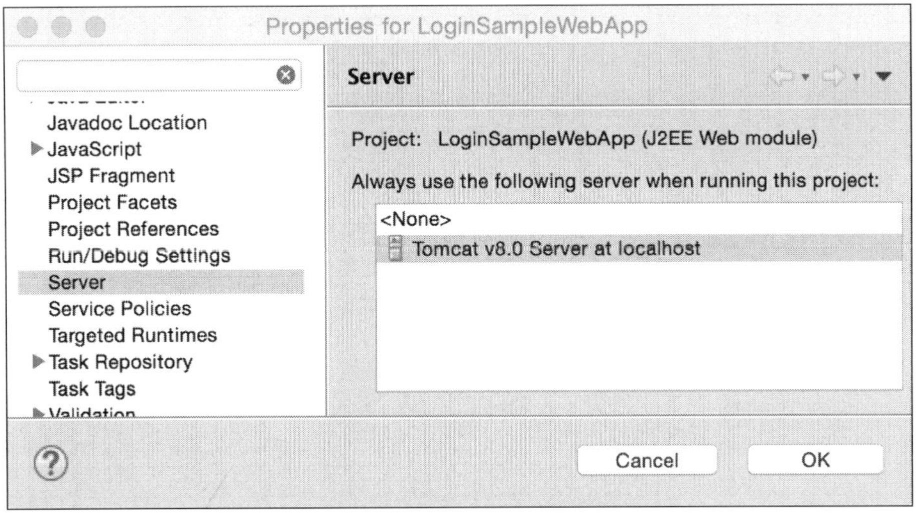

Figure 2.17 Select Server in Project Properties

In the first method, the project is immediately deployed on the server. In the second method, it will be deployed only when you run the project on the server.

1. To run the application, right-click on the project in **Project Explorer** and select **Run As** | **Run on Server**. The first time you will be prompted to restart the server. Once the application is deployed, you will see it under the selected server in the **Servers** view:

Figure 2.18 Project deployed on the server

2. Enter some text other than admin in the username and password boxes and click **Submit**. You should see the error message and the same form displayed again.

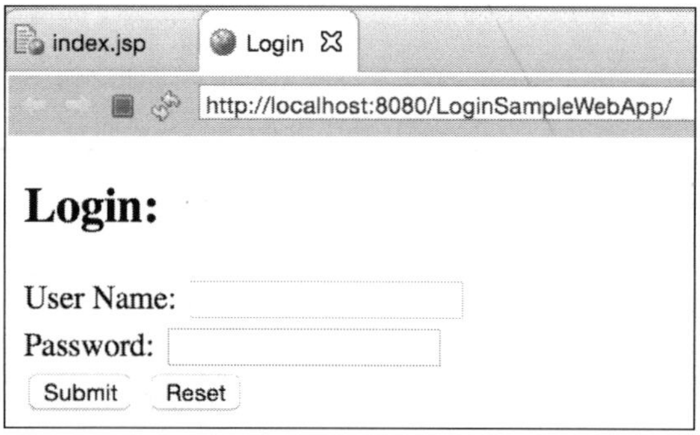

Figure 2.19 Project running in the built-in browser in Eclipse

3. Now enter `admin` as the username and the password and then submit the form. You should see the welcome message.

JSPs are compiled dynamically to Java classes, so if you make any changes in a page, in most cases, you do not have to restart the server; just refresh the page, and Tomcat will recompile the page if it has changed and the modified page would be displayed. In cases when you need to restart the server to apply your changes, Eclipse would prompt you if you want to restart the server.

Using JavaBeans in JSP

The code that we wrote in JSP above does not follow JSP best practices. In general, it is a bad idea to have scriplets (Java code) in JSP. In most large organizations, the UI designer and programmers are different roles performed by different people. Therefore, it is recommended that JSP contains mostly markup tags so that it is easy for a designer to work on page design. The Java code should be in separate classes. It also makes sense from the reusability point of view to move the Java code out of JSP.

You can delegate the processing of the business logic to JavaBeans from JSP. JavaBeans are simple Java objects with attributes and getters and setters for these objects. The naming convention for a getter/setter in JavaBeans is to get/set followed by the name of the attribute, with the first letter of each word in uppercase, also known as CamelCase. For example, if you have a class attribute named `firstName`, then the getter function will be `getFirstName` and the setter will be `setFirstName`.

JSP has a special tag for using JavaBeans – `jsp:useBean`:

```
<jsp:useBean id="name_of_variable" class="name_of_bean_class"
scope="scope_of_bean"/>
```

Scope indicates the lifetime of this bean. Valid values are `application`, `page`, `request`, and `session`.

Scope name	Description
`page`	Bean can be used only in the current page.
`request`	Bean can be used in any page in the processing of the same request. One JSP request can be handled by multiple JSPs if one page forwards the request to another page.
`session`	Bean can be used in the same HTTP session. The session is useful if your application wants to save the user data per interaction with the application, for example, to save items in the shopping cart in an online store application.
`application`	Bean can be used in any page in the same web application. Typically, web applications are deployed in a web application container as **Web Application Archive** (**WAR**) files. In the application scope, all JSPs in a WAR file can use JavaBeans within this scope.

We will move the code to validate the user in our login example to a `JavaBean` class. First, we need to create the `JavaBean` class.

1. In **Project Explorer**, right-click on the `src` folder **New** | **Package** menu option.
2. Create a package named `packt.book.jee_eclipse.ch2.bean`.
3. Right-click on the package, and select the **New** | **Class** menu option.
4. Create a class named `LoginBean`.
5. Create two private **String** members as follows:

```
public class LoginBean {
  private String userName;
  private String password;
}
```

6. Right-click anywhere inside the class (in the editor) and select the **Source | Generate Getters and Setter ...** menu option:

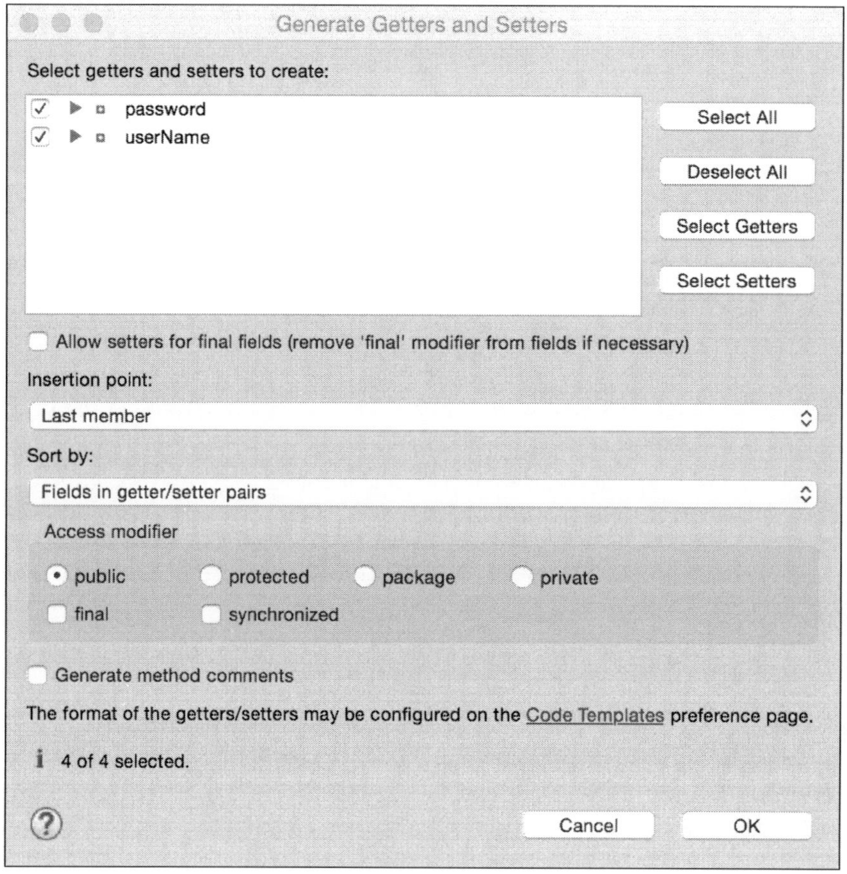

Figure 2.20 Generate getters and setters

7. We want to generate the getters and setters for all members of the class. Therefore, click the **Select All** button and select **Last member** from the drop-down list for **Insertion point** because we want to insert the getters and setters after declaring all member variables.

   You class should now look like this:

```
public class LoginBean {
  private String userName;
  private String password;
  public String getUserName() {
    return userName;
  }
```

```
  public void setUserName(String userName) {
    this.userName = userName;
  }
  public String getPassword() {
    return password;
  }
  public void setPassword(String password) {
    this.password = password;
  }
}
```

8. We will add one more method to it, to validate the username and the password:

```
public boolean isValidUser()
  {
    //Validation can happen here from a number of sources
    //for example, database and LDAP
    //We are just going to hardcode a valid username and
    //password here.
    return "admin".equals(this.userName) &&
           "admin".equals(this.password);
  }
```

This completes our JavaBean for storing user information and validation.

9. We will now use this bean in our JSP and delegate the task of validating a user to this bean. Open `index.jsp`. Replace the Java scriplet just above the `<body>` tag in the preceding code with the following:

```
<%String errMsg = null; %>
<%if ("POST".equalsIgnoreCase(request.getMethod()) && request.
getParameter("submit") != null) {%>
  <jsp:useBean id="loginBean"
  class="packt.book.jee_eclipse.ch2.bean.LoginBean">
    <jsp:setProperty name="loginBean" property="*"/>
  </jsp:useBean>
  <%
    if (loginBean.isValidUser())
    {
      //valid user
      out.println("<h2>Welcome admin !</h2>");
      out.println("You are successfully logged in");
    }
    else
```

```
        {
          errMsg = "Invalid user id or password. Please try again";
        }
      %>
    <%} %>
```

10. Before we discuss what has been changed, note that you can invoke and get code assist for the attributes and values of `<jsp:*>` tags too. If you are not sure where code assist is available, just press *Ctrl* + *Command* + *C*.

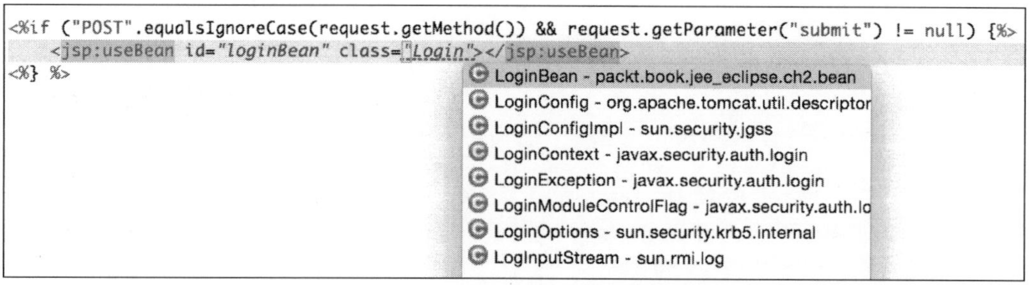

Figure 2.21 Code assist in JSP tags

Notice that Eclipse displays code assist for the JavaBean that we just added.

Now; let's understand what we changed in the code:

- We created multiple scriplets, one for declaration of the `errMsg` variable and two more to start an `if` block and end the same `if` block.
- We added the `<jsp:useBean` tag in the `if` condition. The bean will be created when the condition in the `if` statement is satisfied, that is, when the form is posted by clicking the **Submit** button.
- We used the `<jsp:setProperty>` tag to set the attributes of the bean:

  ```
  <jsp:setProperty name="loginBean" property="*"/>
  ```

  We are setting the values of the member variables of `loginBean`. Further, we are setting the values of all the member variables by specifying `property="*"`. However, where do we specify values? The values are specified implicitly because we have named the members of `LoginBean` to be the same as the fields in the form. Therefore, the JSP runtime gets parameters from a request object and assigns values to the JavaBean members with the same name.

If the member names of JavaBean do not match the request parameters, then you set the values explicitly by using the same tag:

```
<jsp:setProperty name="loginBean" property="userName"
  value="<%=request.getParameter(\"userName\")%>"/>
<jsp:setProperty name="loginBean" property="password"
  value="<%=request.getParameter(\"password\")%>"/>
```

- We then checked whether a user is valid by calling `loginBean.isValidUser()`. The code to handle an error message is the same as that shown in the previous example.

To test the page we have just completed, perform the following steps:

1. Right-click on `index.jsp` in **Project Explorer**.
2. Select the **Run As** | **Run on Server** menu option. Eclipse will prompt you to restart Tomcat.
3. Click the **OK** button to restart Tomcat.

The page will be displayed in the internal Eclipse browser. It should behave in the same way as in the previous example.

Although we have moved the validation of a user to `LoginBean`, we still have a lot of code in Java scriplets. Ideally, we should have as few Java scriplets as possible in JSP. We still have the code for checking conditions and for variable assignments. We can write the same code by using tags so that it is consistent with the remaining tag-based code in JSP and will be easier for a web designer to work on it. This can be achieved using **JSP Standard Tag Library (JSTL)**.

Using JSTL

JSTL tags can be used to replace much of the Java code written in scriplets. JSTL tags are classified in five broad groups:

- **Core**: Covers flow control and variable support among other things
- **XML**: Tags to process an XML document
- **i18n**: Tags to support internationalization
- **SQL**: Tags to access a database
- **Functions**: Tags to perform some of the common string operations

> See `http://docs.oracle.com/javaee/5/tutorial/doc/bnake.html` for more details on JSTL.

We will modify the login JSP to use JSTL so that there are no Java scriplets in it.

1. Download JSTL libraries from `https://jstl.java.net/download.html`.
2. The download page contains links to JSTL API and Implementation. Make sure you download both.

   As of writing this chapter, the latest .jar files are `javax.servlet.jsp.jstl-api-1.2.1.jar` (`http://search.maven.org/remotecontent?filepath=javax/servlet/jsp/jstl/javax.servlet.jsp.jstl-api/1.2.1/javax.servlet.jsp.jstl-api-1.2.1.jar`) and `javax.servlet.jsp.jstl-1.2.1.jar` (`http://search.maven.org/remotecontent?filepath=org/glassfish/web/javax.servlet.jsp.jstl/1.2.1/javax.servlet.jsp.jstl-1.2.1.jar`). Make sure that these files are copied to `WEB-INF/lib`. All .jar files in this folder are added to the `classpath` of the web application.

3. We need to add a declaration for JSTL in our JSP. So, add the following `taglib` declaration below the first page declaration (`<%@ page language="java" ...>`):

   ```
   <%@ taglib prefix="c" uri="http://java.sun.com/jsp/jstl/core" %>
   ```

   The `taglib` declaration contains the URL of the `tag` library and `prefix`. All tags in the tag library are accessed using `prefix` in JSP.

4. Replace `<%String errMsg = null; %>` with the `set` tag of JSTL:

   ```
   <c:set var="errMsg" value="${null}"/>
   <c:set var="displayForm" value="${true}"/>
   ```

   > We have enclosed the value in `${}`. This is called **Expression Language (EL)**. You enclose the Java expression in JSTL in `${}`.

   We have also set a new variable called `displayForm` (initialized to `true`). We will see later where it is used.

5. Replace the following code:

   ```
   <%if ("POST".equalsIgnoreCase(request.getMethod()) &&

   request.getParameter("submit") != null) {%>
   ```

   With the `if` tag of JSTL:

   ```
   <c:if test="${\"POST\".equalsIgnoreCase(pageContext.request

   .method) && pageContext.request.getParameter(\"submit\") !=
   null}">
   ```

> The `request` object is accessed in the JSTL tag via `pageContext`.

6. JavaBean tags go within the `if` tag. There is no change here.

```
<jsp:useBean id="loginBean"
  class="packt.book.jee_eclipse.ch2.bean.LoginBean">
  <jsp:setProperty name="loginBean" property="*"/>
</jsp:useBean>
```

7. We then add tags to call `loginBean.isValidUser()` and based on its return value, to set messages. However, we can't use the `if` tag of JSTL here, because we need to write an `else` statement too. JSTL does not have a tag for `else`. Instead, for multiple *if-else* statements, you need to use the `choose` statement, which is somewhat similar to the Java `switch` statement:

```
<c:choose>
  <c:when test="${!loginBean.isValidUser()}">
    <c:set var="errMsg" value="Invalid user id or password. Please
    try again"/>
  </c:when>
  <c:otherwise>
    <h2><c:out value="Welcome admin !"/></h2>
    <c:out value="You are successfully logged in"/>
    <c:set var="displayForm" value="${false}"/>
  </c:otherwise>
</c:choose>
```

If the user credentials are not valid, we set an error message. Else (the `c:otherwise` tag), we print the welcome message and set the `displayForm` flag to `false`. We don't want to display the login form if the user is successfully logged in.

8. Consider this code:

```
<%if (errMsg != null) { %>
  <span style="color: red;"><%out.print(errMsg); %></span>
<%} %>
```

Replace it with the following code:

```
<c:if test="${errMsg != null}">
  <span style="color: red;">
    <c:out value="${errMsg}"></c:out>
  </span>
</c:if>
```

Here again, we replace the `if` statement in the scriplet with the JSTL `if` tag. Further, we use the `out` tag to print an error message.

9. Finally, we enclose the entire `<body>` content in another JSTL `if` tag:

```
<c:if test="${displayForm}">
<body>
   ...
</body>
</c:if>
```

Here is the complete source code:

```
<%@ page language="java" contentType="text/html; charset=UTF-8"
    pageEncoding="UTF-8"%>
<%@ taglib prefix="c" uri="http://java.sun.com/jsp/jstl/core" %>

<!DOCTYPE html PUBLIC "-//W3C//DTD HTML 4.01 Transitional//EN"
"http://www.w3.org/TR/html4/loose.dtd">
<html>
<head>
<meta http-equiv="Content-Type" content="text/html; charset=UTF-
8">
<title>Login</title>
</head>

<c:set var="errMsg" value="${null}"/>
<c:set var="displayForm" value="${true}"/>
<c:if test="${\"POST\".equalsIgnoreCase(pageContext.request.method)
&& pageContext.request.getParameter(\"submit\") != null}">
  <jsp:useBean id="loginBean"
  class="packt.book.jee_eclipse.ch2.bean.LoginBean">
    <jsp:setProperty name="loginBean" property="*"/>
  </jsp:useBean>
  <c:choose>
    <c:when test="${!loginBean.isValidUser()}">
      <c:set var="errMsg" value="Invalid user id or password.
      Please try again"/>
    </c:when>
    <c:otherwise>
    <h2><c:out value="Welcome admin !"/></h2>
      <c:out value="You are successfully logged in"/>
```

```
        <c:set var="displayForm" value="${false}"/>
      </c:otherwise>
    </c:choose>
  </c:if>

  <c:if test="${displayForm}">
  <body>
    <h2>Login:</h2>
    <!-- Check error message. If it is set, then display it -->
    <c:if test="${errMsg != null}">
      <span style="color: red;">
        <c:out value="${errMsg}"></c:out>
      </span>
    </c:if>
    <form method="post">
      User Name: <input type="text" name="userName"><br>
      Password: <input type="password" name="password"><br>
      <button type="submit" name="submit">Submit</button>
      <button type="reset">Reset</button>
    </form>
  </body>
  </c:if>
  </html>
```

As you can see, there are no Java scriplets in the previous code. All of them are replaced by tags. If a web designer opens this code in any HTML editor, they will be able to edit the HTML code quite easily without any interfering Java code.

One last note before we leave the topic of JSP. In a real-world application, you would probably forward the request to another page after logging in the user successfully, instead of just displaying the welcome message on the same page. You could use the `<jsp:forward>` tag to achieve this.

Implementing login application using Java Servlet

We will now see how to implement a login application using Servlet. Create a new **Dynamic Web Application** in Eclipse as described in the previous section. We will call this `LoginServletApp`.

1. Right-click on the **src** folder under **Java Resources** for the project in **Project Explorer**. Select the **New** | **Servlet** menu option.

2. In the **Create Servlet** wizard, enter the package name as `packt.book.jee_eclipse.book.servlet` and the class name as `LoginServlet`. Then, click **Finish**.

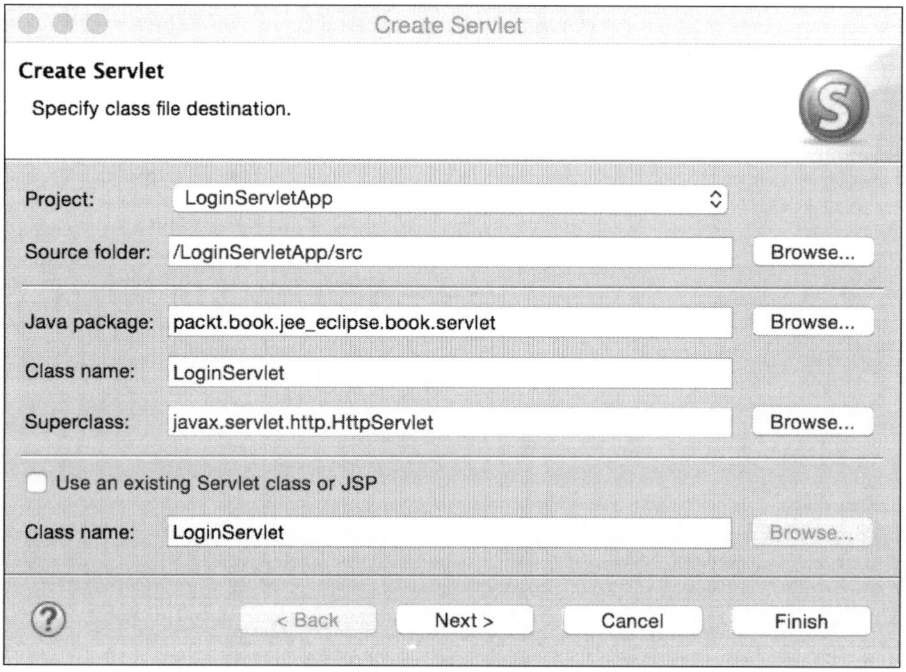

Figure 2.22 Create Servlet wizard

3. The Servlet wizard creates the class for you. Notice the `@WebServlet("/LoginServlet")` annotation just above the class declaration. Before JEE 5, you had to declare servlets in `web.xml` in the `WEB-INF` folder. You can still do that, but you can skip this declaration if you use proper annotations. Using `WebServlet`, we are telling the servlet container that `LoginServlet` is a servlet, and we are mapping it to the following URL path: `/LoginServlet`. Thus, we are avoiding two entries in `web.xml` by using this annotation:
    - `<servlet>`
    - `<servlet-mapping>`

   We will now change the mapping from `/LoginServlet` to just `/login`. Therefore, we will modify the annotation as follows:

```
@WebServlet("/login")
  public class LoginServlet extends HttpServlet {...}
```

4. The wizard also created the `doGet` and `doPost` functions. These functions are overridden from the following base class: `HttpServlet`.

   The `doGet` function is called to create a response for the `Get` request, and `doPost` is called to create a response for the `Post` request.

   We will create the login form in the `doGet` function and process the form data (`Post`) in the `doPost` function. However, since `doPost` may need to display the form in case the user credentials are invalid, we will write the `createForm` function, which could be called from both `doGet` and `doPost`.

5. Add the `createForm` function as follows:

```
protected String createForm(String errMsg) {
  StringBuilder sb = new StringBuilder("<h2>Login</h2>");
  //check whether error message is to be displayed
  if (errMsg != null) {
    sb.append("<span style='color: red;'>")
      .append(errMsg)
      .append("</span>");
  }
  //create form
  sb.append("<form method='post'>\n")
    .append("User Name: <input type='text'
    name='userName'><br>\n")
    .append("Password: <input type='password'
    name='password'><br>\n")
    .append("<button type='submit'
    name='submit'>Submit</button>\n")
    .append("<button type='reset'>Reset</button>\n")
    .append("</form>");

  return sb.toString();
}
```

6. We will now modify the `doGet` function to call the `createForm` function and return it as the response:

```
protected void doGet(HttpServletRequest request,
HttpServletResponse response)
  throws ServletException, IOException {
  response.getWriter().write(createForm(null));
}
```

   We call the `getWrite` method on the response object and write the form content to it by calling the `createForm` function. Note that when we display the form, initially, there is no error message, so we pass a null argument to `createForm`.

7. We will modify `doPost` to process the form content when the user posts the form by clicking on the **Submit** button.

```
protected void doPost(HttpServletRequest request,
  HttpServletResponse response)
  throws ServletException, IOException {
    String userName = request.getParameter("userName");
    String password = request.getParameter("password");

  //create StringBuilder to hold response string
  StringBuilder responseStr = new StringBuilder();
  if ("admin".equals(userName) && "admin".equals(password)) {
    responseStr.append("<h2>Welcome admin !</h2>")
    .append("You are successfully logged in");
  }
  else {
    //invalid user credentials
    responseStr.append(createForm("Invalid user id or password.
    Please try again"));
  }

  response.getWriter().write(responseStr.toString());
}
```

   We first get the username and the password from the request object by calling the `request.getParameter` method. If the credentials are valid, we add a welcome message to the response string; else, we call `createForm` with an error message and add a return value (markup for the form) to the response string.

   Finally, we get the writer object from the response and write the response.

8. Right-click on the `LoginServlet.java` file in **Project Explorer** and select the **Run As | Run on Server** option. We have not added this project to the Tomcat server. Therefore, Eclipse will ask if you want to use the configured server to run this servlet. Click the **Finish** button of the wizard.
9. Since a new web application is deployed in the server, Tomcat needs to restart. Eclipse will prompt you to restart the server. Click **OK**.

When the servlet is opened in the internal browser of Eclipse, notice the URL; it ends with `/login`, which is the mapping that we specified in the servlet annotation. However, you will observe that instead of rendering an HTML form, the page displays the markup text. This is because we missed an important setting on the response object. We did not tell the browser the type of content that we are returning, so the browser assumed it to be text and rendered it as plain text. We need to tell the browser that it is HTML content. We do this by calling `response.setContentType("text/html")` in both the `doGet` and the `doPost` methods. Here is the complete source code:

```
package packt.book.jee_eclipse.book.servlet;
import java.io.IOException;
import javax.servlet.ServletException;
import javax.servlet.annotation.WebServlet;
import javax.servlet.http.HttpServlet;
import javax.servlet.http.HttpServletRequest;
import javax.servlet.http.HttpServletResponse;


/**
 * Servlet implementation class LoginServlet
 */
@WebServlet("/login")
public class LoginServlet extends HttpServlet {
  private static final long serialVersionUID = 1L;

  public LoginServlet() {
    super();
  }
  //Handles HTTP Get requests
  protected void doGet(HttpServletRequest request, HttpServletResponse
response)
    throws ServletException, IOException {
  response.setContentType("text/html");
  response.getWriter().write(createForm(null));
  }
  //Handles HTTP POST requests
  protected void doPost(HttpServletRequest request,
  HttpServletResponse response)
      throws ServletException, IOException {
    String userName = request.getParameter("userName");
    String password = request.getParameter("password");

    //create StringBuilder to hold response string
    StringBuilder responseStr = new StringBuilder();
```

```
        if ("admin".equals(userName) && "admin".equals(password)) {
          responseStr.append("<h2>Welcome admin !</h2>")
            .append("You're are successfully logged in");
        } else {
          //invalid user credentials
          responseStr.append(createForm("Invalid user id or password.
          Please try again"));
        }
        response.setContentType("text/html");
        response.getWriter().write(responseStr.toString());
      }

      //Creates HTML Login form
      protected String createForm(String errMsg) {
        StringBuilder sb = new StringBuilder("<h2>Login</h2>");
        //check if error message to be displayed
        if (errMsg != null) {
          sb.append("<span style='color: red;'>")
            .append(errMsg)
            .append("</span>");
        }
        //create form
        sb.append("<form method='post'>\n")
          .append("User Name: <input type='text'
          name='userName'><br>\n")
          .append("Password: <input type='password'
          name='password'><br>\n")
          .append("<button type='submit'
          name='submit'>Submit</button>\n")
          .append("<button type='reset'>Reset</button>\n")
          .append("</form>");
        return sb.toString();
      }
    }
```

As you can see, it is not very convenient to write HTML markup in Servlet. Therefore, if you are creating a page with a lot of HTML markup, then it is better to use JSP or plain HTML. Servlets are good to process requests that do not need to generate too much markup, for example, controllers in the **Model-View-Controller (MVC)** framework; for processing requests that generate a non-text response; or for creating a web service or web-socket end points.

Creating WAR

Thus far, we have been running our web application from Eclipse, which does all the work of deploying the application to the Tomcat server. This works fine during development, but when you want to deploy it to the test or the production server, you need to create **Web Application Archive (WAR)**. We will see how to create WAR from Eclipse. However, first, un-deploy the existing applications from Tomcat.

1. Go to the **Servers** view, select the application, and right-click and select the **Remove** option.

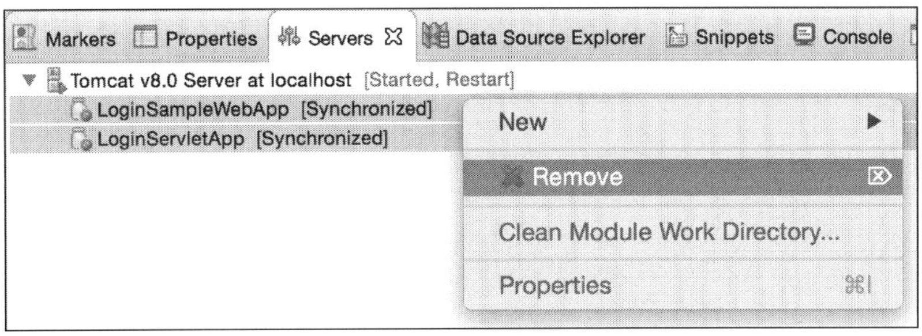

Figure 2.23 Un-deploy a web application from the server

2. Then, right-click on the project in **Project Explorer** and select **Export | WAR file**. Select the destination for the WAR file.

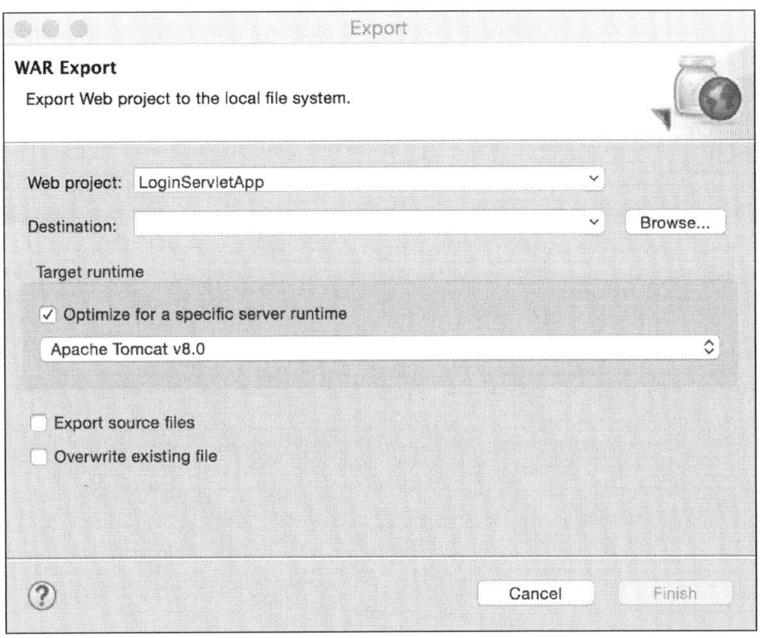

Figure 2.24 Export WAR

3. To deploy the WAR file to Tomcat, copy it to the `<tomcat_home>/webapps` folder.
4. Start the server if it is not already running. If Tomcat is already running, you don't need to restart it.

Tomcat monitors the `webapps` folder, and any WAR file copied to it is automatically deployed. You can verify this by opening the URL of your application in the browser, for example, `http://localhost:8080/LoginServletApp/login`.

Java Server Faces

When working with JSP, we saw that it is not a good idea to mix scriplets with the HTML markup. We solved this problem by using JavaBean. Java Server Faces takes this design further, and in addition to supporting JavaBeans, it provides built-in tags for HTML user controls, which are context aware, can perform validation, and can preserve the state between requests. We will now create the login application using JSF.

1. Create a dynamic web application in Eclipse; let's name it `LoginJSFApp`. In the last page of the wizard, make sure that you check the **Generate web.xml deployment descriptor** box.
2. Download JSF libraries from `https://maven.java.net/content/repositories/releases/org/glassfish/javax.faces/2.2.9/javax.faces-2.2.9.jar` and copy to the `WEB-INF/lib` folder in your project.
3. JSF follows the MVC pattern. In the MVC pattern, the code to generate a user interface (view) is separate from the container of the data (model). The controller acts as the interface between the view and the model. It selects the model for processing a request on the basis of the configuration, and once the model processes the request, it selects the view to be generated and returned to the client, on the basis of the result of the processing in the model. The advantage of MVC is that there is a clear separation of the UI and the business logic (which requires a different set of expertise) so that they can be developed independently to a large extent. In JSP, the implementation of MVC is optional, but JSF enforces the MVC design.

Views in JSF are created as `xhtml` files. The controller is a servlet from the JSF library, and the models are **Managed Beans** (JavaBeans).

We will first configure a controller for JSF. We will add the servlet configuration and mapping in `web.xml`. Open `web.xml` from the `WEB-INF` folder of the project (`web.xml` should have been created for you by the project wizard if you checked the **Generate web.xml deployment descriptor** box. See Step 1). Add the following XML snippet before `</web-app>`:

```
<servlet>
  <servlet-name>JSFServlet</servlet-name>
  <servlet-class>javax.faces.webapp.FacesServlet</servlet-class>
  <load-on-startup>1</load-on-startup>
</servlet>

<servlet-mapping>
  <servlet-name>JSFServlet</servlet-name>
  <url-pattern>*.xhtml</url-pattern>
</servlet-mapping>
```

Note that you can get code assist when creating the above elements by pressing *Ctrl/Command* + *C*.

You can specify any name as `servlet-name`; just make sure that you use the same name in `servlet-mapping`. The class for the servlet is `javax.faces.webapp.FacesServlet`, which is in the JAR file that we downloaded as the JSF libraries and copied to `WEB-INF/lib`. Further, we have mapped any request ending with `.xhtml` to this servlet.

Next, we will create **Managed Bean** for our login page. This is the same as JavaBean that we had written earlier with the addition of JSF-specific annotations.

1. Right-click on the `src` folder under **Java Resources** for the project in **Project Explorer**.
2. Select the **New** | **Class** menu option.
3. Create JavaBean, `LoginBean`, as described in the *Using JavaBeans in JSP* section.
4. Create two members for `userName` and `password`.
5. Create the getters and setters for them. Then, add two annotations as follows:

```
package packt.book.jee_eclipse.bean;
import javax.faces.bean.ManagedBean;
import javax.faces.bean.RequestScoped;

@ManagedBean(name="loginBean")
@RequestScoped
```

```
public class LoginBean {
  private String userName;
  private String password;
  public String getUserName() {
    return userName;
  }
  public void setUserName(String userName) {
    this.userName = userName;
  }
  public String getPassword() {
    return password;
  }
  public void setPassword(String password) {
    this.password = password;
  }
}
```

(You can get code assist for annotations too. Type `@` and press *Ctrl*/*Command* + *C*. Code assist works for the annotation `key-value` attribute pairs too, for example, for the name attribute of the `ManagedBean` annotation).

6. Create a new file called `index.xhtml` inside the `WebContent` folder of the project by selecting the **File** | **New** | **File** menu option. When using JSF, you need to add a few namespace declarations at the top of the file.

```
<html xmlns="http://www.w3.org/1999/xhtml"
  xmlns:f="http://java.sun.com/jsf/core"
  xmlns:h="http://java.sun.com/jsf/html">
```

Here, we are declaring namespaces for JSF built-in tag libraries. We will access tags in the core JSF tag library with the prefix `f` and HTML tags with the prefix h.

7. Add the title and start the `body` tag:

```
<head>
  <title>Login</title>
</head>
<body>
  <h2>Login</h2>
```

> There are corresponding JSF tags for the head and the body, but we do not use any attributes specific to JSF; therefore, we have used simple HTML tags.

8. We then add the code to display an error message, if it is not null.

```
<h:outputText value="#{loginBean.errorMsg}"
              rendered="#{loginBean.errorMsg != null}"
              style="color:red;"/>
```

Here, we use a tag specific to JSF and expression language to display the value of the error message. The `OutputText` tag is similar to the `c:out` tag that we saw in JSTL. We have also added a condition to render it only if the error message in the managed bean is not null. Additionally, we have set the color of this output text.

We have not added the `errorMsg` member to the managed bean yet. Therefore, let's add the declaration, the getter, and the setter. Open the `LoginBean` class and add the following code:

```
private String errorMsg;
public String getErrorMsg() {
  return errorMsg;
}
public void setErrorMsg(String errorMsg) {
  this.errorMsg = errorMsg;
}
```

Note that we access the managed bean in JSF by using the value of the `name` attribute of the `ManagedBean` annotation. Further, unlike JavaBean in JSP, we do not create it by using the `<jsp:useBean>` tag. The JSF runtime creates the bean if it is not already there in the required scope, in this case, the `Request` scope.

9. Let's go back to editing `index.xhtml`. We will now add the following form:

```
<h:form>
  User Name: <h:inputText id="userName"
                value="#{loginBean.userName}"/><br/>
  Password: <h:inputSecret id="password"
                value="#{loginBean.password}"/><br/>
  <h:commandButton value="Submit"
  action="#{loginBean.validate}"/>
</h:form>
```

Many things are happening here. First, we have used the `inputText` tag of JSF to create textboxes for the username and the password. We have set their values with the corresponding members of `loginBean`. We have used the `commandButton` tag of JSF to create the **Submit** button. When the user clicks the **Submit** button, we have set it to call the `loginBean.validate` method (using the `action` attribute).

We haven't defined the validate method in `loginBean`, so let's add that. Open the `LoginBean` class and add the following code:

```
public String validate()
{
  if ("admin".equals(userName) && "admin".equals(password)) {
    errorMsg = null;
    return "welcome";
  } else {
    errorMsg = "Invalid user id or password. Please try
    again";
    return null;
  }
}
```

10. Note that the `validate` method returns a string. How is the return value used? It is used for navigation purposes in JSF. The JSF runtime looks for the JSF file with the same name as the string value returned after evaluating the expression in the `action` attribute of `commandButton`. In the `validate` method, we return `welcome` if the user credentials are valid. We tell the JSF runtime to navigate to `welcome.xhtml` in this case. If the credentials are invalid, we set an error message and return null, in which case, the JSF runtime displays the same page.
11. We will now add the `welcome.xhml` page. It simply contains the welcome message:

```
<html xmlns="http://www.w3.org/1999/xhtml"
      xmlns:f="http://java.sun.com/jsf/core"
      xmlns:h="http://java.sun.com/jsf/html">
  <body>
    <h2>Welcome admin !</h2>
      You are successfully logged in
  </body>
</html>
```

Here is the complete source code of `index.html`:

```
<html xmlns="http://www.w3.org/1999/xhtml"
  xmlns:f="http://java.sun.com/jsf/core"
  xmlns:h="http://java.sun.com/jsf/html">

  <head>
    <title>Login</title>
  </head>
  <body>
```

```
    <h2>Login</h2>
    <h:outputText value="#{loginBean.errorMsg}"
    rendered="#{loginBean.errorMsg != null}"
    style="color:red;"/>
    <h:form>
      User Name: <h:inputText id="userName"
      value="#{loginBean.userName}"/><br/>
      Password: <h:inputSecret id="password"
      value="#{loginBean.password}"/><br/>
    <h:commandButton value="Submit" action="#{loginBean.validate}"/>
    </h:form>
  </body>
  </html>
```

Further, here is the source code of the `LoginBean` class:

```
package packt.book.jee_eclipse.bean;
import javax.faces.bean.ManagedBean;
import javax.faces.bean.RequestScoped;

@ManagedBean(name="loginBean")
@RequestScoped
public class LoginBean {
  private String userName;
  private String password;
  private String errorMsg;
  public String getUserName() {
    return userName;
  }
  public void setUserName(String userName) {
    this.userName = userName;
  }
  public String getPassword() {
    return password;
  }
  public void setPassword(String password) {
    this.password = password;
  }
  public String getErrorMsg() {
    return errorMsg;
  }
  public void setErrorMsg(String errorMsg) {
    this.errorMsg = errorMsg;
  }
```

```
    public String validate()
    {
      if ("admin".equals(userName) && "admin".equals(password)) {
        errorMsg = null;
        return "welcome";
      }
      else {
        errorMsg = "Invalid user id or password. Please try again";
        return null;
      }
    }
  }
```

To run the application, right-click on `index.xhtml` in **Project Explorer** and select the **Run As | Run on Server** option.

JSF can do much more than what we have seen in this small example – it has the support to validate an input and create page templates too. However, these topics are beyond the scope of this book. Visit `http://docs.oracle.com/cd/E11035_01/workshop102/webapplications/jsf/jsf-app-tutorial/Introduction.html` for a tutorial on JSF.

Using Maven for project management

In the projects that we created thus far in this chapter, we have managed many of the project management tasks, such as downloading libraries on which our project depends, adding them to the appropriate folder so that the web application can find it, and exporting the project to create the WAR file for deployment. These are just some of the project management tasks that we have performed so far, but there are many more, which we will see in the subsequent chapters. It helps to have a tool do many of the project management tasks for us so that we can focus on application development. There are some well-known build management tools available for Java, for example, Apache Ant (`http://ant.apache.org/`) and Maven (`http://maven.apache.org/`).

We will now see how to use Maven for project management in this chapter. By following the convention for creating the project structure and allowing projects to define the hierarchy, Maven makes project management easier than Ant. Ant is primarily a build tool, whereas Maven is a project management tool, which does build management too. See `http://maven.apache.org/what-is-maven.html` to understand what Maven can do.

In particular, Maven simplifies dependency management. You saw in the JSF project that we first downloaded the appropriate Jar files for JSF and copied them to the `lib` folder. Maven can automate this. You can configure Maven settings in `pom.xml`. **POM** stands for **Project Object Model**.

Before we use Maven, it is important to understand how it works. Maven uses repositories. Repositories contain plugins for many well-known libraries/projects. A plugin includes the project configuration information, JAR files required to use this project in your own project, and any other supporting artifacts. The default Maven repository is a collection of plugins. You can find a list of plugins in the default Maven repository at `http://maven.apache.org/plugins/index.html`. You can also browse the content of the Maven repository at `http://search.maven.org/#browse`. Maven also maintains a local repository on your machine. This local repository contains only those plugins that your projects have specified dependencies on. On Windows, you will find the local repository at `C:\Users\<username>\.m2`, and on Mac OS X, it is located at `~/.m2`.

You define plugins on which your project depends in the dependencies section of `pom.xml` (we will see the structure of `pom.xml` shortly when we create a Maven project). For example, we can specify a dependency on JSF. When you run the Maven tool, it first inspects all dependencies in `pom.xml`. It then checks whether the dependent plugins with the required versions are already downloaded in the local repository. If not, it downloads them from the central (remote) repository. You can also specify repositories to look in. If you do not specify any repository, then dependencies are searched in the central Maven repository.

We will create a Maven project and explore `pom.xml` in more detail. However, if you are curious to know what `pom.xml` is, then visit `http://maven.apache.org/pom.html#What_is_the_POM`.

The Eclipse JEE version has Maven built-in, so you don't need to download it. However, if you plan to use Maven from outside Eclipse, then download it from `http://maven.apache.org/download.cgi`. In this book, we will use Maven from Eclipse only, so you don't need to download it.

Maven views and preferences in Eclipse JEE

Before we create a Maven project, let's explore the views and preferences specific to Maven in Eclipse.

1. Select the **Window** | **Show View** | **Other...** menu.
2. Type `Maven` in the filter box. You will see two views for **Maven**:

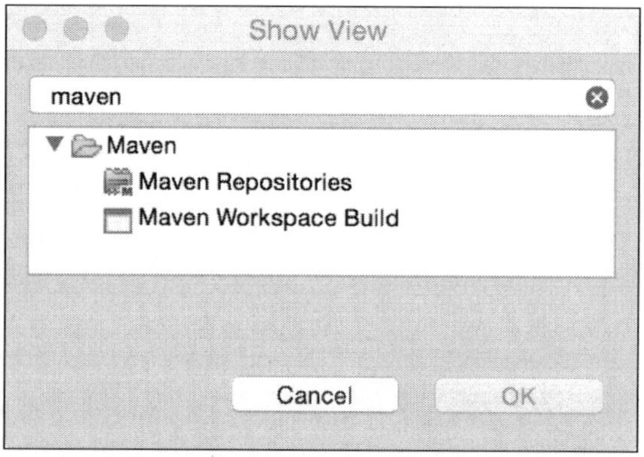

Figure 2.25 Maven views

3. Select the **Maven Repositories** view and click **OK**. This view is opened in the bottom tab window of Eclipse. You can see the location of the local and remote repositories.
4. Right-click on a global repository to see the options to index the repository.

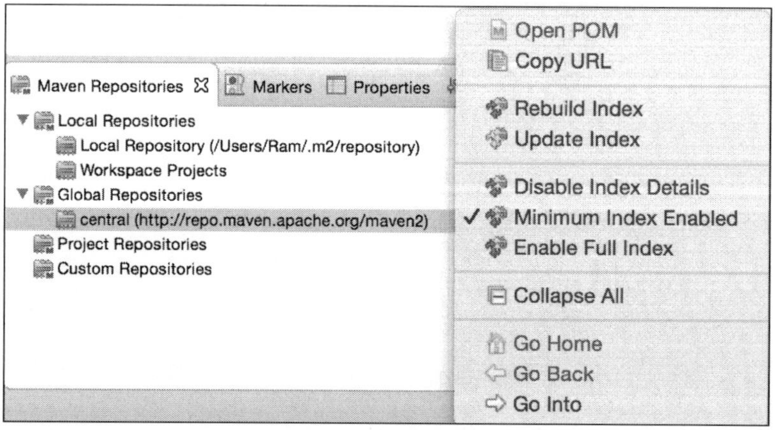

Figure 2.26 The Maven Repositories view

5. Open Eclipse **Preferences** and type `Maven` in the filter box to see all the Maven preferences.

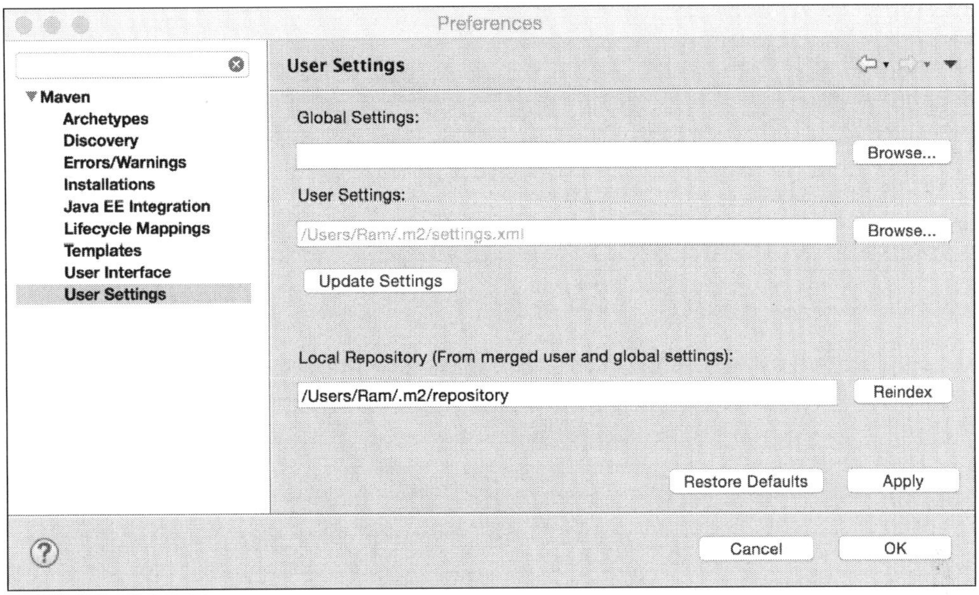

Figure 2.27 Maven Preferences

6. You should set the Maven preferences to refresh repository indexes on startup, so that the latest libraries are available when you add dependencies to your project (we will learn how to add dependencies shortly).
7. Click on the **Maven** node in **Preferences**, and set the following options:

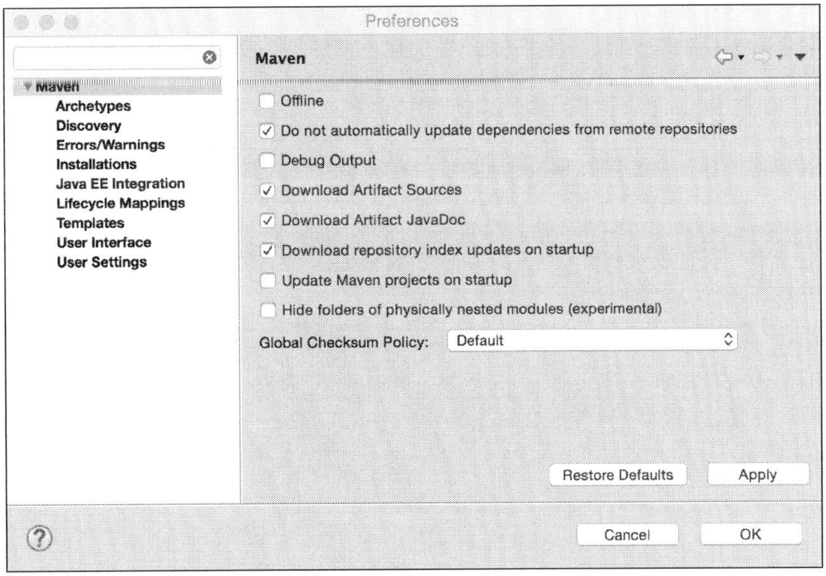

Figure 2.28 Maven Preferences for updating indexes on startup

Creating a Maven project

In the following steps, we will see how to create a Maven project in Eclipse.

1. Select the **New | Maven Project** menu.

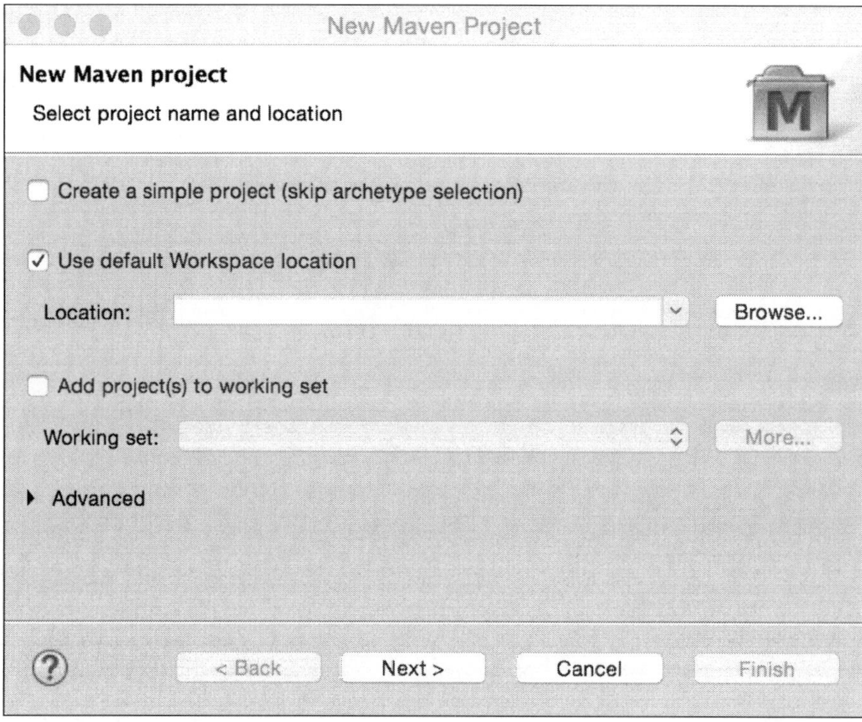

Figure 2.29 Maven New Project wizard

2. Accept all default options and click **Next**. Type `webapp` in the filter box and select **maven-archetype-webapp**.

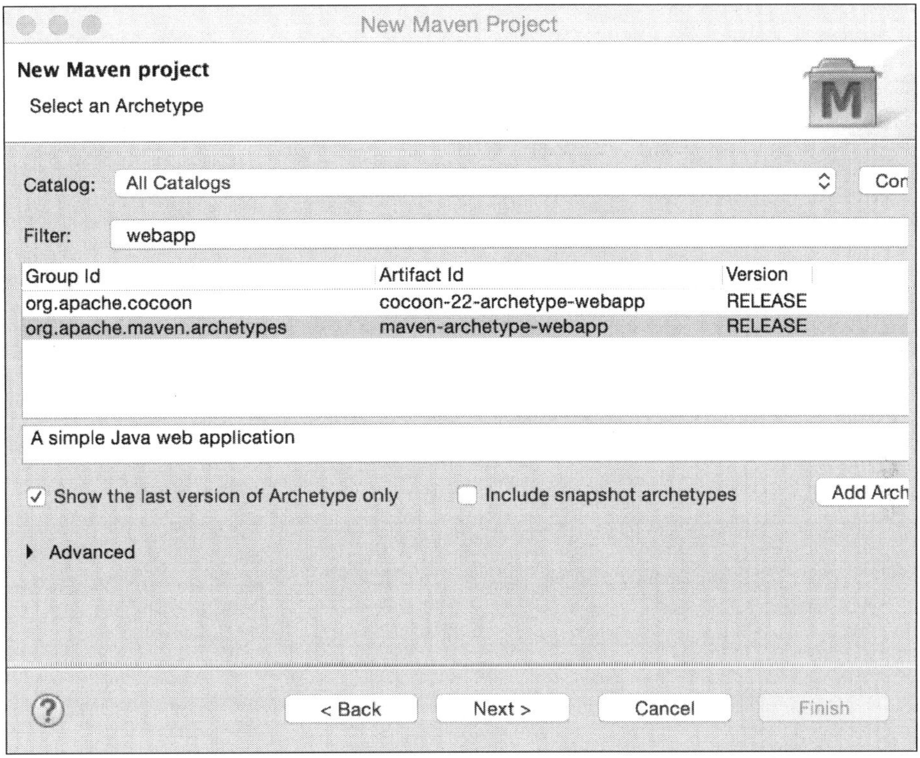

Figure 2.30 Maven New Project - select archetype

Maven Archetype

We selected **maven-archetype-webapp** in the preceding wizard. An archetype is a project template. When you use an archetype for your project, all the dependencies and other Maven project configurations defined in the template (archetype) are imported into your project. See more information about Maven Archetype at `http://maven.apache.org/guides/introduction/introduction-to-archetypes.html`.

Continuing with the **New Maven Project** wizard, click on **Next**. In the **Group Id** field, enter `packt.book.jee_eclipse`. In the **Artifact Id** field, enter `maven_jsf_web_app`.

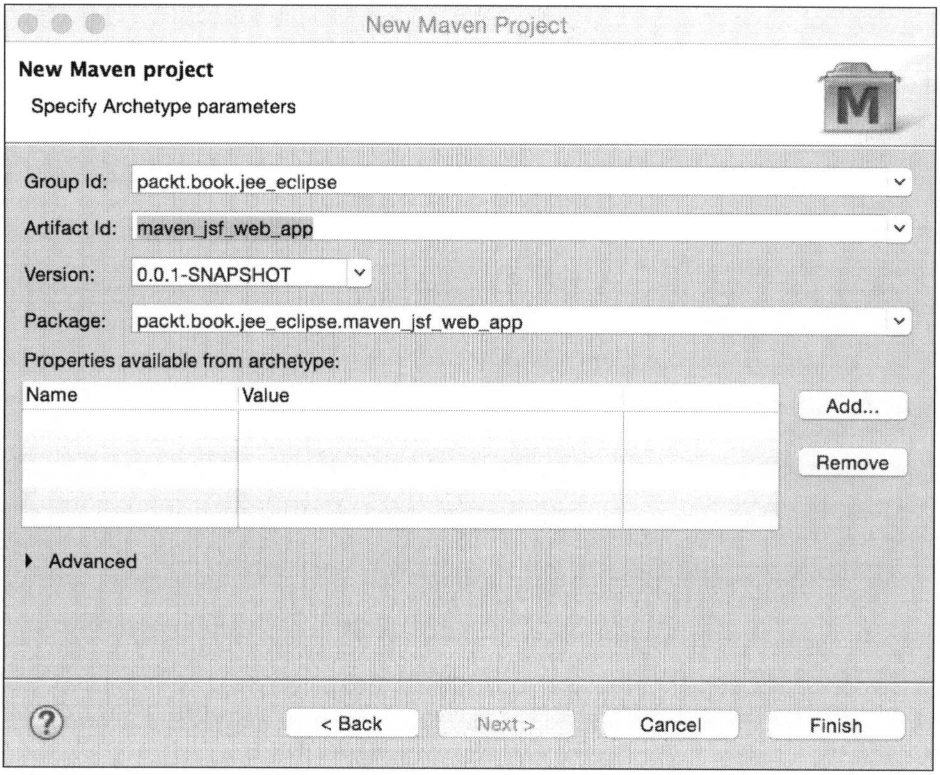

Figure 2.31 New Maven Project - Archetype parameters

Click on **Finish**. The `maven_jsf_web_app` project is added in **Project Explorer**.

Exploring the POM

Open `pom.xml` in the editor and go to the **pom.xml** tab. The following should be the content of the file:

```
<project xmlns="http://maven.apache.org/POM/4.0.0" xmlns:xsi="http://
www.w3.org/2001/XMLSchema-instance"
  xsi:schemaLocation="http://maven.apache.org/POM/4.0.0
  http://maven.apache.org/maven-v4_0_0.xsd">
  <modelVersion>4.0.0</modelVersion>
  <groupId>packt.book.jee_eclipse</groupId>
```

```
  <artifactId>maven_jsf_web_app</artifactId>
  <packaging>war</packaging>
  <version>0.0.1-SNAPSHOT</version>
  <name>maven_jsf_web_app Maven Webapp</name>
  <url>http://maven.apache.org</url>
  <dependencies>
    <dependency>
      <groupId>junit</groupId>
      <artifactId>junit</artifactId>
      <version>3.8.1</version>
      <scope>test</scope>
    </dependency>
  </dependencies>
  <build>
    <finalName>maven_jsf_web_app</finalName>
  </build>
</project>
```

- `modelVersion` in `pom.xml` is the version of Maven.
- `groupId` is the common ID used in a business unit or organization under which projects are grouped together. Although it is not necessary to use the package structure format, it is generally used.
- `artifactId` is the project name.
- `version` is the version number of the project. Version numbers are important when specifying dependencies. You can have multiple versions of a project, and you can specify different version dependencies in different projects. Maven also appends the version number to the JAR, WAR, or EAR file that it creates for the project.
- `packaging` tells Maven what kind of final output we want when the project is built. In this book, we will be using the JAR, WAR, and EAR packaging types, although more types exist.
- `name` is actually the name of the project, but Eclipse shows `artifactid` as the project name in **Project Explorer**.
- `url` is the URL of your project if you are hosting the project information on the web. The default is Maven's URL.
- The `dependencies` section is where we specify the libraries (or other Maven artifacts) that this project depends on. The archetype that we selected for this project has added a default dependency of JUnit to our project. We will learn more about JUnit in *Chapter 5, Unit Testing*.
- `finalName` in the `build` tag indicates the name of the output file (JAR, WAR, or EAR) that Maven generates for your project.

Adding Maven dependencies

The archetype that we selected for the project does not include some of the dependencies required for a JEE web project. Therefore, you might see an error marker in `index.jsp`. We will fix this by adding a dependency for the JEE libraries.

1. With `pom.xml` open in the editor, click on the **Dependencies** tab.
2. Click the **Add** button. This opens the **Select Dependency** dialog.
3. In the filter box, type `javax.servlet` (we want to use servlet APIs in the project).
4. Select the latest version of the API and click on the **OK** button.

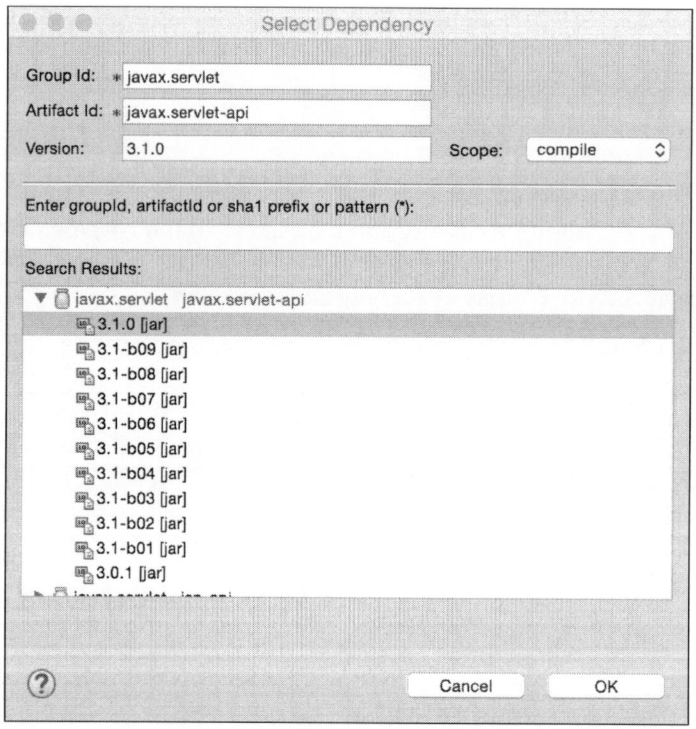

Figure 2.32 Add Servlet API dependency

However, we need JAR files for servlet APIs only at the compile time; at runtime, these APIs are provided by Tomcat. We can indicate this by specifying the scope of the dependency; in this case, setting it to `provided`, which tells Maven to evaluate this dependency for compilation only and not to package it in the WAR file. See `http://maven.apache.org/guides/introduction/introduction-to-dependency-mechanism.html` for more information on dependency scopes.

5. To set the scope of the dependency, select the dependency from the **Dependencies** tab of the POM editor.
6. Click on the **Properties** button. Then, select the **provided** scope from the drop-down list.

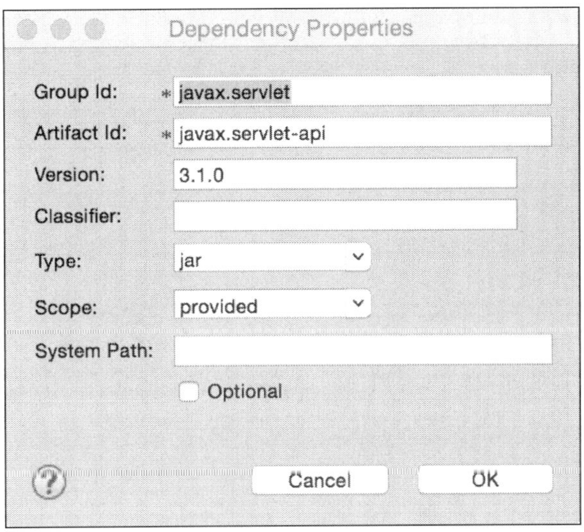

Figure 2.33 Set the Maven dependency scope

7. We now need to add dependencies for JSF APIs and their implementation. Click the **Add** button again, and type `jsf` in the search box.

8. From the list, select `jsf-api` with **Group Id** `com.sun.faces`, and click the **OK** button.

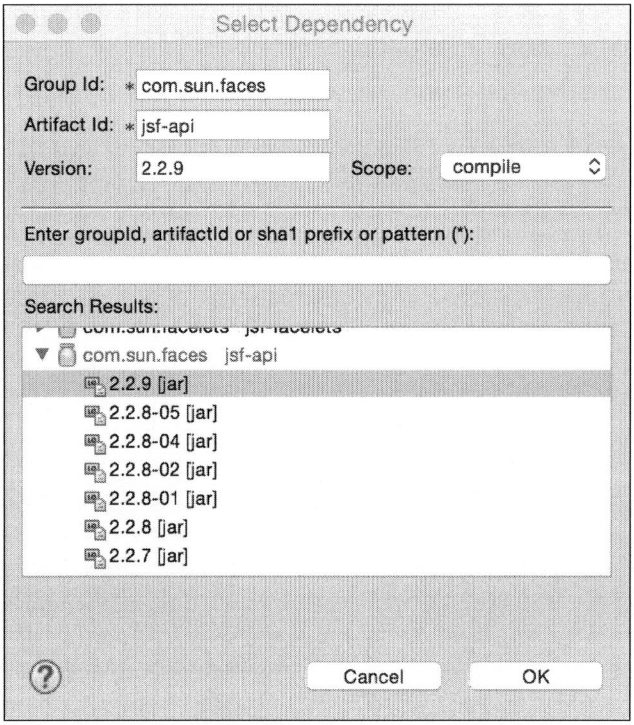

Figure 2.34 Add Maven dependencies for JSF

9. Similarly, add a dependency for `jsf-impl` with **Group Id** `com.sun.faces`.

   The dependencies section in your `pom.xml` should look as follows:

```
<dependencies>
  <dependency>
    <groupId>junit</groupId>
    <artifactId>junit</artifactId>
    <version>3.8.1</version>
    <scope>test</scope>
  </dependency>
  <dependency>
    <groupId>javax.servlet</groupId>
    <artifactId>javax.servlet-api</artifactId>
    <version>3.1.0</version>
    <scope>provided</scope>
  </dependency>
```

```
      <dependency>
        <groupId>com.sun.faces</groupId>
        <artifactId>jsf-api</artifactId>
        <version>2.2.9</version>
        </dependency>
      <dependency>
        <groupId>com.sun.faces</groupId>
        <artifactId>jsf-impl</artifactId>
        <version>2.2.9</version>
      </dependency>
    </dependencies>
```

The Maven project structure

The Maven project wizard creates the `src` and `target` folders under the main project folder. As the name suggests, all source files go under `src`. However, the Java package structure starts under the `main` folder. By convention, Maven expects Java source files under the `java` folder. Therefore, create the `java` folder under `src/main`. The Java package structure starts from the `java` folder, that is, `src/main/java/<java-packages>`. Web content such as HTML, JS, CSS, and JSP go into the `webapp` folder under `src/main`. The compiled classes and other output files generated by the Maven build process are stored in the target folder.

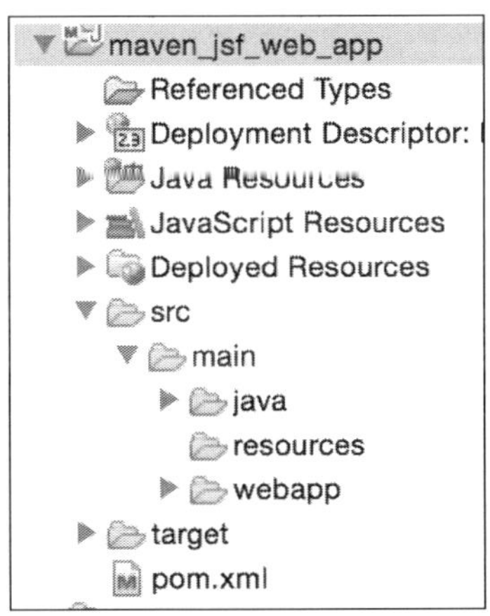

Figure 2.35 Maven web application project structure

The code for our login JSF page is the same as in the previous example of `LoginJSFApp`. Therefore, copy the `packt` folder from the `src` folder of that project to the `src/main/java` folder of this Maven project. This adds `LoginBean.java` to the project. Then, copy `web.xml` from the `WEB-INF` folder to the `src/main/webapp/WEB-INF` folder of this project. Copy `index.xhtml` and `welcome.xhtml` to the `src/main/webapp` folder.

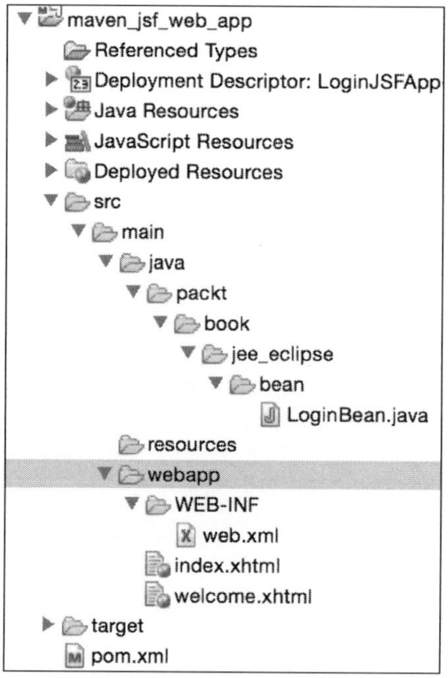

Figure 2.36 Project structure after adding source files

No change is required in the source code. To run the application, right-click on `index.xhtml` and select **Run As | Run on Server**.

We will be using Maven for project management in the rest of this book.

Creating WAR using Maven

In a previous example, we created a WAR file by using the Export option of Eclipse. In a Maven project, you can create WAR by invoking the **Maven Install** plugin. Right-click on the project and select the **Run As | Maven install** option. The WAR file is created in the target folder. You can then deploy the WAR file in Tomcat by copying it to the `webapps` folder of Tomcat.

Summary

In this chapter, we saw how to configure Tomcat in Eclipse. We saw how the same page can be implemented using three different technologies, namely JSP, Servlet, and JSF. All of them can be used for developing any dynamic web application. However, JSP and JSF are more suited to creating a presentation, and servlets are more suited to controllers and end points for a web service and web-socket endpoints. Compared with JSP, JSF enforces the MVC design and provides many additional services. Then, we learnt how to use Maven for many project management tasks.

In the next chapter, we will see how to configure and use source control management systems, particularly SVN and Git.

3

Source Control Management in Eclipse

Source Control Management (**SCM**) is an essential part of software development. By using SCM tools, you make sure that you have access to versions of your code at important milestones. SCM also helps to manage the source code when you are working in a team, by providing you tools to make sure you do not overwrite the work done by others. Whether your project is small or large, whether you are working alone or in a large team, using SCM can benefit you.

Eclipse has had support for integrating various SCM tools for a long time – this includes support for CVS, Microsoft Source Safe, Perforce, and **Subversion** (**SVN**). The recent versions of Eclipse have built in support for Git too. In this chapter, we will see how to use Eclipse plugins for Git and Subversion.

The Eclipse Subversion plugin

In this section, we will see how to install and use SVN Eclipse plugin. We will create a small project and see how to check-in a project to SVN from within Eclipse. We will also see how to sync with the existing SVN repository.

You will need access to SVN repository to follow the steps in this chapter. If you do not have access to a SVN repository, you can choose from some of the free SVN offerings online. This book does not promote or suggest using any particular online SVN hosting, but for the purpose of explaining SVN Eclipse plugin features, the author has used `https://riouxsvn.com`. However, the plugin would wok the same way with any SVN server.

Installing the Eclipse Subversion plugin

Open the **Eclipse Marketplace** by selecting the **Help** | **Eclipse Marketplace** menu. Search for `subversion`.

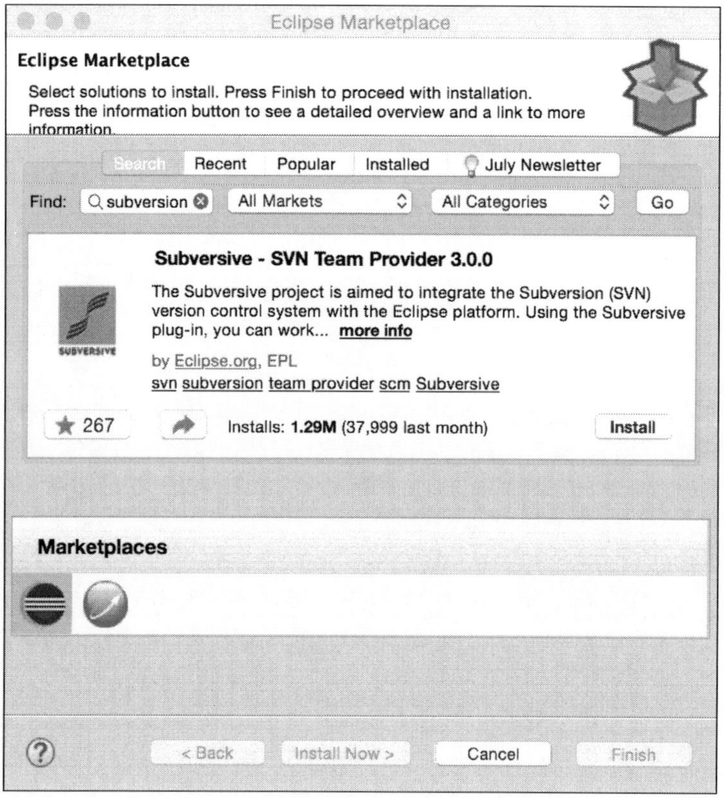

Figure 3.1 Installing the Subversion plugin

Install the plugin. Before we configure the SVN repository in Eclipse, we need to select/install a SVN Connector. Go to Eclipse **Preferences** and type `svn` in the filter box. Then, go to the **SVN Connector** tab.

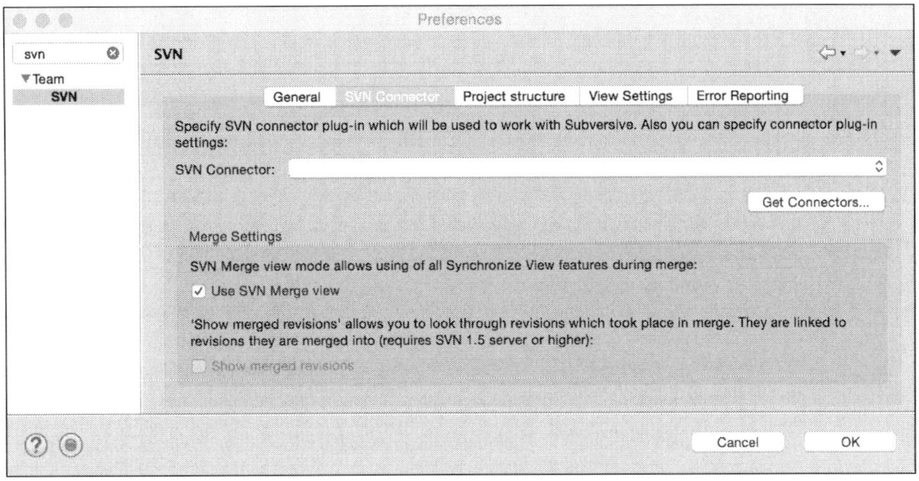

Figure 3.2 SVN Connector preferences

If no connectors are installed, then you will see the **Get Connectors** button. Click the button.

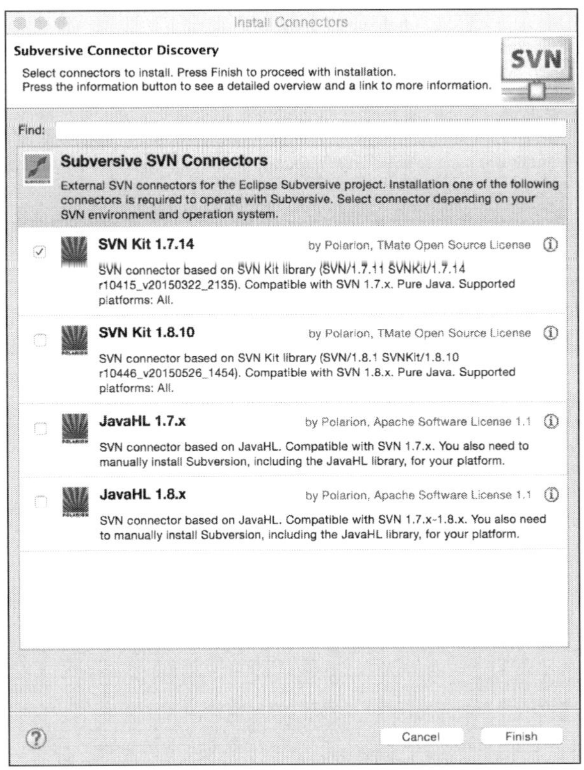

Figure 3.3 The SVN Connector Discovery wizard

Eclipse displays the number of available connectors. We will choose the **SVN Kit** connector and install it (click the **Finish** button).

We will now configure an existing SVN repository in Eclipse. Select the **Window | Open Perspective | Other** menu and then select the **SVN Repository Exploring** perspective.

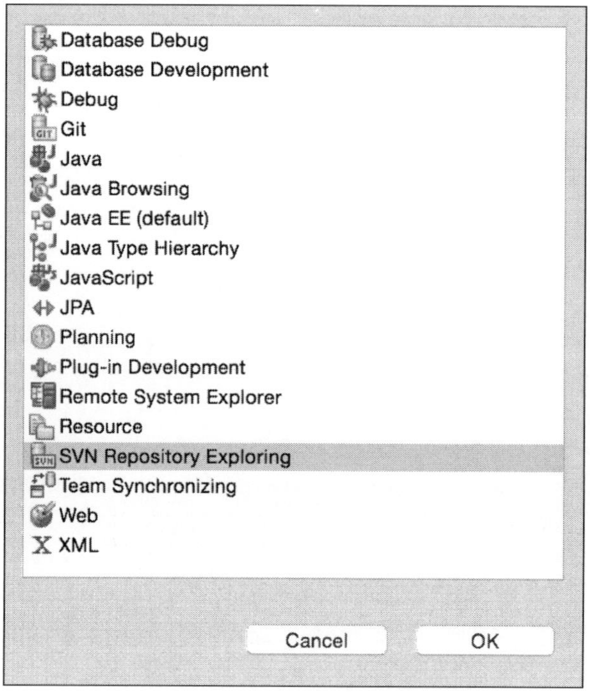

Figure 3.4 Open SVN Perspective

Adding a project to an SVN repository

To add a repository, right-click the **SVN Repositories** view and select **New | Repository Location**.

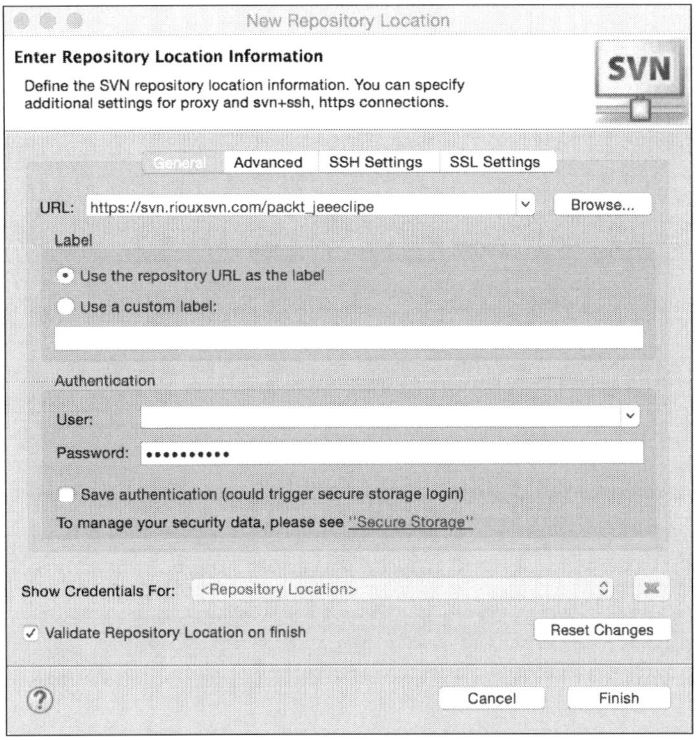

Figure 3.5 Configure SVN repository

Enter the **URL** of your SVN repository, your user name, and the password. If you need to set SSH or SSL information to connect to your SVN repository, then click on the appropriate tab and enter the information. Click **Finish** to add the repository to Eclipse.

Let's now create a simple Java project that we would check into the SVN repository. In this chapter, it is not important what code you write in the project; we are going to use the project only to understand how to check-in the project files to SVN and then see how to sync the project. Create a simple Java project as shown in the following screenshot:

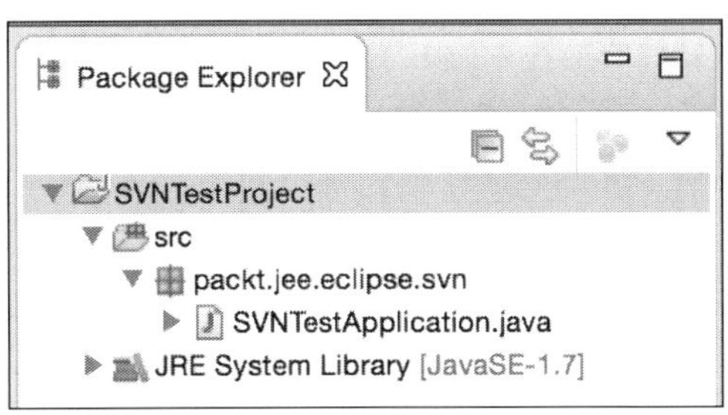

Figure 3.6 A sample project for SVN testing

In the preceding project, we have one source file. The source code is not important at this point. We will now check in this project in SVN. Right-click on the project and select **Team | Share Project**.

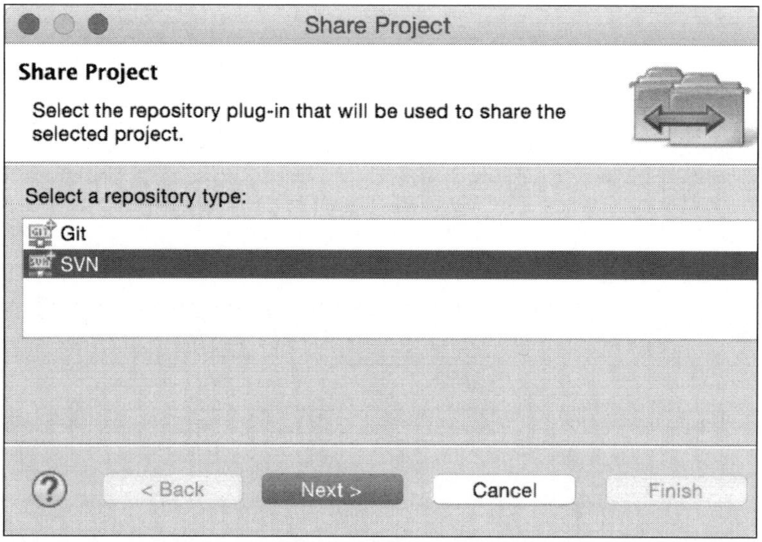

Figure 3.7 Share Project with SVN repository

Select **SVN** and click the **Next** button. The wizard gives you the option to either create a new SVN repository or select an already configured SVN repository.

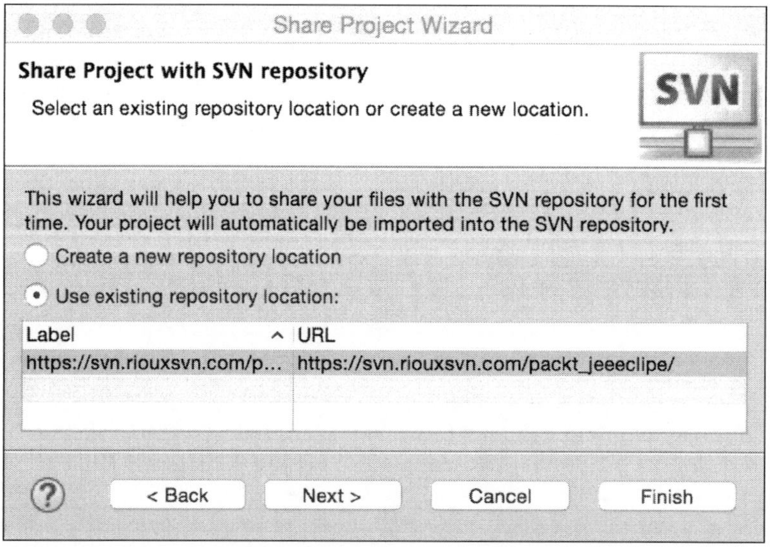

Figure 3.8 Select SVN repository or create a new one

We are going to use the already configured repository. So, select the repository. You can click **Next** and configure the advanced option, but we will keep the configuration simple and click **Finish**. You will be prompted to check-in the existing files in the project.

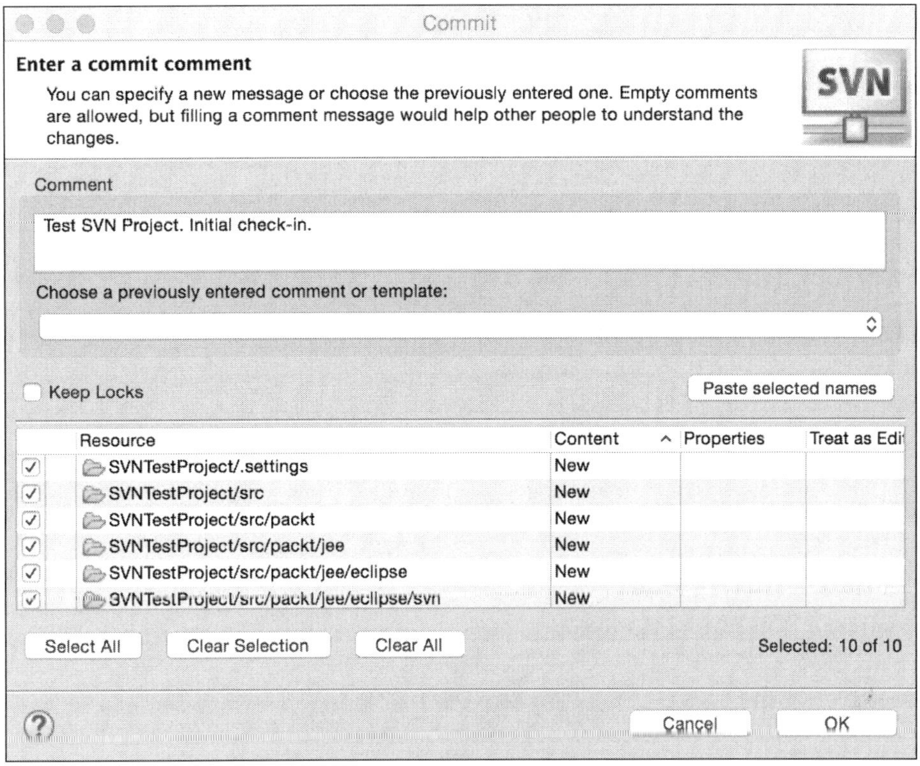

Figure 3.9 Share Project with SVN repository

Select the files you want to check-in and enter the check-in comments. Then click **OK**. To see the checked in files in the SVN repository, switch to the SVN perspective and the **SVN Repositories** view.

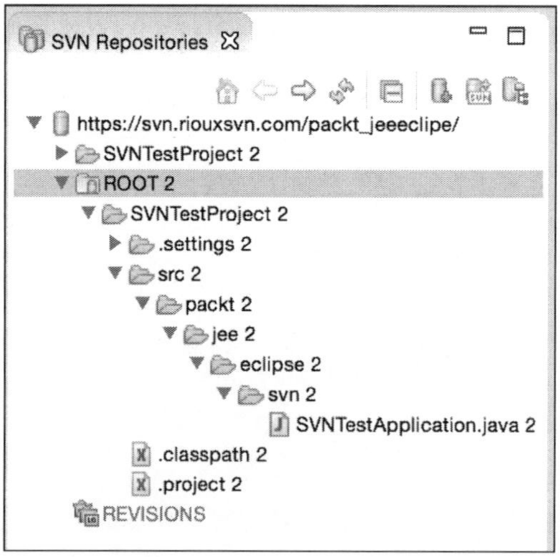

Figure 3.10 Checked-in files in SVN Repositories view

Committing changes to an SVN repository

Let's now modify a file and check-in the changes. Switch back to the **Java** perspective and open `SVNTestApplication.java` from **Package Explorer** or **Navigator**. Modify the file and save the changes. To compare the files or the folders in your working directory with those in the repository, right-click on file/folder/project in `Navigator` and select **Compare With** | **Latest from Repository**. Now that we have modified `SVNTestApplication`, let's see how it differs from the one in the repository.

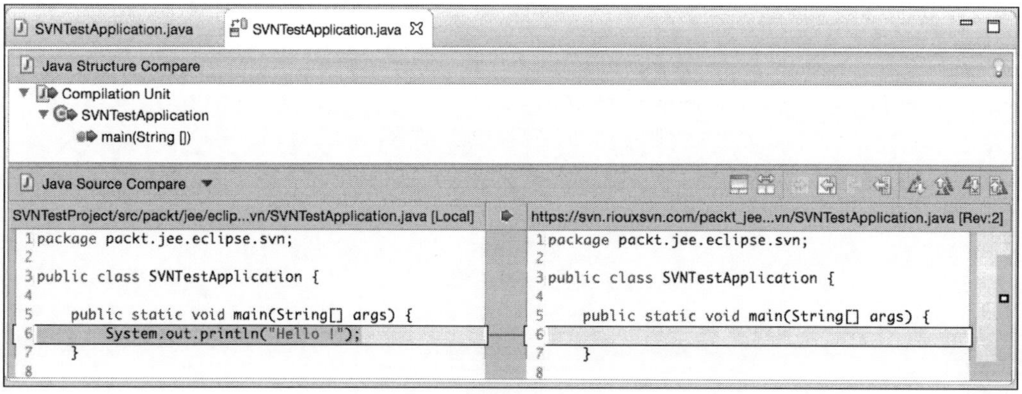

Figure 3.11 Comparing SVN files

Let's add a new file now, say, `readme.txt` in the root of the project. To add the file to the repository, right-click on the file and select **Team** | **Add to Version Control**.

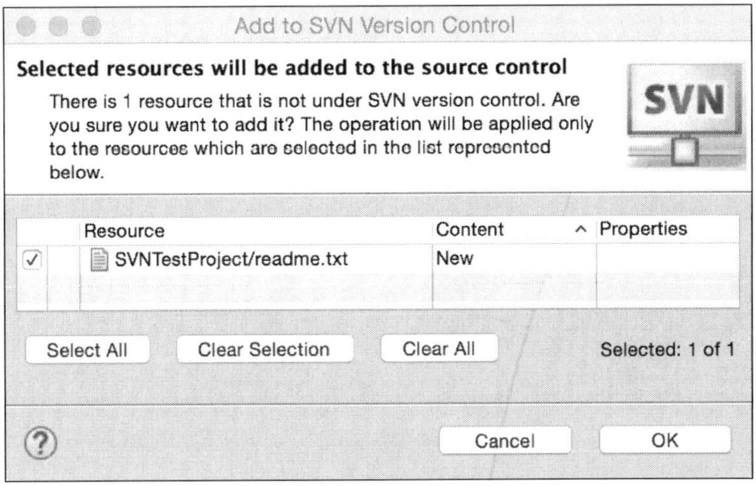

Figure 3.12 Add files to SVN repository

Synchronizing with an SVN repository

To synchronize your local project with the remote repository, click on the project and select **Synchronize with Repository**. This will update the project with files in the remote repository, show files that are new in the local folder, and also show the changed files.

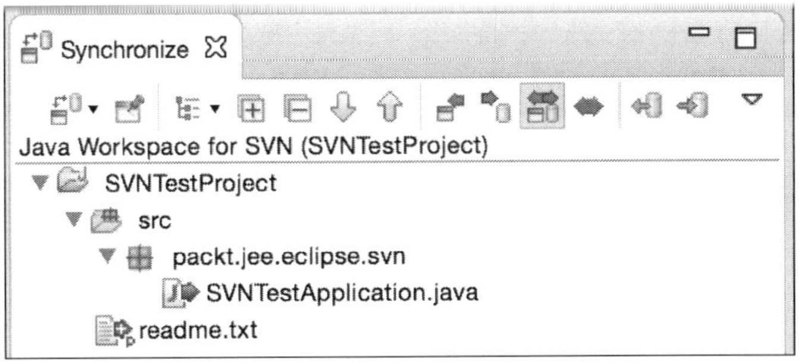

Figure 3.13 The Team Synchronize view

You can filter the list as Incoming Mode (changes from the remote repository), Outgoing Mode (changes in your working directory), or both. As you can see in the preceding image, we have two files that are changed in the working directory, one modified and one new. To commit the changes, right-click on the project and select **Commit**. If you want to commit from **Navigator** or **Package Explorer**, then right-click on the project and select **Team** | **Commit**. Enter the check-in comments and click **OK**. To update the project (receive all the changes from the remote repository), right-click on the project and select **Team** | **Update**.

To see a revision history of the file or folder, right-click **Navigator** or **Package Explorer** and select **Team** | **Show History**.

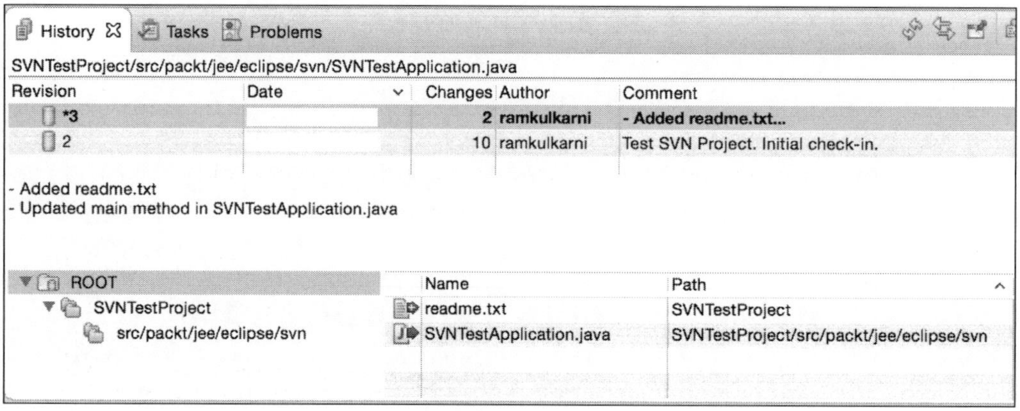

Figure 3.14 SVN file revision history

Checking out a project from SVN

It is easy to check out projects from a SVN repository into a new workspace. In the **SVN Repositories** view, click on the project you want to check out and select the **Check Out** option.

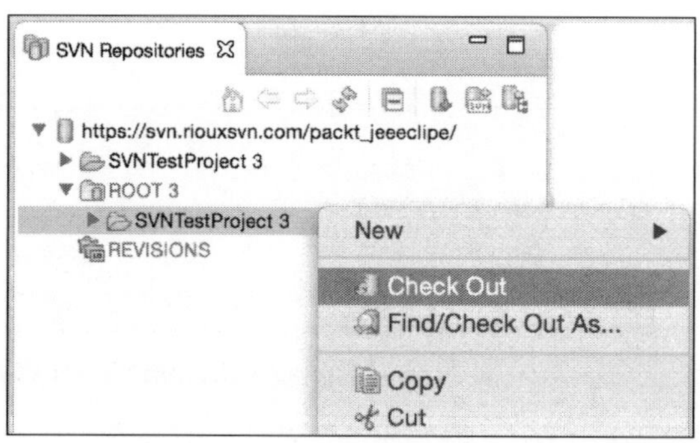

Figure 3.15 SVN file revision history

This option checks out the project in the current workspace. You can also use the import project option to check out the project from SVN. Select the **File | Import** menu option and then select the **SVN | Project from SVN** option.

There are many other features of SVN that you can use from Eclipse. Refer to `http://www.eclipse.org/subversive/documentation.php`.

The Eclipse Git plugin

Recent versions of Eclipse are pre-installed with Eclipse **Git plugin** (**EGit**). If not, you can install the plugin from **Eclipse Marketplace**. Select the **Help | Eclipse Marketplace** option and type `egit` in the **Find** textbox.

Figure 3.16 Searching the EGit plugin in Eclipse Marketplace

If the plugin is already installed, it will be marked as **Installed**.

Adding a project to Git

Git is a distributed repository. Unlike other source management systems, Git maintains a complete local repository too. So you can perform activities such as check-out and check-in in the local repository without connecting to any remote repository. When you are ready to move your code to a remote repository, then you can connect to it and push your files to the remote repository. If you are new to Git, take a look at the following documentation and tutorial:

- `https://git-scm.com/doc`
- `https://www.atlassian.com/git/tutorials/`

Create a simple Java project in the workspace. Again, as in the previous section, what code you write in this project is not important. Create a Java class in the project. We will add this project to Git. Right-click on the project in **Package Explorer** or **Navigator** and select **Team** | **Share Project**.

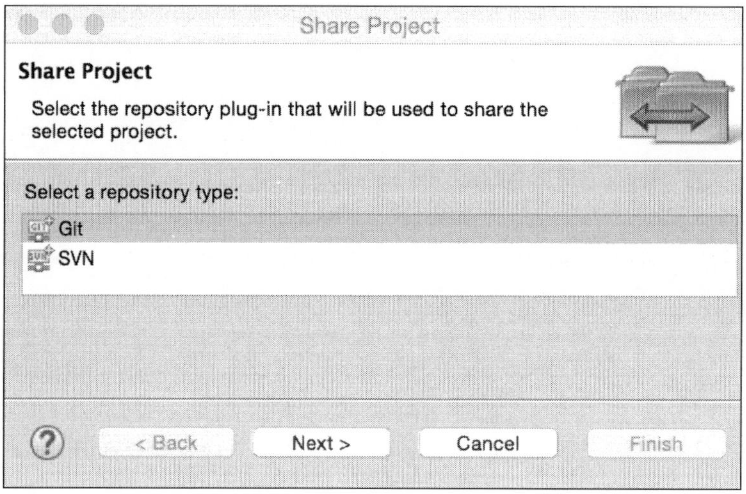

Figure 3.17 Sharing Eclipse project with Git

Select **Git** and click **Next**. Check the box **Use or create repository in parent folder of project**.

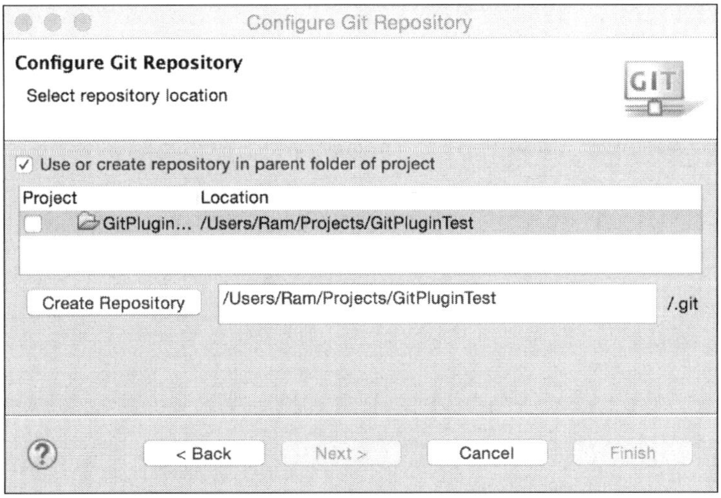

Figure 3.18 Creating a Git repository for a project

Select the project (check the box for the project) and click the **Create Repository** button. Then click **Finish**.

This creates a new Git repository in the project folder. Switch to the Git perspective (or open **Git Repositories** view from the **Window** | **Show View** | **Other** option):

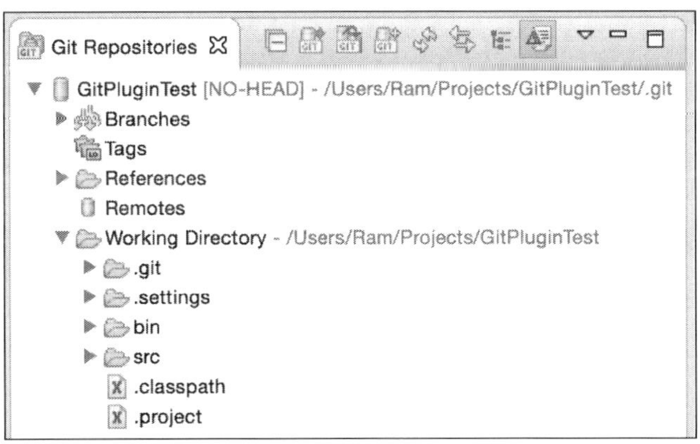

Figure 3.19 Git Repositories view

Committing files in a Git repository

New or modified files are staged for commit. To see the staged files, click on the **Git Staging** tab in the Git perspective.

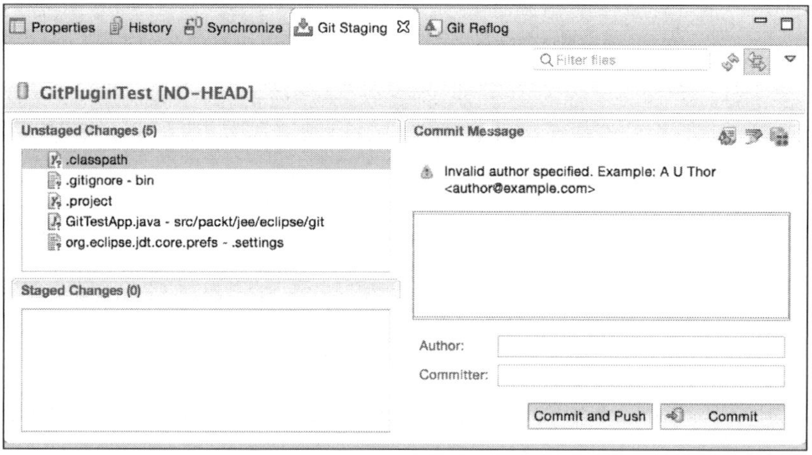

Figure 3.20 The Git Staging view

If you do not want to add a file to the Git repository, then right-click on that file (or multiple files selection) and select the **Ignore** option. Before you commit the files to Git, you need to move **Unstaged Changes** to **Staged Changes**. We are going to add all the files to Git. So select all the files in the **Unstaged** view and drag and drop them in the **Staged Changes** view. It is also recommended to set **Author** name and **Committer**. It is usually in a `Name <email>` format. To set this option at global level in Eclipse (so that you do not have to set these fields at every commit), go to Eclipse **Preferences** and search for `Git`. Then go to the **Team** | **Git** | **Configuration** page, and click the **Add Entry** button.

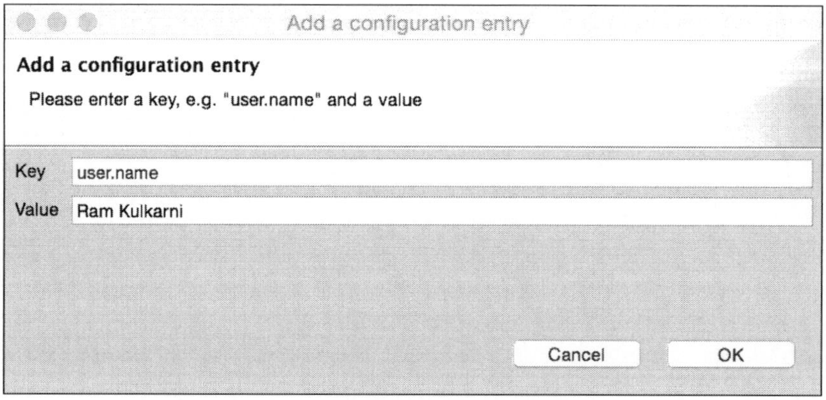

Figure 3.21 Add a Git Configuration entry

Similarly, add the `user.email` entry.

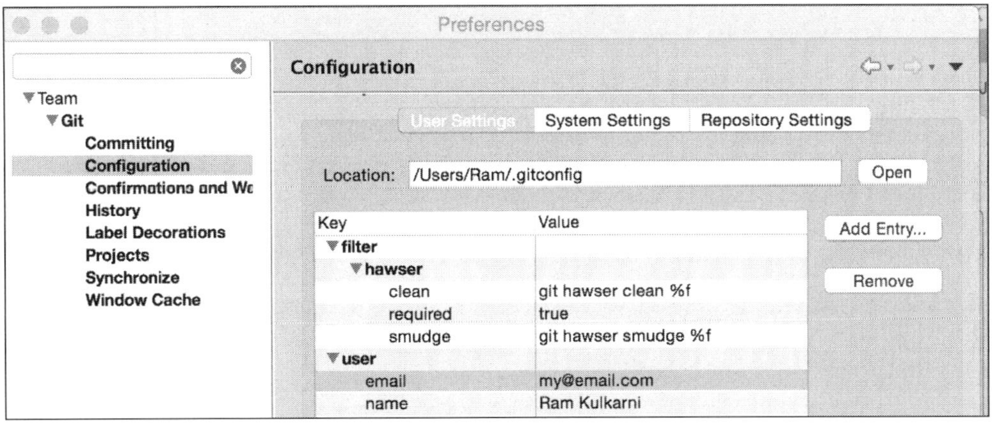

Figure 3.22 Git configurations in Preferences

Coming back to the **Git Staging** view, enter **Author**, **Committer**, and **Commit Message**. Then click the **Commit** button.

Viewing a file difference after modifications

Let's modify the single Java class created in the previous project. If you go to the **Git Staging** view after making changes to the file, you will see that the file appears in the **Unstaged Changes** list. To see what changes have been made to the file since last commit, double-click on the file in the **Git Staging** view.

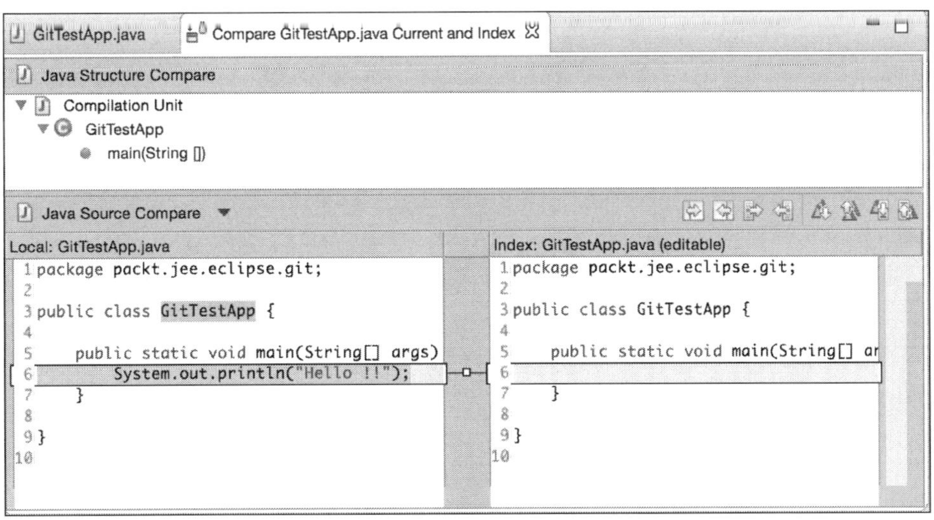

Figure 3.23 Viewing a file difference

To commit these changes, move it to **Staged View**, enter **Commit Message**, and click the **Commit** button. You can also view the file differences by clicking on the file in **Package Explorer** and selecting **Compare With | Head Revision**.

To see the history of changes to the project or file(s)/folder(s), right-click and select **Team | Show in History**.

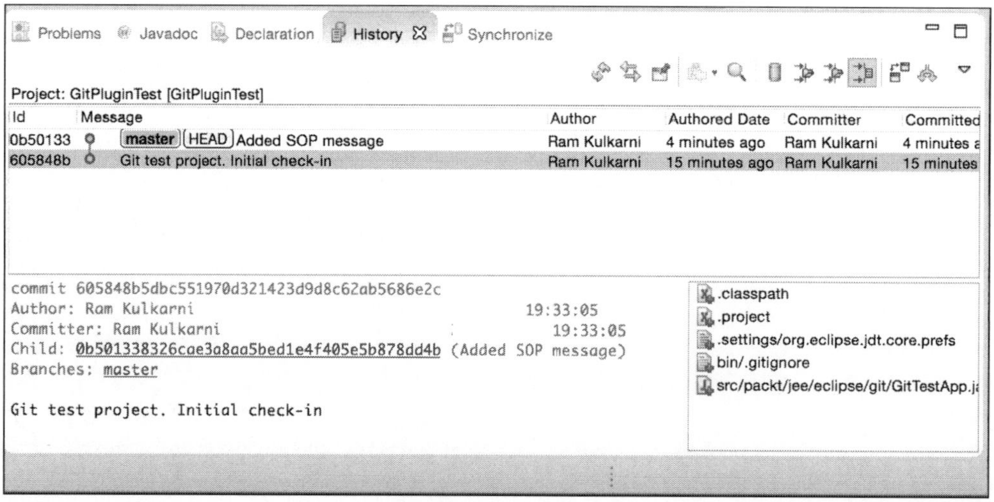

Figure 3.24 Git history view

Creating a new branch

It is typical when you are using source control management to create separate branches for features or even for bug fixes. The idea is that the main or the master branch should always have a working code and you do development on branches which may not be stable. When you finish a feature or fix a bug and know that the branch is stable, then you merge the code from the branch to the master branch.

To create a new branch, go to the **Git Repositories** view and right-click on the repository you want to branch. Then select the **Switch To | New Branch** option.

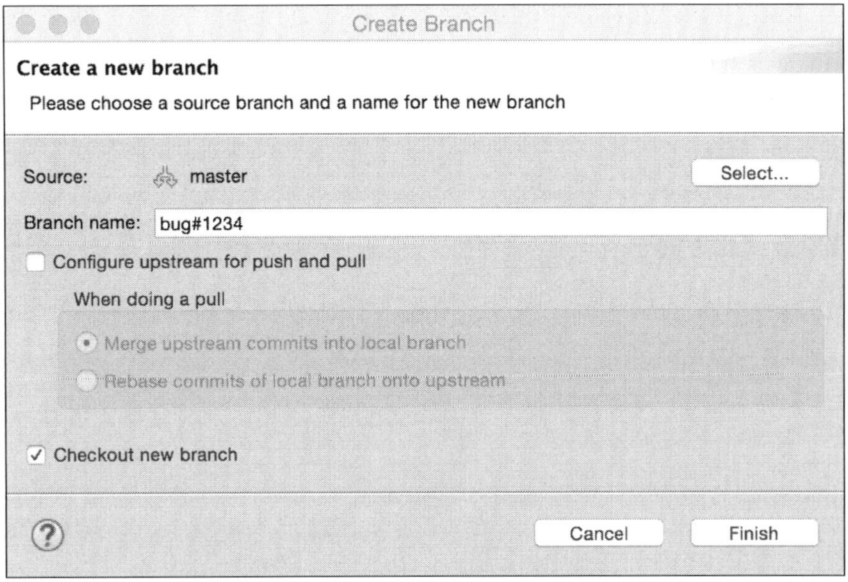

Figure 3.25 Creating a new branch

Note that the **Checkout new branch** box is checked. Because of this option, the new branch becomes the active branch once it is created. Any changes you commit are going to be in this branch and the master branch remains unaffected. Click **Finish** to create the branch.

Let's make some changes to the code, say in the main method of the `GitTestApp` class:

```
public class GitTestApp {

  public static void main(String[] args) {
    System.out.println("Hello Git, from branch bug#1234 !!");
  }
}
```

Commit the preceding changes to the new branch.

Now let's check out the master branch. Right-click on the repository in the **Git Repositories** view and select **Switch To | master**. Open the file you had modified in the new branch. You will observe that the changes you had made to the file are not present. As mentioned previously, any changes you do to branches are not committed to the master branch. You have to explicitly merge the changes.

To merge changes from **branch bug#1234** to the master branch, right click on the repository in the **Git Repositories** view and select **Merge**.

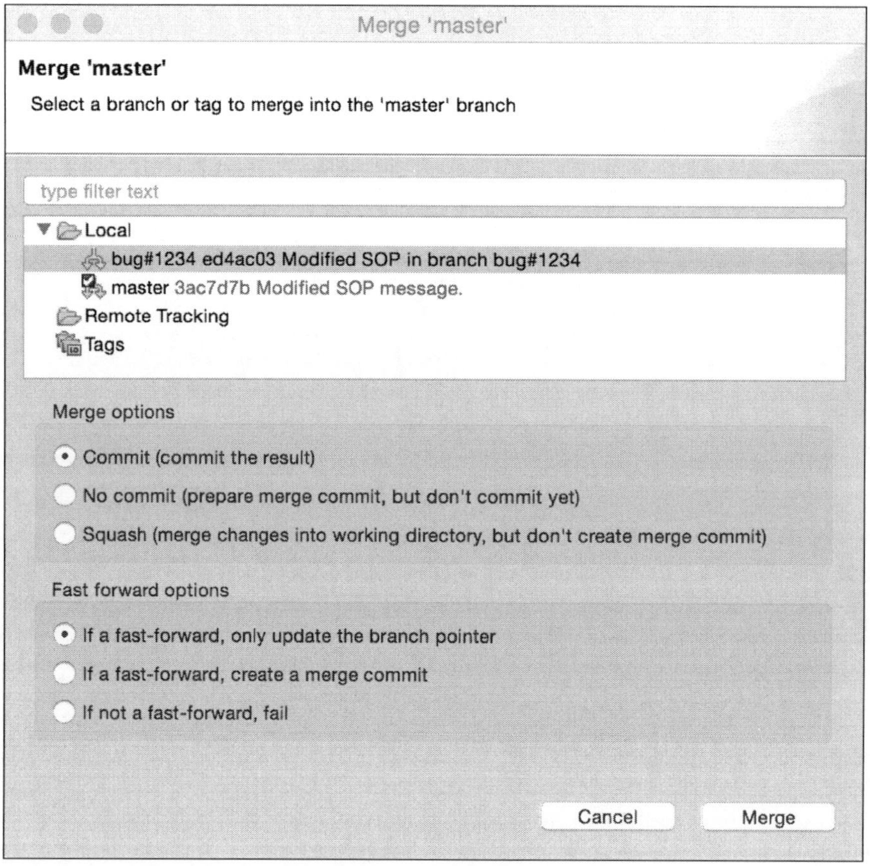

Figure 3.26 Merge Git braches

Select **branch bug#1234**. This branch will be merged in the master branch. Click **Merge**. Git displays the summary of merge. Click **OK** to complete the merge operation. Now the file in the master branch contains the changes done in **branch bug#1234**.

We have merged all the changes from **branch bug#1234** to the master and we no longer need it. So, let's delete **branch bug#1234**. Expand the Branches node in the **Git Repositories** view and right-click on the branch to be deleted (the selected branch should not be the active branch when deleting). Then select the **Delete Branch** menu option.

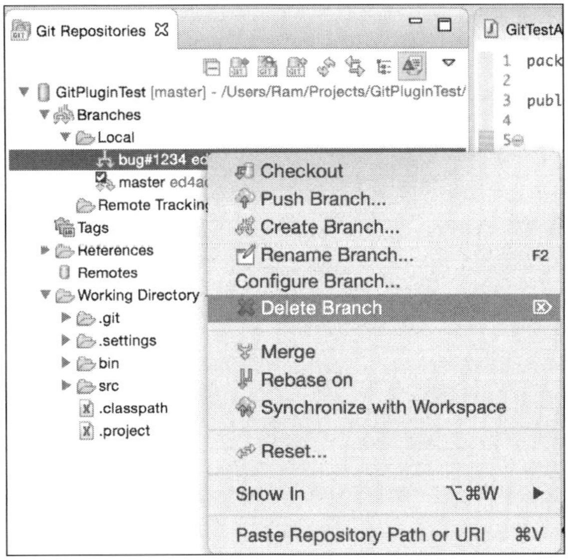

Figure 3.27 Delete Git branch

Committing a project to a remote repository

So far we have been working in the local Git repository. But you may want to push your project to a remote repository if you want to share your code and/or make sure that you do not lose your changes locally. So in this section, we will see how to push a local project to a remote Git repository. If you do not have access to a Git repository, you could create one at `http://www.github.com`. Create a new repository in the remote Git server, named `GitPluginTest`.

In the **Git Repositories** view, right-click on the **Remotes** node and select the **Create Remote** option.

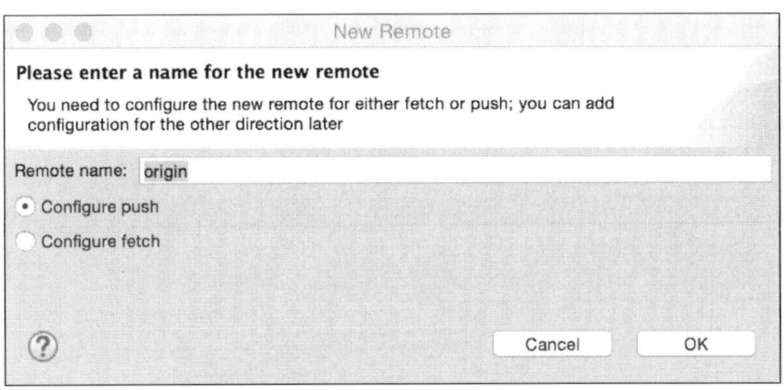

Figure 3.28 Add a remote Git repository

By convention, the name of the remote repository is 'origin'. Click **OK**. In the next page, set up configuration for push. Click on the **Change** button next to the URL textbox.

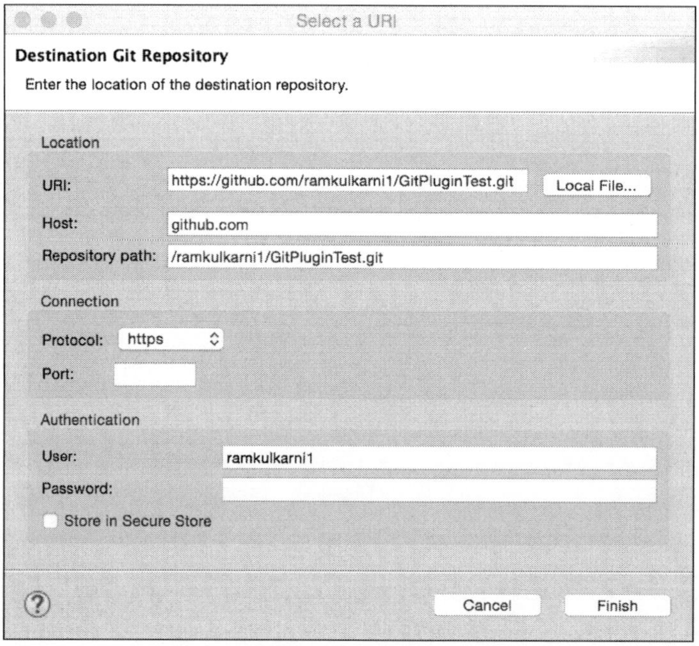

Figure 3.29 Setup a remote Git URI

Enter URI of the remote Git repository. The wizard extracts the host, repository path, and protocol from the URL. Enter your user ID and password and click **Finish**.

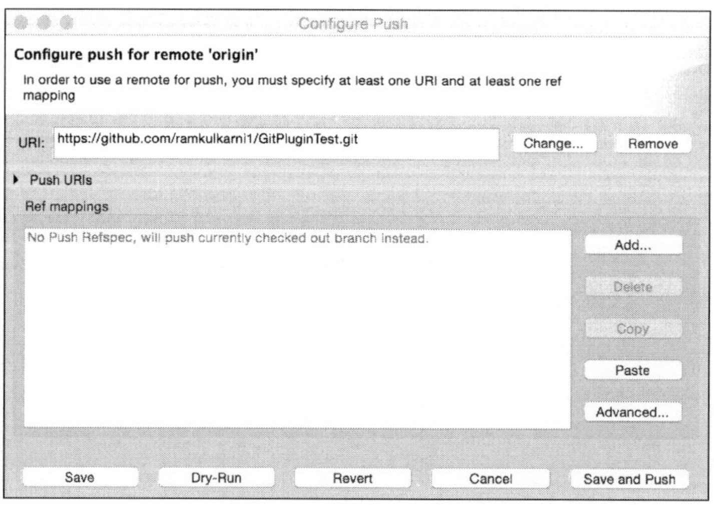

Figure 3.30 Configure a Git push

Click **Save and Push**. This sends files in the local master branch to the remote Git repository.

Pulling changes from a remote repository

As you work in a team, your team members would also be making changes to the remote repository. When you want to get the changes done in the remote repository to your local repository, then you use the Pull option. But before you perform the Pull operation, you need to configure it. In the **Package Explorer**, right-click on the project and select **Team** | **Remote** | **Configure Fetch from Upstream**.

> In Git, both Pull and Fetch can get the changes from a remote repository. However, the Fetch operation does not merge the changes in the local repository. The Pull operation first fetches the changes and then merges in the local repository. If you want to inspect the files before you merge, then select the **Fetch** option.

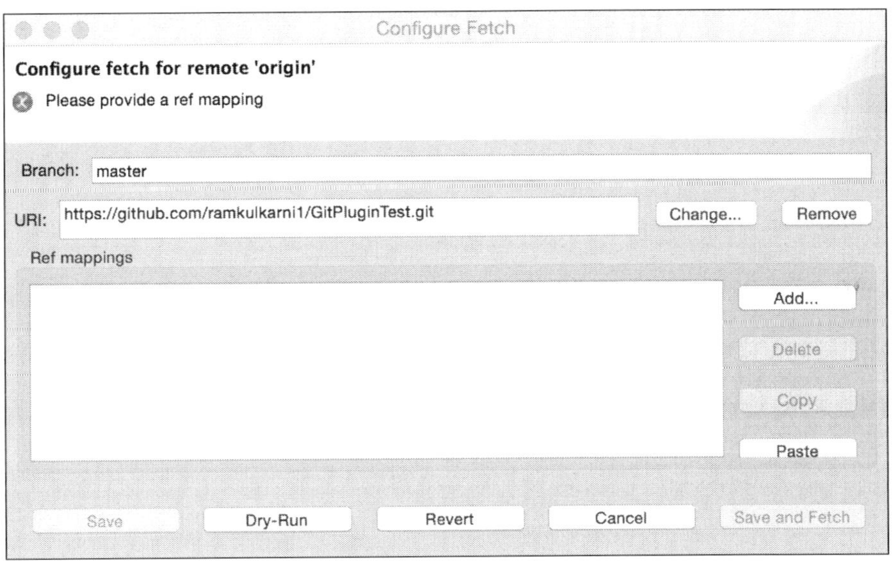

Figure 3.31 Configure Git Fetch

We need to map the local master branch with a branch in the remote repository. This tells the pull operation to fetch the changes from the branch in the remote repository and merge it in the given (in this case, master) local repository. Click the **Add** button.

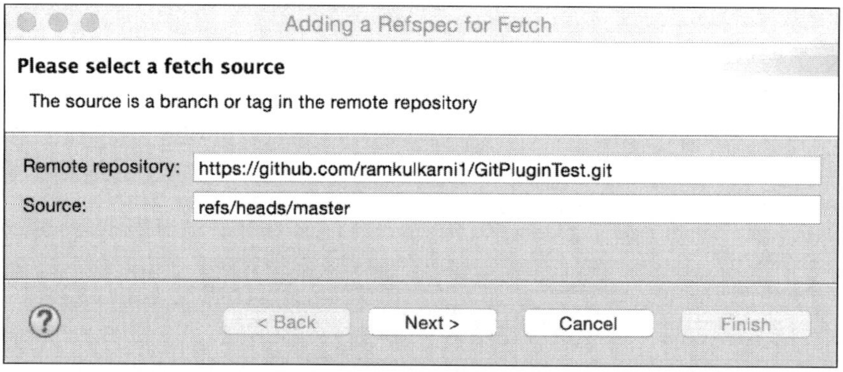

Figure 3.32 Configure Git Fetch

Start typing the name of the branch in the source text box, and the wizard will get the branch information from the remote repository and auto complete it. Click **Next** and then **Finish**. This takes you back to the **Configure Fetch** page with mapping of the branches added to it.

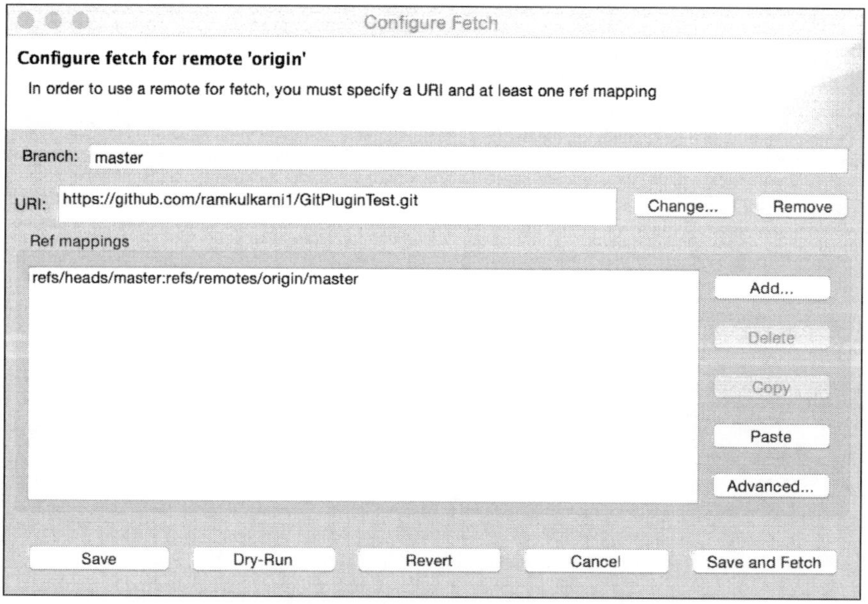

Figure 3.33 Configure Git Fetch with mapping added

Click **Save and Fetch** to pull the changes from the remote repository.

Cloning a remote repository

We saw how to start development using a local Git repository and then push changes to a remote repository. Let's see how we can get an already existing remote Git repository and create a local copy; in other words, we will see how to clone a remote Git repository. The easiest option is to import the remote Git project. Select **File | Import from the main menu and then Git | Projects from Git | Clone URI**.

The wizard display a page similar to *Figure 3.29 Setup remote Git URI*. Enter the URI of the remote repository, the user name, and the password, and then click **Next**. Select a remote branch and click **Next**.

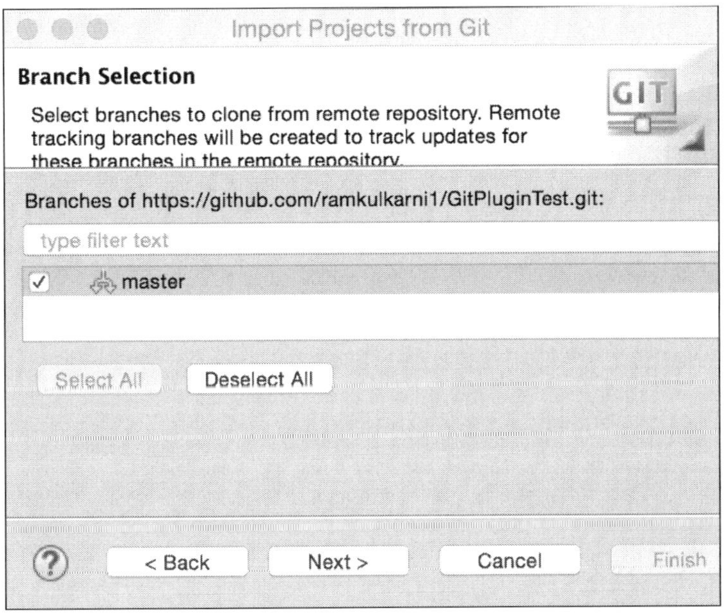

Figure 3.34 Select a Remote branch to clone

Click **Next**.

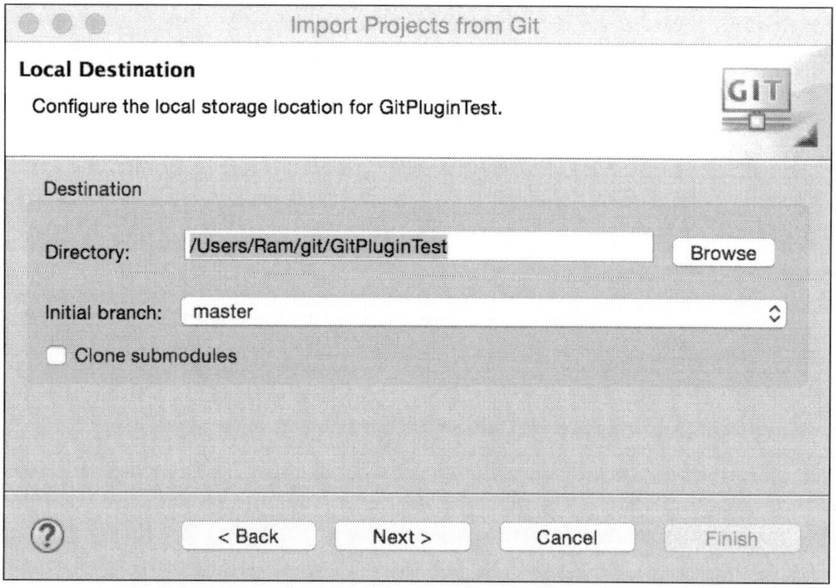

Figure 3.35 Select the location of the cloned project

Select the location where the project is to be saved and click **Next**.

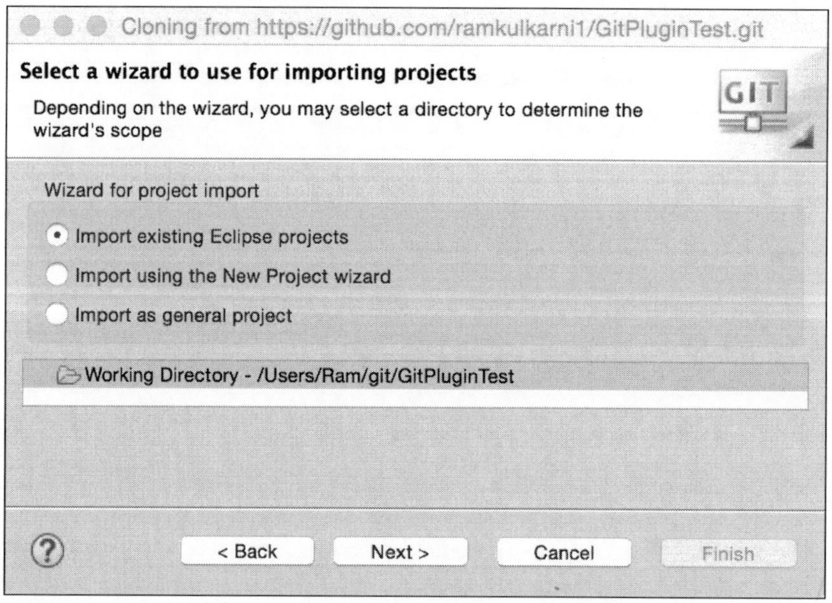

Figure 3.36 Options to import the cloned project

There are three options to import the cloned project. If the remote repository contains the entire Eclipse project then select **Import existing Eclipse projects**, else select either of the remaining two options. Since we have checked in the Eclipse project in the remote repository, we will select the first option. Click **Next** and then **Finish**.

For more information about Eclipse Git plugin, refer to `https://wiki.eclipse.org/EGit/User_Guide`.

Summary

There are Eclipse plugins available for wide variety of SCM systems. In this chapter, we saw how to use Eclipse plugins for SVN and Git. Using these plugins you can perform many of the typical SCM operations, such as checking out source, comparing versions, and committing changes, right within the Eclipse environment. This provides great convenience and can improve your productivity.

In the next chapter, we will see how to create JEE Database application using JDBC and JDO.

4
Creating a JEE Database Application

Most web applications today require access to a database. In this chapter, we will see two ways to access a database from JEE web applications.

- Using JDBC APIs
- Using JPA APIs

JDBC has been part of JDK since version 1.1. It provides uniform APIs to access different relational databases. Between JDBC APIs and the database sits the JDBC driver for this database (either provided by the vendor of the database or some third-party vendor). JDBC translates the common API calls to database-specific calls. The results returned from the database are also converted into objects of common data access classes. Although JDBC APIs require you to write a lot more code to access the database, it is still popular in JEE web applications because of its simplicity of use, flexibility of using database-specific SQL statements, and low learning curve.

JPA is the result of **JSR** 220 (which stands for **Java Specification Request**). JSR is part of the **Java Community Process (JCP)**. One of the problems of using JDBC APIs directly is converting object representation of data to relation data. Object representation is in your JEE application, which needs to be mapped to tables and columns in a relational database. The process is reversed when handling data returned from the relational database. If there is a way to automatically map object-oriented representation of data in web applications to relational data, it would save a lot of developer time. This is also called **Object-relational mapping (ORM)**. Hibernate (`http://hibernate.org/`) is a very popular framework for ORM in Java applications.

Many of the concepts of such popular third-party ORM frameworks were incorporated in JPA. Just as JDBC provides uniform APIs for accessing relational databases, JPA provides uniform APIs for accessing ORM libraries. Third-party ORM frameworks provide an implementation of JPA on top of their framework. The JPA implementation may use the JDBC APIs underneath.

We will explore many features of JDBC and JPA in this chapter as we build applications using these frameworks. In fact, we will build the same application, once using JDBC and then using JPA.

The application that we are going to build is for student-course management. The goal is to take an example that can show how to model relationships between tables and use them in JEE applications. We will use MySQL for the database and Tomcat for the web application container. Although this chapter is about database programming in JEE, we will revisit some of the things we learnt about JSTL and JSF in *Chapter 2, Creating a Simple JEE Web Application*. We will use them to create a user interface for our database web application. Make sure that you have configured Tomcat in Eclipse as described in the *Chapter 2, Creating a Simple JEE Web Application*.

Let's first create a database and the tables for this application.

Creating a database schema

There are many ways of creating database tables and relationships in MySQL:

- You can use **Data Description Language** (**DDL**) statements directly at MySQL Command Prompt from a console
- You can use MySQL Workbench and create tables directly by using the user interface
- You can create an entity-relationship diagram in MySQL Workbench, export it to create a DDL script, and then run this script to create tables and relationships

We will use the third option. If you just want to get a script to create tables and want to skip creating an ER diagram, then jump to the *The script for creating tables and relationships* section.

If you have not already installed MySQL and MySQL Workbench, then refer to *Chapter 1, Introducing JEE and Eclipse*, for instructions.

1. Open MySQL Workbench. Select the **File** | **New Model** menu. A blank model will be created with the option to create ER diagrams.

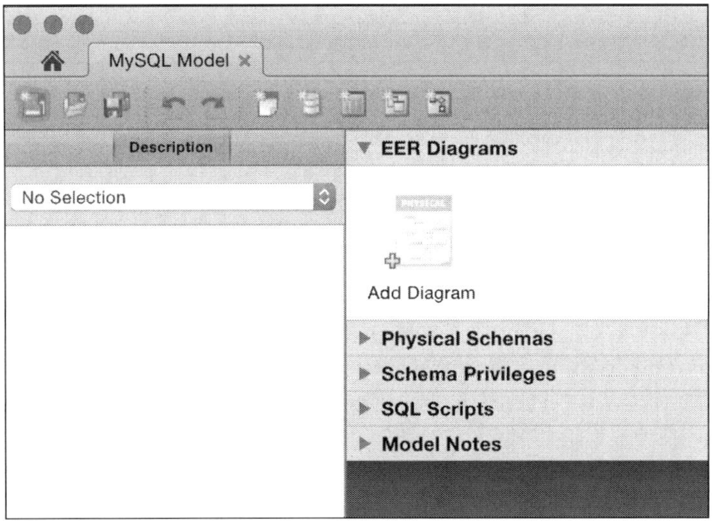

Figure 4.1.Create new MySQL Workbench model

2. Double-click the **Add Diagram** icon; a blank ER diagram will be opened.

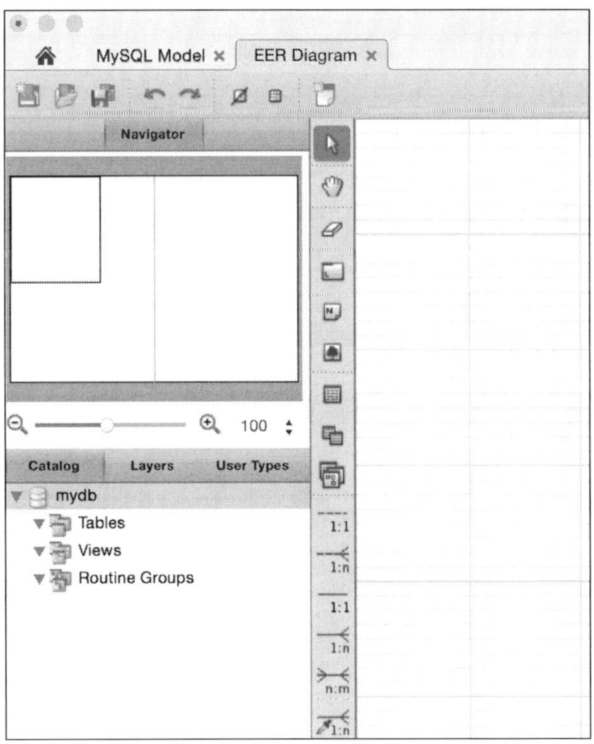

Figure 4.2.Create new ER diagram

3. By default, the new schema is named **mydb**. Double-click on it to open the properties of the schema. Rename the schema as **course_management**.

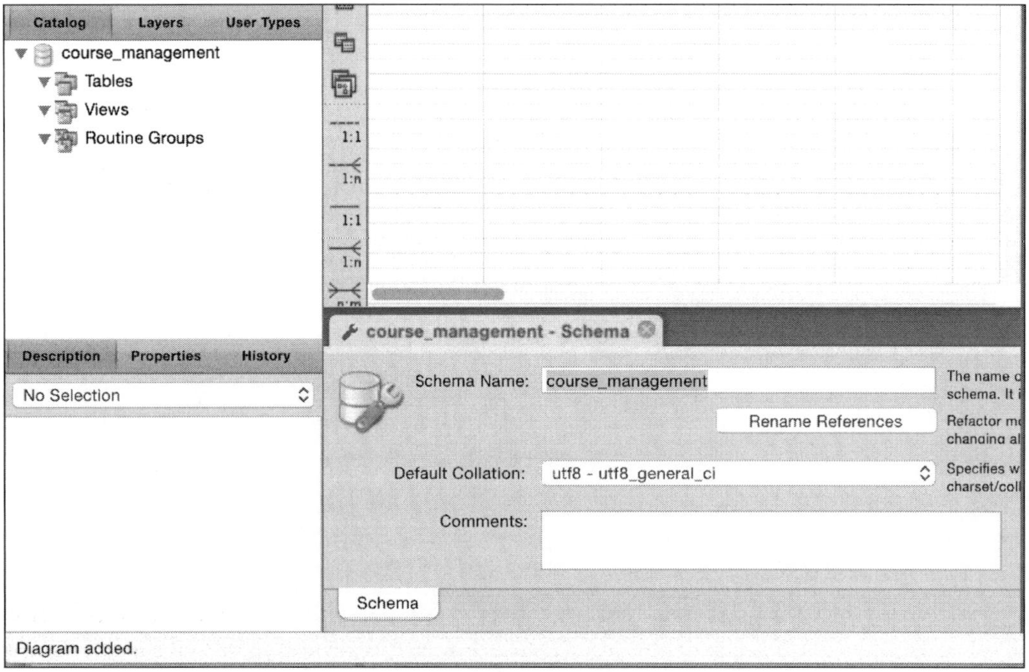

Figure 4.3.Rename schema

4. Hover over the toolbar buttons on the left side of the page, and you will see tool tips about their functions. Click on the button for new table and then click on the blank page. This will insert a new table with the name **table1**. Double-click the table icon to open the properties page of the table. In the **Properties** page, change the name of the table to **Course**.

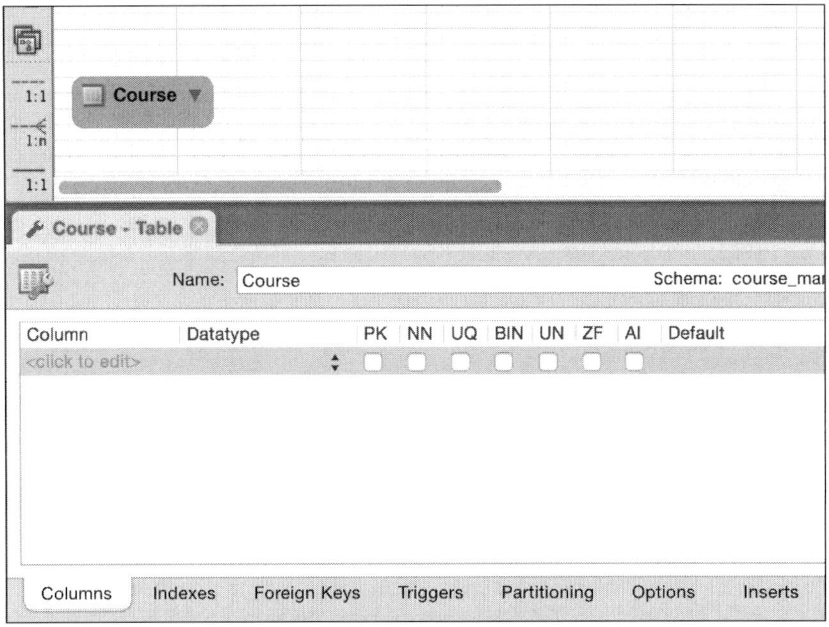

Figure 4.4.Create table in ER diagram

5. We will now create the columns of the table. Double-click in the first column and name it **id**. Check the **PK** (primary key), **NN** (not null), and **AI** (auto increment) checkboxes. Add other columns shown as follows:

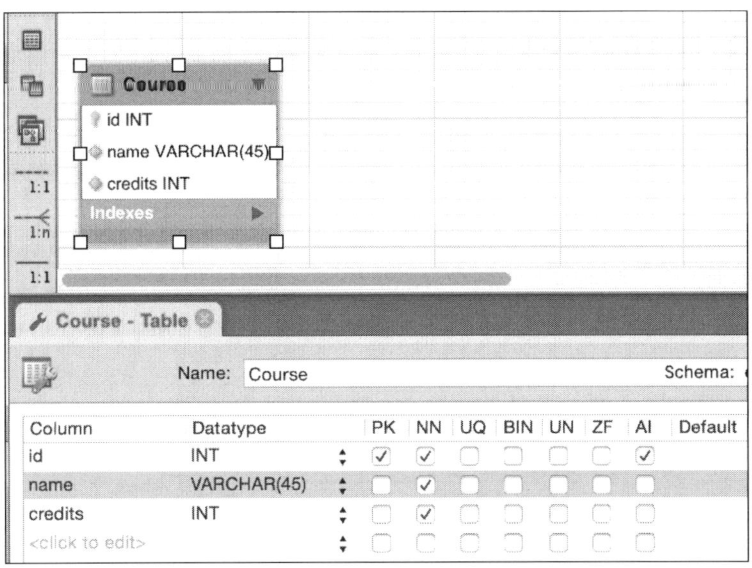

Figure 4.5.Create columns in a table in the ER diagram

6. Create other tables, namely **Student** and **Teacher**, as follows:

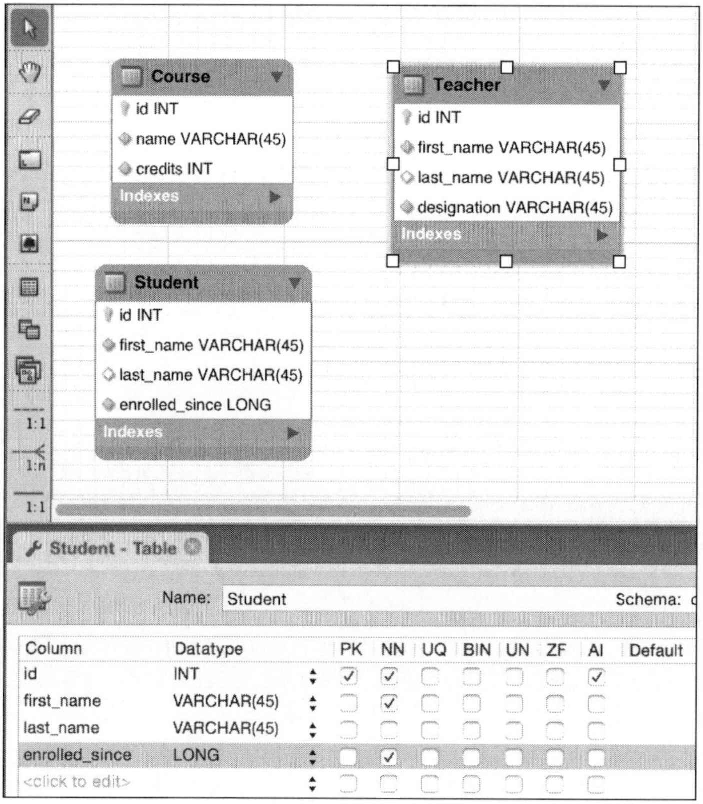

Figure 4.6.Create additional tables

Note that if you want to edit the column properties of any table, then double-click the table in the ER diagram. Just selecting a table by a single click would not change the table selection in the properties page. All columns in all tables are required (not null), except the **last_name** column in the **Student** and **Teacher** tables.

We will now create the relationships between tables. One course can have many students and students can take many courses. So, there is a many-to-many relationship between **Course** and **Student**.

We will assume that one course is taught by only one teacher. However, a teacher can teach more than one courses. Therefore, there is a many-to-one relationship between **Course** and **Teacher**.

Let's now model these relationships in the ER diagram.

1. First, we will create a non-identifying relationship between **Course** and **Teacher**.
2. Click on the non-identifying one-to-many button in the toolbar (dotted lines and **1:n**).
3. Then, click on the **Course** table first and then on the **Teacher** table. It will create a relationship as shown in *Figure 4.7.Create a one-to-many relationship between tables*. Notice that a foreign key **Teacher_id** is created in the **Course** table. We don't want to make the **Teacher_id** field required in **Course**. A course can exist without a teacher in our application. Therefore, double-click on the link joining the **Course** and **Teacher** tables.
4. Then, click on the **Foreign Key** tab.
5. On the **Referenced Table** side, uncheck the mandatory checkbox.

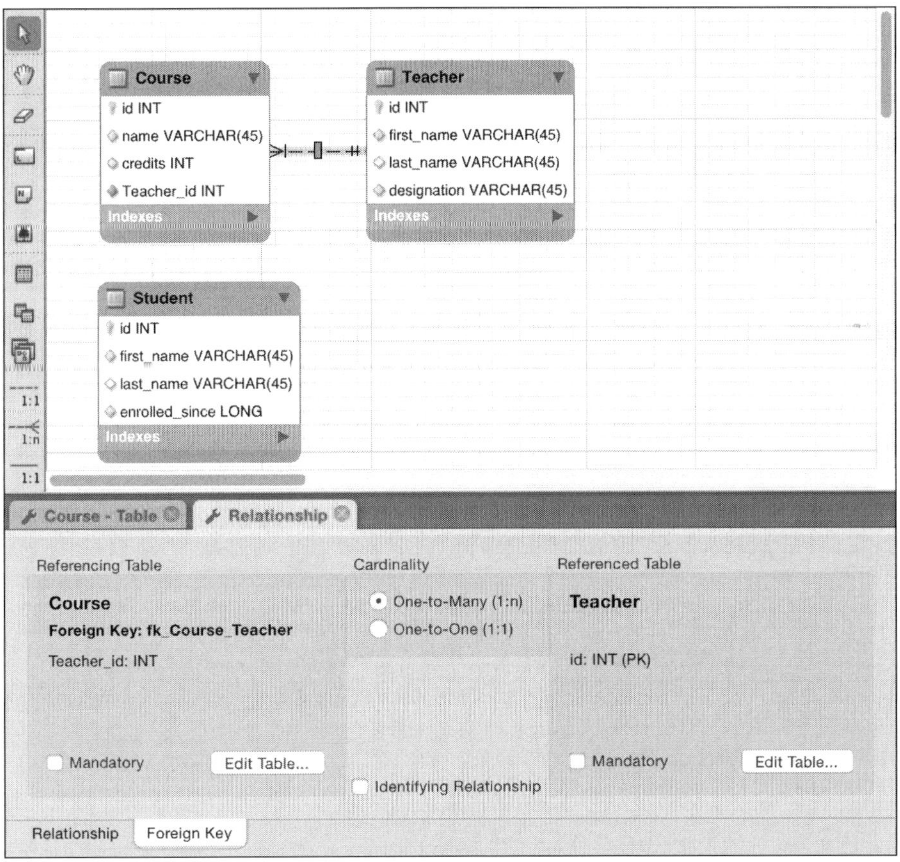

Figure 4.7.Create a one-to-many relationship between tables

The creation of a many-to-many relationship requires a link table to be created. To create a many-to-many relationship between **Course** and **Student**, click on the icon for many-to-many (**n:m**) and then click on the **Course** table and the **Student** table. This will create a third table (link table) called **Course_has_Student**. We will rename this table as **Course_Student**. The final diagram is as shown in the following figure:

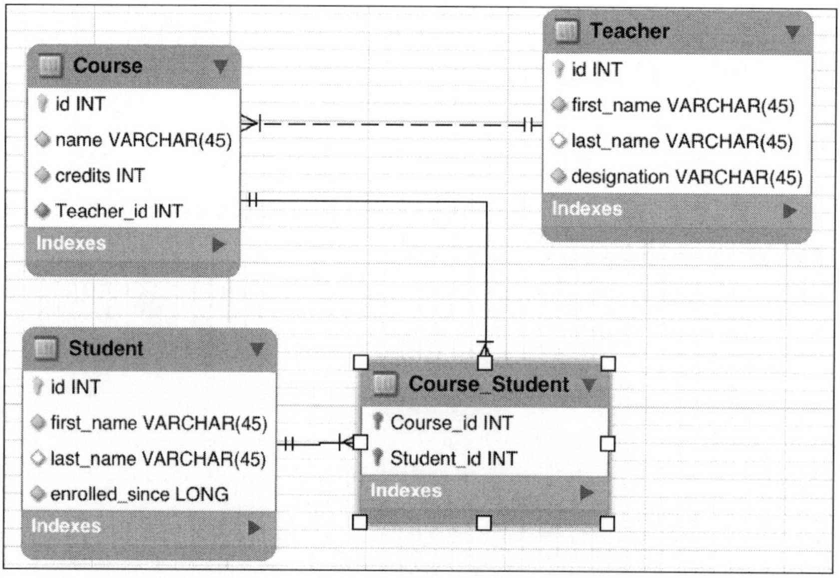

Figure 4.8 ER diagram for the course management example

Follow these steps to create DDL scripts from the preceding ER diagram:

1. To create DDL scripts from this ER diagram, select the **File** | **Export** | **Forward Engineer SQL Create Script...** menu.
2. In the **SQL Export Options** page, select checkboxes for two options:
   - **Generate DROP Statements Before Each CREATE Statement**
   - **Generate DROP SCHEMA**
3. Also, specify the **Output SQL Script File** path if you want to save the script.
4. On the last page of the *Export* wizard, you will see the script generated by MySQL Workbench. Copy this script by clicking the **Copy to Clipboard** button.

The script for creating tables and relationships

The following is the DDL script to create tables and relationships for the course management example.

```
-- MySQL Script generated by MySQL Workbench
-- Sun Mar  8 18:17:07 2015
-- Model: New Model    Version: 1.0
-- MySQL Workbench Forward Engineering

SET @OLD_UNIQUE_CHECKS=@@UNIQUE_CHECKS, UNIQUE_CHECKS=0;
SET @OLD_FOREIGN_KEY_CHECKS=@@FOREIGN_KEY_CHECKS, FOREIGN_KEY_
CHECKS=0;
SET @OLD_SQL_MODE=@@SQL_MODE, SQL_MODE='TRADITIONAL,ALLOW_INVALID_
DATES';

-- -----------------------------------------------------
-- Schema course_management
-- -----------------------------------------------------
DROP SCHEMA IF EXISTS `course_management` ;

-- -----------------------------------------------------
-- Schema course_management
-- -----------------------------------------------------
CREATE SCHEMA IF NOT EXISTS `course_management` DEFAULT CHARACTER SET
utf8 COLLATE utf8_general_ci ;
USE `course_management` ;

-- -----------------------------------------------------
-- Table `course_management`.`Teacher`
-- -----------------------------------------------------
DROP TABLE IF EXISTS `course_management`.`Teacher` ;

CREATE TABLE IF NOT EXISTS `course_management`.`Teacher` (
  `id` INT NOT NULL AUTO_INCREMENT,
  `first_name` VARCHAR(45) NOT NULL,
  `last_name` VARCHAR(45) NULL,
  `designation` VARCHAR(45) NOT NULL,
  PRIMARY KEY (`id`))
ENGINE = InnoDB;


-- -----------------------------------------------------
-- Table `course_management`.`Course`
-- -----------------------------------------------------
```

```
DROP TABLE IF EXISTS `course_management`.`Course` ;

CREATE TABLE IF NOT EXISTS `course_management`.`Course` (
  `id` INT NOT NULL AUTO_INCREMENT,
  `name` VARCHAR(45) NOT NULL,
  `credits` INT NOT NULL,
  `Teacher_id` INT NULL,
  PRIMARY KEY (`id`),
  INDEX `fk_Course_Teacher_idx` (`Teacher_id` ASC),
  CONSTRAINT `fk_Course_Teacher`
    FOREIGN KEY (`Teacher_id`)
    REFERENCES `course_management`.`Teacher` (`id`)
    ON DELETE NO ACTION
    ON UPDATE NO ACTION)
ENGINE = InnoDB;


-- -----------------------------------------------------
-- Table `course_management`.`Student`
-- -----------------------------------------------------
DROP TABLE IF EXISTS `course_management`.`Student` ;

CREATE TABLE IF NOT EXISTS `course_management`.`Student` (
  `id` INT NOT NULL AUTO_INCREMENT,
  `first_name` VARCHAR(45) NOT NULL,
  `last_name` VARCHAR(45) NULL,
  `enrolled_since` MEDIUMTEXT NOT NULL,
  PRIMARY KEY (`id`))
ENGINE = InnoDB;


-- -----------------------------------------------------
-- Table `course_management`.`Course_Student`
-- -----------------------------------------------------
DROP TABLE IF EXISTS `course_management`.`Course_Student` ;

CREATE TABLE IF NOT EXISTS `course_management`.`Course_Student` (
  `Course_id` INT NOT NULL,
  `Student_id` INT NOT NULL,
  PRIMARY KEY (`Course_id`, `Student_id`),
  INDEX `fk_Course_has_Student_Student1_idx` (`Student_id` ASC),
  INDEX `fk_Course_has_Student_Course1_idx` (`Course_id` ASC),
  CONSTRAINT `fk_Course_has_Student_Course1`
    FOREIGN KEY (`Course_id`)
```

```
    REFERENCES `course_management`.`Course` (`id`)
    ON DELETE NO ACTION
    ON UPDATE NO ACTION,
  CONSTRAINT `fk_Course_has_Student_Student1`
    FOREIGN KEY (`Student_id`)
    REFERENCES `course_management`.`Student` (`id`)
    ON DELETE NO ACTION
    ON UPDATE NO ACTION)
ENGINE = InnoDB;


SET SQL_MODE=@OLD_SQL_MODE;
SET FOREIGN_KEY_CHECKS=@OLD_FOREIGN_KEY_CHECKS;
SET UNIQUE_CHECKS=@OLD_UNIQUE_CHECKS;
```

Creating tables in MySQL

Let's now create tables and relationships in the MySQL database by using the script created in the previous section.

Make sure that MySQL is running and there is an open connection to the server from MySQL Workbench (see *Chapter 1, Introducing JEE and Eclipse*, for more details):

1. Create a new query tab (the first button in the toolbar) and paste the preceding script.
2. Execute the query.
3. At the end of the execution, refresh the schemas in the left pane. You should see the **course_management** schema and the tables created in it.

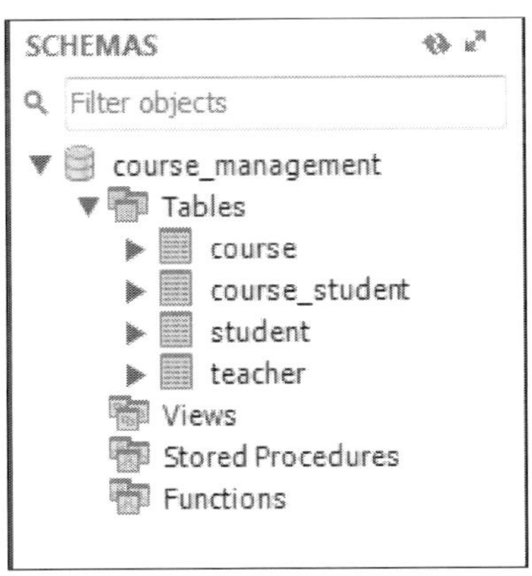

Figure 4.9 MySQL schema for the course management example

Creating a database application using JDBC

In this section, we will use JDBC to create a simple course management web application. We will use the MySQL schema created in the previous section. Further, we will create a web application using Tomcat; we have already seen how to create one in *Chapter 2, Creating a Simple JEE Web Application*. We also learnt how to use JSTL and JSF in the same chapter. In this section, we will use JSTL and JDBC to create the course management application, and in the next section, we will use JSF and JPA to create the same application. We will use Maven (as described in *Chapter 2, Creating a Simple JEE Web Application*) for project management, and of course, our IDE is going to be Eclipse JEE.

Creating a project and setting up Maven dependencies

The following are the steps to create the Maven project for our application:

1. Create a Maven web project as described in *Chapter 2, Creating a Simple JEE Web Application*.
2. Name the project `CourseManagementJDBC`.
3. Add dependencies for Servlet and JSP, but do not add a dependency for JSF.
4. To add a dependency for JSTL, open `pom.xml` and go to the **Dependencies** tab. Click on the **Add** button. Type `javax.servlet` in the search box and select **jstl**.

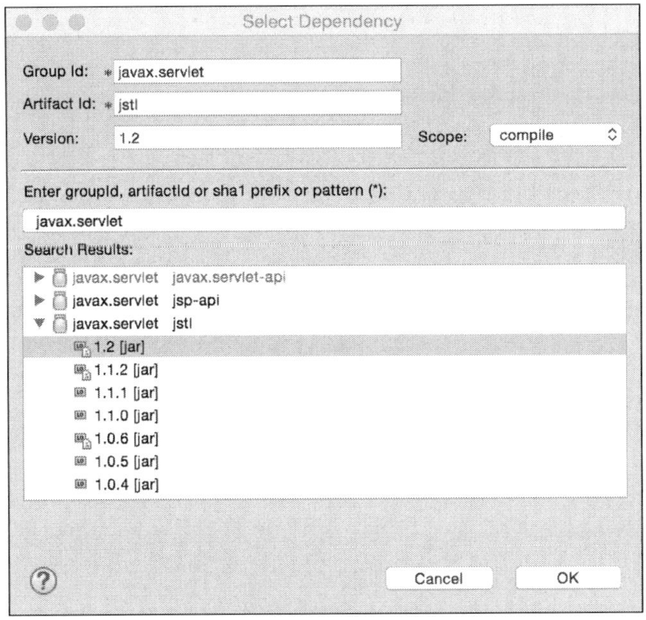

Figure 4.10 Add a dependency for JSTL

5. Add a dependency for the MySQL JDBC driver too.

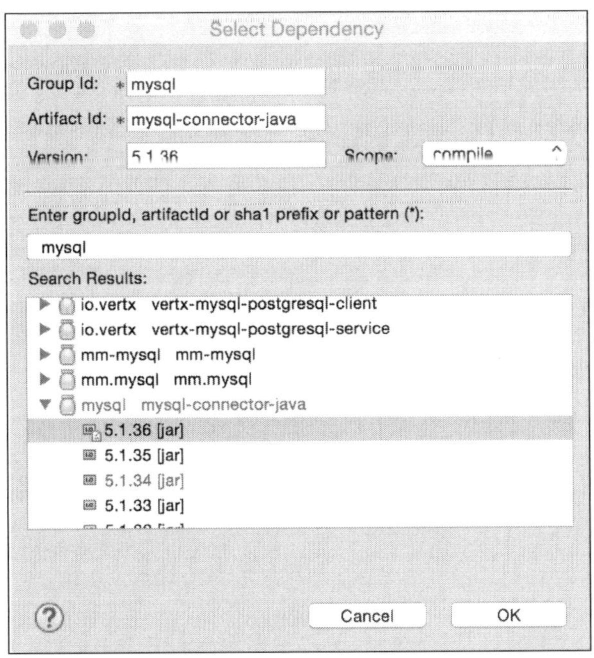

Figure 4.11 Add a dependency for the MySQL JDBC driver

Here is the `pom.xml` file after adding dependencies:

```
<project xmlns="http://maven.apache.org/POM/4.0.0"
  xmlns:xsi="http://www.w3.org/2001/XMLSchema-instance"
  xsi:schemaLocation="http://maven.apache.org/POM/4.0.0
http://maven.apache.org/xsd/maven-4.0.0.xsd">
  <modelVersion>4.0.0</modelVersion>
  <groupId>packt.book.jee.eclipse</groupId>
  <artifactId>CourseManagementJDBC</artifactId>
  <version>1</version>
  <packaging>war</packaging>
  <dependencies>
    <dependency>
      <groupId>javax.servlet</groupId>
      <artifactId>javax.servlet-api</artifactId>
      <version>3.1.0</version>
<scope>provided</scope>
    </dependency>
    <dependency>
      <groupId>javax.servlet</groupId>
      <artifactId>jstl</artifactId>
      <version>1.2</version>
    </dependency>
    <dependency>
      <groupId>mysql</groupId>
      <artifactId>mysql-connector-java</artifactId>
      <version>5.1.34</version>
    </dependency>
    <dependency>
      <groupId>javax.servlet.jsp</groupId>
      <artifactId>jsp-api</artifactId>
      <version>2.2</version>
      <scope>provided</scope>
    </dependency>
  </dependencies>
</project>
```

Note that the dependencies for Servlet and JSP are marked as provided, which means that they will be provided by the web container (Tomcat) and will not be packaged with the application.

A description of how to configure Tomcat and add a project to it is skipped here. Refer to *Chapter 2, Creating a Simple JEE Web Application,* for these details. This section will also not repeat information on how to run JSP pages and about JSTL that were covered in *Chapter 2, Creating a Simple JEE Web Application.*

Creating JavaBeans for data storage

We will first create the JavaBean classes for **Student**, **Course**, and **Teacher**. Since both the student and the teacher are people, we will create a new class called `Person` and have the `Student` and `Teacher` classes extend it. Create these JavaBeans in the `packt.book.jee.eclipse.ch4.beans` package as follows:

- `Course` bean:

```
package packt.book.jee.eclipse.ch4.bean;

public class Course {
  private int id;
  private String name;
  private int credits;
  public int getId() {
    return id;
  }
  public void setId(int id) {
    this.id = id;
  }
  public String getName() {
    return name;
  }
  public void setName(String name) {
    this.name = name;
  }
  public int getCredits() {
    return credits;
  }
  public void setCredits(int credits) {
    this.credits = credits;
  }
}
```

- `Person` bean:

```
package packt.book.jee.eclipse.ch4.bean;

public class Person {
  private int id;
  private String firstName;
  private String lastName;

  public int getId() {
    return id;
```

```
    }
    public void setId(int id) {
      this.id = id;
    }
    public String getFirstName() {
      return firstName;
    }
    public void setFirstName(String firstName) {
      this.firstName = firstName;
    }
    public String getLastName() {
      return lastName;
    }
    public void setLastName(String lastName) {
      this.lastName = lastName;
    }
  }
```

- `Student` bean:

```
package packt.book.jee.eclipse.ch4.bean;

public class Student extends Person {
  private long enrolledsince;

  public long getEnrolledsince() {
    return enrolledsince;
  }

  public void setEnrolledsince(long enrolledsince) {
    this.enrolledsince = enrolledsince;
  }
}
```

- `Teacher` bean:

```
package packt.book.jee.eclipse.ch4.bean;

public class Teacher extends Person {
  private String designation;

  public String getDesignation() {
    return designation;
  }
```

```
    public void setDesignation(String designation) {
      this.designation = designation;
    }
  }
```

Creating JSP to add a course

We will create a JSP page to add a new course. Right-click on the project in **Package Explorer**, and select the **New** | **Other** option. Type `jsp` in the filter box and select **JSP File**. Name the file `addCourse.jsp`. Eclipse will create the file in the `src/main/webapp` folder of the project.

Type the following code in `addCourse.jsp`:

```
<%@ page language="java" contentType="text/html; charset=UTF-8"
    pageEncoding="UTF-8"%>
<%@ taglib prefix="c" uri="http://java.sun.com/jsp/jstl/core" %>

<!DOCTYPE html PUBLIC "-//W3C//DTD HTML 4.01 Transitional//EN"
"http://www.w3.org/TR/html4/loose.dtd">
<html>
<head>
<meta http-equiv="Content-Type" content="text/html; charset=UTF-8">
<title>Add Course</title>
</head>
<body>
  <c:set var="errMsg" value="${null}"/>
  <c:set var="displayForm" value="${true}"/>
  <c:if test="${\"POST\".equalsIgnoreCase(pageContext.request.method)
        && pageContext.request.getParameter(\"submit\") != null}">
    <jsp:useBean id="courseBean" class="packt.book.jee.eclipse.ch4.
bean.Course">
      <c:catch var="beanStorageException">
        <jsp:setProperty name="courseBean" property="*" />
      </c:catch>
    </jsp:useBean>
    <c:choose>
      <c:when test="${!courseBean.isValidCourse() ||
beanStorageException != null}">
        <c:set var="errMsg" value="Invalid course details. Please
        try again"/>
      </c:when>
      <c:otherwise>
        <c:redirect url="listCourse.jsp"/>
```

```
      </c:otherwise>
    </c:choose>
  </c:if>

  <h2>Add Course:</h2>
  <c:if test="${errMsg != null}">
    <span style="color: red;">
      <c:out value="${errMsg}"></c:out>
    </span>
  </c:if>
  <form method="post">
    Name: <input type="text" name="name"> <br>
    Credits : <input type="text" name="credits"> <br>
    <button type="submit" name="submit">Add</button>
  </form>

</body>
</html>
```

Most of the code should be familiar, if you have read *Chapter 2, Creating a Simple JEE Web Application* (see section *Using JSTL*). We have a form to add a course. At the top of the file, we check whether the `post` request is made; if yes, store the content of the form in `courseBean` (make sure that the names of the `form` field are the same as the members defined in the bean). The new tag that we have used here is `<c:catch>`. It is like the *try-catch* block in Java. Any exception thrown from within the body of `<c:catch>` is assigned to the variable name declared in the `var` attribute. Here, we are not doing anything with `beanStorageException`; we are suppressing the exception. When an exception is thrown, the `credits` field of the `Course` bean will remain set to zero and it will be caught in the `courseBean.isValidCourse` method. If the course data is valid, then we redirect the request to the `listCourse.jsp` page by using the JSTL `<c:redirect>` tag.

We need to add the `isValidCourse` method in the `Course` bean. Therefore, open the class in the editor and add the following method:

```
public boolean isValidCourse() {
  return name != null && credits != 0;
}
```

We also need to create `listCourse.jsp`. For now, just create a simple JSP with no JSTL/Java code, and with only one header in the `body` tag:

```
<h2>Courses:</h2>
```

Right-click on `addCourse.jsp` in **Package Explorer**, and select **Run As | Run on Server**. If you have configured Tomcat properly and added your project in Tomcat (as described in *Chapter 2, Creating a Simple JEE Web Application*), then you should see the JSP page running the Eclipse built-in browser. Test the page with both valid and invalid data (a wrong credit value; for example, a non-numeric value). If the data entered is valid, then you would be redirected to `listCourse.jsp`; else, the same page would be displayed with an error message.

Before we start writing the JDBC code, let's learn some fundamental concepts of JDBC.

JDBC concepts

Before performing any operations in JDBC, we need to establish a connection to the database. Here are some of the important classes/interfaces in JDBC for executing SQL statements:

JDBC class/interface	Description
`java.sql.Connection`	Represents the connection between the application and the backend database. Must for performing any action on the database.
`java.sql.DriverManager`	Manages JDBC drivers used in the application. Use the `DriverManager.getConnection` static method to obtain the connection.
`java.sql.Statement`	Used for executing static SQL statements
`java.sql.PreparedStatement`	Used for preparing parameterized SQL statements. SQL statements are pre-compiled and can be executed with different parameters repeatedly.
`Java.sqlCallableStatement`	Used for executing a stored procedure.
`java.sql.ResultSet`	Represents a row in the database table in the result returned after the execution of an SQL query by `Statement` or `PreapredStatement`.

You can find all the interfaces for JDBC at `http://docs.oracle.com/javase/8/docs/api/java/sql/package-frame.html`.

Many of these are interfaces, and concrete implementations of these interfaces are provided by the JDBC drivers.

Creating a database connection

Make sure that the JDBC driver for the database that you want to connect to is downloaded, and is in the class path. In our project, we have already ensured this by adding a dependency in Maven. Maven downloads the driver and adds it to the class path of our web application.

It is always a good practice to make sure that the JDBC driver class is available when the application is running. If it is not, we can set a suitable error message and not perform any JDBC operations. The name of the MySQL JDBC driver class is `com.mysql.jdbc.Driver` (see `http://dev.mysql.com/doc/connector-j/en/connector-j-usagenotes-connect-drivermanager.html`).

```
try {
  Class.forName("com.mysql.jdbc.Driver");
}
catch (ClassNotFoundException e) {
  //log excetion
  //either throw application specific exception or return
  return;
}
```

Then, get the connection by calling the `DriverManager.getConnection` method.

```
try {
  Connection con =
DriverManager.getConnection("jdbc:mysql://localhost:3306/schema_name?"
+
      "user=your_user_name&password=your_password");
//perform DB operations and then close the connection
  con.close();
}
catch (SQLException e) {
  //handle exception
}
```

The argument to `DriverManager.getConnection` is called a connection URL or string. It is specific to the JDBC driver. So, check the documentation of the JDBC driver to understand how to create a connection URL. The preceding URL format is for MySQL. See `http://dev.mysql.com/doc/connector-j/en/connector-j-reference-configuration-properties.html`.

The connection URL contains the following details: the hostname of MySQL, the port on which MySQL is running (default is `3306`), and the schema name (database name that you want to connect to). You can pass the username and the password to connect to the database as the URL parameters.

Creating a connection is an expensive operation. Also, database servers allow a certain maximum number of connections to it, so connections should be created sparingly. It is advisable to cache a database connection and reuse it. However, make sure that you close the connection when you no longer need it, for example, in the final blocks of your code. Later, we will see how to create a pool of connections so that we create a limited number of connections, take them out of the pool when required, perform the required operations, and return them to the pool so that they can be reused.

Executing SQL statements

Use `Statement` for executing static SQL (having no parameters) and `PreparedStatement` for executing parameterized statements (to avoid the risk of SQL Injection, refer to `http://en.wikipedia.org/wiki/SQL_injection` and `https://www.owasp.org/index.php/SQL_injection`).

To execute any `Statement`, you first need to create the statement by using the `Connection` object. You can then perform any SQL operation, such as `create`, `update`, `delete`, and `select`. The `Select` statement (query) returns the `ResultSet` object. Iterate over the `ResultSet` object to get individual rows.

For example, use the following code to get all rows from the `Course` table:

```
Statement stmt = null;
ResultSet rs = null;
try {
  stmt = con.createStatement();
  rs = stmt.executeQuery("select * from Course");

  List<Course> courses = new ArrayList<Course>();
  //Depending on the database that you connect to, you may have to
  //call rs.first() before calling rs.next(). In the case of a MySQL
  //database, it is not necessary to call rs.first()
  while (rs.next()) {
    Course course = new Course();
    course.setId(rs.getInt("id"));
    course.setName(rs.getString("name"));
    course.setCredits(rs.getInt("credits"));
    courses.add(course);
  }
```

```
    }
    catch (SQLException e) {
      //handle exception
      e.printStackTrace();
    }
    finally {
      try {
        if (rs != null)
        rs.close();
        if (stmt != null)
        stmt.close();
      }
      catch (SQLException e) {
        //handle exception
      }
    }
```

Things to note:

- Use `Connection.createStatement ()` to create an instance of `Statement`.
- `Statement.executeQuery` returns `ResultSet`. If the SQL statement is not a query, for example, for the `create`, `update`, and `delete` statements, use `Statement.execute` (which returns `true` if the statement is executed successfully; else, `false`) or `Statement.executeUpdate` (which returns the number of rows affected or zero if none is affected).
- Pass the SQL statement to the `Statement.executeQuery` function. This can be any valid SQL string understood by the database.
- Iterate over `ResultSet` by calling the next method, till it returns `false`.
- Use different variations of the `get` methods (depending on data type of the column) to obtain values of column in the current row that `ResultSet` is pointing to. You can either pass the positional index of the column in SQL that you passed to `executeQuery` or the column name as used in the database table or alias specified in the SQL statement. For example, we would use the following code if we had specified column names in the SQL:

  ```
  rs = stmt.executeQuery("select id, name, credits as
  courseCredit from Course");
  ```

  Then, we could retrieve column values as follows:

  ```
  course.setId(rs.getInt(1));
  course.setName(rs.getString(2));
  course.setCredits(rs.getInt("courseCredit"));
  ```

- Make sure that you close `ResultSet` and `Statement`.

Instead of getting all courses, if you want to get a specific course, you would want to use `PreparedStatement`.

```
PreparedStatement stmt = null;
int courseId = 10;
ResultSet rs = null;
try {
  stmt = con.prepareStatement("select * from Course where id =
  ?");
  stmt.setInt(1, courseId);
  rs = stmt.executeQuery();

  Course course = null;
  if (rs.next()) {
    course = new Course();
    course.setId(rs.getInt("id"));
    course.setName(rs.getString("name"));
    course.setCredits(rs.getInt("credits"));
  }
}
catch (SQLException e) {
  //handle exception
  e.printStackTrace();
}
finally {
  try {
    if (rs != null)
    rs.close();
    if (stmt != null
    stmt.close();
  }
catch (SQLException e) {
    //handle exception
  }
}
```

In this example, we are trying to get the course with ID `10`. We first get an instance of `PreparedStatement` by calling `Connection.prepareStatement`. Note that you need to pass an SQL statement as an argument to this function. Parameters in the query are replaced by the `?` placeholder. We then set the value of the parameter by calling `stmt.setInt`. The first argument is the position of the parameter (it starts from `1`), and the second argument is the value. There are many variations of the `set` method for different data types.

Handling transactions

If you want to perform multiple changes to the database as a single unit, that is, either all changes should be done or none, then you need to start a transaction in JDBC. You start a transaction by calling `Connection. setAutoCommit(false)`. Once all operations are executed successfully, commit the changes to the database by calling `Connection.commit`. If for any reason you want to abort the transaction, call `Connection.rollback()`. Changes are not done in the database until you call `Connection.commit`.

Here is an example of inserting a bunch of courses in the database. Although in a real application, it may not make sense to abort a transaction when one of the courses is not inserted, here, we assume that either all courses must be inserted in the database or none.

```
PreparedStatement stmt = con.prepareStatement("insert into Course
(id, name, credits) values (?,?,?)");

con.setAutoCommit(false);
try {
  for (Course course : courses) {
    stmt.setInt(1, course.getId());
    stmt.setString(2, course.getName());
    stmt.setInt(3, course.getCredits());
    stmt.execute();
  }
  //commit the transaction now
  con.commit();
}
catch (SQLException e) {
  //rollback commit
  con.rollback();
}
```

There is more to learn about transactions than explained here. Refer to Oracle's JDBC tutorial at `http://docs.oracle.com/javase/tutorial/jdbc/basics/transactions.html`.

Using the JDBC database connection pool

As mentioned before, a JDBC database connection is an expensive operation and the connection object should be reused. Connection pools are used for this purpose. Most web containers provide their own implementation of a connection pool along with ways to configure it using JNDI. Tomcat also lets you configure a connection pool using JNDI. The advantage of configuring a connection pool by using JNDI is that the database configuration parameters, such as host name and port remain outside the source code and can be easily modified. See `http://tomcat.apache.org/tomcat-8.0-doc/jdbc-pool.html`.

However, a Tomcat connection pool can also be used without JNDI, as described in the preceding link. In this example, we will use a connection pool without JNDI. The advantage is that you can use the connection pool implementation provided by a third party; your application then becomes easily portable to other web containers. With JNDI, you can also port your application, as long as you create the JNDI context and resources in the web container that you are switching to.

We will add the dependency of the Tomcat connection pool library to Maven's `pom.xml`. Open the `pom.xml` file and add the following dependencies (see *Chapter 2, Creating a Simple JEE Web Application* to know how to add dependencies to Maven):

```
<dependency>
  <groupId>org.apache.tomcat</groupId>
  <artifactId>tomcat-jdbc</artifactId>
  <version>8.0.20</version>
</dependency>
```

Note that you can use any other implementation of the JDBC connection pool. One such connection pool library is HikariCP (`https://github.com/brettwooldridge/HikariCP`).

We also want to move the database properties out of the code. Therefore, create a file called `db.properties` in `src/main/resources`. Maven puts all the files in this folder in the classpath of the application. Add the following properties in `db.properties`:

```
db_host=localhost
db_port=3306
db_name=course_management
db_user_name=your_user_name
db_password=your_password
db_driver_class_name=com.mysql.jdbc.Driver
```

We will create a singleton class to create JDBC connections by using the Tomcat connection pool. Create the `packt.book.jee.eclipse.ch4.db.connection` package and create `DatabaseConnectionFactory` in it:

```
package packt.book.jee.eclipse.ch4.db.connection;

import java.io.IOException;
import java.io.InputStream;
import java.sql.Connection;
import java.sql.SQLException;
import java.util.Properties;

import org.apache.tomcat.jdbc.pool.DataSource;
import org.apache.tomcat.jdbc.pool.PoolProperties;

/**
 * Singleton Factory class to create JDBC database connections
 *
 */
public class DatabaseConnectionFactory {
  //singleton instance
  private static DatabaseConnectionFactory conFactory = new
  DatabaseConnectionFactory();

  private DataSource dataSource = null;

  //Make the construction private
  private DatabaseConnectionFactory() {}

  //



  /**
   * Must be called before any other method in this class.
   * Initializes the data source and saves it in an instance
  variable
   *
   * @throws IOException
   */
  public synchronized void init() throws IOException {
    //Check if init was already called
```

```
    if (dataSource != null)
      return;

      //load db.properties file first
      InputStream inStream =
  this.getClass().getClassLoader().getResourceAsStream("db.properties");
      Properties dbProperties = new Properties();
      dbProperties.load(inStream);
      inStream.close();

      //create Tomcat specific pool properties
      PoolProperties p = new PoolProperties();
  p.setUrl("jdbc:mysql://" + dbProperties.getProperty("db_host") +
  ":" + dbProperties.getProperty("db_port") + "/" +
  dbProperties.getProperty("db_name"));

  p.setDriverClassName(dbProperties.getProperty("db_driver_class_
  name"));
      p.setUsername(dbProperties.getProperty("db_user_name"));
      p.setPassword(dbProperties.getProperty("db_password"));
      p.setMaxActive(10);

      dataSource = new DataSource();
      dataSource.setPoolProperties(p);
    }

    //Provides access to singleton instance
    public static DatabaseConnectionFactory getConnectionFactory() {
      return conFactory;
    }

    //returns database connection object
    public Connection getConnection () throws SQLException {
      if (dataSource == null)
        throw new SQLException("Error initializing datasource");
      return dataSource.getConnection();
    }
  }
```

We must call the `init` method of `DatabaseConnectionFactory` before getting a connection from it. We will create a servlet and load it on startup. Then, we will call `DatabaseConnectionFactory.init` from the `init` method of the servlet.

Create `package packt.book.jee.eclipse.ch4.servlet`, and then, create `InitServlet` in it:

```
package packt.book.jee.eclipse.ch4.servlet;
import java.io.IOException;
import javax.servlet.ServletConfig;
import javax.servlet.ServletException;
import javax.servlet.annotation.WebServlet;
import javax.servlet.http.HttpServlet;

import packt.book.jee.eclipse.ch4.db.connection.
DatabaseConnectionFactory;

@WebServlet(value="/initServlet", loadOnStartup=1)
public class InitServlet extends HttpServlet {
  private static final long serialVersionUID = 1L;

  public InitServlet() {
    super();
  }

  public void init(ServletConfig config) throws ServletException {
    try {
      DatabaseConnectionFactory.getConnectionFactory().init();
    }
    catch (IOException e) {
      config.getServletContext().log(e.getLocalizedMessage(),e);
    }
  }
}
```

Note that we have used the `@WebServlet` annotation to mark this class as a servlet and the `loadOnStartup` attribute is set to `1`, to tell the web container to load this servlet at startup.

Now, we can call the following statement to get the `Connection` object from anywhere in the application:

```
Connection con =
DatabaseConnectionFactory.getConnectionFactory().getConnection();
```

If there are no more connections available in the pool, then the `getConnection` method throws an exception (particularly, in the case of `Tomcat` datasource, it throws `PoolExhaustedException`). When you close the connection that was obtained from the connection pool, then the connection is returned to the pool for reuse.

Saving a course in a database table using JDBC

Now that we have figured out how to use a JDBC connection pool and get a connection from it, let's write the code to save a course to the database.

We will create **Course Data Access Object (CourseDAO)**, which will have the functions required to directly interact with the database. We are thus separating the code to access the database from the UI and business code.

Create `package packt.book.jee.eclipse.ch4.dao`. Create a Java class called `CourseDAO` in it:

```
package packt.book.jee.eclipse.ch4.dao;

import java.sql.Connection;
import java.sql.PreparedStatement;
import java.sql.ResultSet;
import java.sql.SQLException;
import java.sql.Statement;

import packt.book.jee.eclipse.ch4.bean.Course;
import packt.book.jee.eclipse.ch4.db.connection.
DatabaseConnectionFactory;

public class CourseDAO {

  public static void addCourse (Course course) throws SQLException
  {
    //get connection from connection pool
    Connection con =
DatabaseConnectionFactory.getConnectionFactory().getConnection();
    try {
      final String sql = "insert into Course (name, credits)
      values (?,?)";
      //create the prepared statement with an option to get auto-
      generated keys
      PreparedStatement stmt = con.prepareStatement(sql,
      Statement.RETURN_GENERATED_KEYS);
      //set parameters
      stmt.setString(1, course.getName());
      stmt.setInt(2, course.getCredits());

      stmt.execute();
```

```
        //Get auto-generated keys
        ResultSet rs = stmt.getGeneratedKeys();

        if (rs.next())
          course.setId(rs.getInt(1));

        rs.close();
        stmt.close();
      }
      finally {
        con.close();
      }
    }
  }
```

We have already seen how to insert a record by using JDBC. The only new thing in the preceding code is to get an auto-generated ID. Remember that the `id` column in the `Course` table is auto-generated. This is the reason that we did not specify it in the insert SQL:

```
String sql = "insert into Course (name, credits) values (?,?)";
```

When we prepare a statement, we are telling the driver to get the auto-generated ID. Further, after the row is inserted in the table, we get the auto-generated ID by calling

```
ResultSet rs = stmt.getGeneratedKeys();
```

We have already created `addCourse.jsp`. Somehow, `addCourse.jsp` needs to send the form data to CourseDAO in order to save the data to the database. `addCourse.jsp` already has access to the `Course` bean and saves the form data in it. So, it makes sense for the `Course` bean to interface between `addCourse.jsp` and `CourseDAO`. So, we will modify the `Course` bean to add an instance of `CourseDAO` as a member variable and then add a function to add a course to the database by using the instance of `CourseDAO`.

```
public class Course {
....

  private CourseDAO courseDAO = new CourseDAO();

...

  public void addCourse() throws SQLException {
    courseDAO.addCourse(this);
  }
}
```

We will then modify `addCourse.jsp` to call the `addCourse` method of the `Course` bean. We will have to add the code for this after the form is submitted and the data is validated:

```
<c:catch var="addCourseException">
  ${courseBean.addCourse()}
</c:catch>
<c:choose>
  <c:when test="${addCourseException != null}">
    <c:set var="errMsg" value="${addCourseException.message}"/>
  </c:when>
  <c:otherwise>
    <c:redirect url="listCourse.jsp"/>
  </c:otherwise>
</c:choose>
```

One thing to note in the preceding code is the following:

```
${courseBean.addCourse()}
```

You can insert **Expression Language** (**EL**) in JSP as discussed previously. This method does not return anything (it is void method). Therefore, we didn't use the `<c:set>` tag. Further, note that the call is made within the `<c:catch>` tag. If any `SQLException` is thrown from the method, then it will be assigned to the `addCourseException` variable. We then check whether `addCourseException` is set in the `<c:when>` tag. If the value is not null, then it means that the exception was thrown. We set the error message, which is later displayed on the same page. If no error is thrown, then the request is redirected to `listCourse.jsp`. Here is the complete code of `addCourse.jsp` with the preceding changes.

```
<%@ page language="java" contentType="text/html; charset=UTF-8"
    pageEncoding="UTF-8"%>
<%@ taglib prefix="c" uri="http://java.sun.com/jsp/jstl/core" %>

<!DOCTYPE html PUBLIC "-//W3C//DTD HTML 4.01 Transitional//EN"
"http://www.w3.org/TR/html4/loose.dtd">
<html>
<head>
<meta http-equiv="Content-Type" content="text/html; charset=UTF-8">
<title>Insert title here</title>
</head>
<body>
  <c:set var="errMsg" value="${null}"/>
  <c:set var="displayForm" value="${true}"/>
```

```
  <c:if
test="${\"POST\".equalsIgnoreCase(pageContext.request.method)
&& pageContext.request.getParameter(\"submit\") != null}">
  <jsp:useBean id="courseBean"
  class="packt.book.jee.eclipse.ch4.bean.Course">
    <c:catch var="beanStorageException">
    <jsp:setProperty name="courseBean" property="*" />
    </c:catch>
    </jsp:useBean>
    <c:choose>
      <c:when test="${!courseBean.isValidCourse() ||
      beanStorageException != null}">
      <c:set var="errMsg" value="Invalid course details. Please
      try again"/>
      </c:when>
      <c:otherwise>
        <c:catch var="addCourseException">
        ${courseBean.addCourse()}
        </c:catch>
        <c:choose>
          <c:when test="${addCourseException != null}">
          <c:set var="errMsg"
          value="${addCourseException.message}"/>
          </c:when>
          <c:otherwise>
            <c:redirect url="listCourse.jsp"/>
          </c:otherwise>
        </c:choose>
      </c:otherwise>
    </c:choose>
  </c:if>

  <h2>Add Course:</h2>
  <c:if test="${errMsg != null}">
    <span style="color: red;">
      <c:out value="${errMsg}"></c:out>
    </span>
  </c:if>
  <form method="post">
    Name: <input type="text" name="name"> <br>
    Credits : <input type="text" name="credits"> <br>
    <button type="submit" name="submit">Add</button>
  </form>

</body>
</html>
```

Run the page, either in Eclipse or outside (see *Chapter 2, Creating a Simple JEE Web Application* to know how to run JSP in Eclipse and view it in Eclipse's internal browser) and add a couple of courses.

Getting courses from the database table using JDBC

We will now modify `listCourses.jsp` to display the courses that we have added using `addCourse.jsp`. However, we first need to add a method in `CourseDAO` to get the courses from the database.

Note that the `Course` table has a one-to-many relationship with `Teacher`. It stores the teacher id in it. Further, the teacher id is not a required field, so a course can exist in the `Course` table with a null `teacher_id`. To get all the details of a course, we need to get the teacher for the course too. However, we cannot create a simple join in SQL query to get the details of a course and of the teacher for each course, because a teacher may not have been set for the course. In such cases, we use the left outer join, which returns all records from the table on the left side of the join but only matching records from the table on the right side of the join. Here is the SQL statement to get all courses and teachers for each course.

```
select course.id as courseId, course.name as courseName,
  course.credits as credits, Teacher.id as teacherId,
  Teacher.first_name as firstName,Teacher.last_name as lastName,
  Teacher.designation designation
from Course left outer join Teacher on
course.Teacher_id = Teacher.id
order by course.name
```

We will use the preceding query in `CourseDAO` to get all courses. Open the `CourseDAO` class and add the following method:

```
public List<Course> getCourses () throws SQLException {
  //get connection from connection pool
  Connection con =
DatabaseConnectionFactory.getConnectionFactory().getConnection();

  List<Course> courses = new ArrayList<Course>();
  Statement stmt = null;
  ResultSet rs = null;
  try {
    stmt = con.createStatement();
```

```
        //create SQL statement using left outer join
        StringBuilder sb = new StringBuilder("select course.id as
        courseId, course.name as courseName,")
          .append("course.credits as credits, Teacher.id as teacherId,
          Teacher.first_name as firstName, ")
          .append("Teacher.last_name as lastName, Teacher.designation
          designation ")
          .append("from Course left outer join Teacher on ")
          .append("course.Teacher_id = Teacher.id ")
          .append("order by course.name");

    //execute the query
        rs = stmt.executeQuery(sb.toString());

    //iterate over result set and create Course objects
    //add them to course list
        while (rs.next()) {
          Course course = new Course();
          course.setId(rs.getInt("courseId"));
          course.setName(rs.getString("courseName"));
          course.setCredits(rs.getInt("credits"));
          courses.add(course);

          int teacherId = rs.getInt("teacherId");
    //check whether teacher id was null in the table
          if (rs.wasNull()) //no teacher set for this course.
            continue;
          Teacher teacher = new Teacher();
          teacher.setId(teacherId);
          teacher.setFirstName(rs.getString("firstName"));
          teacher.setLastName(rs.getString("lastName"));
          teacher.setDesignation(rs.getString("designation"));
          course.setTeacher(teacher);
        }

        return courses;
      }
    finally {
      try {if (rs != null) rs.close();} catch (SQLException e) {}
      try {if (stmt != null) stmt.close();} catch (SQLException e) {}
      try {con.close();} catch (SQLException e) {}
      }
    }
```

We have used `Statement` to execute the query because it is a static query. We have used `StringBuilder` to build the SQL statement because it is a relatively large query (compared to those that we have written so far) and we would like to avoid a concatenation of string objects, because they are immutable. After executing the query, we iterate over the result set and create the `Course` object and add it to the list of courses, which is returned at the end.

One interesting thing here is the use of `ResultSet.wasNull`. We want to check whether the `teacher_id` field in the `Course` table for that particular row was null. Therefore, immediately after calling `rs.getInt("teacherId")`, we check whether the value fetched by `ResultSet` was null by calling `rs.wasNull`. If `teacher_id` was null, then the teacher was not set for that course, so we continue the loop, skipping the code to create the `Teacher` object.

In the final block, we catch an exception when closing `ResultSet`, `Statement`, and `Connection` and ignoring it.

Let's now add a method in the `Course` bean to fetch courses by calling the `getCourses` method of `CourseDAO`. Open the `Course` bean and add the following method:

```
public List<Course> getCourses() throws SQLException {
  return courseDAO.getCourses();
}
```

We are now ready to modify `listCourse.jsp` to display courses. Open the JSP and replace the existing code with the following:

```
<%@ page language="java" contentType="text/html; charset=UTF-8"
    pageEncoding="UTF-8"%>
<%@ taglib prefix="c" uri="http://java.sun.com/jsp/jstl/core" %>

<!DOCTYPE html PUBLIC "-//W3C//DTD HTML 4.01 Transitional//EN"
"http://www.w3.org/TR/html4/loose.dtd">
<html>
<head>
<meta http-equiv="Content-Type" content="text/html; charset=UTF-8">
<title>Courses</title>
</head>
<body>
  <c:catch var="err">
    <jsp:useBean id="courseBean"
    class="packt.book.jee.eclipse.ch4.bean.Course"/>
    <c:set var="courses" value="${courseBean.getCourses()}"/>
  </c:catch>
  <c:choose>
```

```
      <c:when test="${err != null}">
        <c:set var="errMsg" value="${err.message}"/>
      </c:when>
      <c:otherwise>
      </c:otherwise>
    </c:choose>
    <h2>Courses:</h2>
    <c:if test="${errMsg != null}">
      <span style="color: red;">
        <c:out value="${errMsg}"></c:out>
      </span>
    </c:if>
    <table>
      <tr>
        <th>Id</th>
        <th>Name</th>
        <th>Credits</th>
        <th>Teacher</th>
      </tr>
      <c:forEach items="${courses}" var="course">
        <tr>
          <td>${course.id}</td>
          <td>${course.name}</td>
          <td>${course.credits}</td>
          <c:choose>
            <c:when test="${course.teacher != null}">
              <td>${course.teacher.firstName}</td>
            </c:when>
            <c:otherwise>
              <td></td>
            </c:otherwise>
          </c:choose>
        </tr>
      </c:forEach>
    </table>
  </body>
  </html>
```

Most of the code should be easy to understand because we have used similar code in the previous examples. At the beginning of the script, we create the `Course` bean and get all the courses and assign the course list to a variable called `courses`.

```
<c:catch var="err">
    <jsp:useBean id="courseBean"
    class="packt.book.jee.eclipse.ch4.bean.Course"/>
    <c:set var="courses" value="${courseBean.getCourses()}"/>
</c:catch>
```

To display courses, we create an HTML table and set its headers. One new thing in the preceding code is the use of the `<c:forEach>` JSTL tag to iterate over the list. The `forEach` tag takes the following two attributes:

- List of objects
- Variable name of a single item when iterating over the list

In the preceding case, the list of objects is provided by the `courses` variable that we set at the beginning of the script and we identify a single item in the list with the variable name `course`. We then display the course details and the teacher for the course, if any.

Writing code to add `Teacher` and `Student` and list them is left to the readers as an exercise. The code would be very similar to that for course, of course, with different table and class names.

Completing the add Course functionality

We still haven't completed the functionality for adding a new course; we need to provide an option to assign a teacher to the course when adding a new course. Assuming that you have implemented `TeacherDAO` and added the `addTeacher` and `getTeachers` methods in the `Teacher` bean, we can now complete the add Course functionality.

First, modify `addCourse` in `CourseADO` to save the teacher id for each course, if it is not zero. The SQL statement to insert a record changes as follows:

```
String sql = "insert into Course (name, credits, Teacher_id) values
(?,?,?)";
```

We have added the `Teacher_id` column and the corresponding parameter holder `?`. We will set `Teacher_id` to null if it is zero; else, the actual value:

```
if (course.getTeacherId() == 0)
  stmt.setNull(3, Types.INTEGER);
else
  stmt.setInt(3,course.getTeacherId());
```

We will then modify the `Course` bean to save the teacher id that will be passed along with the `POST` request from the HTML form.

```
public class Course {

  private int teacherId;
  public int getTeacherId() {
```

```
        return teacherId;
    }
      public void setTeacherId(int teacherId) {
        this.teacherId = teacherId;
      }
    }
```

Next, we will modify `addCourse.jsp` to display the drop-down list of teachers when adding a new course. We first need to get the list of teachers. Therefore, we will create a `Teacher` bean and call the `getTeachers` method on it. We will do this just before the **Add Course** header

```
<jsp:useBean id="teacherBean" class="packt.book.jee.eclipse.ch4.bean.
Teacher"/>
<c:catch var="teacherBeanErr">
<c:set var="teachers" value="${teacherBean.getTeachers()}"/>
</c:catch>
<c:if test="${teacherBeanErr != null}">
  <c:set var="errMsg" value="${err.message}"/>
</c:if>
```

Finally, we will display the HTML drop-down list in the form and populate it with the teacher names:

```
Teacher :
<select name="teacherId">
<c:forEach items="${teachers}" var="teacher">
<option value="${teacher.id}">${teacher.firstName}
</option>
</c:forEach>
</select>
```

Download the accompanying code for this chapter to see the complete source code of `CourseDAO` and `addCourse.jsp`.

With this, we conclude our discussion on using JDBC to create web database applications. With the examples that you have seen so far, you should be in a good position to complete the remaining application by adding the functionality to modify and delete the records in the database. The update and delete SQL statements can be executed by `Statement` or `PreparedStatement`, just as the `insert` statements are executed using these two classes.

Using Eclipse Data Source Explorer

It is sometimes useful if you can see the data in the database table from your IDE and can modify it. This is possible in Eclipse JEE by using **Data Source Explorer**. This view is displayed in a tab at the bottom pane, just below editors, in the **Java EE** perspective. If you do not see the view, or have closed the view, you can reopen it by using the **Window** | **Show View** | **Other** menu. Type `data source` in the filter textbox and you should see the view name under the **Data Management** group. Open the view:

Figure 4.12 Data Source Explorer

Right-click on the **Database Connections** node and select **New**. From the list, select **MySQL**.

Figure 4.13 Select MySQL Connection Profile

Click **Next**. If the Drivers list is empty, you haven't configured the driver yet. Click on an icon next to the drop-down list for drivers to open the configuration page.

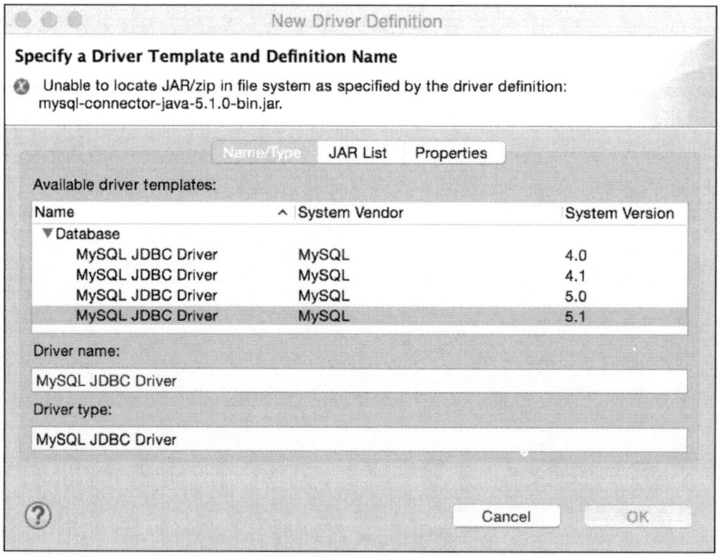

Figure 4.13 JDBC Driver Definition page

Select the MySQL version and click on the **JAR List** tab.

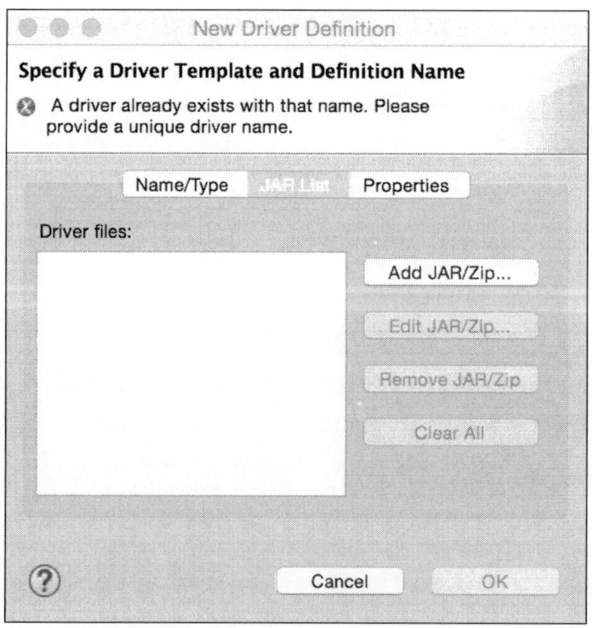

Figure 4.13 JDBC Driver Definition page

Remove any file from the **Driver files** list. Click on the **Add JAR/Zip...** button. This opens the **File Open** dialog. Select the JAR file for the MySQL driver version that you have selected. Since Maven has already downloaded the JAR file for you, you can select it from the local Maven repository. On OS X and Linux, the path is `~/.m2/repository/mysql/mysql-connector-java/<version_num>/mysql_connector_java_version_num/mysql-connector-java-version_num.jar` (`version_num` is a placeholder for the actual version number in the path). On Windows, you can find the Maven repository at `C:\Documents and Settings\{your-username}\.m2`, and then, the relative path for the MySQL driver is the same as in OS X.

If you have trouble finding the JAR in the local Maven repository, you can download the JAR file (for the MySQL JDBC driver) from `http://dev.mysql.com/downloads/connector/j/`.

Once you specify the correct driver JAR file, you need to set the following properties:

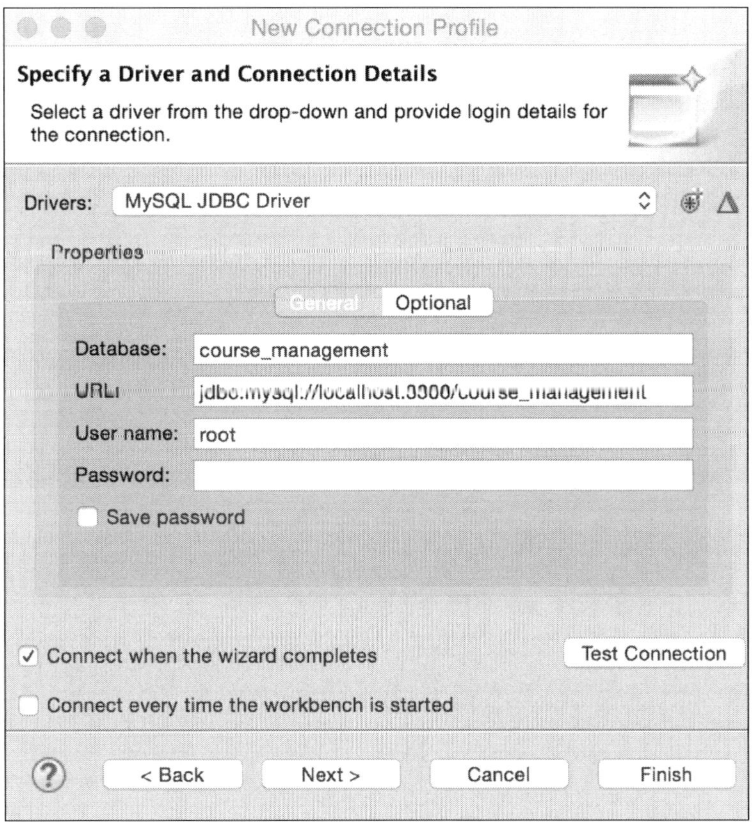

Figure 4.14 Set JDBC driver properties

Click **Next** and then **Finish**. A new database connection will be added in **Data Source Explorer**. You can now browse the database schema and tables.

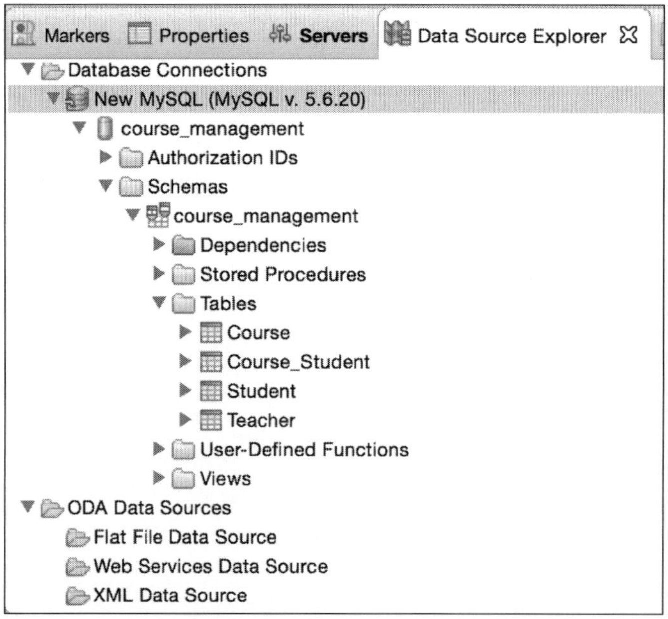

Figure 4.14 Browse tables in Data Source Explorer

Right-click on any table to see the menu options available for different actions.

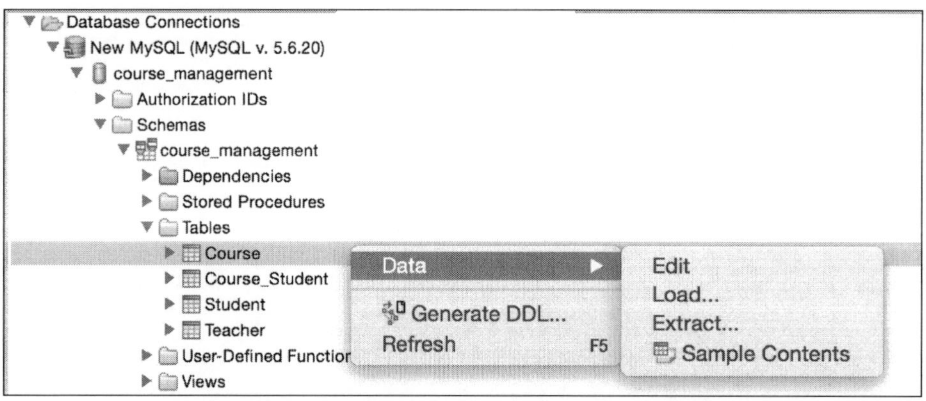

Figure 4.14 Table menu options in Data Source Explorer

Select the **Edit** menu to open a page in the editor where you can see the existing records in the table. You can also modify or add new data in the same page. Select the **Load** option to load data from an external file into the table. Select the **Extract** option to export data from the table.

Creating a database application using JPA

In the previous section, we learnt how to create a Course Management application by using JDBC and JSTL. In this section, we will build the same application using JPA and JSF. We have seen how to create a web application using JSF in *Chapter 2, Creating a Simple JEE Web Application*. We will use much of this learning in this section.

As mentioned at the beginning of this chapter, JPA is an ORM framework, which is now part of the JEE specification. At the time of writing, it is in version 2.1.

We will learn a lot about JPA as we develop our application.

Create a Maven project called `CourseManagementJPA` with the group ID `packt.book.jee_eclipse` and the artefact ID `CourseManagementJPA`. Eclipse JEE has great tools for creating applications using JPA, but you need to convert your project to a JPA project. We will see how to do this later in this section.

Creating the user interface for adding a course using JSF

Before we write any data access code using JPA, let's first create a user interface using JSF. As we have learnt in *Chapter 2, Creating a Simple JEE Web Application*, we need to add Maven dependencies for JSF. Add the following dependencies in `pom.xml`:

```
<dependencies>
  <dependency>
    <groupId>javax.servlet</groupId>
    <artifactId>javax.servlet-api</artifactId>
    <version>3.1.0</version>
    <scope>provided</scope>
  </dependency>
  <dependency>
    <groupId>com.sun.faces</groupId>
    <artifactId>jsf-api</artifactId>
    <version>2.2.9</version>
  </dependency>
  <dependency>
    <groupId>com.sun.faces</groupId>
    <artifactId>jsf-impl</artifactId>
    <version>2.2.9</version>
  </dependency>
</dependencies>
```

We need to add `web.xml`, declare the JSF Servlet, and add the mapping for it. Eclipse provides you a very easy way to add `web.xml` (which should be in the `WEB-INF` folder). Right-click on the project and select the **Java EE Tools | Generate Deployment Descriptor Stub** menu. This creates the `WEB-INF` folder under `src/main/webapp` and creates `web.xml` in the `WEB-INF` folder with the default content. Now, add the following servlet and mapping:

```
<servlet>
  <servlet-name>JSFServlet</servlet-name>
  <servlet-class>javax.faces.webapp.FacesServlet</servlet-class>
  <load-on-startup>1</load-on-startup>
</servlet>
<servlet-mapping>
  <servlet-name>JSFServlet</servlet-name>
  <url-pattern>*.xhtml</url-pattern>
</servlet-mapping>
```

We will now create JavaBeans for `Course`, `Teacher`, `Student`, and `Person`, just as we created them in the previous example for JDBC. Create a `packt.book.jee.eclipse.ch4.jpa.bean` package and create the following JavaBeans:

- `Course.java`

```
package packt.book.jee.eclipse.ch4.jpa.bean;

import java.io.Serializable;
import javax.faces.bean.ManagedBean;
import javax.faces.bean.RequestScoped;

@ManagedBean (name="course")
@RequestScoped
public class Course implements Serializable {
  private static final long serialVersionUID = 1L;

  private int id;
  private String name;
  private int credits;
  private Teacher teacher;

  public int getId() {
    return id;
  }
  public void setId(int id) {
    this.id = id;
  }
```

```
    public String getName() {
      return name;
    }
    public void setName(String name) {
      this.name = name;
    }
    public int getCredits() {
      return credits;
    }
    public void setCredits(int credits) {
      this.credits = credits;
    }
    public boolean isValidCourse() {
      return name != null && credits != 0;
    }
    public Teacher getTeacher() {
      return teacher;
    }
    public void setTeacher(Teacher teacher) {
      this.teacher = teacher;
    }
  }
```

- `Person.java`

```
package packt.book.jee.eclipse.ch4.jpa.bean;

import java.io.Serializable;

public class Person implements Serializable{
  private static final long serialVersionUID = 1L;

  private int id;
  private String firstName;
  private String lastName;

  public int getId() {
    return id;
  }
  public void setId(int id) {
    this.id = id;
  }
  public String getFirstName() {
    return firstName;
  }
```

```
  public void setFirstName(String firstName) {
    this.firstName = firstName;
  }
  public String getLastName() {
    return lastName;
  }
  public void setLastName(String lastName) {
    this.lastName = lastName;
  }
}
```

- `Student.java`

```
package packt.book.jee.eclipse.ch4.jpa.bean;

import javax.faces.bean.ManagedBean;
import javax.faces.bean.RequestScoped;
import java.util.Date;


@ManagedBean (name="student")
@RequestScoped
public class Student extends Person {
  private static final long serialVersionUID = 1L;

  private Date enrolledsince;

  public Date getEnrolledsince() {
    return enrolledsince;
  }

  public void setEnrolledsince(Date enrolledsince) {
    this.enrolledsince = enrolledsince;
  }
}
```

- `Teacher.java`

```
package packt.book.jee.eclipse.ch4.jpa.bean;

import javax.faces.bean.ManagedBean;
import javax.faces.bean.RequestScoped;

@ManagedBean (name="teacher")
@RequestScoped
```

```
public class Teacher extends Person {
  private static final long serialVersionUID = 1L;

  private String designation;

  public String getDesignation() {
    return designation;
  }

  public void setDesignation(String designation) {
    this.designation = designation;
  }
  public boolean isValidTeacher() {
    return getFirstName() != null;
  }
}
```

> All are JSF managed beans in `RequestScope`. Refer to JSF discussion in *Chapter 2, Creating a Simple JEE Web Application* to know more about managed beans and scopes.

These beans are now ready for use in JSF pages. Create a JSF page and name it `addCourse.xhtml`:

```
<html xmlns="http://www.w3.org/1999/xhtml"
    xmlns:f="http://java.sun.com/jsf/core"
    xmlns:h="http://java.sun.com/jsf/html">

  <h2>Add Course:</h2>
  <h:form>
    <h:outputLabel value="Name:" for="name"/>
      <h:inputText value="#{course.name}" id="name"/> <br/>
    <h:outputLabel value="Credits:" for="credits"/>
      <h:inputText value="#{course.credits}" id="credits"/>
    <br/>
    <h:commandButton value="Add" action="
    #{courseServiceBean.addCourse} "/>
  </h:form>

</html>
```

The page uses JSF tags and Managed Beans to get/set values. Notice that the value of an action attribute calls `courseServiceBean`. In the application that we created using JDBC, we had some code to interact with DAOs in the JavaBeans. For example, the `Course` bean had a method for `addCourse`. However, here, we will handle it differently. We will create service bean classes (they are also Managed Beans, just like `Course`) to interact with the data access objects and have the `Course` bean contain only the values set by the user.

Create a package and name it `packt.book.jee.eclipse.ch4.jpa.service_bean`. Create a class called `CourseServiceBean` in this package with the following code:

```
package packt.book.jee.eclipse.ch4.jpa.service_bean;

import javax.faces.bean.ManagedBean;
import javax.faces.bean.ManagedProperty;
import javax.faces.bean.RequestScoped;

import packt.book.jee.eclipse.ch4.jpa.bean.Course;

@ManagedBean(name="courseServiceBean")
@RequestScoped
public class CourseServiceBean {
  @ManagedProperty(value="#{course}")
  private Course course;

  private String errMsg= null;

  public Course getCourse() {
    return course;
  }

  public void setCourse(Course course) {
    this.course = course;
  }

  public String getErrMsg() {
    return errMsg;
  }

  public void setErrMsg(String errMsg) {
    this.errMsg = errMsg;
  }

  public String addCourse() {
```

```
        return "listCourse";
    }
}
```

`CourseServiceBean` is a managed bean including the `errMsg` field (to store any error message during the processing of requests), a method called `addCourse`, and a field called `course`. This field is annotated with `@ManagedProperty`.

The `ManagedProperty` annotation tells the JSF implementation to inject another bean (specified in the `value` attribute) in the current bean. Here, we expect `CourseServiceBean` to have access to the `course` bean at runtime, without instantiating it. This is part of the **Dependency Injection** (**DI**) framework supported by Java EE. We will learn more about the DI framework in Java EE in the later chapters. The `addCourse` function doesn't do much at this point but just returns the `"listCourse"` string. If you want to execute `addCourse.xhtml` at this point, create a simple `listCourse.xml` file with some placeholder content and test `addCourse.xhtml`. We will add more content to `listCourse.xml` later on in this section.

JPA concepts

JPA is an ORM framework in JEE. It provides a set of APIs that the JPA implementation providers are expected to implement. There are many JPA providers, such as **EclipseLink** (`https://eclipse.org/eclipselink/`), Hibernate JPA (`http://hibernate.org/orm/`), and OpenJPA (`http://openjpa.apache.org/`). Before we start writing the persistence code using JPA, it is important to understand some basic concepts of JPA.

Entity

Entity represents a single object instance that is typically related to one table. Any **Plain Old Java Object** (**POJO**) can be converted to entity by annotating the class with `@Entity`. Members of the class are mapped to columns of a table in the database. Entity classes are simple Java classes, so they can extend or include other Java classes or even another JPA entity. We will see an example of this in our application. You can also specify validation rules for members of the Entity class; for example, you can mark a member as not null by using the `@NotNull` annotation. These annotations are provided by Java EE Bean Validation APIs. See `http://docs.oracle.com/javaee/7/tutorial/bean-validation001.htm#GIRCZ` for a list of validation annotations.

EntityManager

The `EntityManager` APIs manages entities. They provide the persistence context in which entities exist. The persistence context also allows you to manage transactions. By using `EntityManager` APIs, you can perform query and write operations on entities. The entity manager can be web container managed (in which case an instance of `EntityManager` is injected by the container), or application managed. In this chapter, we are going to look at an application-managed entity manager. We will visit container-managed entity manager in *Chapter 7, Creating JEE Applications with EJB* when we learn EJBs. The persistence unit of the entity manager defines the database connectivity information and groups entities that become part of the persistence unit. It is defined in a configuration file called `persistence.xml` and is expected to be in `META-INF` in the class path.

`EntityManager` has its own persistence context, which is a cache of entities. Updates to entities are first done in the cache and then pushed to the database when a transaction is committed or when the data is explicitly pushed to the database.

When an application is managing `EntityManager`, it is advisable to have only one instance of `EntityManager` for a persistence unit.

EntityManagerFactory

`EntityManagerFactory` creates `EntityManager`. `EntityManagerFactory` itself is obtained by calling a static `Persistence.createEntityManagerFactory` method. The argument to this function is the `persistence-unit` name that you have provided in `persistence.xml`.

Creating a JPA application

The following are the typical steps in creating a JPA application.

1. Create a database schema (tables and relationships). Optionally, you can create tables and relationships from JPA entities. We will see an example of this. However, it should be mentioned here that although creating tables from JPA entities is fine for development, it is not recommended in the production environment; doing so may result in a non-optimized database model.
2. Create `persistence.xml` and specify the database configurations.
3. Create entities and relationships.
4. Get an instance of `EntityManagerFactory` by calling `Persistence.createEntityManagerFactory`.
5. Create an instance of `EntityManager` from `EntityManagerFactory`.

6. Start a transaction on `EntityManager` if you are performing an insert or update operation on Entity.
7. Perform operations on Entity.
8. Commit the transaction.

Here is an example:

```
EntityManagerFactory factory =
Persistance.Persistence.createEntityManagerFactory("course_
management")
EntityManager entityManager = factory.createEntityManager();
EntityTransaction txn = entityManager.getTransaction();
txn.begin();
entityManager. persist(course);
txn.commit();
```

You can find a description of JPA annotations at `http://eclipse.org/eclipselink/documentation/2.5/jpa/extensions/annotations_ref.htm`. JPA tools in Eclipse EE make adding many of the annotations very easy, as we will see in this section.

Creating a new MySQL schema

For this example, we will create a separate MySQL schema (we won't use the same schema that we created for the JDBC application, although it is possible). Open MySQL Workbench and connect to your MySQL database (see *Chapter 1, Introducing JEE and Eclipse*, if you do not know how to connect to the MySQL database from MySQL Workbench).

Right-click in the **Schema** window and select **Create Schema...**.

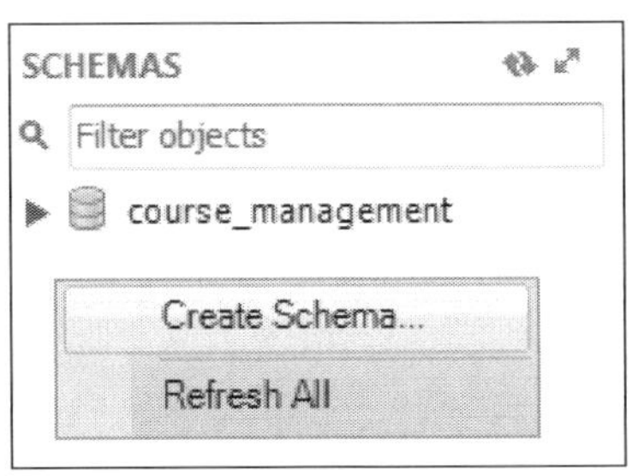

Figure 4.19 Create New MySQL schema

Name the new schema `course_management_jpa` and click **Apply**. We are going to use this schema for the JPA application.

Setting up a Maven dependency for JPA

In this example, we will use EclipseLink (`https://eclipse.org/eclipselink/`) for the JPA implementation. We will use a MySQL JDBC driver and a Bean Validation framework for validating the members of entities. Finally, we will use Java annotations provided by JSR0250. So, let's add Maven dependencies for all these:

```
<dependency>
  <groupId>org.eclipse.persistence</groupId>
  <artifactId>eclipselink</artifactId>
  <version>2.5.2</version>
</dependency>
<dependency>
  <groupId>mysql</groupId>
  <artifactId>mysql-connector-java</artifactId>
  <version>5.1.34</version>
</dependency>
<dependency>
  <groupId>javax.validation</groupId>
  <artifactId>validation-api</artifactId>
  <version>1.1.0.Final</version>
</dependency>
<dependency>
  <groupId>javax.annotation</groupId>
  <artifactId>jsr250-api</artifactId>
  <version>1.0</version>
</dependency>
```

Converting a project into a JPA project

Many JPA tools become active in Eclipse JEE only if the project is a JPA project. Although we have created a Maven project, it is easy to add an Eclipse JPA facet to it.

1. Right-click on the project and select **Configure** | **Convert to JPA Project**.

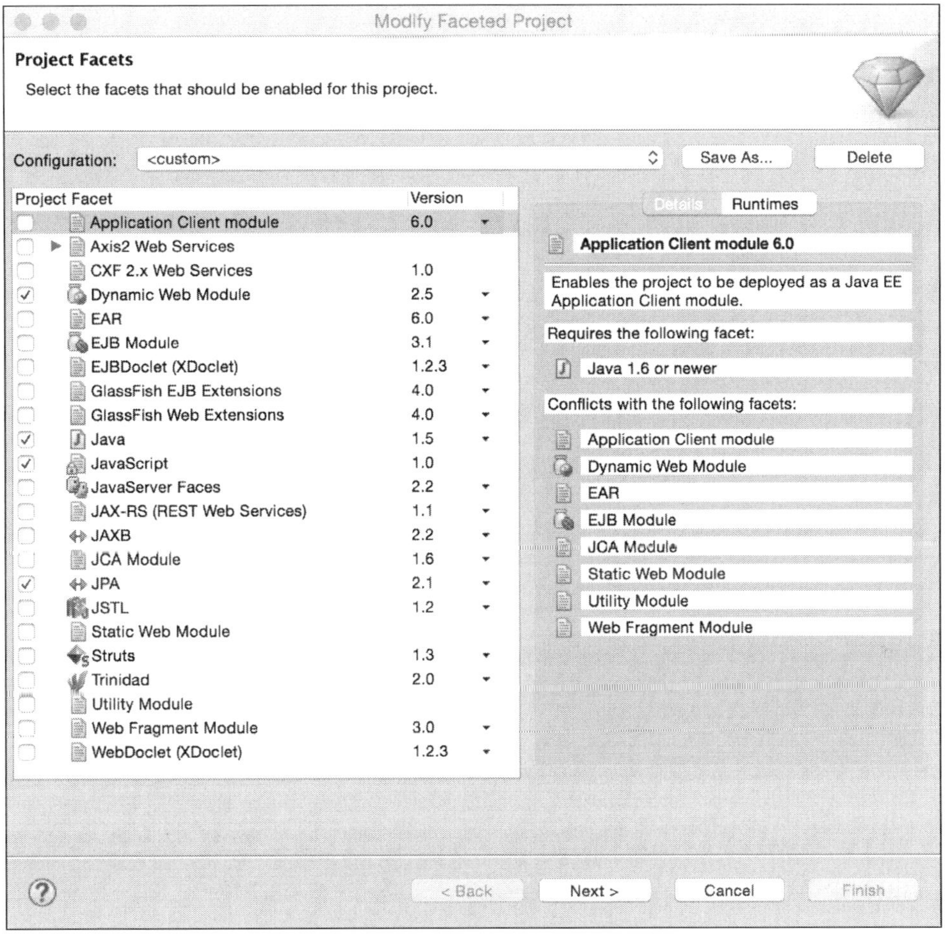

Figure 4.20 Add a JPA facet to a project

2. Make sure JPA is selected.
3. In the next page, select **EclipseLink 2.5.x** as the platform.
4. For the JPA implementation type, select **Disable Library Configuration**.

5. The drop-down list for **Connection** lists any connections you have configured in the **Data Source Explorer**. For now, do not select any connection. At the bottom of the page, select the **Discover Annotated Classes Automatically** option.

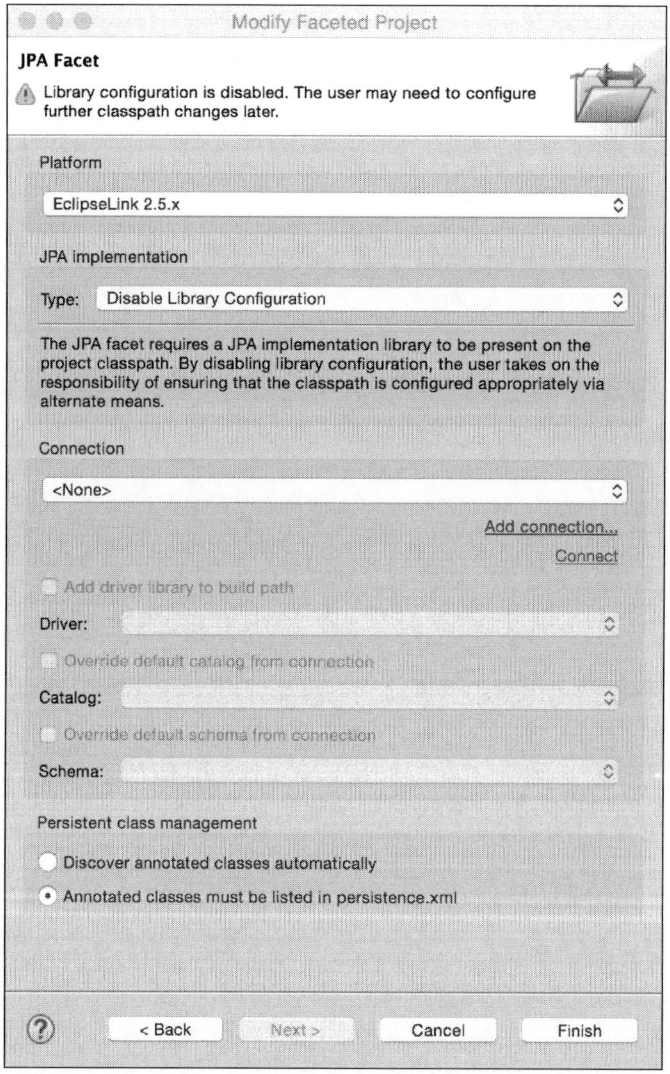

Figure 4.21 Configure a JPA facet (need to change the image with Discover ... option | Ram)

6. Click **Finish**.
7. Notice that the **JPA Content** group is created under the project and `persistence.xml` is created in it. Open `persistence.xml` in the editor.

8. Click on the **Connection** tab and change **Transaction type** to **Resource Local**. We have selected **Resource Local** because in this chapter, we are going to manage `EntityManager`. If you want a JEE container to manage `EntityManager`, then you should set **Transaction type** to **JTA**. We will see an example of the JTA transaction type in *Chapter 7, Creating JEE Applications with EJB*.
9. Enter the EclipseLink connection pool attributes according to the following screenshot and save the file.

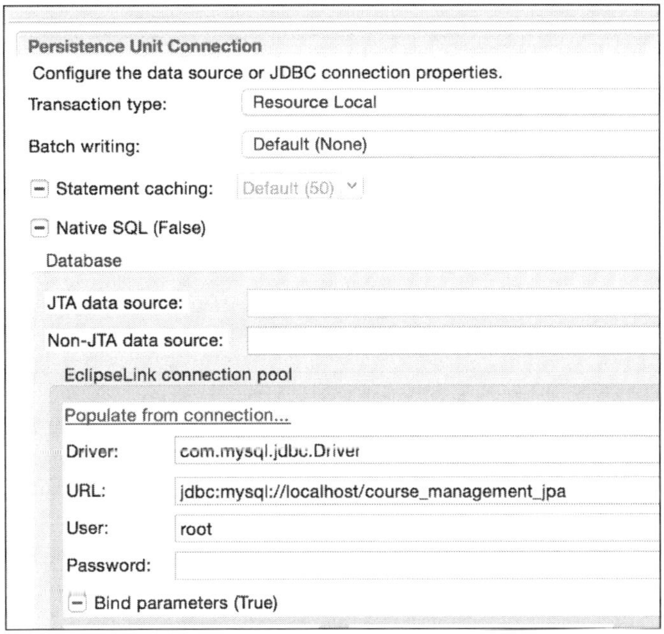

Figure 4.22 Setup Persistence Unit Connection

10. Next, click on the **Schema Generation** tab. Here, we will set the options to generate database tables and relationships from entities. Select the options according to the following screenshot:

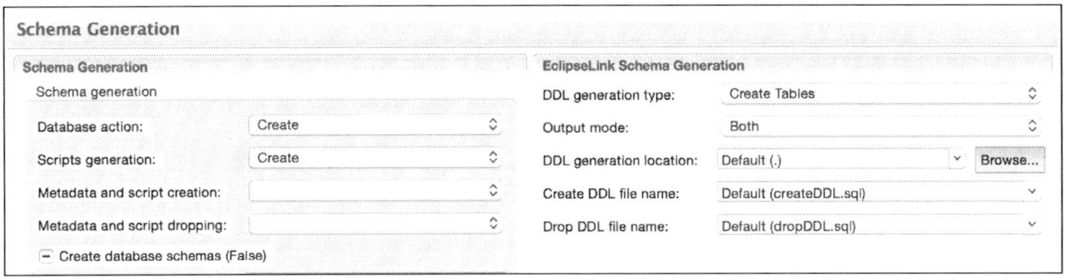

Figure 4.23 Setup Schema Generation options of Persistence Unit

Here is the code of the `persistenace.xml` file for the previous settings:

```
<?xml version="1.0" encoding="UTF-8"?>
<persistence version="2.1" xmlns="http://xmlns.jcp.org/xml/ns/
persistence" xmlns:xsi="http://www.w3.org/2001/XMLSchema-instance"
xsi:schemaLocation="http://xmlns.jcp.org/xml/ns/persistence http://
xmlns.jcp.org/xml/ns/persistence/persistence_2_1.xsd">
  <persistence-unit name="CourseManagementJPA" transaction-
type="RESOURCE_LOCAL">
    <properties>
      <property name="javax.persistence.jdbc.driver"
      value="com.mysql.jdbc.Driver"/>
      <property name="javax.persistence.jdbc.url"
      value="jdbc:mysql://localhost/course_management_jpa"/>
      <property name="javax.persistence.jdbc.user" value="root"/>
      <property name="javax.persistence.schema-
      generation.database.action" value="create"/>
      <property name="javax.persistence.schema-
      generation.scripts.action" value="create"/>
<property name="eclipselink.ddl-generation" value="create-
tables"/>
      <property name="eclipselink.ddl-generation.output-mode"
value="both"/>
    </properties>
  </persistence-unit>
</persistence>
```

Creating entities

We have already created JavaBeans for `Course`, `Person`, `Student`, and `Teacher`. We will now convert them to JPA entities by using the `@Entity` annotation. Open `Course.java` and add the following annotations:

```
@ManagedBean (name="course")
@RequestScoped
@Entity
public class Course implements Serializable
```

The same bean can act as a managed bean for JSF and an entity for JPA. Note that if the name of the class is different from the table name in the database, you will need to specify the `name` attribute of the `@Entity` annotation. For example, if our `Course` table were called `SchoolCourse`, then the entity declaration would be as follows:

```
@Entity(name="SchoolCourse")
```

To specify the primary key of the `Entity`, use the `@Id` annotation. In the `Course` table, `id` is the primary key and is auto-generated. To indicate the auto-generation of the value, use the `@GeneratedValue` annotation. Use the `@column` annotation to indicate that the member variable corresponds to a column in the table. Therefore, the annotations for `id` are as follows:

```
@Id
@GeneratedValue(strategy=GenerationType.IDENTITY)
@Column(name="id")
private int id;
```

You can specify the validations for a column by using the Bean Validation framework annotation, as mentioned earlier. For example, the course name should not be null:

```
@NotNull
@Column(name="name")
private String name;
```

Further, the minimum value of credits should be `1`:

```
@Min(1)
@Column(name="credits")
private int credits;
```

> In the preceding examples, the `@Column` annotation is not necessary to specify the name of the column if the field name is the same as the column name.

If you are using JPA entities to create tables and want to exactly specify the type of columns, then you can use the `columnDefinition` attribute of the `@Column` annotation; for example, to specify a column of type `varchar` with length `20`, you could use `@Column(columnDefinition="VARCHAR(20)")`. Refer to `http://docs.oracle.com/javaee/7/api/javax/persistence/Column.html` to see all the attributes of the `@Column` annotation.

We will add more annotations to `Course Entity` as needed later. For now, let's turn our attention to the `Person` class. This class is the parent class of the `Student` and `Teacher` classes. However, in the database, there is no `Person` table and all the fields of `Person` and `Student` are in the `Student` table and the same for the `Teacher` table. So, how do we model this in JPA? Well, JPA supports the inheritance of entities and provides control over how they should be mapped to database tables. Open the `Person` class and add the following annotations:

```
@Entity
@Inheritance(strategy=TABLE_PER_CLASS)
public abstract class Person implements Serializable { …
```

We are not only identifying the `Person` class as Entity, but we are also saying that it is used for inheritance (using `@Inheritance`). The inheritance strategy decides how tables are mapped to classes. There are three possible strategies:

- `SINGLE_TABLE`: In this case, fields of the parent and child classes would be mapped to the table of the parent class. If we use this strategy, then the fields of `Parent`, `Student`, and `Teacher` will be mapped to table mapped to by the `Person` entity.
- `TABLE_PER_CLASS`: In this case, each concrete class (non-abstract class) is mapped to a table in the database. All the fields of the parent class are also mapped to the table mapped to the child class. For example, all the fields of `Person` and `Student` will be mapped to columns in the `Student` table. Since `Person` is marked as abstract, no table will be mapped by the `Person` class. It exists only to provide inheritance support in the application.
- `JOINED`: In this case, the parent and its children are mapped to separate tables. For example, `Person` will be mapped to the `Person` table and `Student` and `Teacher` would be mapped to the corresponding tables in the database.

On the basis of the schema that we created for the JDBC application, we have the `Student` and `Teacher` tables with all the required columns and there is no `Person` table. Therefore, we have selected the `TABLE_PER_CLASS` strategy here.

See more information about entity inheritance in JPA at `http://docs.oracle.com/javaee/7/tutorial/persistence-intro002.htm#BNBQN`.

The `id`, `firstName`, and `lastName` fields in the `Person` table are shared by `Student` and `Teacher`. Therefore, we need to mark them as columns in tables and set the primary key. Hence, add the following annotations to the fields in the `Person` class:

```
@Id
@GeneratedValue(strategy=GenerationType.IDENTITY)
@Column(name="id")
private int id;

@Column(name = "first_name")
@NotNull
private String firstName;

@Column(name = "last_name")
private String lastName;
```

Here, the column names in the table do not match the class fields. Therefore, we have to specify the name attribute in the `@Column` annotations.

Let's now mark the `Student` class as `Entity`:

```
@Entity
@ManagedBean (name="student")
@RequestScoped
public class Student extends Person implements Serializable
```

The `Student` class has a `Date` field called `enrolledSince`, which is of the `java.util.Date` type. However, JDBC and JPA use the `java.sql.Date` type. If you want JPA to automatically convert `java.sql.Date` to `java.util.Date`, then you need to mark the field with the `@Temporal` annotation:

```
@Temporal(DATE)
@Column(name="enrolled_since")
private Date enrolledSince;
```

Open the `Teacher` class and add the `@Entity` annotation to it.

```
@Entity
@ManagedBean (name="teacher")
@RequestScoped
public class Teacher extends Person implements Serializable
```

Then, map the `designation` field in the class:

```
@NotNull
@Column(name="designation")
private String designation;
```

We have now added annotations for all tables and their fields that do not participate in table relationships. We will now model the relationships between tables in our classes.

Configuring entity relationships

First, we will model the relationship between `Course` and `Teacher`. There is a one-to-many relationship between them: one teacher may teach a number of courses. Open `Course.java` in the editor. Open the JPA perspective in Eclipse JEE (the **Window** | **Open Perspective** | **JPA** menu).

Configuring a many-to-one relationship

With `Course.java` open in the editor, click on the **JPA Details** tab in the bottom window (just below the editor window). In `Course.java`, click on the `teacher` member variable. The **JPA Details** tab shows the details of this attribute:

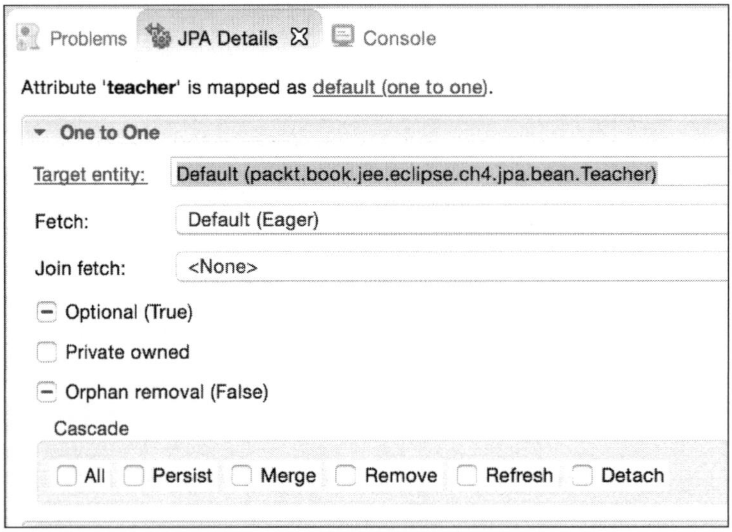

Figure 4.24 JPA details of an entity attribute

Target entity is auto-selected (as `Teacher`) because we have marked `Teacher` as an entity and the type of `teacher` field is the `Teacher` entity.

However, Eclipse has assumed a one-to-one relationship between `Course` and `Teacher`, which is not correct. There is a many-to-one relationship between `Course` and `Teacher`. To change this, click on the **(one_to_one)** hyperlink at the top of the **JPA Details** view and select **Many To One** in the **Mapping Type Selection** dialog box.

Select only the **Merge** and **Refresh** cascade options; else, duplicate entries will be added in the `Teacher` table for every `Teacher` that you selected for a `Course`. See `https://docs.oracle.com/javaee/7/tutorial/persistence-intro001.htm#BNBQH` for more details on entity relationships and cascade options.

When you select the **Merge** and **Refresh** cascade options, the `cascade` attribute added to the annotation is added to the `teacher` field in the `Course` entity:

```
@ManyToOne(cascade = { MERGE, REFRESH })
private Teacher teacher;
```

Scroll down in the **JPA Details** page to see **Joining Strategy**. This determines how columns in the `Course` and `Teacher` tables are joined.

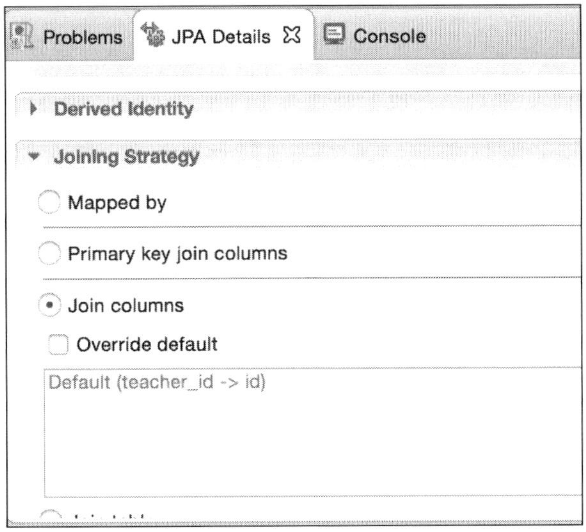

Figure 4.25 Editing Joining Strategy in an entity relationship

Note that the default joining strategy is that the `teacher_id` column in the `Course` table maps to the `id` column in the `Teacher` table. Eclipse has just guessed `teacher_id` (the appended `id` to the `teacher` field in the `Course` entity), but if we had a different join column in the `Course` table, for example, `teacherId`, then we would need to override the default join columns. Click on the **Override default** checkbox and then on the **Edit** button on the right side of the textbox.

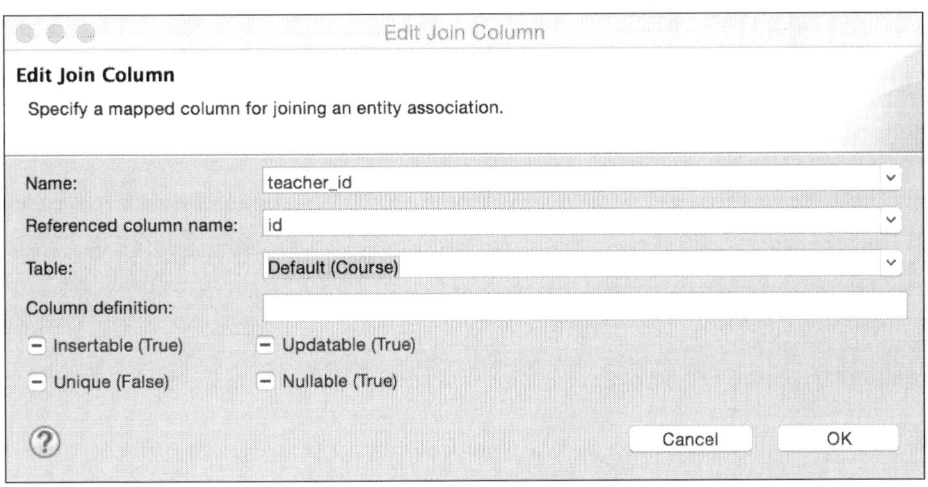

Figure 4.26 Editing Join Column

Since, in our case, the default options match the table columns, we will keep them unchanged. When you select the **Override default** checkbox above, the `@JoinColumn` annotation is added to the `teacher` field in Course Entity:

```
@JoinColumn(name = "teacher_id", referencedColumnName = "id")
@ManyToOne(cascade = { MERGE, REFRESH })
private Teacher teacher;
```

All the required annotations for the `teacher` field are now added.

Configuring a many-to-many relationship

We will now configure the `Course` and `Student` entities for a many-to-many relationship (a course can have many students, and one student can take many courses).

Many-to-many relations could be unidirectional or bidirectional. For example, you may only want to track students enrolled in courses (so the `Course` entity will have a list of students) and not students taking courses (the `Student` entity does not keep a list of courses). This is a unidirectional relationship where only the `Course` entity knows about the students, but the `Student` entity does not know about courses).

In a bidirectional relationship, each entity knows about the other one. Therefore, the `Course` entity will keep a list of students and the `Student` entity will keep a list of courses. We will configure the bidirectional relationship in this example.

A many-to-many relationship also has one owning side and the other inverse side. You can mark either entity in the relationship as the owning entity. From the configuration point of view, the inverse side is marked by the `mappedBy` attribute to the `@ManyToMany` annotation.

In our application we will make `Student` as the owning side of the relationship and `Course` as the inverse side. A many-to-many relationship in the database needs a join table, which is configured in the owning entity by using the `@JoinTable` annotation.

We will first configure the many-to-many relationship in the `Course` entity. Add a member variable in `Course` to hold a list of `Student` entities and add the getter and the setter for it.

```
private List<Student> students;
public List<Student> getStudents() {
  return students;
}
public void setStudents(List<Student> students) {
  this.students = students;
}
```

Then, click on the `students` field (added previously) and notice the settings in the **JPA Details** view:

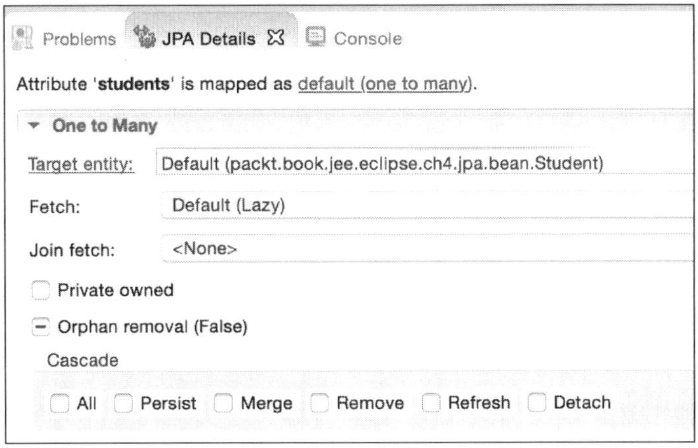

Figure 4.27 Default JPA details for the students field in Course Entity

Because the students field is a list of `Student` entities, Eclipse has assumed a one-to-many relationship (see the link at the top of the **JPA Details** view). We need to change this. Click on the **one_to_many** link and select **Many To Many**.

Check the **Merge** and **Refresh** cascade options. Since we are putting the `Course` entity on the inverse side of the relationship, select **Mapped By** as **Joining Strategy**. Enter `courses` in the **Attributes** text field. The compiler will show an error for this because we don't have the courses field in the `Student` entity yet. We will fix this shortly. The JPA settings for the `students` field should be as follows:

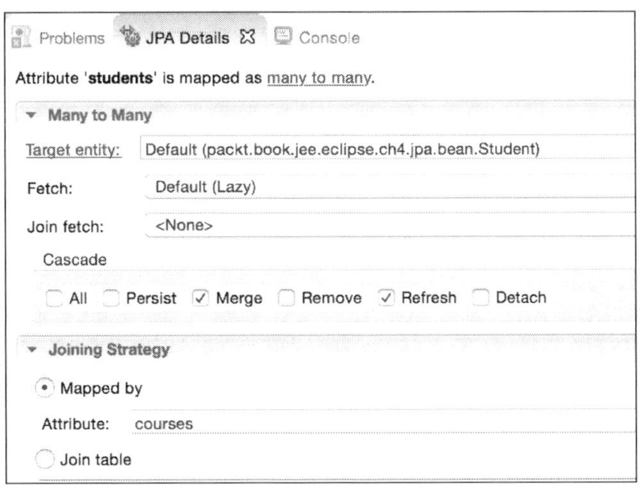

Figure 4.28 Modified JPA settings for the students field in Course Entity

Further, annotations for the `students` field in the `Course` entity should be as follows:

```
@ManyToMany(cascade = { MERGE, REFRESH }, mappedBy = "courses")
private List<Student> students;
```

Open `Student.java` in the editor. Add the `courses` field and the getter and the setter for it. Click on the `courses` field in the file and change the relationship from one-to-many to many-to-many in the **JPA Details** view (as described above for the `students` field in the `Course` entity). Select the **Merge** and **Refresh** cascade options. In the **Joining Strategy** section, make sure that the **Join table** option is selected. Eclipse creates the default join table by concatenating the owning table and the inverse table separated by an underscore (in this case, `Student_Course`). Change this to **Course_Student** to make it consistent with the schema that we created for the JDBC application.

In the **Join columns** section, select the **Override default** checkbox. Eclipse has named the join columns as `students_id->id`, but again, in the **Course_Student** table, we had created in the JDBC application, we had named the `student_id` column. So, click the **Edit** button and change the name to **student_id**.

Similarly, change **Inverse join columns** from `courses_id->id` to `course_id->id`. After these changes, **JPA Details** for the `courses` field should be as follows:

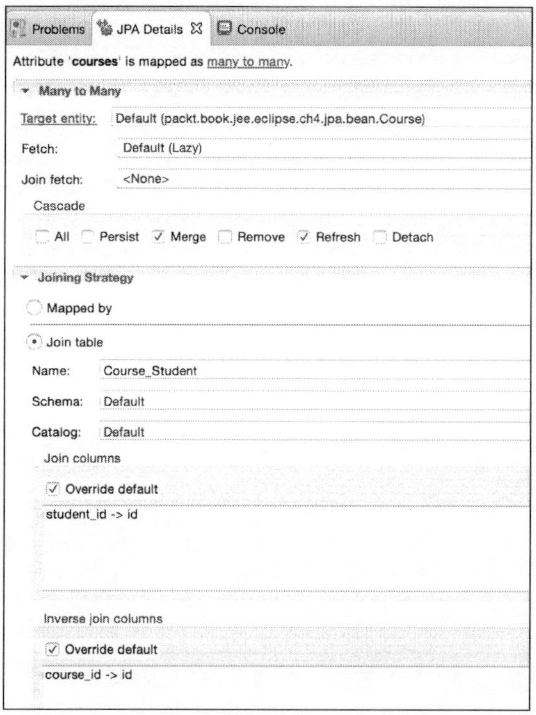

Figure 4.29 JPA Details for the courses field in Student Entity

The previous settings create the following annotations for the `courses` field should be as follows:

```
@ManyToMany(cascade = { MERGE, REFRESH })
@JoinTable(name = "Course_Student", joinColumns = @JoinColumn(name =
"student_id", referencedColumnName = "id"), inverseJoinColumns =
@JoinColumn(name = "course_id", referencedColumnName = "id"))

List<Course> courses;
```

We have set all the entity relationships required for our application. Download the accompanying code for this chapter to see the complete source code for the `Course`, `Student`, and `Teacher` entities.

We need to add the entities that we created above in `persistence.xml`. Open the file and make sure that the **General** tab is open. In the **Managed Classes** session, click the **Add** button. Type the name of entity that you want to add (for example, `Student`) and select the class from the list. Add all the four entities that we have created.

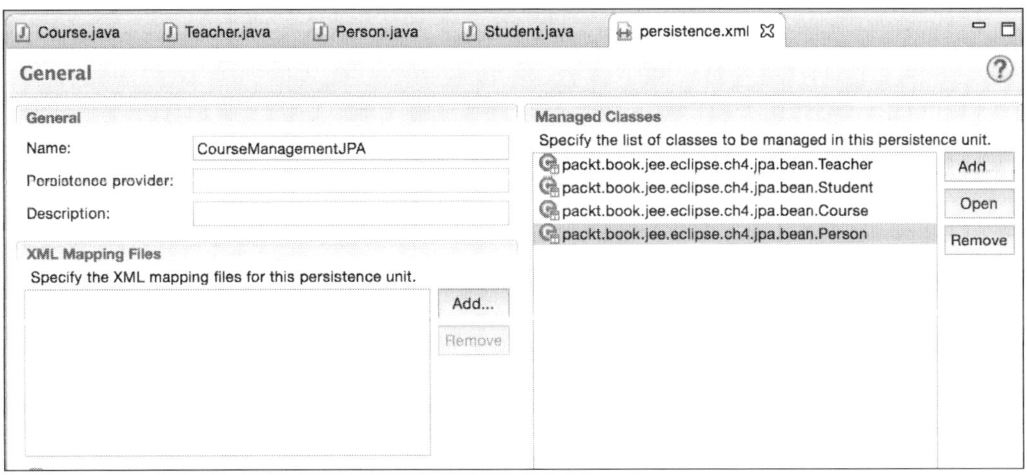

Figure 4.30 Add entities in persistence.xml

Creating database tables from entities

Follow these steps to create database tables from entities and relationships that we have modeled.

1. Right-click on the project and select **JPA Tool** | **Generate Tables from Entities**.

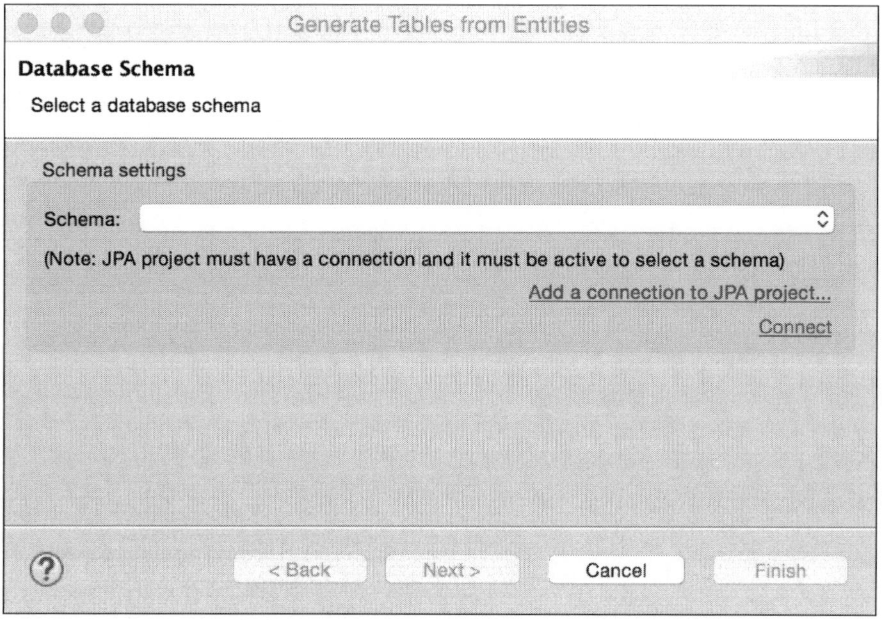

Figure 4.31 JPA Details for the courses field in Student Entity

2. Because we haven't configured any schema for our JPA project, the **Schema** dropdown will be empty. Click the **Add a connection to JPA project** link.

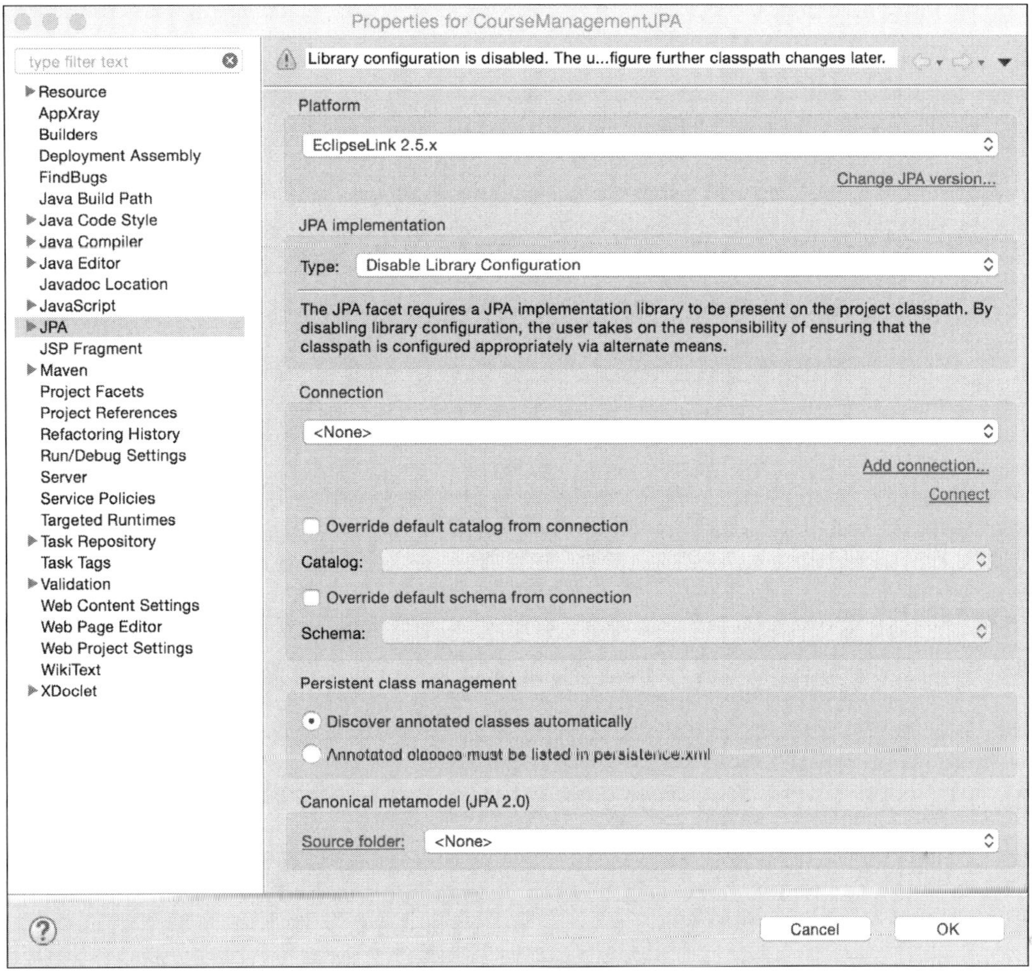

Figure 4.32 JPA project properties

3. Click the **Add connection** link and create a connection to the `course_management_jpa` schema that we had created. We have already seen how to create a connection to the MySQL schema in the *Using Eclipse Data Source Explorer* section.

4. Select `course_management_jpa` in the dropdown shown in *Figure 4.30 Add entities in persistence.xml* and click **Next**.

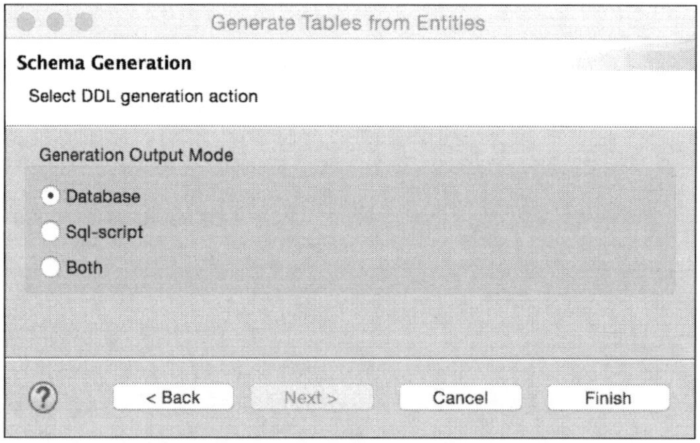

Figure 4.33 Schema Generation from entities

5. Click **Finish**.

Eclipse generates DDL scripts for creating tables and relationships and executes these scripts in the selected schema. Once the script ID is run successfully, open the **Data Source Explorer** view (see the previous *Using Eclipse Data Source Explorer* section) and browse tables in the **course_management_jpa** connection. Make sure that the tables and fields are created according to the entities that we have created.

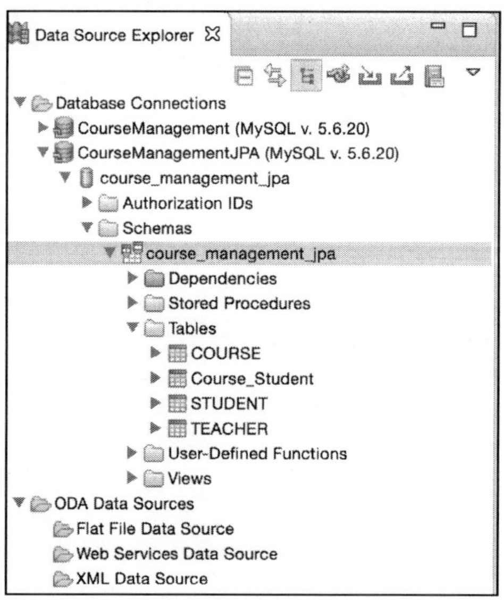

Figure 4.34 Tables created from JPA entities

This feature of Eclipse and JPA makes it very easy to update the database as you modify your entities.

Using JPA APIs to manage data

We will now create classes that use JPA APIs to manage data for our application: course management. We will create service classes for the **Course**, **Teacher**, and **Student** entities and add methods that directly access the database though JPA APIs.

As mentioned in the *JPA concepts* section, it is a good practice to cache an instance of `EntityManagerFactory` in our application. Further, Managed Beans of JSF act as an interface between the UI and the backend code, and as a conduit to transfer data between the UI and the data access objects. Therefore, they must have an instance of the data access objects (which use JPA to access data from the database). To cache an instance of `EntityManagerFactory`, we will create another Managed Bean, whose only job is to make the `EntityManagerFactory` instance available to other Managed Beans.

Therefore, create an `EntityManagerFactoryBean` class in the `packt.book.jee.eclipse.ch4.jpa.service_bean` package. This package contains all the managed beans. `EntityManagerFactoryBean` creates an instance of `EntityManagerFactory` in the constructor and provides a getter method:

```
package packt.book.jee.eclipse.ch4.jpa.service_bean;

import javax.faces.bean.ApplicationScoped;
import javax.faces.bean.ManagedBean;
import javax.persistence.EntityManagerFactory;
import javax.persistence.Persistence;

//Load this bean eagerly, i.e., before any request is made
@ManagedBean(name="emFactoryBean", eager=true)
@ApplicationScoped
public class EntityManagerFactoryBean {

  private EntityManagerFactory entityManagerFactory;

  public EntityManagerFactoryBean() {
    entityManagerFactory =
Persistence.createEntityManagerFactory("CourseManagementJPA");
  }
```

```
    public EntityManagerFactory getEntityManagerFactory() {
      return entityManagerFactory;
    }

  }
```

Note the argument passed in the following:

```
entityManagerFactory =
Persistence.createEntityManagerFactory("CourseManagementJPA");
```

This is the name of the persistence unit in `persistence.xml`.

Now, let's write service classes that actually use the JPA APIs to access database tables.

Create a package called `packt.book.jee.eclipse.ch4.jpa.service`. Create a new class named `CourseService`. Every service class will need access to `EntityManagerFactory`. So, create a private member variable as follows:

```
private EntityManagerFactory factory;
```

Constructor takes an instance of `EntityManagerFactoryBean` and gets the reference of `EntityManagerFactory` from it.

```
public CourseService(EntityManagerFactoryBean factoryBean) {
  this.factory = factoryBean.getEntityManagerFactory();
}
```

We will add a function to get all `courses` from the database:

```
public List<Course> getCourses() {
  EntityManager em = factory.createEntityManager();
  CriteriaBuilder cb = em.getCriteriaBuilder();
  CriteriaQuery<Course> cq = cb.createQuery(Course.class);
  TypedQuery<Course> tq = em.createQuery(cq);
  List<Course> courses = tq.getResultList();
  em.close();
  return courses;
}
```

Note how `CriteriaBuilder`, `CriteriaQuery`, and `TypesQuery` are used to get all the courses. It is a type-safe way to execute a query. See `http://docs.oracle.com/javaee/7/tutorial/persistence-criteria.htm#GJITV` for a detailed discussion on how to use the JPA criteria APIs. We could have done the same thing using **Java Query Language (JQL)** - `http://www.oracle.com/technetwork/articles/vasiliev-jpql-087123.html`, but it is not type safe. However, here is an example of using JQL to write the `getCourses` function:

```
public List<Course> getCourses() {
  EntityManager em = factory.createEntityManager();
  List<Course> courses = em.createQuery("select crs from Course
crs").getResultList();
  em.close();
  return courses;
}
```

Add a method to insert a course in the database:

```
public void addCourse (Course course) {
  EntityManager em = factory.createEntityManager();
  EntityTransaction txn = em.getTransaction();
  txn.begin();
  em.persist(course);
  txn.commit();
}
```

The code is quite simple. We get the entity manager and then start a transaction because it is an `update` operation. Then, we call the `persist` method on `EntityManager` by passing an instance of `Course` to save. Then, we commit the transaction. Methods to update and delete are also simple. Here is the entire source code of `CourseService`:

```
package packt.book.jee.eclipse.ch4.jpa.service;

import java.util.List;

import javax.persistence.EntityManager;
import javax.persistence.EntityManagerFactory;
import javax.persistence.EntityTransaction;
import javax.persistence.TypedQuery;
import javax.persistence.criteria.CriteriaBuilder;
import javax.persistence.criteria.CriteriaQuery;

import packt.book.jee.eclipse.ch4.jpa.bean.Course;
import packt.book.jee.eclipse.ch4.jpa.service_bean.
EntityManagerFactoryBean;

public class CourseService {
  private EntityManagerFactory factory;

  public CourseService(EntityManagerFactoryBean factoryBean) {
    factory = factoryBean.getEntityManagerFactory();
  }
```

```
    public List<Course> getCourses() {
      EntityManager em = factory.createEntityManager();
      CriteriaBuilder cb = em.getCriteriaBuilder();
      CriteriaQuery<Course> cq = cb.createQuery(Course.class);
      TypedQuery<Course> tq = em.createQuery(cq);
      List<Course> courses = tq.getResultList();
      em.close();
      return courses;
    }

  public void addCourse (Course course) {
      EntityManager em = factory.createEntityManager();
      EntityTransaction txn = em.getTransaction();
      txn.begin();
      em.persist(course);
      txn.commit();
  }

    public void updateCourse (Course course) {
      EntityManager em = factory.createEntityManager();
      EntityTransaction txn = em.getTransaction();
      txn.begin();
      em.merge(course);
      txn.commit();
    }

    public Course getCourse (int id) {
      EntityManager em = factory.createEntityManager();
      return em.find(Course.class, id);
    }

    public void deleteCourse (Course course) {
      EntityManager em = factory.createEntityManager();
      EntityTransaction txn = em.getTransaction();
      txn.begin();
      Course mergedCourse = em.find(Course.class, course.getId());
      em.remove(mergedCourse);
      txn.commit();
    }
  }
```

Create the `StudentService` and `TeacherService` classes with the following methods:

```
public class StudentService {
  private EntityManagerFactory factory;

  public StudentService (EntityManagerFactoryBean factoryBean) {
    factory = factoryBean.getEntityManagerFactory();
  }

  public void addStudent (Student student) {
    EntityManager em = factory.createEntityManager();
    EntityTransaction txn = em.getTransaction();
    txn.begin();
    em.persist(student);
    txn.commit();
  }

  public List<Student> getStudents() {
    EntityManager em = factory.createEntityManager();
    CriteriaBuilder cb = em.getCriteriaBuilder();
    CriteriaQuery<Student> cq = cb.createQuery(Student.class);
    TypedQuery<Student> tq = em.createQuery(cq);
    List<Student> students = tq.getResultList();
    em.close();
    return students;
  }

}

public class TeacherService {
  private EntityManagerFactory factory;

  public TeacherService (EntityManagerFactoryBean factoryBean) {
    factory = factoryBean.getEntityManagerFactory();
  }

  public void addTeacher (Teacher teacher) {
    EntityManager em = factory.createEntityManager();
    EntityTransaction txn = em.getTransaction();
    txn.begin();
    em.persist(teacher);
    txn.commit();
  }

  public List<Teacher> getTeacher() {
    EntityManager em = factory.createEntityManager();
```

```
    CriteriaBuilder cb = em.getCriteriaBuilder();
    CriteriaQuery<Teacher> cq = cb.createQuery(Teacher.class);
    TypedQuery<Teacher> tq = em.createQuery(cq);
    List<Teacher> teachers = tq.getResultList();
    em.close();
    return teachers;
  }

  public Teacher getTeacher (int id) {
    EntityManager em = factory.createEntityManager();
    return em.find(Teacher.class, id);
  }
}
```

Wiring the user interface with a JPA service class

Now that we have all data access classes ready, we need to connect the user interface that we have created for adding a course, `addCourse.xhtml`, to pass data and get data from the JPA service classes. As mentioned previously, we are going to do this by using Managed Beans, in this case, `CourseServiceBean`.

`CourseServiceBean` will need to create an instance of `CourseService` and call the `addCourse` method. Open `CourseServiceBean` and create a member variable as follows:

```
private CourseService courseService ;
```

We also need an instance of the `EntityManagerFactoryBean` Managed Bean that we created in the earlier section.

```
@ManagedProperty(value="#{emFactoryBean}")
private EntityManagerFactoryBean factoryBean;
```

The `factoryBean` instance is injected by the JSF runtime and is available only after the managed bean in completely constructed. However, for this bean to be injected, we need to provide a setter method. Therefore, add a setter method for `factoryBean`. We can have JSF call a method of our bean after it is fully constructed by annotating the method with `@PostConstruct`. Therefore, let's create a method called `postConstruct`:

```
@PostConstruct
public void init() {
  courseService = new CourseService(factoryBean);
}
```

Then, modify the `addCourse` method to call our service method:

```
public String addCourse() {
  courseService.addCourse(course);
  return "listCourse";
}
```

Since our `listCourse.xhtml` page will need to get a list of courses, let's add the `getCourses` method too in `CourseServiceBean`:

```
public List<Course> getCourses() {
  return courseService.getCourses();
}
```

Here is the `CourseServiceBean` after the abovementioned changes:

```
@ManagedBean(name="courseServiceBean")
@RequestScoped
public class CourseServiceBean {

  private CourseService courseService ;

  @ManagedProperty(value="#{emFactoryBean}")
  private EntityManagerFactoryBean factoryBean;

  @ManagedProperty(value="#{course}")
  private Course course;

  private String errMsg= null;

  @PostConstruct
  public void init() {
    courseService = new CourseService(factoryBean);
  }

  public void setFactoryBean(EntityManagerFactoryBean factoryBean)
  {
    this.factoryBean = factoryBean;
  }

  public Course getCourse() {
    return course;
  }
```

```
    public void setCourse(Course course) {
      this.course = course;
    }

    public String getErrMsg() {
      return errMsg;
    }

    public void setErrMsg(String errMsg) {
      this.errMsg = errMsg;
    }

    public String addCourse() {
      courseService.addCourse(course);
      return "listCourse";
    }

    public List<Course> getCourses() {
      return courseService.getCourses();
    }

}
```

Finally, we will write the code to display the list of courses in `listCourse.xhtml`. We have already created this file but not the code to display the courses.

```
<html xmlns="http://www.w3.org/1999/xhtml"
    xmlns:f="http://java.sun.com/jsf/core"
    xmlns:h="http://java.sun.com/jsf/html"
    xmlns:c="http://java.sun.com/jsp/jstl/core">

    <h2>Courses:</h2>
    <h:form>
      <h:messages style="color:red"/>
    <h:dataTable value="#{courseServiceBean.courses}"
    var="course">
      <h:column>
        <f:facet name="header">ID</f:facet>
        <h:outputText value="#{course.id}"/>
      </h:column>
      <h:column>
        <f:facet name="header">Name</f:facet>
        <h:outputText value="#{course.name}"/>
      </h:column>
```

```
        <h:column>
          <f:facet name="header">Credits</f:facet>
          <h:outputText value="#{course.credits}"
          style="float:right" />
        </h:column>
      </h:dataTable>
    </h:form>

    <h:panelGroup rendered="#{courseServiceBean.courses.size() ==
    0}">
      <h3>No courses found</h3>
    </h:panelGroup>

    <c:if test="#{courseServiceBean.courses.size() > 0}">
      <b>Total number of courses
        <h:outputText value="#{courseServiceBean.courses.size()}"/>
      </b>
    </c:if>
    <p/>
    <h:button value="Add" outcome="addCourse"/>
  </html>
```

Because of space constraints, we will not discuss how to add a functionality to delete/update courses or to create a course with the `Teacher` field selected. Please download the complete source code for the examples discussed in this chapter to see the complete working applications.

Summary

In this chapter, we learnt how to build web applications that require data access from a relational database. First, we built a simple Course Management application using JDBC and JSTL, and then, the same application was built using JPA and JSF.

JPA is preferred to JDBC because you end up writing a lot less code. The code to map object data to relational data is created for you by the JPA implementation. However, JDBC is still being used in many web applications because it is simpler to use. Although JPA has a moderate learning curve, JPA tools in Eclipse EE can make using JPA APIs a bit easier, particularly configuring entities, relationships, and `persistence.xml`.

In the next chapter, we will deviate a bit from our discussion on JEE and see how to write and run unit tests for Java applications. We will also see how to measure code coverage after running unit tests.

5
Unit Testing

Testing of software that you develop is a very important part of the overall software development cycle. There are many types of testing, and each one has a specific purpose. Each one varies in the scope of testing. Some of the examples of testing are functional testing, integration testing, scenario testing, and unit testing.

Of all these types, unit tests are the narrowest in scope and are typically coded and executed by developers. Each unit test is meant to test a specific and small piece of functionality (typically, a method in a class) and is expected to execute without any external dependencies. Here are some of the reasons why you should write good unit tests:

- Catch bugs early. If you find a bug in functional or integration testing, which have a much wider scope of testing, then it might be difficult to isolate the code that caused the bug. However, it is much easier to catch and fix bugs in unit testing, because unit tests, by definition, work in a narrow scope, and if a test fails, you know exactly where to go and fix the issue.
- Unit tests can help you catch any regression that you might have introduced when editing the code. There are good tools and libraries available for automating the execution of unit tests. For example, by using build tools such as Ant and Maven, you can execute a unit test at the end of a successful build so that you immediately know if the changes that you have made have broken any previously working code.

As mentioned previously, writing unit tests and executing them is typically the responsibility of a developer. Therefore, most IDEs have good built-in support for writing and executing unit tests. Eclipse JEE is no exception. It has built-in support for JUnit, which is a popular unit testing framework for Java.

In this chapter, we will see how to write unit tests for Java applications by using tools available in Eclipse JEE. We will discuss how to write and execute JUnit tests for the course management web application that we built in *Chapter 4, Creating a JEE Database Application*. However, first, here is a quick introduction to JUnit.

JUnit

JUnit test classes are separate Java classes from the classes you want to test. Each test class can contain many test cases, which are just methods marked to be executed when JUnit tests are executed. A test suite is a collection of test classes.

The convention is to assign the test class the same name as that of the class you want to test and append `Test` to this name. For example, if you want to test the `Course` class from the previous chapter, then you would create a JUnit test class and name it `CourseTest`. The test case (method) name starts with `test` followed by the name of the method in the class that you want to test; for example, if you want to test the `validate` method in the `Course` class, then you would create the `testValidate` method in the `CourseTest` class. Test classes are also created in the same package as the package in which the classes to be tested are present. In Maven projects, test classes are typically created under the `src/test/java` folder. The convention is to create the same package structure in the test folder as in the `src/main/java` folder.

JUnit supports annotations to mark unit tests and test suites. Here is a simple test case for the `Course` class:

```
/**
* Test for {@link Course}
*/
Class CourseTest {
  @Test
  public void testValidate() {
    Course course = new Course();
    Assert.assertFalse(course.validate());
    course.setName("course1")
    Assert.assetFalse(course.validate());
    Course.setCredits(-5);
    Assert.assetFalse(course.validate());
    course.setCredits(5);
    Assert.assertTrue(course.validate());
  }
}
```

Let's say the `validate` method checks whether the course name is not null and credits is greater than zero.

The test case is marked with the `@Test` annotation. This case creates an instance of the `Course` class and then calls the `Assert.assertFalse` method to make sure that the `validate` method returns `false`, because the name and credits are not set and they will have their default values, which are `null` and `0`, respectively. `Assert` is a class provided by the JUnit library and has many assert methods to test many conditions (see `http://junit.sourceforge.net/javadoc/org/junit/Assert.html`). The method then sets only the name and again does the same validation and expects the method to return `false`, because credits is still zero. Finally, the test case sets both name and credits and calls the `Assert.assertTrue` method to ensure that `course.validate()` returns `true`. If any of the assertions fail, then the test case fails.

Other than `@Test`, you can use the following annotations provided by JUnit:

- `@Before` and `@After`: Functions annotated with these annotations are executed before and after each test. You may want to initialize resources in `@Before` and free them in `@After`.
- `@BeforeClass` and `@AfterClass`: Similar to `@Before` and `@After` but instead of being called per test, these methods are called once per test class. A method with the `@BeforeClass` annotation is called before any of the test cases in that class are executed and that with `@AfterClass` is called after all the test cases are executed.

You can find more annotations of JUnit at `http://junit.org/javadoc/latest/org/junit/package-summary.html`.

Creating and executing unit tests using Eclipse EE

We will take the JDBC version of the course management application that we developed in *Chapter 4, Creating a JEE Database Application*, because it is simple to understand. Let's start with a simple test case for validating a course. The following is the source code of `Course.java`:

```
package packt.book.jee.eclipse.ch5.bean;

import java.sql.SQLException;
import java.util.List;

import packt.book.jee.eclipse.ch5.dao.CourseDAO;

public class Course {
  private int id;
```

```
    private String name;
    private int credits;
    private Teacher teacher;
    private int teacherId;
    private CourseDAO courseDAO = new CourseDAO();

    public int getId() {
      return id;
    }
    public void setId(int id) {
      this.id = id;
    }
    public String getName() {
      return name;
    }
    public void setName(String name) {
      this.name = name;
    }
    public int getCredits() {
      return credits;
    }
    public void setCredits(int credits) {
      this.credits = credits;
    }
    public boolean isValidCourse() {
      return name != null && credits != 0;
    }
    public Teacher getTeacher() {
      return teacher;
    }
    public void setTeacher(Teacher teacher) {
      this.teacher = teacher;
    }
    public void addCourse() throws SQLException {
      courseDAO.addCourse(this);
    }
    public List<Course> getCourses() throws SQLException {
      return courseDAO.getCourses();
    }
    public int getTeacherId() {
      return teacherId;
    }
    public void setTeacherId(int teacherId) {
      this.teacherId = teacherId;
    }
  }
```

Creating a unit test case

Maven projects follow certain conventions; the entire application source in a Maven project is in the `src/main/java` folder, and unit tests are expected to be in the `src/test/java` folder. In fact, when you create a Maven project in Eclipse, it creates the `src/test/java` folder for you. We are going to create our test cases in this folder. We are going to create the same package structure for the test classes as those for the application source; that is, to test the `packt.book.jee.eclipse.ch5.bean.Course` class, we will create the `packt.book.jee.eclipse.ch5.bean` package under the `src/test/java` folder and then create a JUnit test class called `CourseTest`.

1. Right-click on the `src/test/java` folder in **Package Explorer** in Eclipse and select **New** | **JUnit Test Case** (if you do not find this option in the menu, select **New** | **Other** and type `junit` in the filter textbox. Then, select the **JUnit Test Case** option).
2. Type the package name as `packt.book.jee.eclipse.ch5.bean` and the class name as `CourseTest`.
3. Click the **Browse** button next to the **Class under test** textbox. Type `course` in the filter box and select the `Course` class.

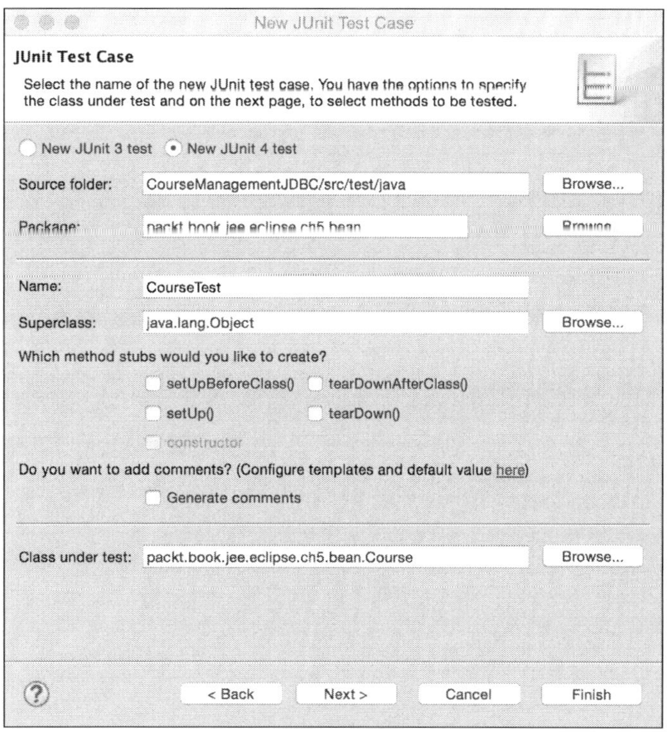

Figure 5.1 JUnit Test Case wizard

4. Click **Next**.
5. The page shows methods in the class (`Course`) for which we want to create test cases. Select the methods that you want to create test cases for.
6. We don't want to test the getters and setters because they are simple methods and don't do much other than just setting or getting member variables. Presently, we will create a test case for only one method: `isValidTestCase`. Therefore, select the checkbox for this method.

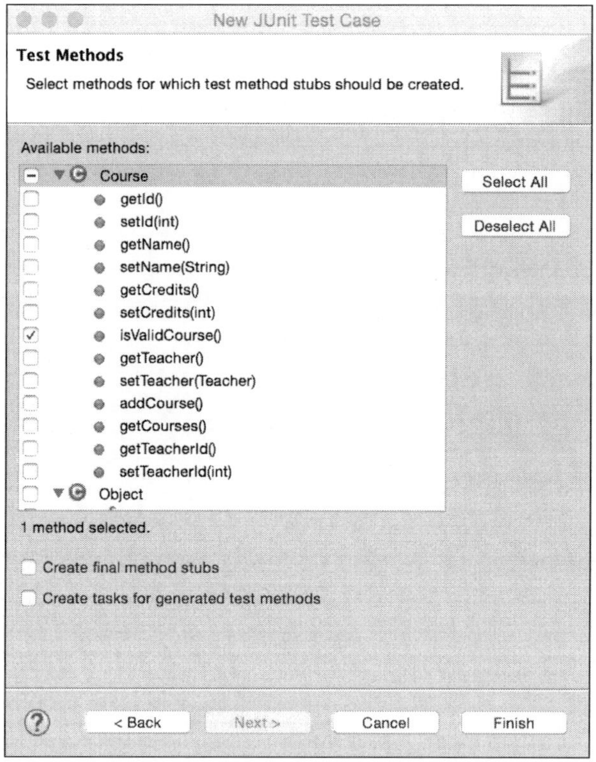

Figure 5.2 Select methods for test cases

7. Click **Finish**. Eclipse checks whether the JUnit libraries are included in your project, and if not, prompts you to include them:

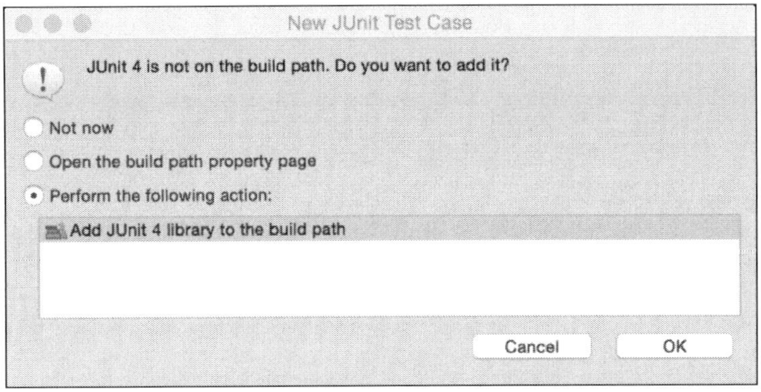

Figure 5.3 Include JUnit libraries in the project

8. Click **OK**. Eclipse creates the package that we specified and the test class with one method/test case called `testIsValidCourse`. Note that the method is annotated with `@Test`, indicating that it is a JUnit test case.

How do we test whether `isValidCourse` works as expected? We create an instance of the `Course` class, set some values that we know are valid or not, call the `isValidateCourse` method, and compare the result with the expected result. JUnit provides many methods in the `Assert` class to compare the actual results obtained by calling test methods with the expected results. So, let's add the test code to the `testIsValidCourse` method:

```
package packt.book.jee.eclipse.ch5.bean;
import org.junit.Assert;
import org.junit.Test;
public class CourseTest {

  @Test
  public void testIsValidCourse() {
    Course course = new Course();
    //First validate without any values set
    Assert.assertFalse(course.isValidCourse());
    //set  name
    course.setName("course1");
    Assert.assertFalse(course.isValidCourse());
    //set zero credits
    course.setCredits(0);
    Assert.assertFalse(course.isValidCourse());
    //now set valid credits
    course.setCredits(4);
    Assert.assertTrue(course.isValidCourse());
  }

}
```

We first create an instance of `Course`, and without setting any of its values, call the `isValidCourse` method. We know that it is not a valid course because name and credits are required fields in a valid course. So, we check whether the returned value of `isValidCourse` is false by calling the `Assert.assertFalse` method. We then set the name and check again, expecting the instance to be an invalid course. Then, we set `0` credit value in `Course`, and finally, we set `4` credits for `Course`. Now, `isValidCourse` is expected to return `true` because both name and credits are valid. We verify this by calling `Assert.assertTrue`.

Running a unit test case

Let's run this test case in Eclipse. Right-click on the file or anywhere in the project in **Package Explorer** and select the **Run As** | **Junit Test** menu. Eclipse finds all unit tests in the project, executes them, and shows the result in the JUnit view:

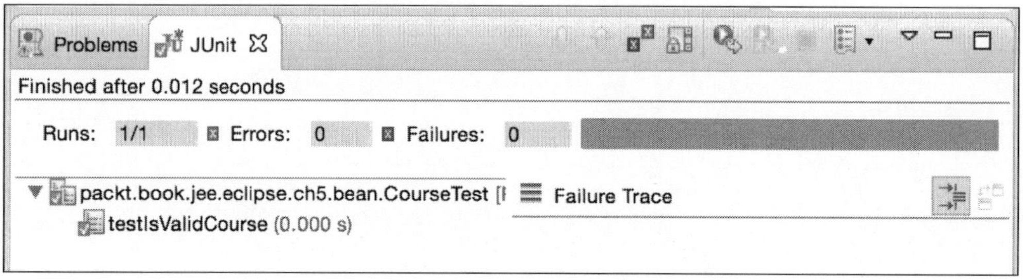

Figure 5.4 JUnit results view

This view shows a summary of the test cases run. In this case, it has run one test case, which was successful. The green bar shows that all test cases were executed successfully.

Now, let's add one more check in the method:

```
@Test
public void testIsValidCourse() {
  ...
  //set empty course name
  course.setName("");
  Assert.assertFalse(course.isValidCourse());
}
```

Run the test case again.

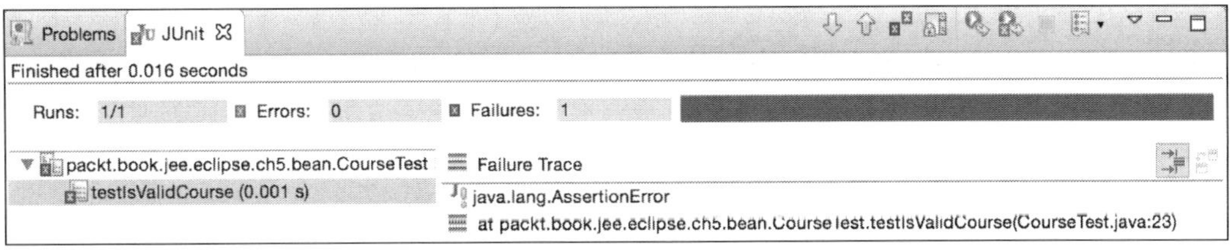

Figure 5.5 JUnit results view showing the failed test

The test case failed now because `course.isValidCourse()` returned `true` when the course name was set to an empty string, whereas the test case expected the instance to be an invalid course. So, we need to modify the `isValidCourse` method of the `Course` class to fix this failure:

```
public boolean isValidCourse() {
  return name != null && credits != 0 && name.trim().length() > 0;
}
```

We have added the condition to check the length of the name field. This should fix the test case failure. You can run the test case again and verify.

Running a unit test case using Maven

You can run unit test cases using Maven too. In fact, the install target of Maven runs unit tests too. However, you can run only unit tests. Right-click on the project in **Package Explorer** and select **Run As** | **Maven** | **Test**.

You might see the following error in the console:

```
java.lang.NoClassDefFoundError: org/junit/Assert
  at packt.book.jee.eclipse.ch5.bean.CourseTest.testIsValidCourse
(CourseTest.java:10)
Caused by: java.lang.ClassNotFoundException: org.junit.Assert
  at java.net.URLClassLoader$1.run(URLClassLoader.java:366)
  at java.net.URLClassLoader$1.run(URLClassLoader.java:355)
  at java.security.AccessController.doPrivileged(Native Method)
```

The reason for this error is that we haven't added a dependency on JUnit for our maven project. Add the following dependency in `pom.xml`:

```
<dependency>
  <groupId>junit</groupId>
  <artifactId>junit</artifactId>
  <version>4.12</version>
</dependency>
```

Refer to the *Using Maven for project management* section in *Chapter 2, Creating a Simple JEE Web Application*, to learn how to add dependencies to a Maven project.

Run the Maven test again; this time, the test should pass.

Mocking external dependencies for unit tests

Unit tests are meant to execute without external dependencies. We can certainly write methods at a granular level such that the core business logic methods are totally separate from methods that have external dependencies. However, sometimes, this is not practical and we may have to write unit tests for code that is closely dependent on methods that access external systems.

For example, let's assume that we have to add a method in our `Course` bean to add students to the course. We will also mandate that the course has an upper limit on the number of students that it can enroll, and once this limit is reached, no more students will be enrolled. Therefore, we add the following method to the `Course` bean:

```
public void addStudent (Student student)
    throws EnrolmentFullException, SQLException {
  //get current enrolement first
  int currentEnrolment = courseDAO.getNumStudentsInCourse(id);
  if (currentEnrolment >= getMaxStudents())
    throw new EnrolmentFullException("Course if full. Enrolment
closed");
  courseDAO.enrolStudentInCourse(id, student.getId());
}
```

The `addStudent` method first finds the current enrolment in the course. For this, it queries the database by using the `CourseDAO` class. It then checks whether the current enrolment is less than the maximum enrolment. Then, it calls the `enrollStudentInCourse` method of `CourseDAO`.

The `addStudent` method has an external dependency. It depends on successful access to an external database. We can write a unit test for this function as follows:

```
@Test
public void testAddStudent() {
  //create course
  Course course = new Course();
  course.setId(1);
```

```
    course.setName("course1");
    course.setMaxStudents(2);
    //create student
    Student student = new Student();
    student.setFirstName("Student1");
    student.setId(1);
    //now add student
    try {
      course.addStudent(student);
    } catch (Exception e) {
      Assert.fail(e.getMessage());
    }
  }
```

The `testAddStudent` method is meant to check whether the `addStudent` method works fine if all external dependencies are satisfied; in this case, it means that a database connection is established, the database is up and running if it is a server, and the tables are configured properly. If we want to verify that the functionality to enroll a student in a course works by taking into account all dependencies, then we should write a functional test. Unit tests need to only check whether code that does not depend on external dependencies works fine; in this case, it is a trivial check to verify whether the total enrolment is less than the maximum allowed enrolment. This is a simple example, but in real applications, you might have a lot more complex code to test.

The problem with the previous unit test is that we may have false failures, from the perspective of unit testing because the database could be down or might not be configured correctly. One solution is to mock external dependencies; we can mock calls to a database (in this case, calls to `CourseDAO`). Instead of making real calls to the database, we can create stubs that will return some mock data or perform a mock operation. For example, we can write a mock function for the `getNumStudentsInCourse` method of `CourseDAO` that returns some hardcoded value. However, we don't want to modify the application source code to add mock methods. Fortunately, there are open source frameworks that let us mock dependencies in unit tests. Next, we will see how to mock dependencies by using a popular framework called Mockito (`http://mockito.org/`).

Using Mockito

At a very high level, we can use Mockito to do two things:

- Provide wrapper implementation over dependent methods in classes
- Verify that these wrapper implementations are called

We specify the wrapper implementation by using a static method of Mockito:

```
Mockito.when(object_name.method_name(params)).thenReturn(return_value);
```

Further, we verify whether the wrapper method was called by calling another static method of Mockito:

```
Mockito.verify(object_name,
Mockito.atLeastOnce()).method_name(params);
```

To use Mockito in our project, we need to add a dependency on it in our `pom.xml`.

```
<dependency>
  <groupId>org.mockito</groupId>
  <artifactId>mockito-core</artifactId>
  <version>1.10.19</version>
</dependency>
```

Before we start writing a unit test case by using Mockito, we will make a small change in the `Course` class. Currently, `CourseDAO` in the `Course` class is private and there are no setters for it. Add the setter method (`setCourseDAO`) in the `Course` class:

```
public void setCourseDAO(CourseDAO courseDAO) {
  this.courseDAO = courseDAO;
}
```

Now, let's rewrite our test case using Mockito.

First, we need to tell Mockito which method calls we want to mock and what action should be taken in the mocked function (for example, return a specific value). In our example, we would like to mock methods in `CourseDAO` that are called from the `Course.addStudent` method, because methods in the `CourseDAO` access database and we want our unit tests to be independent of the data access code. Therefore, we create a mocked (wrapper) instance of `CourseDAO` by using Mockito:

```
CourseDAO courseDAO = Mockito.mock(CourseDAO.class);
```

Then, we tell Mockito which specific methods in this object to mock. We want to mock `getNumStudentsInCourse` and `getNumStudentsInCourse`.

```
try {
Mockito.when(courseDAO.getNumStudentsInCourse(1)).thenReturn(60);
Mockito.doNothing().when(courseDAO).enrollStudentInCourse(1, 1);
} catch (SQLException e) {
  Assert.fail(e.getMessage());
}
```

The code is in a *try-catch* block because the `getNumStudentsInCourse` and `getNumStudentsInCourse` methods throw `SQLException`. This will not happen when we mock the method because the mocked method will not call any SQL code. However, since the signature of these methods indicate that `SQLException` can be thrown from these methods, we have to call them in *try-catch* to avoid compiler errors.

The first statement in the `try` block tells Mockito that when the `getNumStudentsInCourse` method is called on the `courseDAO` object with parameter `1` (course ID), then it should return `60` from the mocked method.

The second statement tells Mockito that when `enrollStudentInCourse` is called on the `courseDAO` object with arguments `1` (course ID) and `1` (student ID), then it should do nothing. We don't really want to insert any record in the database from the unit test code.

We will now create the `Course` and `Student` objects and call the `addStudent` method of `Course`. This code is similar to the one we wrote in the preceding test case.

```
Course course = new Course();
course.setCourseDAO(courseDAO);

course.setId(1);
course.setName("course1");
course.setMaxStudents(60);
//create student
Student student = new Student();
student.setFirstName("Student1");
student.setId(1);
//now add student
course.addStudent(student);
```

Note that the course ID and student ID that we used when creating the `Course` and `Student` objects, respectively, should match the arguments that we passed to `getNumStudentsInCourse` and `enrollStudentInCourse` when mocking the methods.

We have set that the maximum number of students to be allowed in this course should be `60`. When mocking `getNumStudentsInCourse`, we asked Mockito to also return `60`. Therefore, the `addStudent` method should throw an exception because the course is full. We will verify this by adding the `@Test` annotation later.

At the end of the test, we want to verify that the mocked method was actually called.

```
try {
  Mockito.verify(courseDAO,
Mockito.atLeastOnce()).getNumStudentsInCourse(1);
```

```
} catch (SQLException e) {
  Assert.fail(e.getMessage());
}
```

The preceding code verifies that `getNumStudentsInCourse` of `courseDAO` was called at least once by Mockito when running this test.

Here is the complete test case, including the `@Test` annotation attribute, to make sure that the function throws an exception:

```
  @Test (expected = EnrollmentFullException.class)
  public void testAddStudentWithEnrollmentFull() throws Exception
  {
    CourseDAO courseDAO = Mockito.mock(CourseDAO.class);
    try {
Mockito.when(courseDAO.getNumStudentsInCourse(1)).thenReturn(60);
Mockito.doNothing().when(courseDAO).enrollStudentInCourse(1, 1);
    } catch (SQLException e) {
      Assert.fail(e.getMessage());
    }
    Course course = new Course();
    course.setCourseDAO(courseDAO);

    course.setId(1);
    course.setName("course1");
    course.setMaxStudents(60);
    //create student
    Student student = new Student();
    student.setFirstName("Student1");
    student.setId(1);
    //now add student
    course.addStudent(student);

    try {
      Mockito.verify(courseDAO,
      Mockito.atLeastOnce()).getNumStudentsInCourse(1);
    } catch (SQLException e) {
      Assert.fail(e.getMessage());
    }

    //If no exception was thrown then the test case was successful
    //No need of Assert here
  }
```

Run the unit tests. All tests should pass. Here is a similar test case that makes Mockito return the current enrolment number of `59` and makes sure that a student is enrolled successfully:

```
@Test
public void testAddStudentWithEnrollmentOpen() throws Exception
{
  CourseDAO courseDAO = Mockito.mock(CourseDAO.class);
  try {
Mockito.when(courseDAO.getNumStudentsInCourse(1)).thenReturn(59);
Mockito.doNothing().when(courseDAO).enrollStudentInCourse(1, 1);
  } catch (SQLException e) {
    Assert.fail(e.getMessage());
  }
  Course course = new Course();
  course.setCourseDAO(courseDAO);

  course.setId(1);
  course.setName("course1");
  course.setMaxStudents(60);
  //create student
  Student student = new Student();
  student.setFirstName("Student1");
  student.setId(1);
  //now add student
  course.addStudent(student);

  try {
    Mockito.verify(courseDAO,
    Mockito.atLeastOnce()).getNumStudentsInCourse(1);
    Mockito.verify(courseDAO,
    Mockito.atLeastOnce()).enrollStudentInCourse(1,1);
  } catch (SQLException e) {
    Assert.fail(e.getMessage());
  }

  //If no exception was thrown then the test case was successful
  //No need of Assert here
}
```

Note that this test case does not expect any exceptions to be thrown (if an exception is thrown, then the test case fails). We can also verify that the mocked method called `enrollStudentInCourse` is called. We did not verify this in the previous test case because an exception was thrown before calling this method in the `Course.addStudent` method.

There are many topics of JUnit that we have not covered in this section. You are encouraged to read the JUnit documentation at `https://github.com/junit-team/junit/wiki`. In particular, the following topics might be of interest to you:

- JUnit test suites. You can aggregate test cases from different test classes in a suite. Find more information about test suites at `https://github.com/junit-team/junit/wiki/Aggregating-tests-in-suites`.
- Parameterized test cases at `https://github.com/junit-team/junit/wiki/Parameterized-tests`.
- If you are using Apache Ant for building your project, then take a look at JUnit Ant task - `https://ant.apache.org/manual/Tasks/junit.html`.

Calculating test coverage

Unit tests tell you if your application code behaves as expected. Unit tests are important to maintain code quality and catch errors early in the development cycle. However, this goal is at risk if you do not write enough unit tests to test your application code or if you have not tested all possible input conditions in the test cases and the exception paths. To measure the quality and adequacy of your test cases, you need to calculate the coverage of your test cases. In simple terms, coverage tells you what percentage of your application code was touched by running your unit tests. There are different measures to calculate coverage:

- Number of lines covered
- Number of branches (created using the `if`, `else`, `elseif`, `switch`, and `try/catch` statements)
- Number of functions covered

Together, these three measures give a fair measurement of the quality of your unit tests. There are many code coverage tools for Java. In this chapter, we will take a look at an open source code coverage tool called JaCoCo (`http://www.eclemma.org/jacoco/`). JaCoCo also has an Eclipse plugin (`http://www.eclemma.org/`), and we can use it from right within Eclipse.

You can either install the JaCoCo plugin by using the update URL (`http://update.eclemma.org/`) or from Eclipse Marketplace. To install it using the update site, select the **Help | Install New Software** menu. Click the **Add** button and enter the name of the update site (you can give any name) and update URL:

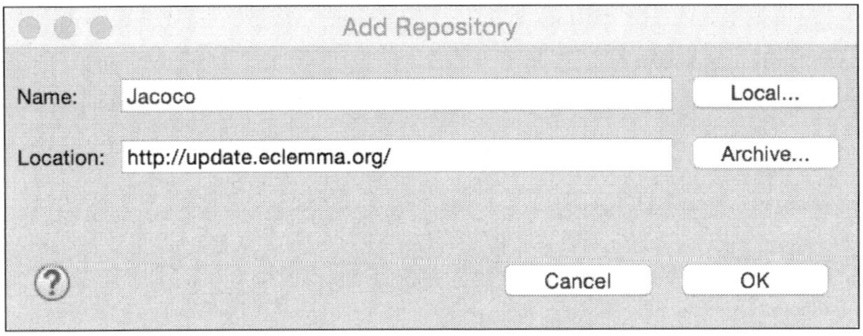

Figure 5.6 Add an update site for JaCoCo

Then, follow the instructions to install the plugin.

Alternatively, you can install it from the marketplace. Select the **Help** | **Eclipse Marketplace** menu. Type `EclEmma` in the find textbox, and click the **Go** button.

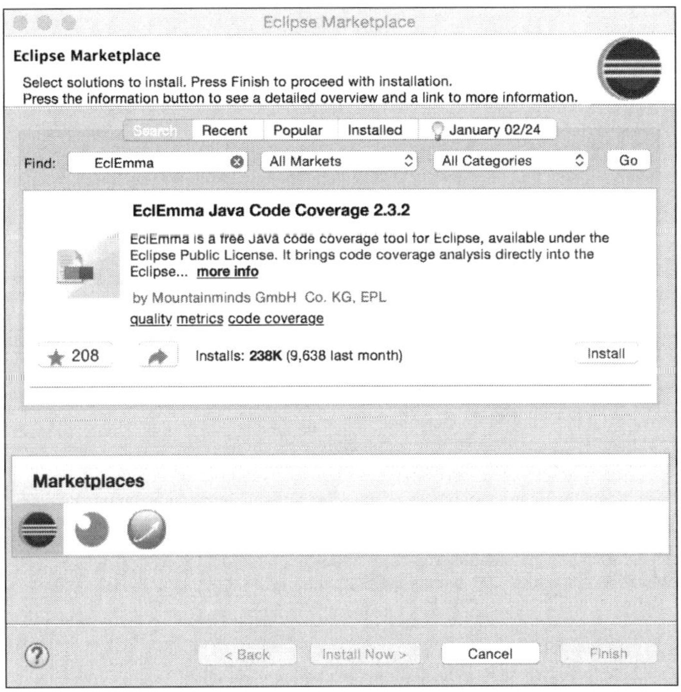

Figure 5.7 Install the EclEmma Code Coverage plugin from the marketplace

Click the **Install** button and follow the instructions to install the plugin.

To verify that the plugin is installed properly, open **Window** | **Show View** | **Other**. Type `coverage` in the filter box and make sure that the **Coverage** (under **Java** category) view is available. Open the view.

To run a unit test with coverage, right-click on the project in **Package Explorer** and select **Coverage As | JUnit Test**. After the tests are run, the coverage information is displayed in the **Coverage** view.

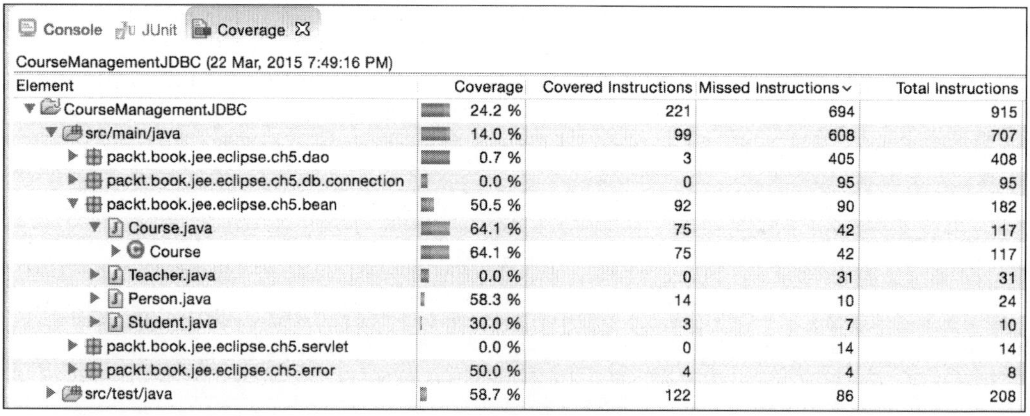

Element	Coverage	Covered Instructions	Missed Instructions	Total Instructions
CourseManagementJDBC	24.2 %	221	694	915
src/main/java	14.0 %	99	608	707
packt.book.jee.eclipse.ch5.dao	0.7 %	3	405	408
packt.book.jee.eclipse.ch5.db.connection	0.0 %	0	95	95
packt.book.jee.eclipse.ch5.bean	50.5 %	92	90	182
Course.java	64.1 %	75	42	117
Course	64.1 %	75	42	117
Teacher.java	0.0 %	0	31	31
Person.java	58.3 %	14	10	24
Student.java	30.0 %	3	7	10
packt.book.jee.eclipse.ch5.servlet	0.0 %	0	14	14
packt.book.jee.eclipse.ch5.error	50.0 %	4	4	8
src/test/java	58.7 %	122	86	208

Figure 5.8 Coverage results

How to interpret these results? Overall, at the project level, the coverage is **24.2%**. This means that out of all the code that we have written in this application, out unit test case has touched only **24.2%**. Then, there is the coverage percentage at the package level and the class level.

Double-click on `Course.java` in the **Coverage** view to see which lines are covered in this file. The following is a part of the file where the red lines denote code that is not covered and the green lines, the code that is covered.

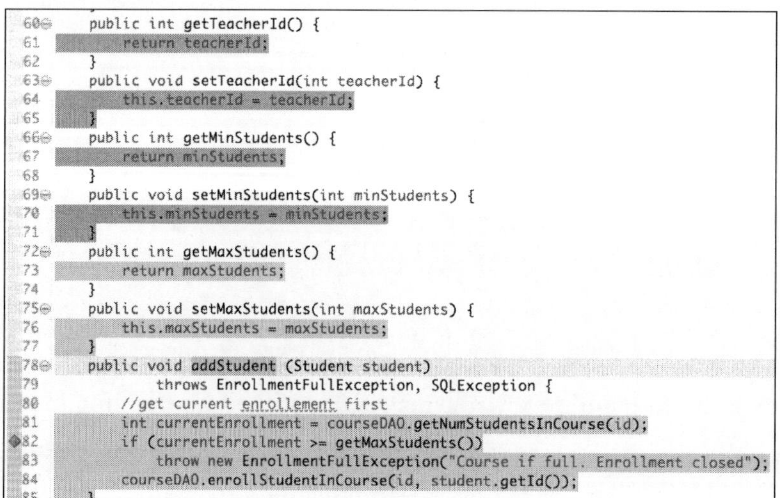

```
    public int getTeacherId() {
        return teacherId;
    }
    public void setTeacherId(int teacherId) {
        this.teacherId = teacherId;
    }
    public int getMinStudents() {
        return minStudents;
    }
    public void setMinStudents(int minStudents) {
        this.minStudents = minStudents;
    }
    public int getMaxStudents() {
        return maxStudents;
    }
    public void setMaxStudents(int maxStudents) {
        this.maxStudents = maxStudents;
    }
    public void addStudent (Student student)
            throws EnrollmentFullException, SQLException {
        //get current enrollement first
        int currentEnrollment = courseDAO.getNumStudentsInCourse(id);
        if (currentEnrollment >= getMaxStudents())
            throw new EnrollmentFullException("Course if full. Enrollment closed");
        courseDAO.enrollStudentInCourse(id, student.getId());
    }
```

Figure 5.9 Line coverage details

We have written unit tests for `addStudent`, and the coverage of this class is **100%**, which is good. We haven't used all the setters and getters in our unit tests, so some of them are not covered.

As you can see, the coverage results help you understand places in your code for which unit tests are not written or which are partially covered by unit tests. Using this data, you can add unit tests for the code that is not covered. Of course, you may not want all lines to be covered if the code is very simple, such as the getters and the setters in the above class.

In *Figure 5.8 Coverage results*, observe that the coverage tool has analyzed the test classes too. Typically, we don't want to measure coverage on test classes; we want to measure the coverage of the application code by running the test classes. To exclude the test classes from this analysis, right-click on the project and select **Coverage As** | **Coverage Configurations**. Click on the **Coverage** tab and select only **src/main/java**.

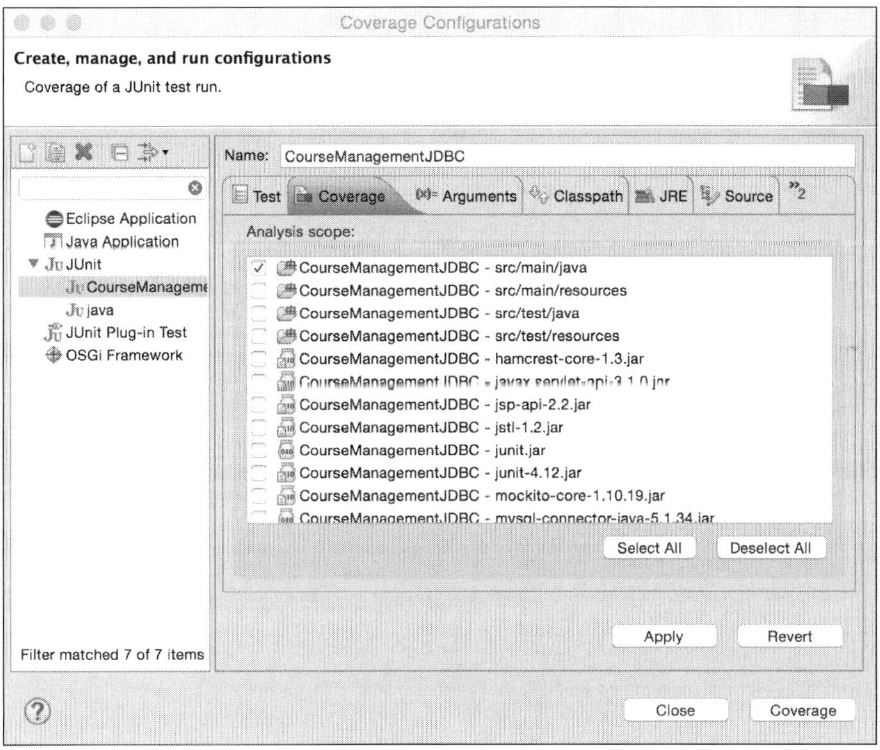

Figure 5.10 Coverage configuration

Click **Coverage** to run coverage with the new settings. You will see in the **Coverage** view that the test classes do not appear in the report and that the overall test coverage on the project has also dropped.

If you want to run coverage using Maven, then refer to `http://www.eclemma.org/jacoco/trunk/doc/maven.html`. In particular, take a look at `pom.xml` (`http://jacoco.org/jacoco/trunk/doc/examples/build/pom-it.xml`), which creates reports for the JUnit and JaCoCo coverage.

Summary

Writing unit tests is an important part of application development. Unit tests help you catch bugs in your application at a very early stage; they also help you catch any regression because of the subsequent code changes. JUnit and Eclipse provide an easy way to integrate unit tests in your development workflow. Eclipse also creates a nice report in the JUnit view that makes it easy to identify the failed tests and jump to the line in the code where the test failed.

Unit tests are meant to be executed without any external dependencies. Libraries such as Mockito help you to mock any external dependencies.

Use coverage tools such as JaCoCo to know the quality of the unit tests that you have written. Coverage tools tell you the percentage of application code that is covered by your unit tests. You can also see in each class which lines are covered by your unit tests and which are not. Such a report can help you to decide whether you need to write more unit test cases or modify the existing unit test cases to cover important code that your unit tests have not tested.

In the next chapter, we will see how to debug a Java application from Eclipse. The chapter will also explain how to connect to a remote JEE server for debugging.

6

Debugging a JEE Application

Debugging is an unavoidable part of application development. Unless the application is very simple, chances are that it is not going to work as expected in the very first attempt and you will spend time trying to find out the reasons. In very complex applications, in fact, application developers might end up spending more time debugging than writing application code. Problems may not necessarily exist in your code, but may exist in the external system on which your application depends, and you may even find that you have to debug your application. Debugging a complex piece of software requires skill, which can be developed with experience. However, it also needs good support from the application runtime and IDE.

There are different ways to debug applications. You might just put the `System.out.println()` statements in your code and print values of variables, or just a message that the execution of the application has reached a certain point. If the application is small or simple, this might work but may not be a good idea when debugging large and complex applications. You also need to remember to remove such debug statements before moving the code to staging or production. If you have written unit tests and if some of the unit tests fail, then that might give you some idea about the problems in your code. However, in many cases, you may want to monitor the execution of code at the line level or the function level and check the values of variables at that line or in that function. This requires support from the language runtime and a good IDE that helps you visualize and control the debugging process. Fortunately, Java has an excellent debugger and Eclipse JEE provides great support for debugging Java code.

In this chapter, we are going to learn how to debug a JEE application using Eclipse JEE. We will use the same Course Management application that we built in *Chapter 4, Creating a JEE Database Application*, for debugging. The debugging technique described in this chapter can be applied to remotely debug any Java application, and not necessarily restricted to the JEE applications.

Debugging a remote Java application

You might have debugged standalone Java applications from Eclipse. You set breakpoints in the code, run the application in the debug mode from Eclipse, and then, can debug the application in steps. Debugging remote Java applications is a bit different, particularly when it comes to how you launch the debugger. In the case of a local application, the debugger launches the application. In the case of a remote application, it is already launched and you need to connect the debugger to it. In general, if you want to allow remote debugging for an application, you need to run the application using the following parameters:

```
-Xdebug -Xrunjdwp:transport=dt_socket,address=9001,server=y,suspend=n
```

Here:

- `Xdebug` enables debugging
- `Xrunjdwp` runs the debugger implementation of **JDWP** (which stands for **Java Debug Wire Protocol**)

Instead of `-Xdebug -Xrunjdwp`, you can also use `-agentlib:jdwp` for JRE 1.5 and above, for example:

```
-agentlib:jdwp=transport= dt_socket,address=9001,server=y,suspend=n
```

Here:

- `transport=dt_socket` starts a socket server at `address=9001` (this can be any free port) to receive debugger commands and send responses.
- `server=y` tells the JVM if it is a server or a client, in the context of debugger communication. Use the `y` value for the remote application to be debugged.
- `suspend=n` tells the JVM to not wait for the debugger client to attach to it. If the value is `y`, then the JVM will wait before executing the main class till the debugger client attaches to it. Setting the `y` value for this option may be useful in cases where you want to debug, for example, the initialization code of servlets that are loaded upon the startup of a web container. In such cases, if you do not choose to suspend the application till the debugger connects to it, the code that you want to debug might get executed before the debugger client attaches to it.

Debugging a web application using Tomcat in Eclipse EE

We have already learnt how to configure Tomcat in Eclipse EE and deploy a web application in it from Eclipse (refer to the *Configure Tomcat in Eclipse* and *Running JSP in Tomcat* sections in *Chapter 2, Creating JEE Project*). We will use the Course Management application that we created in *Chapter 4, Creating a JEE Database Application*, using JDBC for debugging.

Starting Tomcat in debug mode

If you want to debug a remote Java process, you need to start the process by using the debug parameters. However, if you have configured Tomcat in Eclipse EE, you don't need to do this manually. Eclipse takes care of launching Tomcat in the debug mode. To start Tomcat in the **Debug** mode, select the server in the **Servers** view and click the **Debug** button in the Server view. Alternatively, right-click on the server and select **Debug** from the menu. Make sure that the project that you want to debug is already added to Tomcat; in this case, the project is `CourseManagementJDBC`.

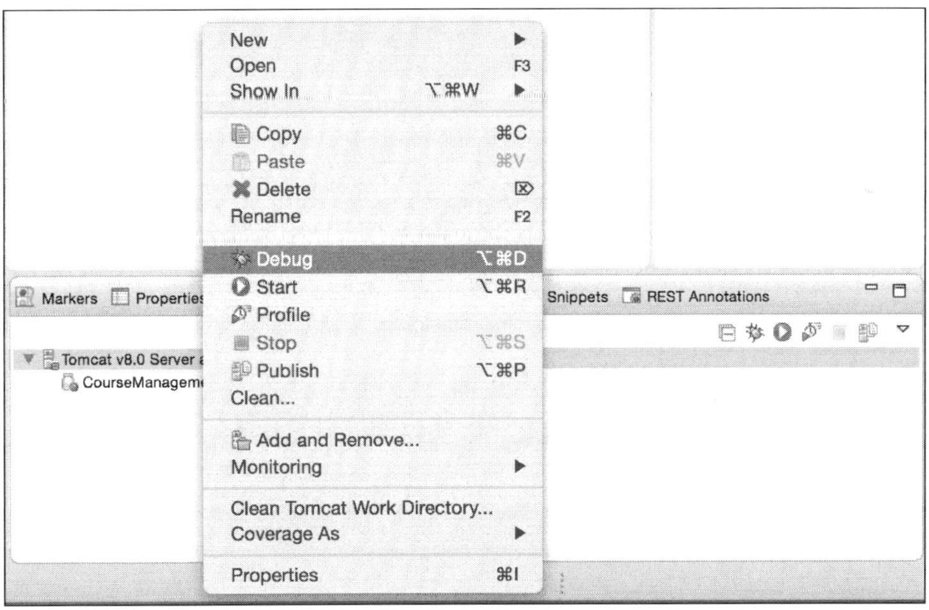

Figure 6.1 Start Tomcat in the debug mode

Once Tomcat is started in the debug mode, its status changes to **Debugging**.

Figure 6.2 Tomcat running in the debug mode

Setting breakpoints

Let's now set breakpoints in the code before we launch the `CourseManagement` application. Open `CourseDAO` from the `CourseManagementJDBC` project and double-click in the left margin of the first line in the `getCourses` method.

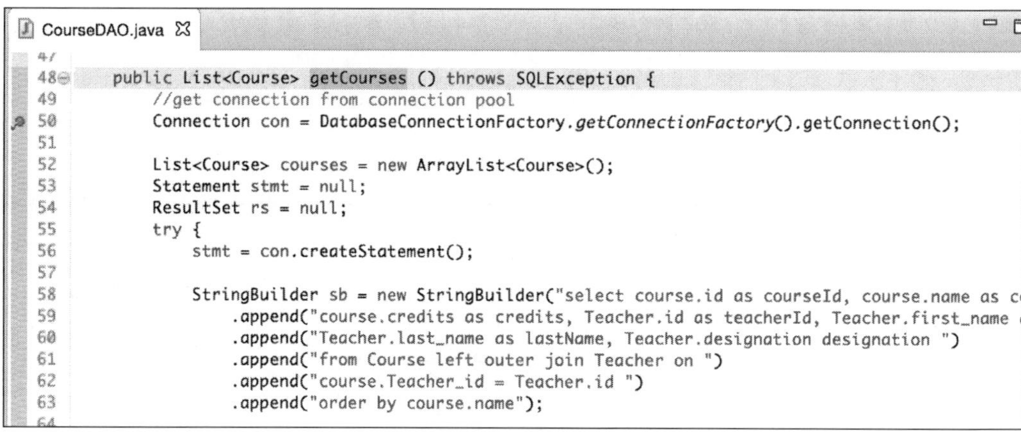

Figure 6.3 Set a breakpoint

Another way to set a breakpoint at a line is to right-click in the left margin and select **Toggle Breakpoint**.

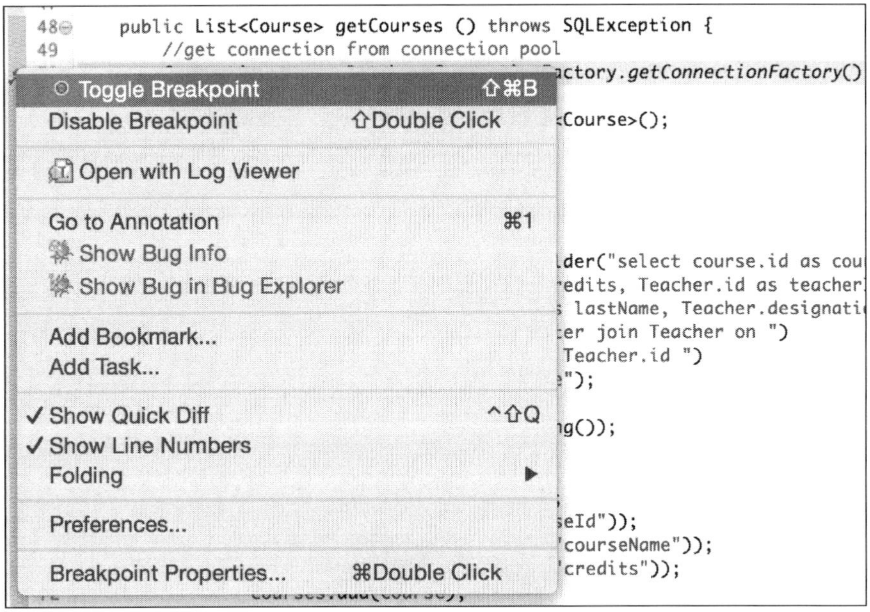

Figure 6.4 Toggle breakpoints using the menu

You can also set the breakpoint at the method level. Just place the caret inside any method, and select the **Run | Toggle Method Breakpoint** menu. This is equivalent to setting a breakpoint at the first line of the method. This is preferred over setting a breakpoint at the first line of the method when you always want to stop at the beginning of the method. The debugger will always stop at the first statement in the method even if you later add more code at the beginning of the method.

Another useful breakpoint option is to set it when any an exception occurs during program execution. Often, you may not want to set a breakpoint at a specific location but may want to investigate why an exception is happening. If you do not have access to the stack trace of the exception, you can just set a breakpoint for the exception and run the program again. Next time, the execution will stop at the code location where the exception occurred. This makes it easy to debug exceptions. To set a breakpoint for an exception, select **Run** | **Java Breakpoint Exception** and select the `Exception` class from the list.

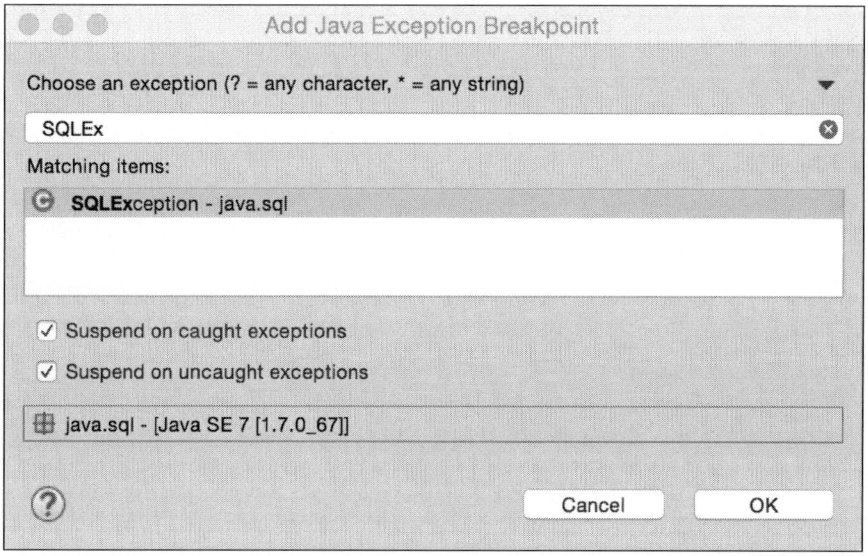

Figure 6.5 Set a breakpoint at an exception

Running an application in debug mode

Let's now run the `listCourse.jsp` page in the debug mode. In **Project Navigator**, go to `src/main/webapp/listCourse.jsp` and right-click. Select **Debug As** | **Debug on Server**. Eclipse might prompt you to use the existing debug server.

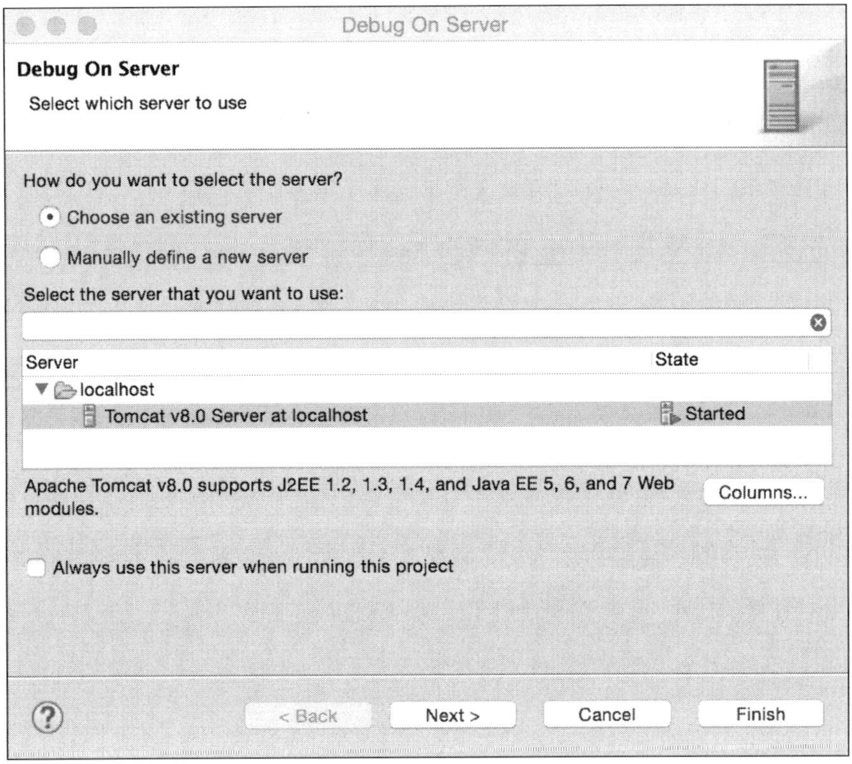

Figure 6.6 Use the existing debug server

Click **Finish**. Eclipse asks you if you want to switch to the **Debug** perspective (refer to *Chapter 1, Introducing JEE and Eclipse* for discussion on Eclipse perspectives).

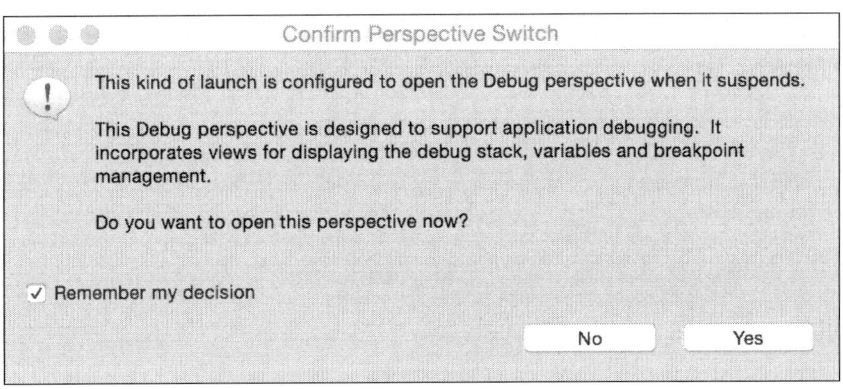

Figure 6.7 Auto switching to the Debug perspective

Eclipse switches to the **Debug** perspective. Eclipse tries to open the page in the internal Eclipse browser, but it won't display the page immediately. Recall that `listCourse.jsp` calls `Course.getCourses()`, which in turn calls `CourseDAO.getCourses()`. We have set a breakpoint in the `CourseDAO.getCourses()` method, so the execution of the page stops there.

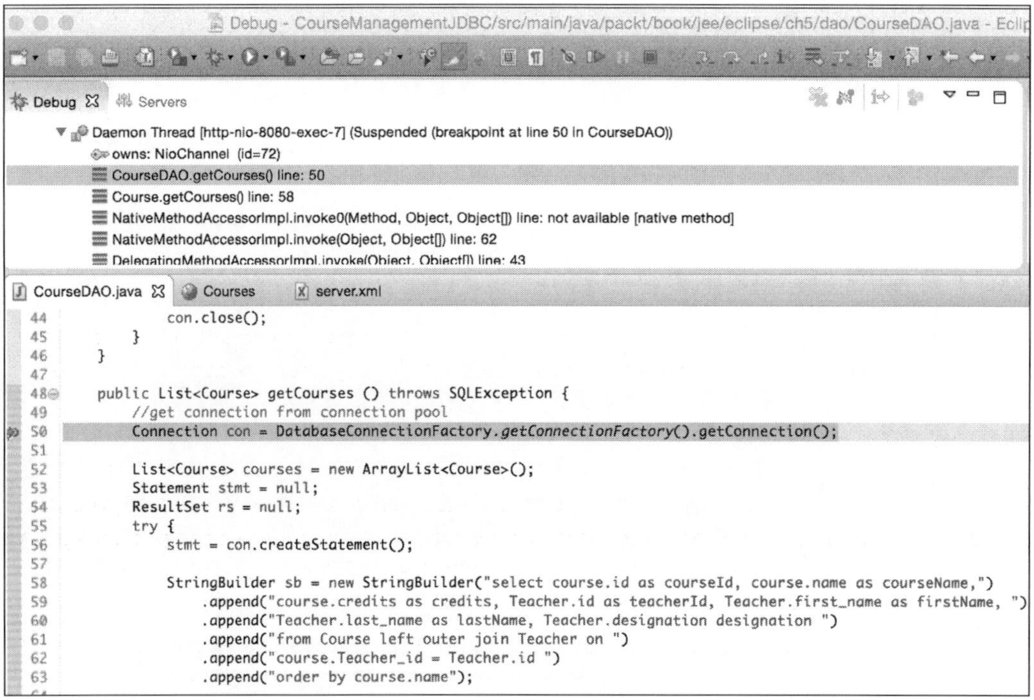

Figure 6.8 Debugger paused at a breakpoint

Performing step operations and inspecting variables

You can now perform different step operations (step over, step in, and step out) by using the toolbar icons at the top, or using keyboard shortcuts. Drop-down the **Debug** menu to know the menu and toolbar shortcuts for debugging. Typically, you would inspect variables or perform step operations to verify whether the execution flow is correct and then continue the execution by pressing the **Resume** button or the menu/keyboard shortcut.

In the preceding **Debug** window the editor, you can see all threads and inspect the stack frames of each thread, when the debugger is suspended. Stack frames of a thread show you the path of program execution in that thread until the point that the debugger was suspended after hitting a breakpoint or due to step operations. In a multithreaded application, such as Tomcat web container, more than one thread might have been suspended at a time and they might have different stack frames. When debugging a multi-threaded application, make sure that you have selected the required thread in the **Debug** window before selecting options to step over/in/out or resume.

Often, you step into a method and realize that the values are not what you expect and you want to re-run statements in the current method to investigate. In such cases, you can drop to any previous stack frame and start over.

For example, let's say, in the above example, we step into the `DatabaseConnectionFactory.getConnectionFactory().getConnection` method. When we perform step-in, the debugger first steps into the `getConnectionFactory` method, and in the next step-in operation, it steps into the `getConnection` method. Suppose that when we are in the `getConnection` method, we want to go back and check what happened in the `getConnectionFactory` method that we might have missed earlier (although in this simple example, not much happens in the `getConnectionFactory` method, it should just serve as an example). We can go back to the `getCourses` method and start over the execution of `getConnectionFactory` and `getConnection`. In the **Debug** view, right-click on the `CourseDAO.getCourses()` stack frame and select **Drop to Frame**, as shown in the following screenshot:

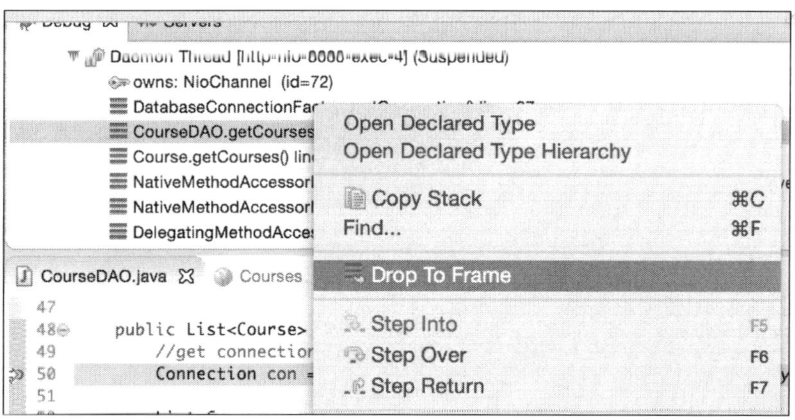

Figure 6.9 Drop to Frame

The debugger discards all the stack frames above the selected frame and execution drops back to the selected frame, in this case, in the `getCourses` method of `CourseDAO`. You can then step over again into the `getConnection` method. Note that only stack variables and their values are discarded when you drop to frame. Any changes made to reference objects that are not in the stack are not rolled back.

Inspecting variable values

Let's now step over a few statements till we are in the while loop to create the Course objects from the data returned by the result set. In the top-right window, you will find the Variables view, which displays variables applicable at that point of execution.

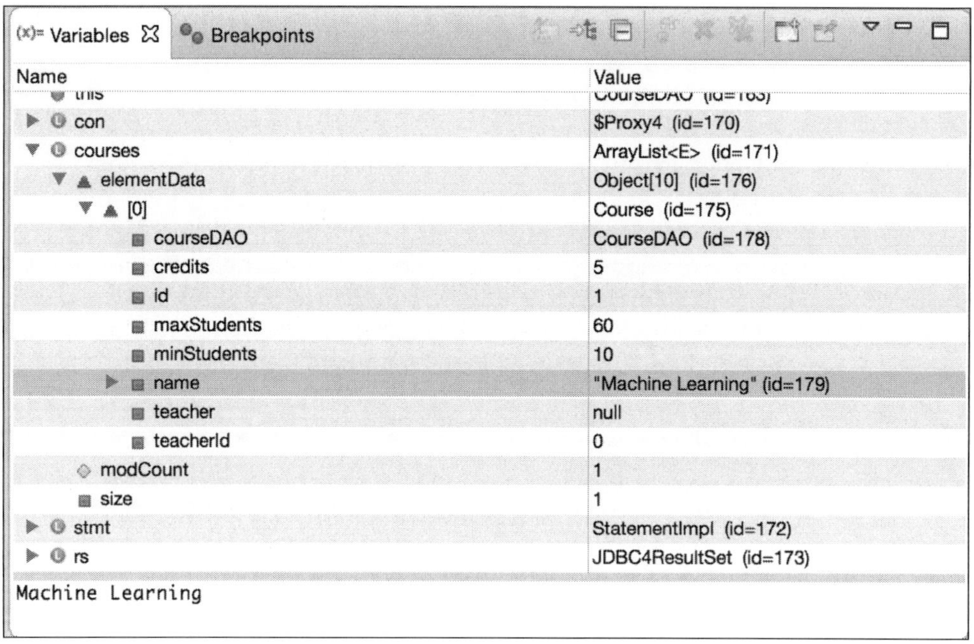

Figure 6.10 Debugger paused at a breakpoint

You can inspect variables in the previous methods calls too by changing the selection in the **Debug** view: click on any previous method call (stack frame) and the **Variables** view displays variables valid for the selected method. You can change the value of any variable, including the values of the member variables of the objects. For example, in *Figure 6.8 Debugger paused at a breakpoint*, we can change the value of the course name from `"Machine Learning"` to `"Machine Learning - Part1"`. To change the variable value, right-click on the variable in the **Variables** view and select **Change Value**.

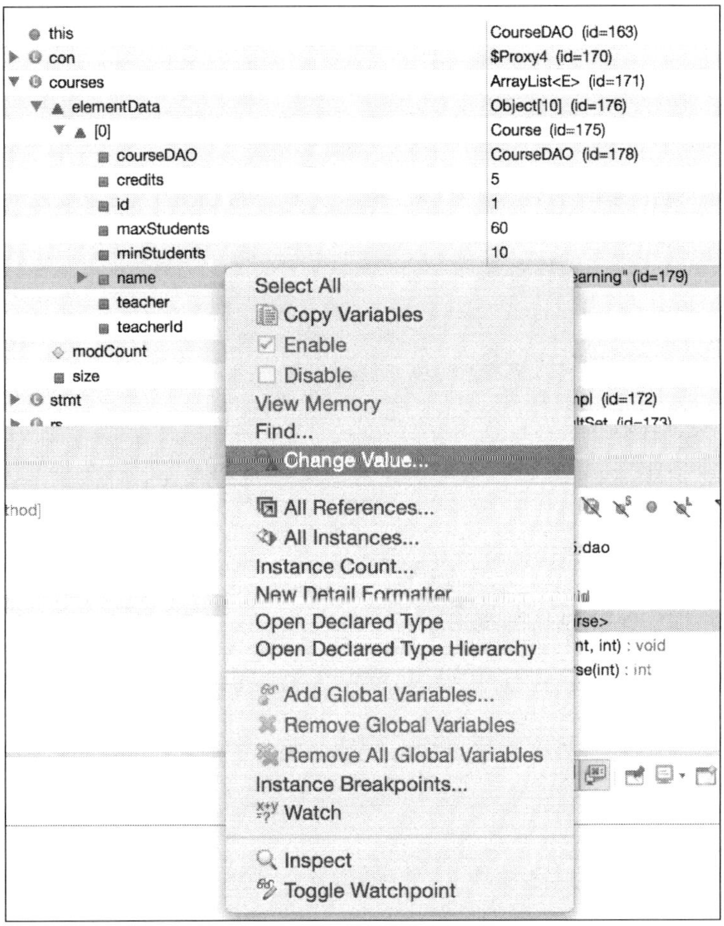

Figure 6.11 Change a variable's value during debugging

You don't have to go to the **Variables** view to check a variable's value every time. There is a quick way: just hover over the cursor on the variable in editor and Eclipse pops up a window showing the variable's value.

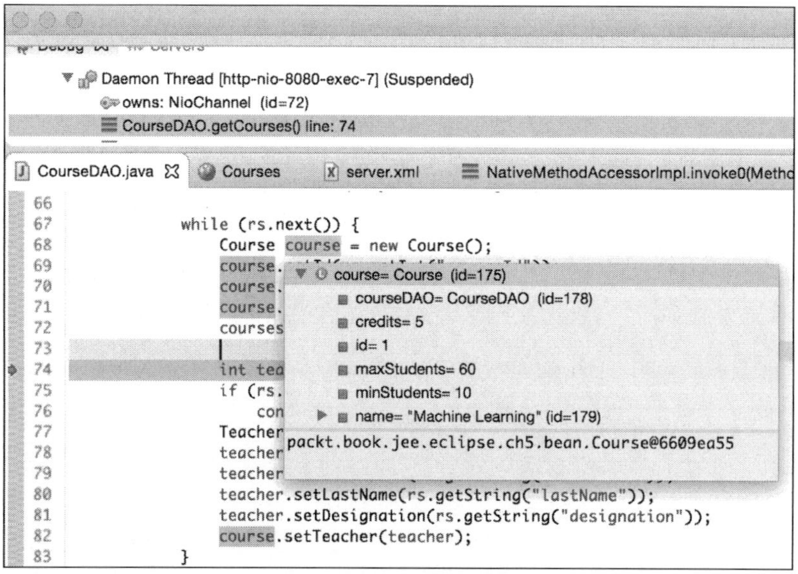

Figure 6.12 Inspect variable

You can also right-click on a variable and select the **Inspect** option to see the variable's values. However, you cannot change the value when you select the **Inspect** option.

If you want to see the value of a variable frequently (for example, a variable in a loop), you can add the variable to the watchlist. It is a more convenient option than trying to search for the variable in the **Variables** view. Right-click on a variable and select the **Watch** option from the menu. The **Watch** option adds the variable to the **Expressions** view (its default location is next to the **Breakpoints** view at the top right) and displays its value.

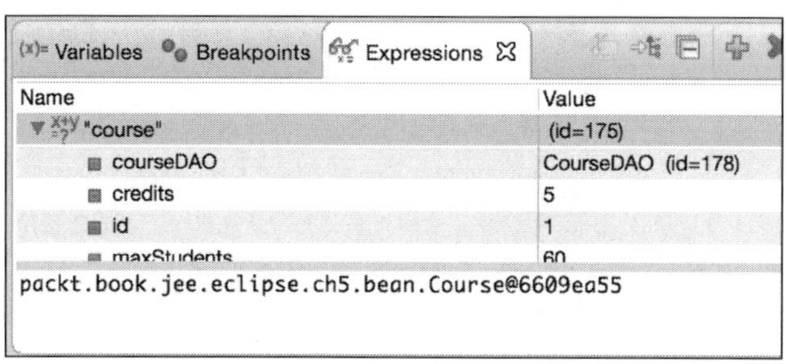

Figure 6.13 Inspect a variable

The use of the **Expressions** view is not limited to watching variable values. You can watch any valid Java expression, such as an arithmetic expression, or even method calls. Click on the plus icon in the **Expressions** view and add an expression.

Debugging an application in an externally configured Tomcat

Thus far, we have debugged our application using Tomcat configured within Eclipse. When we launched Tomcat in the **Debug** mode, Eclipse took care of adding the JVM parameters for the debugging to the Tomcat launch script. In this section, we will see how to launch an external (to Eclipse) Tomcat instance and connect to it from Eclipse. Although we are going to debug a remote instance of Tomcat, information in this section can be used for connecting to any remotely running Java program that is launched in the debug mode. We have already seen the debug parameters to pass when launching a remote application in the debug mode.

Launching Tomcat externally in the debug mode is not too difficult. Tomcat startup scripts already have an option to start Tomcat in the **Debug** mode; you just need to pass the appropriate parameter. From the Command Prompt, change the folder to `<TOMCAT_HOME>/bin` and type the following command in Windows:

```
>catalina.bat jpda start
```

And on Mac and Linux:

```
$./catalina.sh jpda start
```

Passing the `jpda` argument sets the default values to all the required debug parameters. The default debug port is `8000`. If you want to change it, either modify `catalin.bat/catalin.sh` or set the environment variable called `JPDA_ADDRESS`, use the following code:

In Windows:

```
>set JPDA_ADDRESS=9001
```

On Mac and Linux:

```
$export JPDA_ADDRESS=9001
```

Similarly, you can set `JPDA_SUSPEND` to `y` or `n` to control whether the debugger should wait for the client to connect before executing the `main` class.

To connect the debugger from Eclipse to a remote instance, select the **Run | Debug Configuration ...** menu. Right-click on the **Remote Java Application** node in the list view on the left and select **New**.

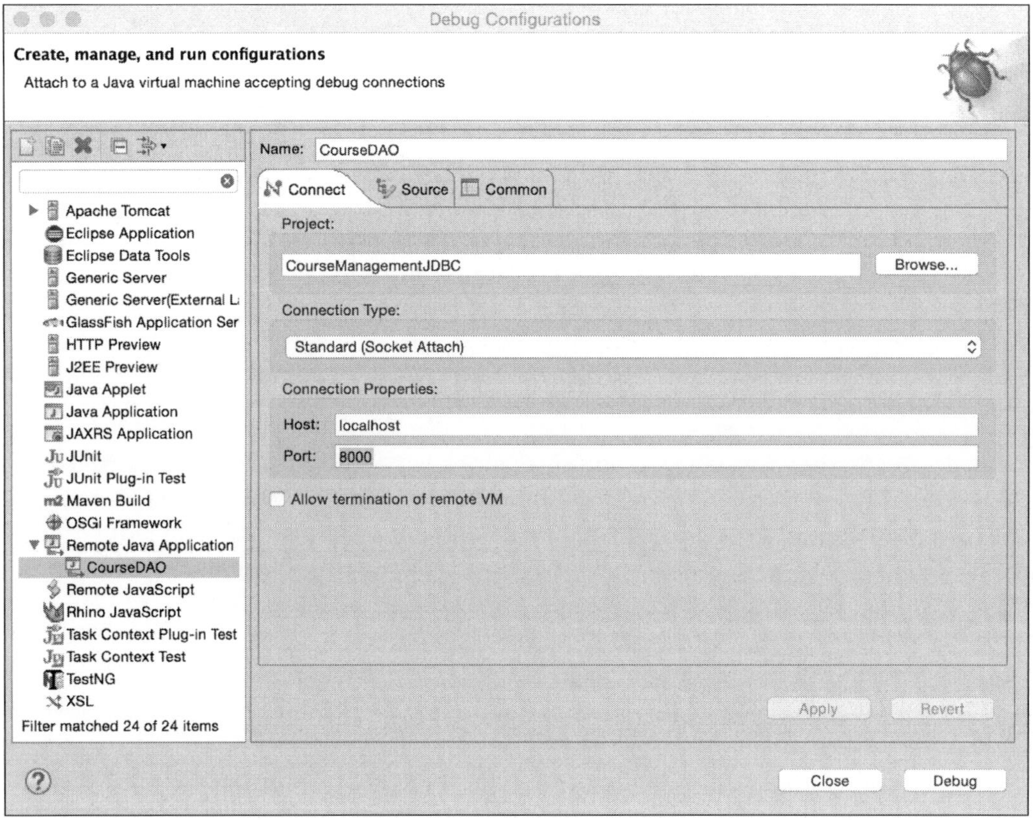

Figure 6.14 Inspect a variable

Set the appropriate **Project** and **Port** (the same as the one you selected to start Tomcat in the **Debug** mode, that is, default `8000`) and click **Debug**. If the debug connection is successful, Eclipse will switch to the debug perspective. From here on, the process of debugging is the same as that explained earlier.

Using Debugger to know the status of a program execution

We have seen how to use the debugger to verify the execution flow of a program (using the step operations) and to inspect variables. You can also use the debugger to know the status of the running program. For example, a web request is taking too long and you want to know where exactly the execution is stuck. You can use the debugger to find this. It is similar to taking the thread dump of a running program, but much easier than the methods used to get the thread dump. Let's assume that our method `CourseDAO.getCourses` is taking a long time to execute. Let's simulate this by using a couple of `Thread.sleep` calls:

```
public List<Course> getCourses () throws SQLException {
  //get connection from connection pool
  Connection con =
DatabaseConnectionFactory.getConnectionFactory().getConnection();

  try {
    Thread.sleep(5000);
  } catch (InterruptedException e) {}


  List<Course> courses = new ArrayList<Course>();
  Statement stmt = null;
  ResultSet rs = null;
  try {
    stmt = con.createStatement();

    StringBuilder sb = new StringBuilder("select course.id as
    courseId, course.name as courseName,")
      .append("course.credits as credits, Teacher.id as teacherId,
      Teacher.first_name as firstName, ")
      .append("Teacher.last_name as lastName, Teacher.designation
      designation ")
      .append("from Course left outer join Teacher on ")
      .append("course.Teacher_id = Teacher.id ")
      .append("order by course.name");
```

```
        rs = stmt.executeQuery(sb.toString());

        while (rs.next()) {
          Course course = new Course();
          course.setId(rs.getInt("courseId"));
          course.setName(rs.getString("courseName"));
          course.setCredits(rs.getInt("credits"));
          courses.add(course);

          int teacherId = rs.getInt("teacherId");
          if (rs.wasNull()) //no teacher set for this course.
            continue;
          Teacher teacher = new Teacher();
          teacher.setId(teacherId);
          teacher.setFirstName(rs.getString("firstName"));
          teacher.setLastName(rs.getString("lastName"));
          teacher.setDesignation(rs.getString("designation"));
          course.setTeacher(teacher);
        }

        try {
          Thread.sleep(5000);
        } catch (InterruptedException e) {}


        return courses;
      } finally {
        try {if (rs != null) rs.close();} catch (SQLException e) {}
        try {if (stmt != null) stmt.close();} catch (SQLException e)
    {}
        try {con.close();} catch (SQLException e) {}
      }
    }
```

Start Tomcat in the debug mode, and run `listCourses.jsp` in the **Debug** mode. Because we have put in the `Thread.sleep` statements, the request will take time. Go to the **Debug** view where the threads and stack frames are displayed. Click on the first node under the Tomcat debug configuration node and select the **Suspend** option, as shown in the following screenshot:

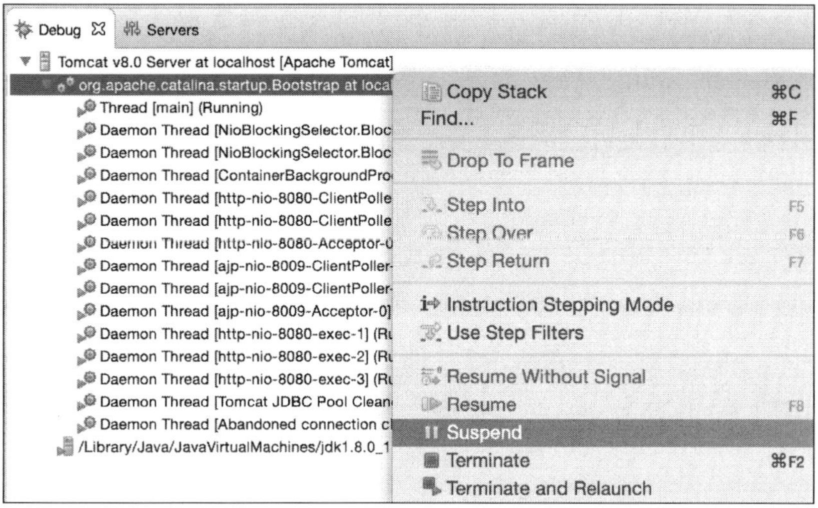

Figure 6.15 Suspend program execution

The debugger pauses the execution of all threads in the program. You can then see the status of each thread by expanding the thread nodes. You will find one of the threads executing the `CourseDAO.getCourse` method and the statement that it was executing before being suspended:

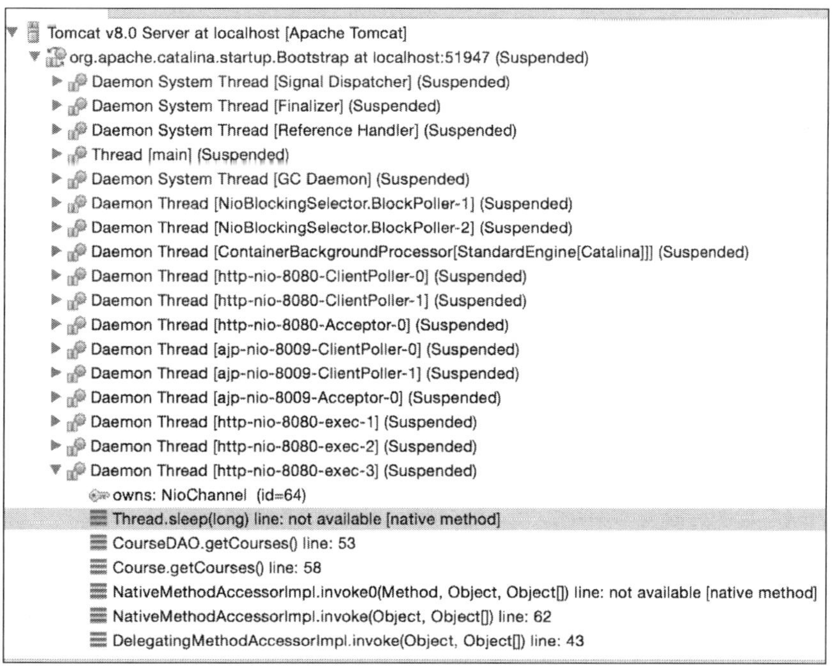

Figure 6.16 Status of suspended threads

As shown in the preceding *Figure 6.16 Status of suspended threads*, `CourseDAO.getCourses` is suspended at the `Thread.sleep` statement. You can even inspect variables at each stack frame when the program is suspended. By suspending the program and inspecting the state of threads and stack frames, you might be able to find the bottlenecks in your application.

Summary

Good support for debugging from language runtime and IDE can considerably reduce the time required for debugging. Java runtime and Eclipse provide excellent support for debugging remote applications. To debug a remote application, launch it with the debug parameters for JVM and connect Eclipse Debugger to it. You can then debug the remote application just as you would debug the local one - set breakpoints, perform step operations, and inspect variables. You can also change the variable values in the application when its execution is suspended.

In the next chapter, we will see how to develop JEE applications using EJBs. We will use the GlassFish server in the next chapter. Although this chapter explained the debugging of JEE applications deployed in Tomcat, you can use the same techniques in the GlassFish server.

7
Creating JEE Applications with EJB

Recall the architecture of database applications in *Chapter 4, Creating a JEE Database Application*. We had JSP or a JSF page calling a JSP bean or a managed bean. The beans then called DAOs to execute the data access code. This separated code for the user interface, business logic, and the database nicely. This would work for small or medium applications but may prove to be a bottleneck in large enterprise applications; the application may not scale very well. If the processing of business logic is time consuming then it would make more sense to distribute it on different servers for better scalability and resilience. If the code for the user interface, business logic, and data access is all on the same machine, then it may affect the scalability of the application; that is, it may not perform well under load.

Using **Enterprise Java Beans** (**EJBs**) for implementing business logic is ideal in scenarios where you want components processing the business logic to be distributed across different servers. However, this is just one of the advantages of EJB. Even if you use EJBs on the same server as the web application, you may gain from a number of services that the EJB container provides to applications through EJBs; you can specify the security constraints for calling EJB methods declaratively (using annotations) and can easily specify transaction boundaries (specify which method calls form a part of one transaction) by using annotations. Further, the container handles the lifecycle of EJBs, including the pooling of certain types of EJB objects so that more objects can be created when the load on the application increases.

In *Chapter 4, Creating a JEE Database Application*, we created a Course Management web application using simple Java beans. In this chapter, we will create the same application using EJBs and deploy it on the GlassFish 4 server. However, before this, we need to understand some basic concepts of EJBs.

Types of EJB

The EJB can be of the following types according to the EJB3 specification:

- Session bean
    - Stateful session bean
    - Stateless session bean
    - Singleton session bean
- Message-driven bean

We will discuss the details of **message-driven bean** (**MDB**) in a later chapter when we talk about the asynchronous processing of requests in a JEE application. In this chapter, we will focus on session beans.

Session bean

In general, session beans are meant to contain methods to execute the main business logic of enterprise applications. Any **POJO** (which stands for **Plain Old Java Object**) can be annotated with the appropriate EJB3-specific annotations to make it session bean. Session beans come in three types.

Stateful session bean

One stateful session bean serves requests for one client only. There is one-to-one mapping between the stateful session bean and the client. Therefore, stateful beans can hold the state data for the client between multiple method calls. In our Course Management application, we could use a stateful bean for holding Student data (student profile and courses taken by her) after a student logs in. The state maintained by the stateful bean is lost when the server restarts or when the session times out. Since there is one stateful bean per client, using a stateful bean might impact the scalability of the application.

We use the `@Stateful` annotation to create a stateful session bean.

Stateless session bean

A stateless session bean does not hold any state information for the client. Therefore, one session bean can be shared across multiple clients. The EJB container maintains pools of stateless beans, and when a client request comes, it takes out a bean from the pool, executes methods, and returns the bean to the pool again. Stateless session beans provide excellent scalability because they can be shared and need not be created for each client.

We use the `@Stateless` annotation to create a stateless session bean.

Singleton session bean

As the name suggests, there is only one instance of a singleton bean class in the EJB container (this is true in the clustered environment too; each EJB container will have an instance of a singleton bean). This means that they are shared by multiple clients, and they are not pooled by EJB containers (because there can be only one instance). Since a singleton session bean is a shared resource, we need to manage concurrency in it. Java EE provides two concurrency management options for singleton session beans, namely container-managed concurrency and bean-managed concurrency. Container-managed concurrency can be easily specified by annotations. See `https://docs.oracle.com/javaee/7/tutorial/ejb-basicexamples002.htm#GIPSZ` for more information on managing concurrency in singleton session beans. The use of a singleton bean could have an impact on the scalability of the application if there are resource contentions in the code.

We use the `@Singleton` annotation to create a singleton session bean.

Accessing session bean from the client

Session beans can be designed to be accessed locally (within the same application as session beans) or remotely (from a client running in a different application or JVM) or both. In the case of remote access, session beans are required to implement a remote interface. For local access, session beans can implement a local interface or implement no interface (the no-interface view of a session bean). The remote and local interfaces that the session bean implements are sometimes also called business interfaces because they typically expose the primary business functionality.

Creating a no-interface session

To create a session bean with the no-interface view, create a POJO and annotate it with the appropriate EJB annotation type and `@LocalBean`. For example, we can create a local stateful student bean as follows:

```
import javax.ejb.LocalBean;
import javax.ejb.Singleton;

@Singleton
@LocalBean
public class Student {
...
}
```

Accessing session bean using dependency injection

You can access session beans by either using the `@EJB` annotation (for dependency injection) or performing the **JNDI** (which stands for **Java Naming and Directory Interface**) lookup. EJB containers are required to make the JNDI URLs of EJBs available to clients.

Dependency injection of session beans using `@EJB` works only for managed components, that is, components of the application whose lifecycle is managed by the EJB container. When a component is managed by the container, it is created (instantiated) and destroyed by the container. You do not create managed components by using the `new` operator. JEE-managed components that support the direct injection of EJBs are Servlets, managed beans of JSF pages, and EJBs themselves (one EJB can have another EJB injected into it). Unfortunately, you cannot have a web container inject EJBs in JSPs or JSP beans. Further, you cannot have EJBs injected into any custom classes that you create and that are instantiated using the `new` operator. Later in the chapter, we will see how to use JNDI to access EJBs from objects that are not managed by the container.

We could use a student bean (created previously) from a managed bean of JSF as follows:

```
import javax.ejb.EJB;
import javax.faces.bean.ManagedBean;

@ManagedBean
public class StudentJSFBean {
  @EJB
  private Student studentEJB;
}
```

Note that if you create EJB with the no-interface view, then all public methods in that EJB will be exposed to clients. If you want to control what methods could be called by clients, then you should implement a business interface.

Creating session bean using the local business interface

The business interface for EJB is a simple Java Interface with either the `@Remote` or the `@Local` annotation. Therefore, we can create a local interface for a student bean as follows:

```
import java.util.List;
import javax.ejb.Local;

@Local
public interface StudentLocal {
  public List<Course> getCourses();
}
```

Further, we can implement a session bean as follows:

```
import java.util.List;
import javax.ejb.Local;
import javax.ejb.Stateful;

@Stateful
@Local
public class Student implements StudentLocal {
  @Override
  public List<CourseDTO> getCourses() {
    //get courses are return
...
  }
}
```

Clients can access the `Student` EJB only through the local interface.

```
import javax.ejb.EJB;
import javax.faces.bean.ManagedBean;

@ManagedBean
public class StudentJSFBean {
  @EJB
  private StudentLocal student;
}
```

A session bean can implement multiple business interfaces.

Accessing session bean using the JNDI lookup

Although accessing EJB using dependency injection is the easiest way, it works only if the container manages the class that accesses the EJB. If you want to access EJB from a POJO that is not a managed bean, then dependency injection will not work. Another scenario where dependency injection does not work is when EJB is deployed in a separate JVM (could be on a remote server). In such cases, you will have to access EJB using JNDI lookup (visit https://docs.oracle.com/javase/tutorial/jndi/ for more information on JNDI.).

JEE applications could be packaged in **EAR** (which stands for **enterprise application archive**), which contains a .jar file for EJBs and a .war file for web applications (and a lib folder containing libraries required for both). If, for example, the name of an EAR file is CourseManagement.ear and the name of the EJB JAR in it is CourseManagementEJBs.jar, then the name of the application is CourseManagement (name of the EAR file) and the module name is CourseManagementEJBs. The EJB container uses these names to create a JNDI URL for the lookup EJBs. A global JNDI URL for EJB is created as follows:

```
"java:global/<application_name>/<module_name>/<bean_name>![<bean_
interface>]"
```

- java:global indicates that it is a global JNDI URL.
- <application_name> is typically the name of the EAR file.
- <module_name> is the name of the EJB JAR.
- <bean_name> is the name of the EJB bean class.
- <bean_interface> is optional if EJB has a no-interface view, or if EJB implements only one business interface. Else, it is a fully qualified name of a business interface.

EJB containers are also required to publish two more variations of JNDI URLs for each EJB. These are not global URLs, which means that they can't be used to access EJBs from clients that are not in the same JEE application (in the same EAR).

- "java:app/[<module_name>]/<bean_name>![<bean_interface>]"
- "java:module/<bean_name>![<bean_interface>]"

The first URL can be used if the EJB client is in the same application, and the second URL can be used if the client is in the same module (the same .jar file as the EJB).

Before you look up any URL in a JNDI server, you need to create InitialContext, which includes information, among other things, such as the host name of the JNDI server and the port on which it is running. If you create `InitialContext` in the same server, then there is no need to specify these attributes.

```
InitialContext initCtx  = new InitialContext();
Object obj = initCtx.lookup("jndi_url");
```

We can use the following JNDI URLs to access no-interface (`LocalBean`) `Student` EJB (assuming that the name of the EAR file is `CourseManagement` and the name of the `.jar` file for EJBs is `CourseManagementEJBs`).

URL	When to use
`java:global/CourseManagement/CourseManagementEJBs/Student`	The client can be anywhere in the EAR file, because we use a global URL. Note that we haven't specified the interface name because we are assuming that a student bean provides the no-interface view in this example.
`java:app/CourseManagementEJBs/Student`	The client can be anywhere in the EAR. We skipped the application name because the client is expected to be in the same application, because the namespace of the URL is `java:app`.
`java:module/Student`	The client must be in the same `.jar` file as EJB.

We can use the following JNDI URLs for accessing Student EJB that implemented a local interface called `StudentLocal`:

URL	When to use
`java:global/CourseManagement/CourseManagementEJBs/Student!packt.jee.book.ch6.StudentLocal`	The client can be anywhere in the EAR file, because we use a global URL.
`java:global/CourseManagement/CourseManagementEJBs/Student`	The client can be anywhere in the EAR. We skipped the interface name because the bean implements only one business interface. Note that the object returned from this call will be of the `StudentLocal` type, and not the `Student` type.

URL	When to use

`java:app/CourseManagementEJBs/Student`
Or
`java:app/CourseManagementEJBs/Student!packt.jee.book.ch6.StudentLocal`
	The client can be anywhere in the EAR. We skipped the application name because the JNDI namespace is `java:app`.

`java:module/Student`
Or
`java:module/Student!packt.jee.book.ch6.StudentLocal`
	The client must be in the same EAR as the EJB.

Here is an example of how we can call a student bean with a local business interface from one of the objects (that is not managed by the web container) in our web application:

```
InitialContext ctx = new InitialContext();
StudentLocal student = (StudentLocal) ctx.loopup
("java:app/CourseManagementEJBs/Student");
return student.getCourses(id) ; //get courses from Student EJB
```

Creating session bean using a remote business interface

If a session bean that you create is going to be accessed by a client object that is not in the same JVM as the bean, then the bean needs to implement a remote business interface. You create a remote business interface by using the `@Remote` annotation.

```
import java.util.List;
import javax.ejb.Remote;

@Remote
public interface StudentRemote {
  public List<CourseDTO> getCourses();
}
```

The EJB implementing the remote interface is also annotated with `@Remote`.

```
@Stateful
@Remote
public class Student implements StudentRemote {
  @Override
  public List<CourseDTO> getCourses() {
    //get courses are return
...
  }
}
```

Remote EJBs can be injected into managed objects in the same application by using the `@EJB` annotation. For example, a JSF bean can access the previously mentioned student bean (in the same application) as follows:

```
import javax.ejb.EJB;
import javax.faces.bean.ManagedBean;

@ManagedBean
public class StudentJSFBean {
  @EJB
  private StudentRemote student;
}
```

Accessing a remote session bean

We can use the following JNDI URLs for accessing the remote `Student` EJB:

URL	When to use
`java:global/CourseManagement/CourseManagementEJBs/Student!packt.jee.book.ch6.StudentRemote`	The client can be in the same application or remote. In case of a remote client, we need to set up proper `InitialContext` parameters.
`java:global/CourseManagement/CourseManagementEJBs/Student`	The client can be in the same application or remote. We skipped the interface name because the bean implements only one business interface.

URL	When to use

`java:app/CourseManagementEJBs/Student`
Or
`java:app/CourseManagementEJBs/Student!packt.jee.book.ch6.StudentRemote`
	The client can be anywhere in the EAR. We skipped the application name because the JNDI namespace is `java:app`.

`java:module/Student`
Or
`java:module/Student!packt.jee.book.ch6.StudentRemote`
	The client must be in the same EAR as the EJB.

To access EJBs from a remote client, you need to use a JNDI lookup method. Further, you need to set up `InitialContext` with certain properties; some of them are JEE application server specific. See `https://glassfish.java.net/javaee5/ejb/EJB_FAQ.html#nonJavaEEwebcontainerRemoteEJB` for information on the properties to be set in GlassFish. If the remote EJB and the client are both deployed in GlassFish (different instances of GlassFish), then you can look up the remote EJB as follows:

```
Properties jndiProperties = new Properties();
jndiProperties.setProperty("org.omg.CORBA.ORBInitialHost",
"<remote_host>");
//target ORB port. default is 3700 in Glassfish
jndiProperties.setProperty("org.omg.CORBA.ORBInitialPort",
"3700");

InitialContext ctx = new InitialContext(jndiProperties);
StudentRemote student =
(StudentRemote)ctx.lookup("java:app/CourseManagementEJBs/Student");
return student.getCourses();
```

Configuring the GlassFish server in Eclipse

We are going to use the GlassFish application server in this chapter. We have already seen how to install GlassFish in the *Installing GlassFish server* section of *Chapter 1, Introducing JEE and Eclipse*.

We will first configure the GlassFish server in Eclipse JEE.

1. To configure the GlassFish server in Eclipse EE, make sure that you are in the **Java EE** perspective in Eclipse. Right-click in the **Servers** view and select **New | Server**.

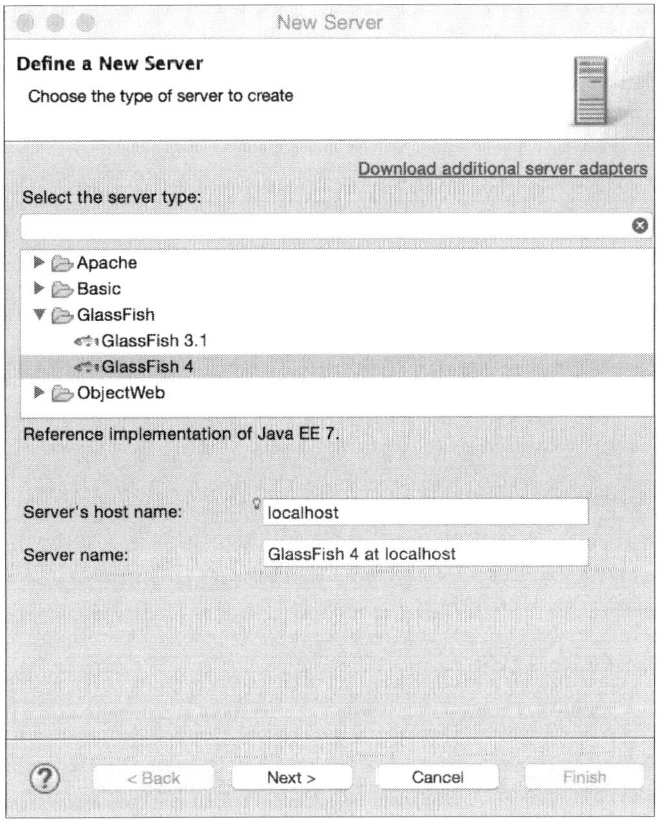

Figure 7.1 Define GlassFish 4 server in Eclipse EE

2. Select the **GlassFish 4** server and click **Next**.

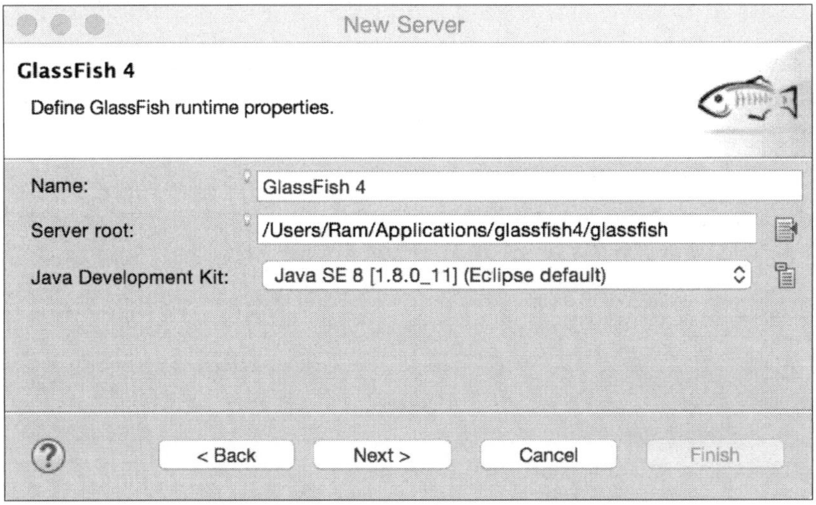

Figure 7.2 Define GlassFish runtime properties

3. Enter the path of the GlassFish 4 server on your local machine in the **Server Root** field and click **Next**.

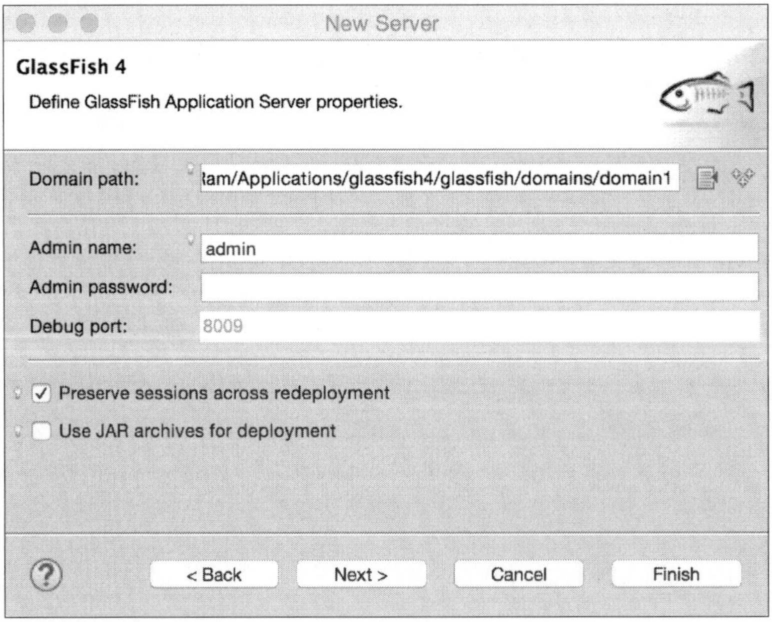

Figure 7.3 Define GlassFish server properties

4. The default domain after you install GlassFish is `domain1`. If you have not changed the default domain in GlassFish after installation, then accept all the default options on this page, or change the values appropriately. We will assume that the domain name is the default one, that is, `domain1`. Click **Next**.
5. The next page allows you to deploy the existing Java EE projects in GlassFish 4. We don't have any projects to add at this point, so just click **Finish**.
6. The server is added to the **Servers** view. Right-click on the server and select **Start**. If the server is installed and configured properly, then the server status should change to **Started**.
7. To open the admin page of the server, right-click on the server and select **GlassFish | View Admin Console**. The admin page is opened in the built-in Eclipse browser. You can browse to the server home page by opening the `http://localhost:8080` URL. `8080` is the default GlassFish port.

Creating the CourseManagement application using EJB

Now, let's create the `CourseManagement` application that we created in *Chapter 4, Creating a JEE Database Application* by using EJBs. In *Chapter 4, Creating a JEE Database Application* we created service classes (which were POJOs) for writing the business logic. We will replace them with EJBs. We will start with creating Eclipse projects for EJBs.

Creating an EJB project in Eclipse

EJBs are packaged in a JAR file. Web applications are packaged in a **WAR** (which stands for **Web Application Archive**). If EJBs are to be accessed remotely, then the client needs to have access to business interfaces. Therefore, EJB business interfaces and shared objects are packaged in a separate JAR, called EJB client JAR. Further, if EJB and the web application are to be deployed as one single application, then they need to be packaged in **EAR** (which stands for **Enterprise Application Archive**).

So, in most cases an application with EJBs is not a single project but four different projects:

1. EJB project that creates EJB JAR.
2. EJB client project that contains business classes and shared (between EJB and client) classes.

3. Web project that generates WAR.
4. EAR project that generates EAR containing EBJ JAR, EJB client JAR, and WAR.

You can create each of these projects independently and integrate them. However, Eclipse gives you the option to create an EJB project, an EJB client project, and an EAR project with one wizard.

1. Select **File** | **New** | **EJB Project**. Type `CourseManagementEJBs` in the **Project name** textbox. Make sure that **Target runtime** is `Glassfish 4` and **EJB module version** is `3.2` or later. From the **Configuration** drop-down list, select `Default Configuration for Glassfish 4`. In the **EAR membership** group, check the **Add project to an EAR** box.

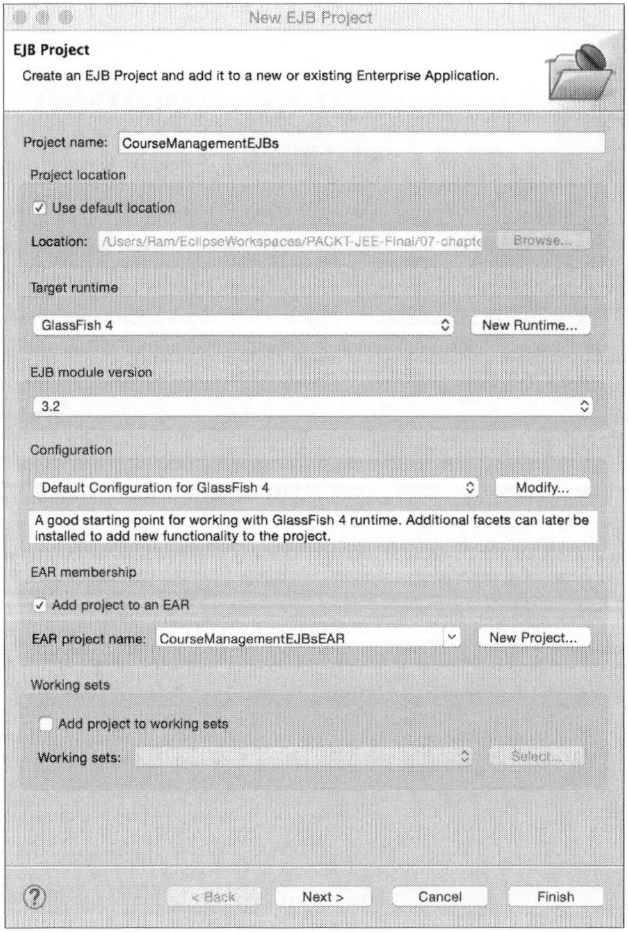

Figure 7.4 New EJB Project wizard

2. Select **Next**. On the next page, specify the source and output folders for the classes. Leave the defaults unchanged on this page.

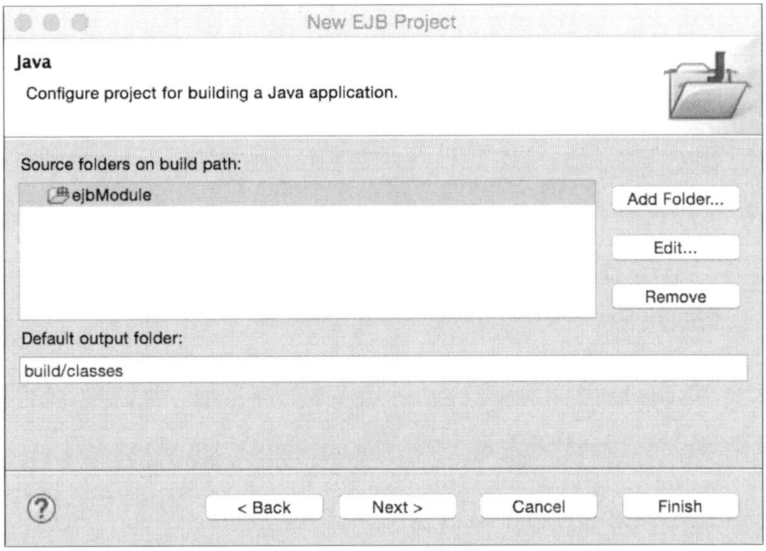

Figure 7.5 Select source and output folders

3. The source Java files in this project would be created in the `ejbModule` folder. Click **Next**.

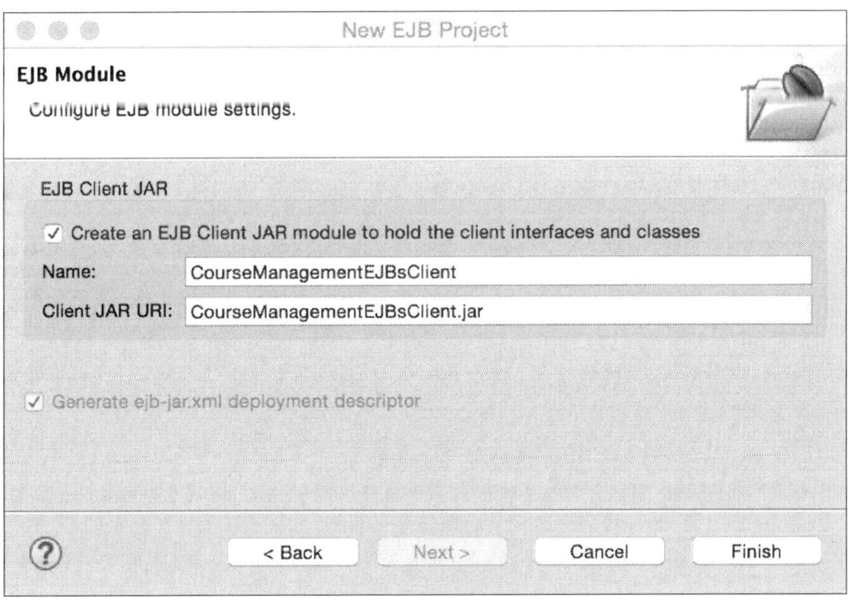

Figure 7.6 Create EJB client project

4. Eclipse gives an option to create an EJB client project. Select the option and click **Finish**.
5. Since we are building a web application, we will create a web project. Select **File | Dynamic Web Project**. Set the project name as `CourseManagementWeb`.

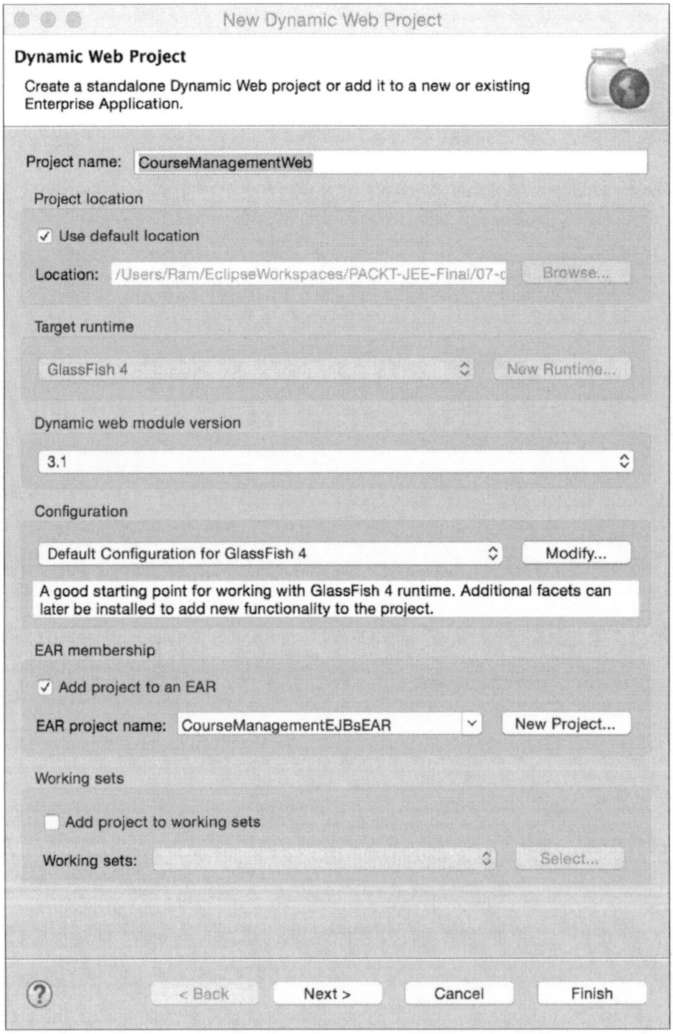

Figure 7.7 New Dynamic Web Project

6. Select the **Add Project to an EAR** checkbox. Since we have only one EAR project in the workspace, Eclipse selects this project from the drop-down list. Click **Finish**.

We now have the following four projects in the workspace.

Figure 7.8 Course Management projects

In the course management application, we will create a stateless EJB called `CourseBean`. We will use JPA (which stands for Java Persistence APIs) for data access and create `Course` entity. See *Chapter 4, Creating a JEE Database Application*, for details on using JPA. The `CourseManagementEJBClient` project will contain the EJB business interface and shared classes. In `CourseManagementWeb`, we will create a JSF page and a managed bean that will access `Course` EJB in the `CourseManagementEJBs` project to get a list of courses.

Configuring datasource in GlassFish 4

In *Chapter 4, Creating a JEE Database Application* we created the JDBC datasource locally in the application. In this chapter, we will create a JDBC datasource in GlassFish 4. The GlassFish 4 server is not packaged with the JDBC driver for MySQL. So, we need to place the `.jar` file for `MySQLDriver` in the path where GlassFish can find it. You can place such external libraries in the `lib/ext` folder of the GlassFish domain in which you will deploy your application. For this example, we will copy the JAR in `<glassfish_home>/glassfish/domains/domain1/lib/ext`.

If you do not have the MySQL JDBC driver, you can download it from `http://dev.mysql.com/downloads/connector/j/`.

1. Open the GlassFish admin console, either by right-clicking on the server in the **Servers** view and selecting **GlassFish** | **View Admin Console** (this opens admin console inside Eclipse) or browsing to `http://localhost:4848` (`4848` is the default port to which the GlassFish admin console application listens). In the admin console, select **Resources** | **JDBC** | **JDBC Connection Pools**. Click the **New** button in the **JDBC Connection Pool** page of GlassFish.

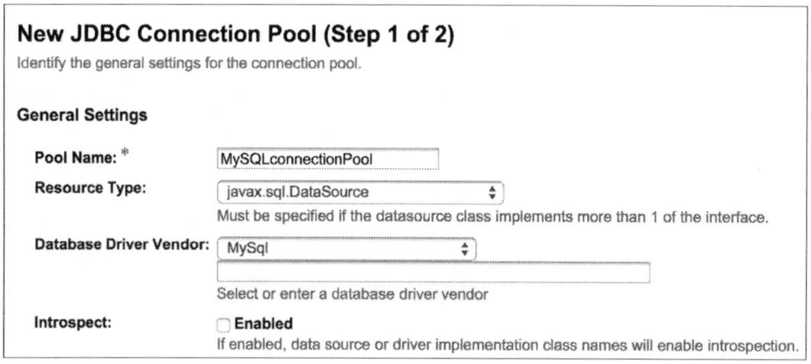

Figure 7.9 Create JDBC Connection Pool in GlassFish

2. Set **Pool Name** as `MySQLconnectionPool` and select `javax.sql.Datasource` as **Resource Type**. Select `MySql` from the **Database Driver Vendor** list and click **Next**. In the next page, select the correct **Datasource Classname** (`com.mysql.jdbc.jdbc2.optional.MysqlDatasource`) on the basis of our selection of the MySQL database in the previous page.

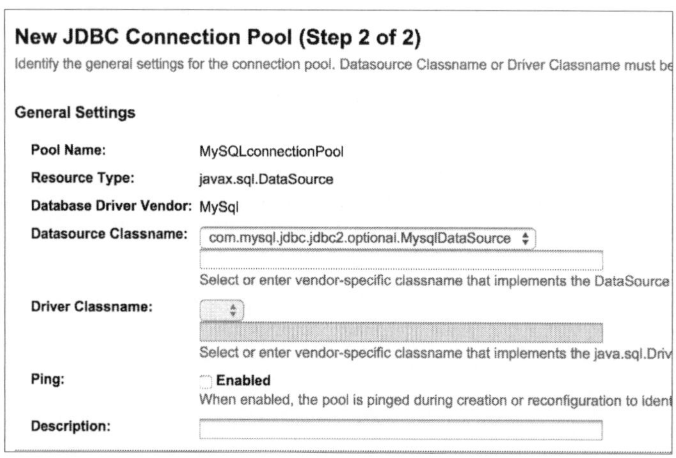

Figure 7.10 JDBC Connection Pool settings 2 in GlassFish

3. We need to set the host name, port, user name, and password of MySQL. Scroll down the page to the **Additional Properties** section.

Port/PortNumber	3306
DatabaseName	<schemaname_of_coursemanagement> for example, course_management. See *Chapter 4, Creating a JEE Database Application* for details on creating the MySQL schema for the Course Management database.
Password	MySQL database password.
URL/Url	jdbc:mysql://:3306/<database_name> for example, jdbc:mysql://:3306/course_management
ServerName	localhost
User	MySQL username

4. Click **Finish**. The new connection pool is added to the list in the left pane. Click on the newly added connection pool. In the **General** tab, click on the **Ping** button and make sure that the ping is successful.

Figure 7.11 Test JDBC Connection Pool in GlassFish

5. Next, we need to create a JNDI resource for this connection pool so that it can be accessed from the client application. Select the **Resources** | **JDBC** | **JDBC Resources** node in the left pane. Click the **New** button to create a new JDBC resource.

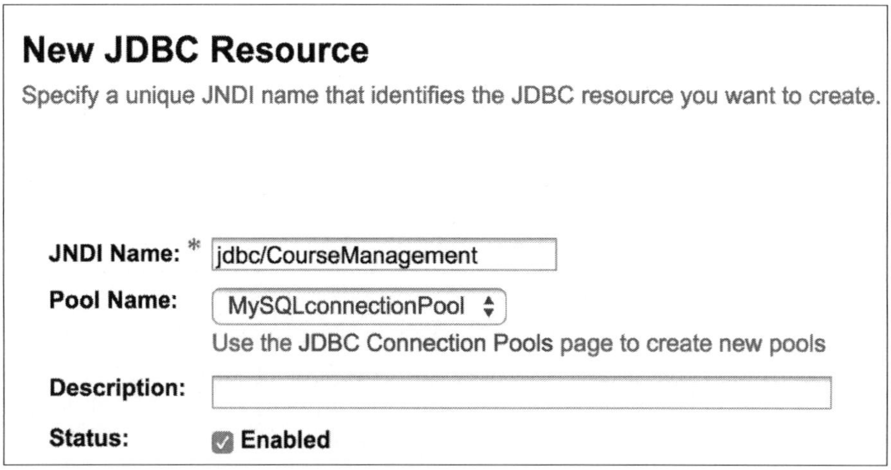

Figure 7.12 Test JDBC Connection Pool in GlassFish

6. Set **JNDI Name** as `jdbc/CourseManagement`. From the **Pool Name** drop-down list, select the connection pool that we created for MySQL, `MySQLconnectionPool`. Click **Save**.

Configuring JPA

We will now configure our EJB project to use JPA to access the MySQL database. We have already seen how to enable JPA for an Eclipse project in *Chapter 4, Creating a JEE Database Application*.

However, we will briefly cover the steps here again.

1. Right-click on the `CourseManagementEJBs` project in **Project Explorer** and select **Configure** | **Convert to JPA Project**. Eclipse opens the **Project Facets** window.

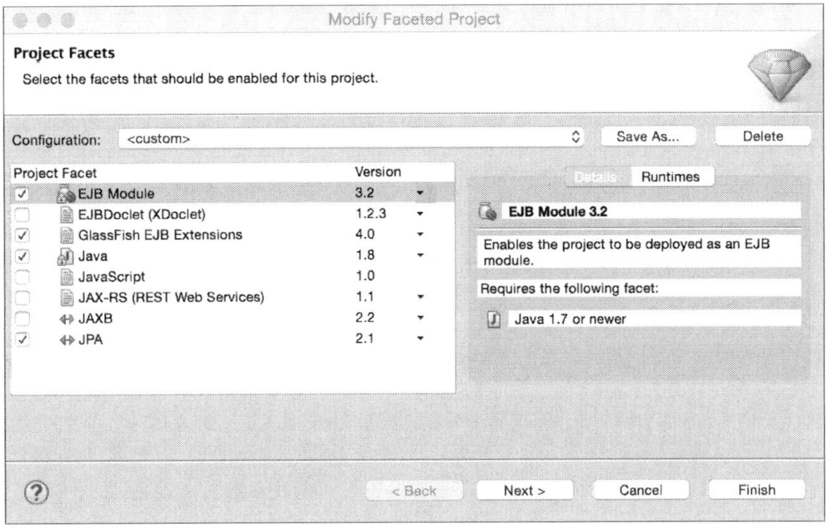

Figure 7.13 Eclipse Project Facets

2. Click **Next** to go to the **JPA Facet** page.

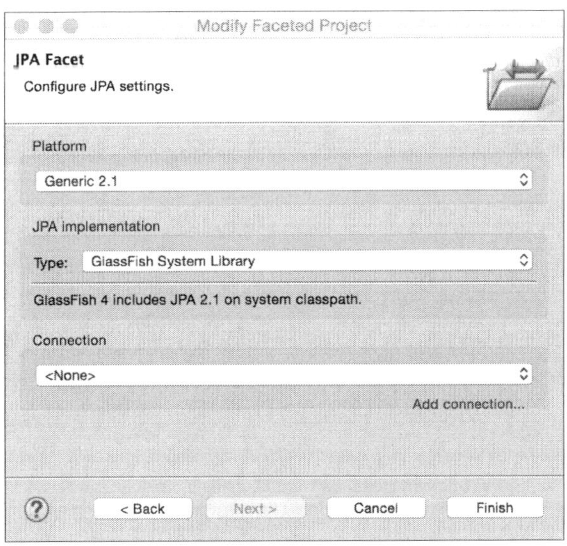

Figure 7.14 JPA Facet

Keep the default values unchanged, and click **Finish**. Eclipse adds `persistence.xml` required by JPA to the project, under the **JPA Content** group in **Project Explorer**. We need to configure the JPA datasource in `persistence.xml`. Open `persistence.xml` and click on the **Connection** tab. Set **Transaction Type** to `JTA`. In the **JTA datasource** textbox, type JNDI name that we set up for our MySQL database in the previous section, as `jdbc/CourseManagement`. Save the file. Note that the actual location of `persistence.xml` is `ejbModule/META-INF`.

Now, let's create a database connection in Eclipse and link it with the JPA properties of the project so that we can create JPA entities from the database tables. Right-click on the `CourseManagementEJBs` project and select **Properties**. This opens the **Project Properties** window. Click on the **JPA** node. Click on the **Add connection** link just below the **Connection** drop-down box. We have already seen how to set up a database connection in the *Using Eclipse Data Source Explorer* section of *Chapter 4, Creating a JEE Database Application*. However, we will quickly recap the steps:

1. In the **Connection Profile** window, select MySQL.

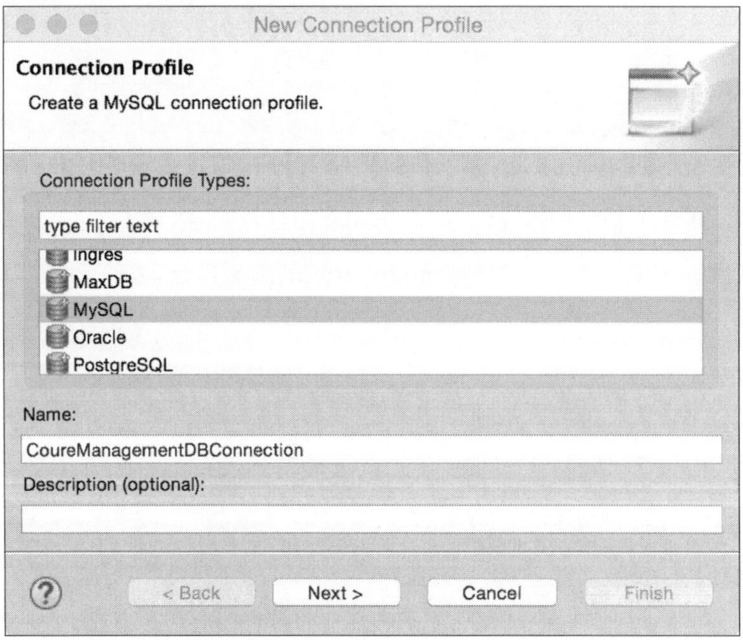

Figure 7.15 New DB Connection Profile

2. Type `CourseManagementDBConnection` in the name textbox and click **Next**. In the **New Connection Profile** window, click on the new connection profile button (the circle next to the **Drivers** drop-down box) to open the **New Driver Definition** window. Select the appropriate **MySQL JDBC Driver** version and click on the **JAR List** tab. Remove any existing `.jar` file from the list if you see an error, and click on the **Add JAR/Zip** button. Browse to the MySQL JDBC driver JAR that we saved in the `<glassfish_home>/glassfish/domains/domain1/lib/ext` folder. Click **OK**. Back in the **New Connection Profile** window, enter the database name, modify the connection URL, and enter **User name** and **Password**.

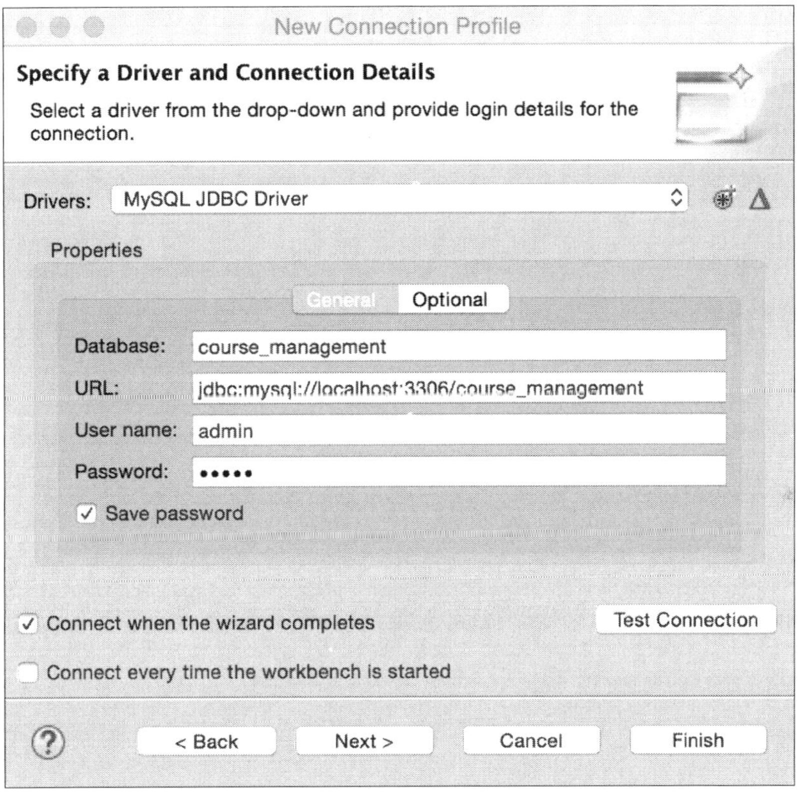

Figure 7.16 Configure MySQL Database Connection

3. Select the **Save password** checkbox. Click the **Test Connection** button and make sure that the test is successful. Click the **Finish** button. Back on the JPA properties page, the new connection is added and the appropriate schema is selected.

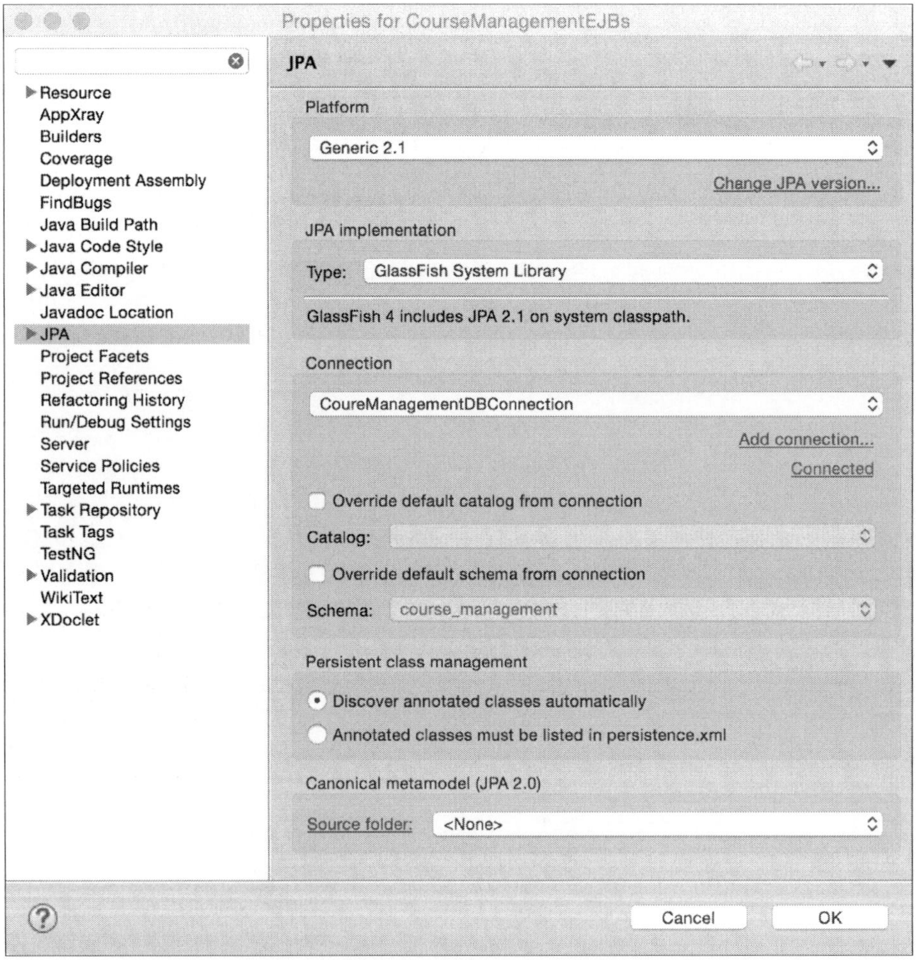

Figure 7.17 Connection Added to JPA project properties

4. Click **OK** to save the changes.

Creating a JPA entity

We will now create an entity class for `Course` by using Eclipse JPA tools.

1. Right-click on the `CourseManagementEJBs` project, and select **JPA Tool | Generate Entities from Tables**.

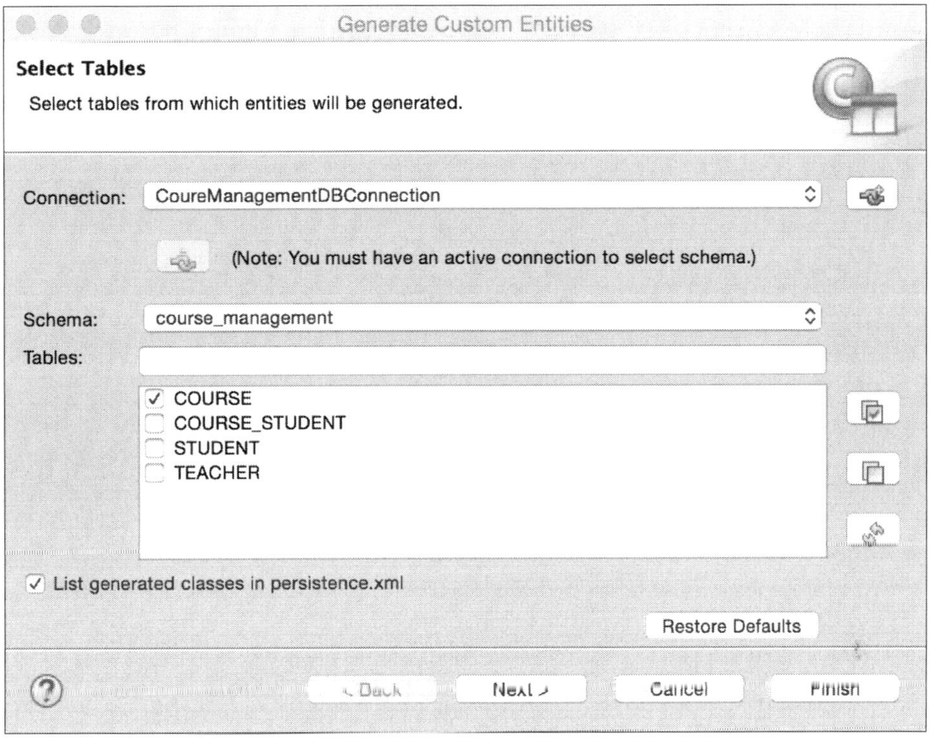

Figure 7.18 Create entity from table

2. Select the **Course** table and click **Next**. Click **Next** in the **Table Associations** window. On the next page, select `identity` as **Key generator**.

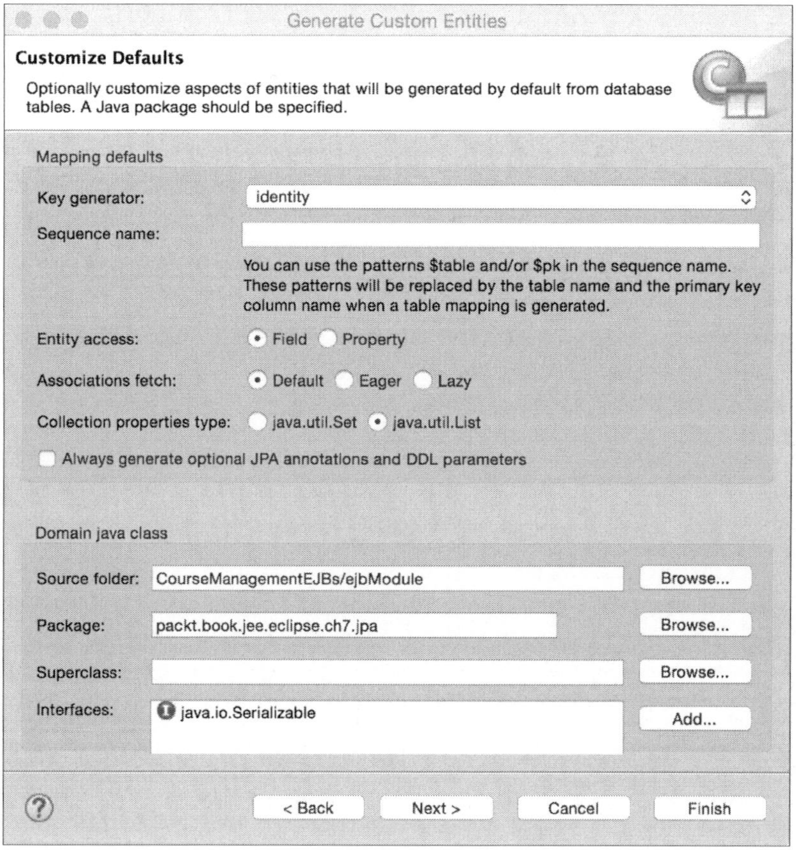

Figure 7.19 Customize JPA entity details

3. Enter the package name. We do not want to change anything on the next page, so click **Finish**. Notice that the wizard creates a `findAll` query for the class that we can use to get all courses.

```
@Entity
@NamedQuery(name="Course.findAll", query="SELECT c FROM
Course c")
public class Course implements Serializable { …}
```

Creating stateless EJB

We will now create stateless EJB.

1. Right-click on the `ejbModule` folder of the `CourseManagementEJBs` project and select **New** | **Session Bean (3.x)**. Type `packt.book.jee.eclipse.ch7.ejb` in the **Java package** textbox and `CourseBean` in **Class name**. Select the **Remote** checkbox.

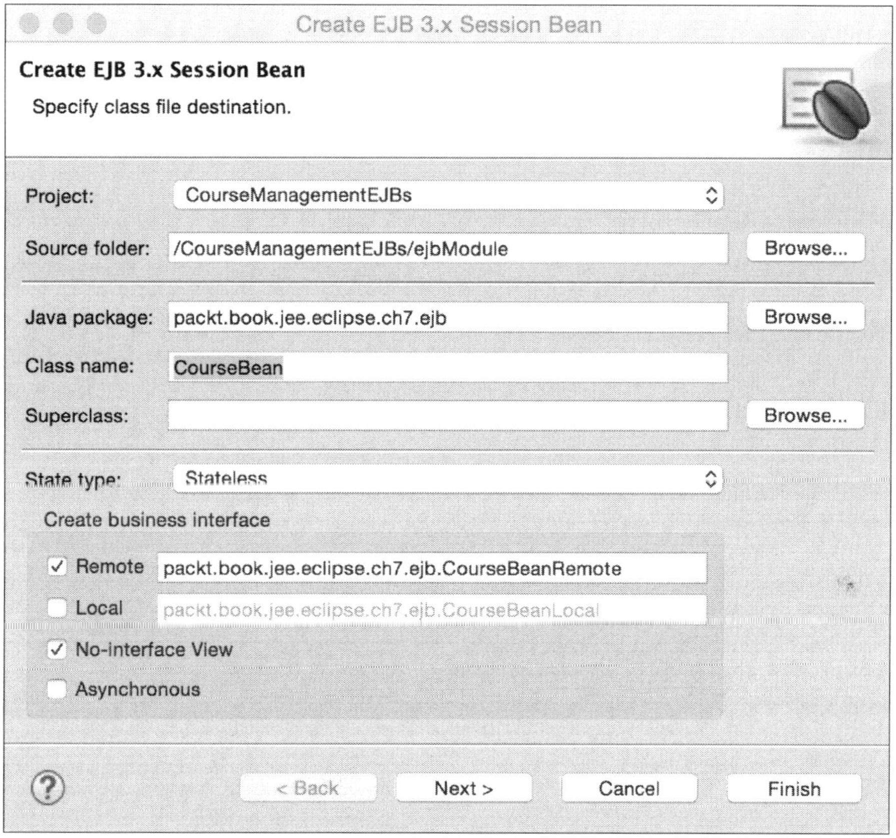

Figure 7.20 Create stateless session bean

2. Click **Next**. No change is required on the next page.

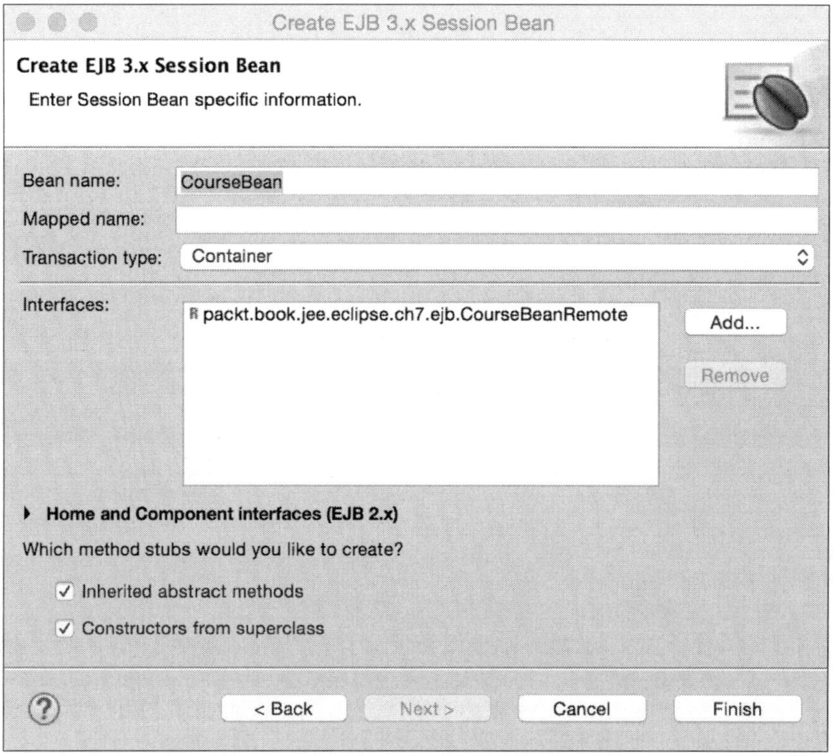

Figure 7.21 Stateless session bean information

3. Click **Finish**. The `CourseBean` class is created with the `@Stateless` and `@Localbean` annotations. The class also implements the `CourseBeanRemote` interface, which is defined in the `CourseManagementEJBClient` project because it is a shared interface (a client calling EJB needs to access this interface).

```
@Stateless
@LocalBean
public class CourseBean implements CourseBeanRemote {
    public CourseBean() {
    }
}
```

The interface is annotated with `@Remote`.

```
@Remote
public interface CourseBeanRemote {

}
```

Now, the question is how do we return `Course` information from EJB? EJB would call JPA APIs to get the instances of `Course` entity, but do we want EJB to return the instances of `Course` entity or should it return the instances of lightweight DTO (which stands for data transfer object)? Each has its own advantages. If we return `Course` entity, then we do not need to transfer data between objects, which we will have to in case of DTO (transfer the data of entity to the corresponding DTO). However, passing entities between layers may not be a good idea if the EJB client is not in the same application, and you may not want to expose your data model to external applications. Further, by passing back JPA entities, you are forcing the client application to depend on JPA libraries in its implementation.

DTOs are lightweight, and you can expose only those fields that you want your clients to use. However, you will have to transfer data between entities and DTOs.

If your EJBs are going to be used by the client in the same application, then it could be easier to transfer Entities to the client from EJB. However, if your client is not part of the same EJB application or when you want to expose EJB as a web service (we will see how to create web services in *Chapter 9, Creating Web Services*), then you may need to use DTOs.

In our application, we will see an example of both the approaches, that is, the EJB method returning JPA entities as well as DTOs. Remember that we have created `CourseBean` as a remote as well as a local bean (no-interface view). Implementation of the remote interface method will return DTOs and that of the local method will return JPA entities.

We will add the `getCourses` method to the EJB. We will create `CourseDTO`, a data transfer object, which is a POJO and returns instances of that from `getCourses`. This DTO needs to be in the `CourseManagementEJBsClient` project because it will be a shared class between EJB and its client.

Create the following class in the `packt.book.jee.eclipse.ch7.dto` package in the `CourseManagementEJBsClient` project:

```
package packt.book.jee.eclipse.ch7.dto;

public class CourseDTO {
  private int id;
  private int credits;
  private String name;
  public int getId() {
    return id;
  }
  public void setId(int id) {
    this.id = id;
  }
  public int getCredits() {
    return credits;
  }
  public void setCredits(int credits) {
    this.credits = credits;
  }
  public String getName() {
    return name;
  }
  public void setName(String name) {
    this.name = name;
  }
}
```

Add the following method to `CourseBeanRemote`:

```
public List<CourseDTO> getCourses();
```

We need to implement this method in CourseBean EJB. To get the courses from the database, the EJB needs to first get an instance of `EntityManager`. Recall that in *Chapter 4, Creating a JEE Database Application* we created `EntityManagerFactory` and got an instance of `EntityManager` from it. Then, we passed this instance of `EntityManager` to the service class, which actually got the data from the database by using JPA APIs.

JEE application servers make injecting `EntityManager` very easy. You just need to create an `EntityManager` field in EJB and annotate it with `@PersistenceContext(unitName="<name_as_specified_in_persistence.xml>")`. The `unitName` attribute is optional if there is only one persistence unit defined in `persistence.xml`. Open the `CourseBean` class and add the following declaration:

```
@PersistenceContext
EntityManager entityManager;
```

EJBs are managed objects, and the EJB container injects `EntityManager` after the EJBs are created. This is a part of the JEE feature called **CDI** (which stands for **Context and Dependency Injection**). See `https://docs.oracle.com/javaee/7/tutorial/partcdi.htm#GJBNR` for information on CDI.

We will add a function to `CourseBean` EJB that will return a list of `Course` entities. This function will be called by the `getCourses` method in the same EJB, which will then convert the list of entities to DTOs and can also be called by a web application, because the EJB exposes the no-interface view (by using the `@LocalBean` annotation).

```
public List<Course> getCourseEntities() {
//Use named query created in Course entity using @NameQuery
annotation.
      TypedQuery<Course> courseQuery =
entityManager.createNamedQuery("Course.findAll", Course.class);
      return courseQuery.getResultList();
}
```

After implementing the `getCourses` method (defined in our remote business interface called `CourseBeanRemote`), we have `CourseBean` as follows:

```
@Stateless
@LocalBean
public class CourseBean implements CourseBeanRemote {
  @PersistenceContext
  EntityManager entityManager;

    public CourseBean() {
    }

    public List<Course> getCourseEntities() {
      //Use named query created in Course entity using @NameQuery
      annotation.
```

```
        TypedQuery<Course> courseQuery =
entityManager.createNamedQuery("Course.findAll", Course.class);
        return courseQuery.getResultList();
      }

    @Override
    public List<CourseDTO> getCourses() {
      //get course entities first
      List<Course> courseEntities = getCourseEntities();

      //create list of course DTOs. This is the result we will
      return
      List<CourseDTO> courses = new ArrayList<CourseDTO>();

      for (Course courseEntity : courseEntities) {
        //Create CourseDTO from Course entity
        CourseDTO course = new CourseDTO();
        course.setId(courseEntity.getId());
        course.setName(courseEntity.getName());
        course.setCredits(course.getCredits());
        courses.add(course);
      }
      return courses;
    }
  }
```

Creating JSF and managed bean

We will now create a JSF page to display courses and a managed bean that will call the `getCourses` method of `CourseEJB`. See the *Java Server Faces* section in *Chapter 2, Creating a Simple JEE Web Application* for the details of JSF.

As discussed in *Chapter 2, Creating a Simple JEE Web Application* we need to add JSF Servlet and mapping to `web.xml`. Open `web.xml` from the `CourseManagementWeb` project. You can open this file either by double-clicking the **Deployment Descriptor | CourseManagementWeb** node or from the `WebContent\Web-INF` folder. Add the following servlet declaration and mapping (within the `web-app` node):

```
<servlet>
  <servlet-name>JSFServlet</servlet-name>
  <servlet-class>javax.faces.webapp.FacesServlet</servlet-class>
  <load-on-startup>1</load-on-startup>
```

```
</servlet>

<servlet-mapping>
  <servlet-name>JSFServlet</servlet-name>
  <url-pattern>*.xhtml</url-pattern>
</servlet-mapping>
```

The `CourseManagementWeb` project needs to access the business interface of EJB, which is in `CourseManagementEJBsClient`. So, we need to add the reference of `CourseManagementEJBsClient` to `CourseManagementWeb`. Open the project properties of `CourseManagementWeb` (right-click on the `CourseManagementWeb` project) and select **Java Build Path**. Click on the **Projects** tab, and click **Add**. Select `CourseManagementEJBsClient` from the list and click **OK**.

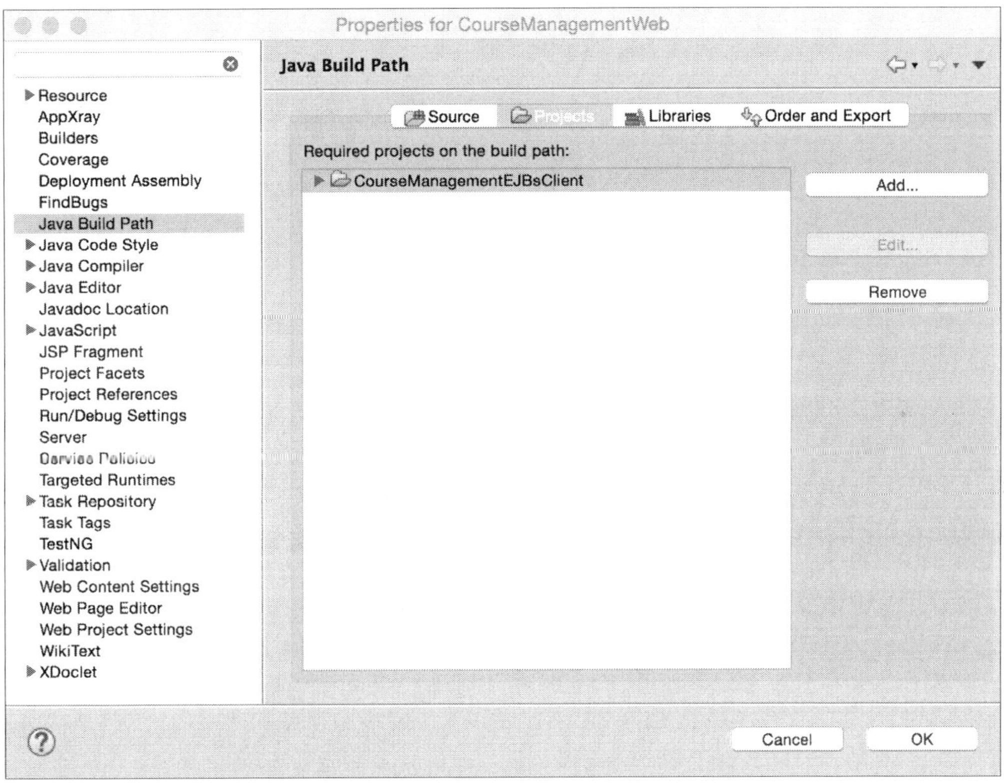

Figure 7.22 Add project reference

Now, let's now create a managed bean for JSF. Create the `CourseJSFBean` class in the `packt.book.jee.eclipse.ch7.web.bean` package in the `CourseManagementWeb` project (Java source files go in the `src` folder under the **Java Resources** group).

```
import java.util.List;
import javax.ejb.EJB;
import javax.faces.bean.ManagedBean;
import packt.book.jee.eclipse.ch7.dto.CourseDTO;
import packt.book.jee.eclipse.ch7.ejb.CourseBeanRemote;

@ManagedBean(name="Course")
public class CourseJSFBean {
  @EJB
  CourseBeanRemote courseBean;

  public List<CourseDTO> getCourses() {
    return courseBean.getCourses();
  }
}
```

JSF beans are managed beans, so we can have a container inject EJB by using the `@EJB` annotation. We referenced `CourseBean` with its remote interface, `CourseBeanRemote`.

We then created a method called `getCourses` that calls a method with the same name on `Course` EJB and returns the list of `CourseDTO` objects. Note that we have set the name attribute in the `@ManagedBean` annotation. This managed bean would be accessed from JSF with the variable name `Course`.

We will now create a JSF page, `course.xhtml`. Right-click on the **WebContent** group in the `CourseManagementWeb` project, and select **New** | **File**. Create `courses.xhtml`. Add the following content to it:

```
<html xmlns="http://www.w3.org/1999/xhtml"
 xmlns:f="http://java.sun.com/jsf/core"
 xmlns:h="http://java.sun.com/jsf/html">

<head>
```

```
    <title>Courses</title>
  </head>
  <body>
    <h2>Courses</h2>
    <h:dataTable value="#{Course.courses}" var="course">
        <h:column>
        <f:facet name="header">Name</f:facet>
        #{course.name}
      </h:column>
        <h:column>
        <f:facet name="header">Credits</f:facet>
        #{course.credits}
      </h:column>
    </h:dataTable>
  </body>
  </html>
```

The page uses the `dataTable` tag (`https://docs.oracle.com/javaee/7/javaserver-faces-2-2/vdldocs-jsp/h/dataTable.html`), which receives the data to populate from the `Course` managed bean (which is actually the `CourseJSFBean` class). `Course.courses` in the expression language syntax is a shortcut for `Course.getCourses()`. This results in the call `getCourses` method of the `CourseJSFBean` class.

Each element of the list returned by `Course.courses`, which is `List` of `CourseDTO`, is represented by the `course` variable (in the `var` attribute value). We then display the name and the credits of each course in the table by using the `column` child tag.

Running the example

Before we can run the example, we need to start GlassFish server and deploy our JEE application in it.

1. Start the GlassFish server.

2. Once it is started, right-click on the GlassFish server in the **Servers** view and select the **Add and Remove ...** menu option.

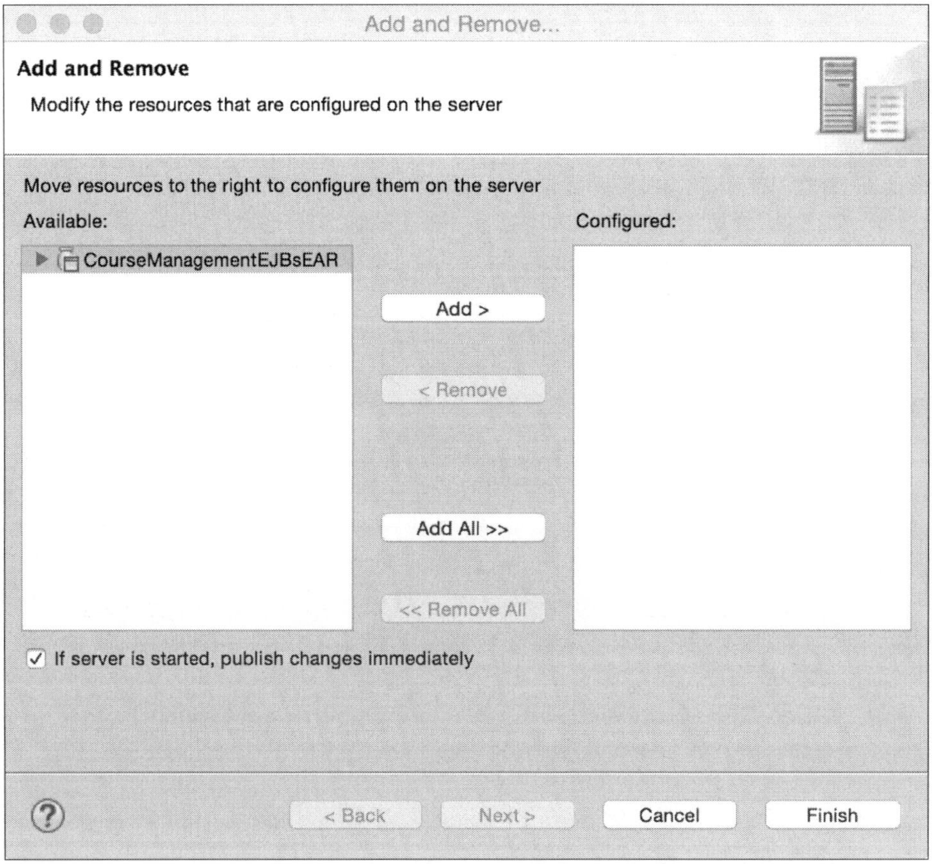

Figure 7.23 Add project to GlassFish for deployment

3. Select the EAR project and click on the **Add** button. Then, click **Finish**. The selected EAR application will be deployed in the server.

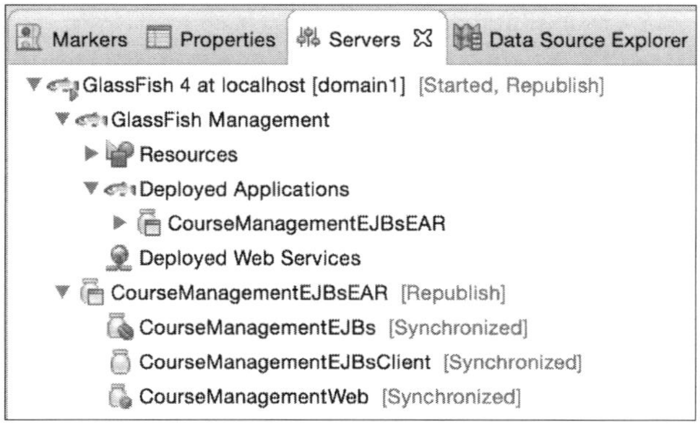

Figure 7.24 Application deployed in GlassFish

4. To run the JSF page, `course.xhtml`, right-click on it in **Project Explorer** and select **Run As | Run on Server**. The page would be opened in the internal Eclipse browser and courses in the MySQL database would be displayed on the page.

Note that we could use `CourseBean` (EJB) as a local bean in `CourseJSFBean` because they are in the same application deployed on the same server. To do this, add a reference of the `CourseManagementEJBs` project in the build path of `CourseManagementWeb` (open the project properties of `CourseManagementWeb`, select **Java Build Path**, select the **Projects** tab, and click the **Add** button. Select the `CourseManagementEJBs` project and add its reference).

Then, in the `CourseJSFBean` class, remove the declaration of `CourseBeanRemote` and add one for `CourseBean`.

```
//@EJB
//CourseBeanRemote courseBean;

@EJB
CourseBean courseBean;
```

When you make any changes in the code, the EAR project needs to be redeployed in the GlassFish server. In the Servers view, you can check whether redeployment is needed by checking the status of the server. If it is **[Started, Synchronized]**, then no redeployment is needed. However, if it is **[Started, Republish]**, then redeployment is required. Just click on the server node and select the **Publish** menu option.

Creating EAR for deployment outside Eclipse

We saw how to deploy an application to GlassFish from Eclipse. This works fine during development, but finally, you will need to create an EAR file for deployment to the external server. To create the EAR file from the project, right-click on the EAR project (in our example, it is `CourseManagementEJBsEAR`) and select **Export** | **EAR file**.

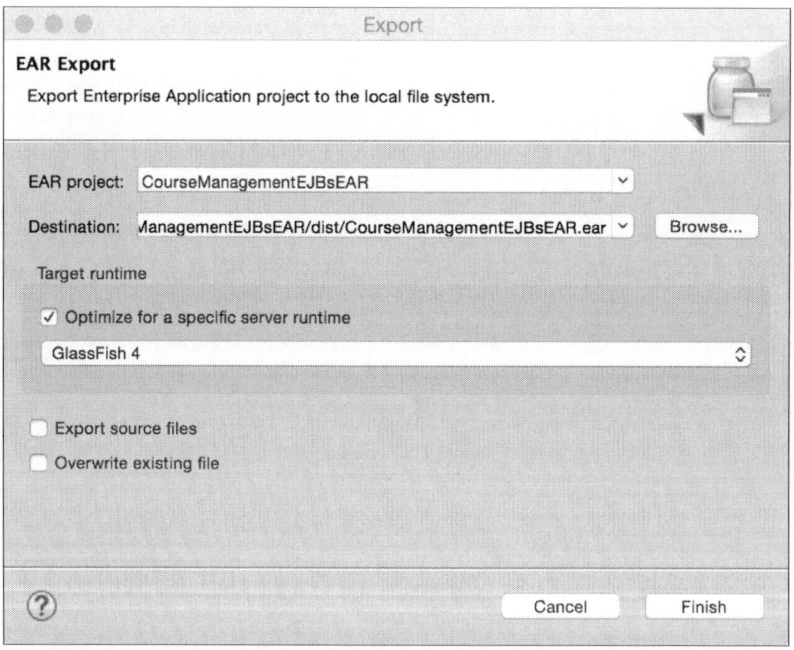

Figure 7.25 Exporting to EAR file

Select the destination folder, and click **Finish**. This file can then be deployed in GlassFish by using the management console or by copying it to the `autodeploy` folder in GlassFish.

Creating a JEE project using Maven

In this section, we will discuss how to create JEE projects with EJBs using Maven. Creating Maven projects may be preferable than Eclipse JEE projects because builds can be automated. We have seen many details of creating EJBs, JPA entities, and other classes in the previous section, so we won't repeat all this information here. We have also seen how to create Maven projects in *Chapter 2, Creating a Simple JEE Web Application* and *Chapter 3, Source Control Management in Eclipse* so the basic details of creating a Maven project will not be repeated either. We will focus mainly on how to create EJB projects using Maven. We will create the following projects:

- `CourseManagementMavenEJBs`: This project contains EJBs
- `CourseManagementMavenEJBClient`: This project contains shared interfaces and objects between an EJB project and the client projects
- `CourseManagementMavenWAR`: This is a web project containing a JSF page and a managed bean
- `CourseManagementMavenEAR`: This project creates an EAR file that could be deployed in GlassFish
- `CourseManagement`: This project is an overall parent project that builds all the previously mentioned projects

We still start with `CourseManagementMavenEJBs`. This project should generate an EJB JAR file. Create a Maven project with the following details:

Group ID	`packt.book.jee.eclipse.ch7.maven`
Artifact ID	`CourseManagementMavenEJBClient`
Version	`1`
Packaging	`Jar`

We need to add a dependency of JEE APIs to our EJB project. We add a dependency of `javax.javaee-api`. Since we are going to deploy this project in GlassFish, which comes with its own JEE implementation and libraries, we will scope this dependency as provided. Add the following in `pom.xml`:

```
<dependencies>
  <dependency>
    <groupId>javax</groupId>
    <artifactId>javaee-api</artifactId>
    <version>7.0</version>
```

```
        <scope>provided</scope>
    </dependency>
</dependencies>
```

When we create EJBs in this project, we need to create local or remote business interfaces in a shared project (client project). Therefore, we will create `CourseManagementMavenEJBClient` with the following details:

Group ID	`packt.book.jee.eclipse.ch7.maven`
Artifact ID	`CourseManagementMavenEJBs`
Version	`1`
Packaging	`Jar`

This shared project also needs to access EJB annotations. So, add the same dependency for `javax.javaee-api` that we added previously to the `pom.xml` file of the `CourseManagementMavenEJBClient` project.

We will create the `packt.book.jee.eclipse.ch7.ejb` package in this project and create a remote interface. Create the `CourseBeanRemote` interface (just as we created in the *Creating stateless EJB* section). Further, create a `CourseDTO` class in the `packt.book.jee.eclipse.ch7.dto` package. This class is the same as the one we created in the *Creating stateless EJB* section.

We are going to create a `Course` JPA entity in `CourseManagementMavenEJBs`. Before we do that, let's convert this project to the JPA project. Right-click on the project in **Package Explorer** and select **Configure | Convert to JPA Project**. In the JPA configuration wizard, select the following JPA facet details:

Platform	`Generic 2.1`
JPA Implementation	`Disable Library Configuration`

JPA wizard creates a `META-INF` folder in the `src` folder of the project and creates `persistence.xml`. Open `persistence.xml` and click on the **Connection** tab. We have already created a MySQL datasource in GlassFish (see the *Configuring datasource in GlassFish 4* section). Enter the JNDI name of the datasource, `jdbc/CourseManagement`, in the **JTA data source** field.

Create a `Course` entity in `packt.book.jee.eclipse.ch7.jpa`, as described in the *Creating a JPA entity* section. Before we create EJB in this project, let's add an EJB facet to this project. Right-click on the project and select Properties. Click on the **Project Facets** group and check the **EJB Module** checkbox. Set the version to the latest one (as of writing this chapter, the latest version was 3.2). We will now create an implementation of the remote session bean interface that we created previously. Right-click on the `CourseManagementMavenEJBs` project, and select the **New | Session Bean** menu. Create an EJB class with the following details:

Java package	`packt.book.jee.eclipse.ch7.ejb`
Class name	`CourseBean`
State type	`Stateless`

Do not select any business interface, because we have already created the business interface in the `CourseManagementMavenEJBClient` project. Click **Next**. On the next page, select `CourseBeanRemote`. You will see Eclipse showing errors because `CourseManagementMavenEJBs` does not know about `CourseManagementMavenEJBClient`, which contains the `CourseBeanRemote` interface, used by `CourseBean` in the EJB project. Adding the Maven dependency (in `pom.xml`) of `CourseManagementMavenEJBClient` in `CourseManagementMavenEJBs` and implementing the `getCourses` method in the EJB class should fix the compilation errors. A complete implementation of `CourseBean` as described in the *Creating stateless EJB* section. Make sure that EJB is marked as `Remote`:

```
@Stateless
@Remote
public class CourseBean implements CourseBeanRemote {
...
}
```

Now, let's create a web application project for course management by using Maven. Create a Maven project with the following details:

Group ID	`packt.book.jee.eclipse.ch7.maven`
Artifact ID	`CourseManagementMavenWebApp`
Version	`1`
Packaging	`War`

To create `web.xml` for this project, right-click on the project and select **Java EE Tools | Generate Deployment Descriptor Stub**. The `web.xml` file is created in the `src/main/webapp/WEB-INF` folder. Open `web.xml` and add the Servlet definition and mapping for JSF (see the *Creating JSF and managed bean* section). Add a dependency of the `CourseManagementMavenEJBClient` project and `javax.javaee-api` in the `pom.xml` file of the `CourseManagementMavenWebApp` project so that the web project has access to the EJB business interface declared in the shared project and to the EJB annotations.

Now, create `CourseJSFBean` in the web project as described in the *Creating JSF and managed bean* section. Note that this will reference the remote interface of EJB in the managed bean as follows:

```
@ManagedBean(name="Course")
public class CourseJSFBean {
  @EJB
  CourseBeanRemote courseBean;

  public List<CourseDTO> getCourses() {
    return courseBean.getCourses();
  }
}
```

Create `course.xhtml` in the `webapp` folder as described in the *Creating JSF and managed bean* section.

We will now create `CourseManagementMavenEAR`. Create a Maven project with the following details:

Group ID	`packt.book.jee.eclipse.ch7.maven`
Artifact ID	`CourseManagementMavenEAR`
Version	`1`
Packaging	`Ear`

You will have to type `ear` in the Packaging file; there is no `ear` option in the drop-down list. Add a dependency of `web`, `ejb`, and client projects to the `pom.xml` file of the EAR project as follows:

```
<dependencies>
  <dependency>
    <groupId>packt.book.jee.eclipse.ch7.maven</groupId>
```

```
        <artifactId>CourseManagementMavenEJBClient</artifactId>
        <version>1</version>
      <type>jar</type>
      </dependency>
      <dependency>
        <groupId>packt.book.jee.eclipse.ch7.maven</groupId>
        <artifactId>CourseManagementMavenEJBs</artifactId>
        <version>1</version>
        <type>ejb</type>
      </dependency>
      <dependency>
        <groupId>packt.book.jee.eclipse.ch7.maven</groupId>
        <artifactId>CourseManagementMavenWebApp</artifactId>
        <version>1</version>
        <type>war</type>
      </dependency>
    </dependencies>
```

Make sure to set `<type>` of each dependency properly. You also need to update JNDI URLs for any name changes.

Maven does not have built-in support to package EAR. However, there is a Maven plugin for EAR. You can find details of this plugin at `https://maven.apache.org/plugins/maven-ear-plugin/` and `https://maven.apache.org/plugins/maven-ear-plugin/modules.html`. We need to add this plugin to our pom.xml and configure its parameters. Our EAR file will contain JARs for EJB and client projects and WAR for web projects. Right-click on `pom.xml` of the EAR project, and select **Maven | Add Plugin**. Type `ear` in the filter box, and select the latest plugin version under **maven-ear-plugin**. Make sure that you also install the **maven-acr-plugin** plugin. Configure the EAR plugin in the `pom.xml` details as follows:

```
  <build>
    <plugins>
      <plugin>
         <groupId>org.apache.maven.plugins</groupId>
         <artifactId>maven-acr-plugin</artifactId>
         <version>1.0</version>
         <extensions>true</extensions>
      </plugin>

      <plugin>
        <groupId>org.apache.maven.plugins</groupId>
```

```
          <artifactId>maven-ear-plugin</artifactId>
          <version>2.10</version>
          <configuration>
             <version>6</version>
          <defaultLibBundleDir>lib</defaultLibBundleDir>
          <modules>
          <webModule>
          <groupId>packt.book.jee.eclipse.ch7.maven</groupId>
          <artifactId>CourseManagementMavenWebApp</artifactId>
          </webModule>
          <ejbModule>
          <groupId>packt.book.jee.eclipse.ch7.maven</groupId>
          <artifactId>CourseManagementMavenEJBs</artifactId>
          </ejbModule>
          < jarModule >
          <groupId>packt.book.jee.eclipse.ch7.maven</groupId>
          <artifactId>CourseManagementMavenEJBClient</artifactId>
          </ jarModule >
          </modules>
          </configuration>
        </plugin>
        </plugins>
      </build>
```

At any time when modifying `pom.xml` if Eclipse may display the following error:

```
Project configuration is not up-to-date with pom.xml. Run Maven-
>Update Project or use Quick Fix…
```

In such a case, right-click on the project and select **Maven | Update Project**.

The last project that we create in this section is `CourseManagement`, which will be a container project for all other EJB projects. When this project is installed, it should build and install all the contained projects. Create a Maven project with the following details:

Group ID	packt.book.jee.eclipse.ch7.maven
Artifact ID	CourseManagement
Version	1
Packaging	Pom

Open `pom.xml` and click on the **Overview** tab. Expand the **Modules** group, and add all other projects as modules. This adds the following modules in `pom.xml`:

```
<modules>
  <module>../CourseManagementMavenEAR</module>
  <module>../CourseManagementMavenEJBClient</module>
  <module>../CourseManagementMavenEJBs</module>
  <module>../CourseManagementMavenWebApp</module>
</modules>
```

Right-click on the `CourseManagement` project and select **Run As | Maven Install**. This builds all EJB projects, and an EAR file is created in the target folder of the `CourseManagementMavenEAR` project. You can deploy this EAR in GlassFish from the management console, or you can right-click on the configured GlassFish server in the **Servers** view of Eclipse, select the **Add and Remove ...** option, and deploy the EAR project from right within Eclipse. Browse to `http://localhost:8080/CourseManagementMavenWebApp/course.xhtml` to see the list of courses displayed by the `course.xhtml` JSF page.

Summary

EJBs are ideal for writing business logic in web applications. They can act as the perfect bridge between web interface components such as JSF, Servlet, or JSP and data access objects such as JDO. EJBs can be distributed across multiple JEE application servers (this could improve application scalability), and their lifecycle is managed by the container. EJBs can be easily injected into managed objects or can be looked up by using JNDI.

Eclipse JEE makes creating and consuming EJBs very easy. Just like we saw how Tomcat can be configured and managed within Eclipse, the JEE application server GlassFish could also be managed by applications deployed from within Eclipse.

In the next chapter, we will discuss how to create web applications by using Spring MVC. Although Spring is not part of JEE, it is a popular framework to implement MVC in JEE web applications; it can work with many of the JEE specifications.

8
Creating Web Applications with Spring MVC

Although this book is about JEE and Eclipse, and Spring MVC is not a part of JEE, it would be worthwhile to understand the Spring MVC framework. Spring MVC is a very popular framework for creating web applications and can be used with other JEE technologies, such as Servlet, JSP, JPA, and EJBs. In this chapter, we will see in detail how to create web applications by using Spring MVC, JDBC, JPA, and JSPs.

JEE does support MVC out of the box, if you use JSF. Refer to *Java Server Faces* in *Chapter 2, Creating a Simple JEE Web Application*, for details. However, there is a difference in the design of JSP and Spring MVC. JSF is a component-based MVC framework. It is designed so that the user interface designer can create pages by assembling reusable components that are either provided by JSF or custom developed. Spring MVC is a request response based MVC framework. If you are familiar with writing JSP or Servlets, then Spring MVC would be an easier framework to use than JSF. You can find a good description of component-based MVC (as implemented by JSF) and request-response-based MVC (as implemented by Spring MVC) by Ed Burns at `http://www.oracle.com/technetwork/articles/java/mvc-2280472.html`.

Before we see how Spring MVC works, we need understand what an MVC framework is. MVC stands for Model-View-Controller framework. We are going to refer to the MVC framework in the context of Java web applications only, although it should be mentioned here that MVC is often used in desktop applications too.

- **Model**: Model contains data that will be used by View to create the output. In the example that we have been following in this book, of the Course Management application, if you have a `Course` class that contains information about the course to be displayed in a page, then the `Course` object can be called the model.

Some definitions of MVC include classes that also implement business logic in the Model layer. For example, the `CourseService` class that takes the `Course` object and calls `CourseDAO` to save `Course` in the database could also be considered a part of the Model layer.

- **View**: View is a page that is displayed to the user. JSP that displays a list of courses could be considered a part of the View layer. View holds a reference to the Model object and uses the data to create the page that users see in browsers.
- **Controller**: Controller is the glue between Model and View. It handles the request, calls Model to handle business logic, and makes Model objects available to View to create the user interface. Controller could be a Servlet, as in the case of JSF or could be POJOs (as in the case of Spring MVC). When controllers are POJO, they get called, typically, by DispatcherServlet.

MVC provides the separation of concerns; that is, the code for the user interface and the business logic is separate. Because of this, the UI and the business layer can be modified independently to a great extent. Of course, since the UI usually displays the data generated by the business layer, it is not always possible to make changes to each of the data elements independent of the others. Developers of appropriate skills can work on each layer independently. A UI expert need not be too worried about how the business layer is implemented and vice versa.

Dependency injection

Spring MVC is a part of the overall Spring framework. The core feature of the Spring framework is **dependency injection** (**DI**). Almost all other features of the Spring framework use DI. Objects managed by the dependency injection framework are not directly instantiated in the code (by using, for example, new operator). Let's call them managed objects. These objects are created by a DI framework, such as Spring. Because objects are created by a framework, the framework has a lot more flexibility in deciding how to set values in the object and from where to get them. For example, your **Data Access Object** (**DAO**) class might need an instance of a database connection factory object. However, instead of instantiating in the DAO class, you just tell the DI framework that when it instantiates the DAO, it has to set the value of the connection pool factory object. Of course, the parameters for the connection pool factory will have to be configured somewhere and be known to the DI framework.

When a class instantiates another class, there is a tight dependency. Such design could be a problem if you want to test classes independent of others. For example, you may want to test a class that has business logic, but one which also refers to DAO, which in turn depends on a JDBC connection object. When testing the first class, you will have to instantiate DAO and configure the connection pool. As we saw in *Chapter 5, Unit Testing*, unit tests should be able to run without an external dependency. One way to achieve this is by using DI. Instead of instantiating the DAO class, our class could refer to an interface that is implemented by DAO and have the DI framework inject the implementation of this interface at runtime. When you are unit testing this class, the DI framework can be configured to inject a mock object that implements the required interface. So, DI enables loose coupling between objects.

Dependency injection in Spring

Because DI is at the core of the Spring framework, let's spend some time understanding how it works in Spring. We will create a standalone application for this purpose. Create a simple Maven project. Add the following dependency for the Spring framework:

```
<dependency>
  <groupId>org.springframework</groupId>
  <artifactId>spring-context</artifactId>
  <version>4.1.6.RELEASE</version>
</dependency>
```

Replace the preceding version number with the latest version of Spring. Classes managed by the DI container of Spring are called beans or components. You can either declare beans in an XML file or you can annotate a class in the source file. We will use annotations in this chapter. However, even though we use annotations, we need to specify the minimum configuration in an XML file. So, create a XML file in the `src/main/resource` folder of your project and name it `context.xml`. The reason that we are creating this file in the `src/main.resource` folder is that the files in this folder are made available in the classpath. Therefore, add the following content to `context.xml`:

```
<?xml version="1.0" encoding="UTF-8"?>
<beans xmlns="http://www.springframework.org/schema/beans"
    xmlns:xsi="http://www.w3.org/2001/XMLSchema-instance"
```

```
     xmlns:context="http://www.springframework.org/schema/context"
    xsi:schemaLocation="http://www.springframework.org/schema/beans
         http://www.springframework.org/schema/beans/spring-
         beans.xsd
         http://www.springframework.org/schema/context
         http://www.springframework.org/schema/context/spring-
         context.xsd">

  <context:component-scan base-package="packt.jee.eclipse.spring"
  />
</beans>
```

By using the `<context:component-scan>` tag, we are telling the Spring framework to scan the `base-package` folder and then, look for classes annotated with `@Component` and recognize them as managed classes so that they can be made available when injecting dependencies. In the preceding example, all classes in the `packt.jee.eclipse.spring` package (and its sub packages) would be scanned to identify components.

Information read from the configuration file must be saved in an object. In Spring, it is saved in an instance of the `ApplicationContext` interface. There are different implementations of `ApplicationContext`. We will be using the `ClassPathXmlApplicationContext` class, which looks for the configuration XML file in the classpath.

We will now create two Spring components. The first one is `CourseDAO`, and the second is `CourseService`. Although we won't write any business logic in these classes (the purpose of this example is to understand how DI works in Spring), assume that `CourseDAO` could have the code to access the database and `CourseService` calls `CourseDAO` to perform the database operations. So, `CourseService` is dependent on `CourseDAO`. To keep the code simple, we will not create an interface for `CourseDAO` but will have a direct dependency. Create the `CourseDAO` class as follows:

```
package packt.jee.eclipse.spring;

import org.springframework.stereotype.Component;

@Component
public class CourseDAO {

}
```

We will have no methods in `CourseDAO`, but as mentioned above, it could have methods to access the database. `@Component` marks this class as managed by Spring. Now, create the `CourseService` class. This class needs an instance of `CourseDAO`.

```
package packt.jee.eclipse.spring;

import org.springframework.beans.factory.annotation.Autowired;
import org.springframework.stereotype.Component;

@Component
public class CourseService {

  @Autowired
  private CourseDAO courseDAO;

  public CourseDAO getCourseDAO() {
    return courseDAO;
  }
}
```

We have declared a member variable called `courseDAO` and annotated it with `@Autowired`. This tells Spring to look for a component in its context (of the `CourseDAO` type) and assign that to the `courseDAO` member.

We will now create the main class. It creates `ApplicationContext`, gets the `CourseService` bean, calls the `getCourseDAO` method, and then checks whether it was injected properly. Create the `SpringMain` class.

```
package packt.jee.eclipse.spring;

import org.springframework.context.ApplicationContext;
import org.springframework.context.support.
ClassPathXmlApplicationContext;

public class SpringMain {

  public static void main (String[] args) {
    //create ApplicationContext
    ApplicationContext ctx = new
    ClassPathXmlApplicationContext("context.xml");
    //Get bean
    CourseService courseService = (CourseService)
    ctx.getBean("courseService");
```

```
        //Get and print CourseDAO. It should not be null
        System.out.println("CourseDAO = " +
        courseService.getCourseDAO());
      }
    }
```

We first create an instance of `ClassPathXmlApplicationContext`. The configuration XML file is passed as the argument to the constructor. We then get the `courseService` bean/component. Notice the naming convention when specifying bean name; it is the class name with the first letter in lowercase. We then get and print the value of `CourseDAO`. The value won't show any meaningful information, but if the value is not null, then it would mean that the Spring DI container has injected this value properly. Note that we have not instantiated `CourseDAO`; it is the Spring DI container that instantiates and injects this object.

In the preceding code, we saw an example of injecting objects at the member declaration (this is also called property injection). We can have this object injected in the constructors too.

```
@Component
public class CourseService {

  private CourseDAO courseDAO;

  @Autowired
  public CourseService (CourseDAO coueseDAO) {
    this.courseDAO = coueseDAO;
  }

  public CourseDAO getCourseDAO() {
    return courseDAO;
  }
}
```

Notice that the `@Autowired` annotation is moved to the constructor and the single constructor argument is autoinjected. You can also have the object injected in a setter.

```
@Component
public class CourseService {

  private CourseDAO courseDAO;

  @Autowired
```

```
    public void setCourseDAO (CourseDAO courseDAO) {
      this.courseDAO = courseDAO;
    }

    public CourseDAO getCourseDAO() {
      return courseDAO;
    }
  }
```

Component scopes

You can specify the scope for your components. The default scope is singleton, which means that there will be only one instance of the component in the context. Every request for this component will be served with the same instance. The other scopes are as follows:

- **Prototype**: Each request for a component is served with a new instance of that class.
- **Request**: Valid for web applications. Single instance of a component class created for each HTTP request.
- **Session**: Single instance of a component class created for each HTTP session. Used in web applications.
- **Global session**: Single instance of a component class created for the global HTTP session. Used in portlet applications.
- **Application**: Single instance of a component class in a web application. The instance is shared by all sessions in this application.

See `http://docs.spring.io/spring/docs/current/spring-framework-reference/html/beans.html#beans-factory-scopes` for more information on component scopes in Spring.

If the component to be injected was not instantiated at the time that it was requested, then Spring creates an instance of the component. In the previous example, we have not specified the scope of the `CourseDAO` component, so the same instance would be injected if there is another request for injecting `CourseDAO`. You can specify the scope in the `@Component` annotation. You can also specify the component name if you want to override the default name that Spring gives to the component.

To see if a single instance of a component is injected when no scope is specified, let's change the main method in the `SpringMain` class and make two calls to the `getBean` method:

```
public static void main (String[] args) {
  //create ApplicationContext
  ApplicationContext ctx = new
  ClassPathXmlApplicationContext("context.xml");
  //call and print ctx.getBean first time
  System.out.println("Course Service 1 - " +
  ctx.getBean("courseService"));
  System.out.println("Course Service 2 - " +
  ctx.getBean("courseService"));
}
```

Run the application and you should see the same instance of the `courseService` bean printed. Let's change scope of the `CourseService` component.

```
@Component
@Scope(ConfigurableBeanFactory.SCOPE_PROTOTYPE)
public class CourseService {
  //content remains the same
}
```

Run the application again; this time, you should see different instances of the `CourseService` component.

When Spring sees the `@Autowire` annotation, it tries to find the component by type. In the preceding example, `courseDAO` is annotated with `@Autowire`. Spring tries to find a component of the `courseDAO` type; it finds an instance of `CourseDAO` and injects it. But what if there are multiple instances of a class in the context? In such a case, we can use the `@Qualifier` annotation to uniquely identify components. Let's now create an `ICourseDAO` interface, which will be implemented by two components, namely `CourseDAO` and `CourseDAO1`.

```
public interface ICourseDAO {
}
```

`CourseDAO` implements `ICourseDAO` and is uniquely qualified as `"courseDAO"`.

```
@Component
@Qualifier("courseDAO")
public class CourseDAO implements ICourseDAO {
}
```

`CourseDAO1` implements `ICourseDAO` and is uniquely qualified as `"courseDAO1"`.

```
@Component
@Qualifier("courseDAO1")
public class CourseDAO1 implements ICourseDAO {
}
```

In the `CourseService` class, we will use a qualifier to uniquely identify whether we want `CourseDAO` or `CourseDAO1` to be injected.

```
@Component
public class CourseService {

  @Autowired
  private @Qualifier("courseDAO1") ICourseDAO courseDAO;

  public ICourseDAO getCourseDAO() {
    return courseDAO;
  }
}
```

The qualifier can also be specified at the method argument. For example:

```
@Autowired
public void setCourseDAO (@Qualifier("courseDAO1") ICourseDAO
courseDAO) {
  this.courseDAO = courseDAO;
}
```

We have covered the basics of dependency injection in Spring. However, Spring offers a lot more options and features for dependency injection than we have covered here. We will see more DI features as and when required in this chapter. Visit `http://docs.spring.io/spring/docs/current/spring-framework-reference/html/beans.html` for more information about dependency injection in Spring.

Installing the Spring Tool Suite

Spring Tool Suite (**STS**) is a set of tools for creating Spring applications. It can be either installed as a plugin to an existing installation of Eclipse JEE or can be installed standalone. The standalone version of STS is also packaged with Eclipse EE, so all Eclipse features for Java EE development are available in STS too. You can download STS from `https://spring.io/tools`. Since we have already installed Eclipse EE, we will install STS as a plugin. The easiest way to install an STS plugin is from **Eclipse Marketplace**. Select the **Help** | **Eclipse Marketplace** menu.

Type `Spring Tool Suite` in the find box, and click the **Go** button.

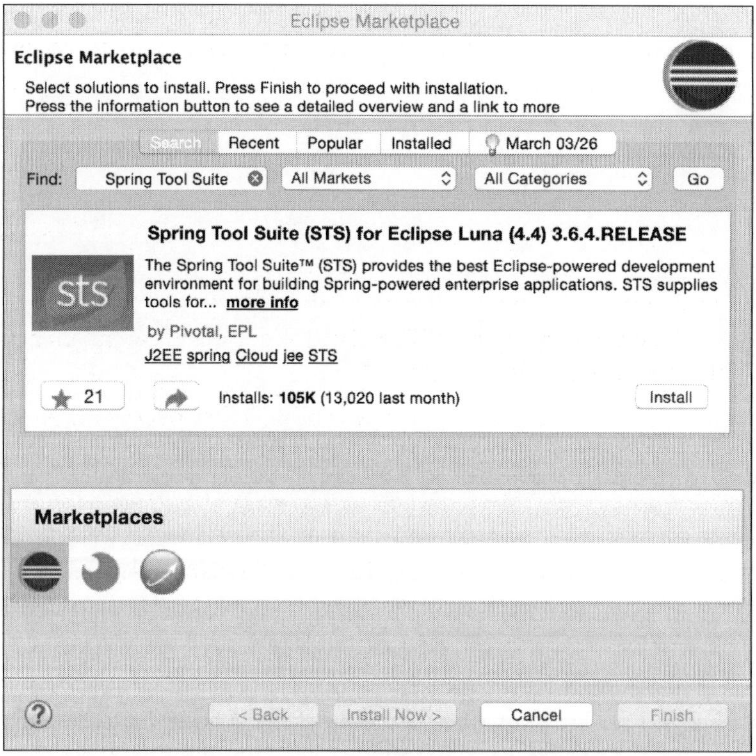

Figure 8.1 Search STS in Eclipse Marketplace

Click **Install**. The next page shows the features of STS that will be installed. Click **Confirm** to install the selected features.

Creating a Spring MVC application

Spring MVC can be used for creating web applications. It provides an easy framework to map an incoming web request to a handler class (controller) and create dynamic HTML. It provides an implementation of the MVC pattern. The controller, models, POJOs, and views can be created using JSP, JSTL, XSLT, and even JSF. However, in this chapter, we will focus on creating views using JSP and JSTL. You can find the Spring web documentation at `http://docs.spring.io/spring/docs/current/spring-framework-reference/html/spring-web.html` for details.

A web request is handled by four layers in Spring MVC

- **Front controller**: This is a Spring Servlet configured in `web.xml`. Based on the request URL pattern, it passes requests to Controller.
- **Controller**: These are POJOs annotated with `@Controller`. For each controller that you write you need to specify a URL pattern that the controller is expected to handle. Sub-URL patterns can be specified at the method level too. We will see examples of this later. Controller has access to Model and to the HTTP request and response objects. Controller can delegate the processing of a request to other business handler objects, get results, and populate the Model object that is made available to View by Spring MVC.
- **Model**: These are data objects. The Controller and View layers can set and get data from model objects.
- **View**: These are typically JSPs, but Spring MVC supports other types of views too. See **View technologies** in Spring documentation at `http://docs.spring.io/spring/docs/current/spring-framework-reference/html/view.html`.

We will learn Spring MVC in this chapter through examples, as we have been learning in some other chapters in this book. We will create a part of the same Course Management application by using Spring MVC. The application will display a list of courses with options to add, remove, and modify them.

Creating a Spring project

First, make sure that you have installed STS. In Eclipse EE, select the **File** | **New** | **Spring Project** menu. Enter the project name, and select the **Spring MVC Project** template.

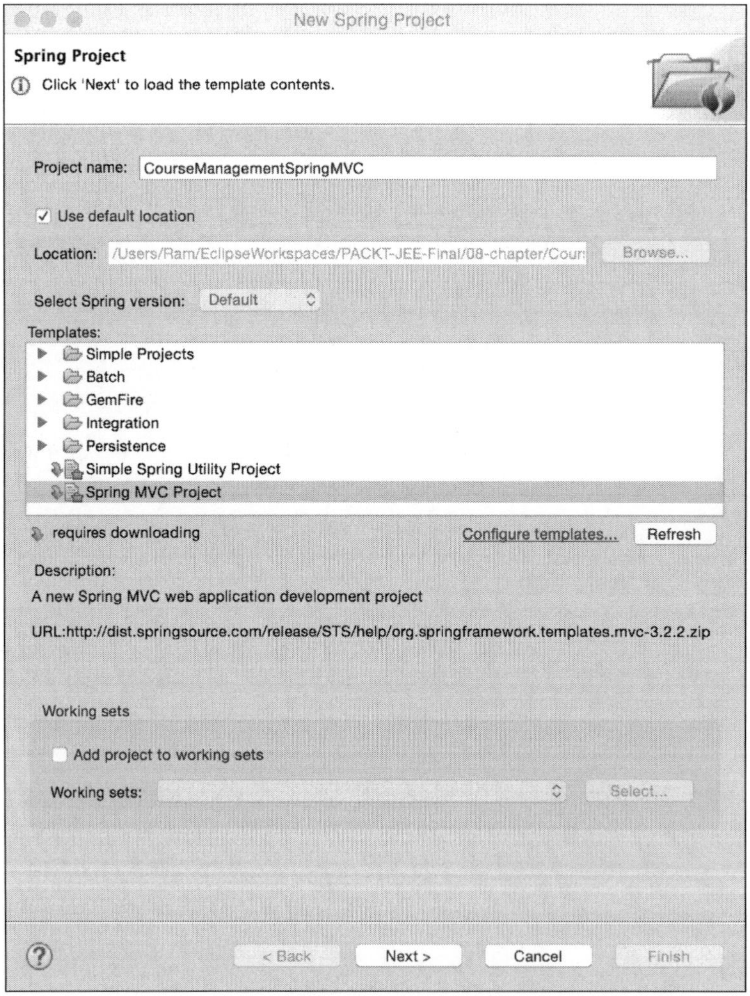

Figure 8.2 Select Spring MVC project template

Click **Next**. The next page would ask you to enter a top-level package name.

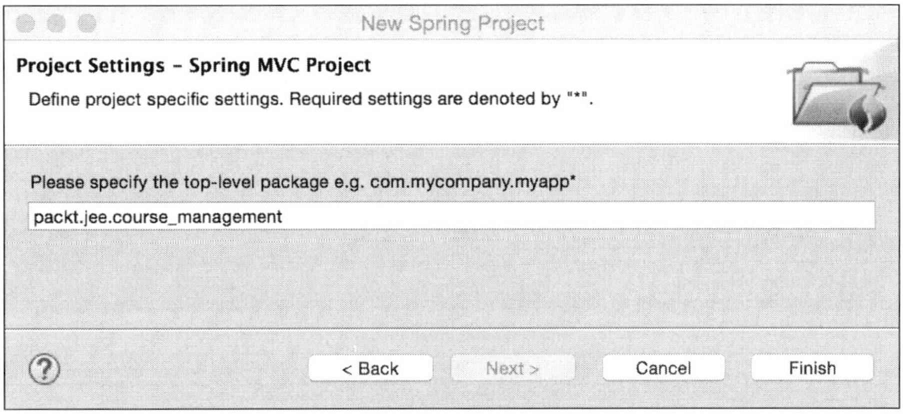

Figure 8.3 Enter top-level package

Whatever you enter as a top-level package, the wizard takes the third sub-package as the application name. When the application is deployed in a server, the application name becomes the context name. For example, if you enter the package name as `packt.jee.course_management`, then `course_management` becomes the application name and the base URL of the application, on a local machine, would be `http://localhost:8080/course_management/`.

Click **Finish**. This creates a Maven project with the required libraries for Spring MVC.

Understanding files created by the Spring MVC project template

Let's examine some of the files created by the template.

- `src/main/webapp/WEB-INF/web.xml`: A front controller Servlet is declared here along with other configurations:

```
<!-- Processes application requests -->
<servlet>
  <servlet-name>appServlet</servlet-name>
  <servlet-
class>org.springframework.web.servlet.DispatcherServlet</servlet-
class>
  <init-param>
    <param-name>contextConfigLocation</param-name>
```

```
    <param-value>/WEB-INF/spring/appServlet/servlet-
    context.xml</param-value>
  </init-param>
  <load-on-startup>1</load-on-startup>
</servlet>
```

`DispatcherServlet` is the front controller Servlet. It is passed the path of the context (XML) file for configuring Spring DI. Recall that in the standalone Spring application, we had created `context.xml` to configure dependency injection. The `DispatcherServlet` Servlet is mapped to handle requests to this web application.

- `src/main/webapp/WEB-INF/spring/appServlet/servlet-context.xml`: Context configuration for Spring DI. Some of the notable configuration parameters in this file are as follows:

  ```
  <annotation-driven />
  ```

  This enables annotations for configuring dependency injection at the class level.

  ```
  <resources mapping="/resources/**" location="/resources/" />
  ```

Static files, such as CSS, JavaScript, and images can be placed in the `resources` folder (`src/main/webapp/resources`).

```
<beans:bean
class="org.springframework.web.servlet.view.
InternalResourceViewResolver">
  <beans:property name="prefix" value="/WEB-INF/views/" />
  <beans:property name="suffix" value=".jsp" />
</beans:bean>
```

This tells Spring to use the `InternalResourceViewResolver` class to resolve views. Properties of this bean tell the `InternalResourceViewResolver` class to look for the `view` files in the `/WEB-INF/views` folder. Further, views will be JSP files, as indicated by the suffix property. Our views will be the JSP files in the `src/main/webapp/WEB-INF/views` folder.

```
<context:component-scan base-package="packt.jee.course_management" />
```

This tells Spring to scan the `packt.book.jee` package and its sub-packages for searching components (annotated by `@Component`).

The default template also creates one controller and one view. The controller class is `HomeController` in the package that you specified in the Spring project wizard (in our example, it is `packt.jee.course_management`). Controller in Spring MVC is called by the dispatcher Servlet. Controllers are annotated by `@Controller`. To map the request path to Controller, you use the `@RequestMapping` annotation. Let's see the code generated by the template in the `HomeController` class.

```
@Controller
public class HomeController {

  private static final Logger logger =
  LoggerFactory.getLogger(HomeController.class);

  /**
   * Simply selects the home view to render by returning its name.
   */
  @RequestMapping(value = "/", method = RequestMethod.GET)
  public String home(Locale locale, Model model) {
    logger.info("Welcome home! The client locale is {}.", locale);

    Date date = new Date();
    DateFormat dateFormat =
DateFormat.getDateTimeInstance(DateFormat.LONG, DateFormat.LONG,
locale);

    String formattedDate = dateFormat.format(date);

    model.addAttribute("serverTime", formattedDate );

    return "home";
  }

}
```

The `home` method is annotated with `@RequestMapping`. The value of mapping is `/`, which tells the dispatcher Servlet to send all requests coming its way to this method. The `method` attribute tells the dispatcher to call the `home` method only for the HTTP request of the `GET` type. The `home` method takes two arguments, namely `Locale` and `Model`; both are injected at runtime by Spring. The `@RequestMapping` annotation also tells Spring to insert any dependencies when calling the `home` method, and hence, `locale` and `model` are autoinjected.

The method itself does not do much; it gets the current date-time and sets it as an attribute in the Model. Any attributes set in the model are available to view (JSP). Method returns a string `"home"`. This value is used by Spring MVC to resolve a view to be displayed. `InternalResourceViewResolver` that we saw in `servlet-context.xml` above resolves this as `home.jsp` in the `/WEB-INF/views` folder. `home.jsp` has the following code in the `<body>` tag.

```
<P>  The time on the server is ${serverTime}. </P>
```

The `serverTime` variable is coming from the Model object set in the `home` method of `HomeController`.

To run this project, we need to configure a server in Eclipse and add this project to the server. Refer to the *Configuring Tomcat in Eclipse* and *Running JSP in Tomcat* sections in *Chapter 2, Creating a Simple JEE Web Application.*

Once you configure Tomcat and add the project to it, start the server. Then, right-click on the project and select **Run As** | **Run on Server**. You should see a **hello** message with the timestamp displayed in the internal Eclipse browser. The URL in the browser's address bar should be `http://localhost:8080/course_management/`, assuming that Tomcat is deployed on port `8080` and the context name (derived from the top-level package name) is `course_management`. If you want to change the default context name or remove the context, that is, deploy the application in the root context, then open the project properties (right-click on the project and select **Properties**) and go to **Web Project Settings**. You can change the context root name or remove it from this page.

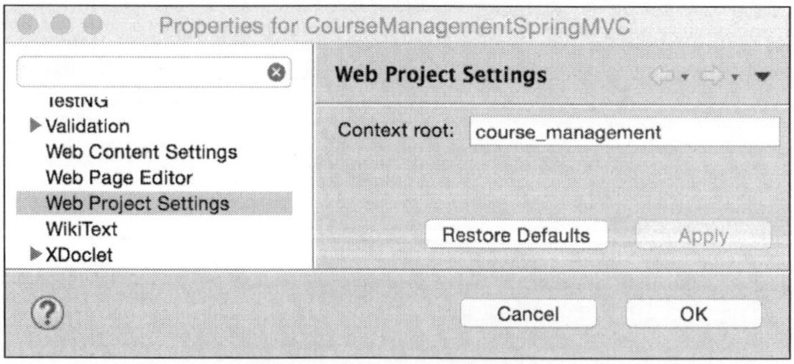

Figure 8.4 Context Root setting

For our course management application, we are not going to need the `HomeController` class and `home.jsp`, so you can go ahead and delete these files.

Spring MVC application using JDBC

In this section, we will build a part of the course management application using Spring MVC and JDBC. The application will display a list of courses and options for adding, deleting, and modifying courses. We will continue using the project that we created in the previous section. We will learn many of the features of Spring for data access using JDBC as we go along.

First, we will configure our datasource. We will use the same MySQL database that we created in the *Creating a database schema* section in *Chapter 4, Creating a JEE Database Application*.

Configuring datasource

In Spring, you can configure a JDBC datasource either in Java code or in the XML configuration (context) file. Before we see how to configure a datasource, we need to add some dependencies in Maven. In this chapter, we will use Apache's Commons DBCP component for connection pooling (recall that in Chapter 4, *Creating a JEE Database Application*, we had selected the Hikari connection pool). Visit `https://commons.apache.org/proper/commons-dbcp/` for details of Apache DBCP. In addition to adding a dependency for Apache DBCP, we need to add dependencies for Spring JDBC and the MySQL JDBC driver. Add the following dependencies to pom.xml of the project:

```
<!-- Spring JDBC -->
<dependency>
  <groupId>org.springframework</groupId>
  <artifactId>spring-jdbc</artifactId>
  <version>${org.springframework-version}</version>
</dependency>

<!-- Apache DBCP -->
<dependency>
  <groupId>commons-dbcp</groupId>
  <artifactId>commons-dbcp</artifactId>
  <version>1.4</version>
</dependency>

<!-- MySQL -->
<dependency>
  <groupId>mysql</groupId>
  <artifactId>mysql-connector-java</artifactId>
  <version>5.1.35</version>
</dependency>
```

If you want to create a datasource in Java code, you can do so as follows:

```
DriverManagerDataSource dataSource = new
DriverManagerDataSource();
dataSource.setDriverClassName("com.mysql.jdbc.Driver");
dataSource.setUrl("jdbc:mysql://localhost:3306/course_management");
dataSource.setUsername("your_user_name");
dataSource.setPassword("your_password");
```

However, we will configure a datasource in the XML configuration file. Open `servlet-context.xml` (you will find it in the `src/main/webapp/WEB-INF/spring/appServlet` folder), and add the following bean:

```
<beans:bean id="dataSource"
  class="org.apache.commons.dbcp.BasicDataSource" destroy-
method="close">
    <beans:property name="driverClassName"
value="com.mysql.jdbc.Driver"/>
  <beans:property name="url"
value="jdbc:mysql://localhost:3306/course_management" />
  <beans:property name="username" value="your_user_name"/>
  <beans:property name="password" value="your_password"/>
</beans:bean>
```

If you are wondering what *bean* means, it is the same as the component that we created in examples in an earlier section. We have so far created a component by using annotations, but the component and the bean can be declared in the XML file too. In fact, this is how it used to be in earlier versions till support for annotations was added in Spring. You can find more information about Spring beans at `http://docs.spring.io/spring/docs/current/spring-framework-reference/html/beans.html#beans-definition`. In a real-world application, you may want to encrypt database passwords before specifying them in the configuration file. One way to decrypt a password before sending it to the database is to create a wrapper class for the datasource (in the previous example, create a wrapper for `org.apache.commons.dbcp.BasicDataSource`) and override the `setPassword` method, where you can decrypt the password.

If you want to keep the database connection parameters separate from the Spring configuration, then you can use the `properties` file. Spring provides a consistent way to access resources such as the `properties` file. Just as you can access web URLs by using the `http` protocol prefix or the file URL by using the `file` protocol prefix, Spring allows you to access resources in the classpath by using the `classpath` prefix. For example, if we create the `jdbc.properties` file and save it in one of the folders in the classpath, then we could access it as `classpath:jdbc.properties`.

Visit `http://docs.spring.io/spring/docs/current/spring-framework-reference/html/resources.html` for detailed information on accessing resources using Spring. The Spring resource URL formats can be used in configuration files or Spring APIs where the resource location is expected.

Spring also provides a convenient tag to load the properties file in the context config XML. You can access the values of properties in the `property` file in the config XML by using the `${property_name}` syntax.

We will move the database connection properties to a file in this example. Create `jdbc.properties` in the `src/main/resources` folder. Maven makes this folder available in the classpath, so we can access it by using the Spring resource format in the XML configuration file.

```
jdbc.driverClassName=com.mysql.jdbc.Driver
jdbc.url=jdbc:mysql://localhost:3306/course_management
jdbc.username=your_user_name
jdbc.password=your_password
```

We will load this properties file from `servlet-context.xml` by using the `property-placeholder` tag.

```
<context:property-placeholder location="classpath:jdbc.properties"/>
```

Notice that the location of the `property` file is specified using the Spring resource format. In this case, we ask Spring to look for the `jdbc.properties` file in the classpath. Further, because the `src/main/resources` folder is in the classpath (where we have saved `jdbc.properties`), it should be loaded by Spring.

Further, we will modify the `datasource` bean declaration to use the property values.

```
<beans:bean id="dataSource"
  class="org.apache.commons.dbcp.BasicDataSource" destroy-
method="close">
    <beans:property name="driverClassName"
value="${jdbc.driverClassName}"/>
  <beans:property name="url" value="${jdbc.url}" />
  <beans:property name="username" value="${jdbc.username}"/>
  <beans:property name="password" value="${jdbc.password}"/>
</beans:bean>
```

Note that the order of the `property-placeholder` tag and where the properties are used does not matter. Spring loads the entire XML configuration file before replacing the `property` references with their values.

Using the Spring JDBCTemplate class

Spring provides a utility class called `JDBCTemplate` that makes it easy to perform many operations using JDBC. It provides convenient methods to execute SQL statements, map results of a query to an object (using the `RowMapper` class), close a database connection at the end of database operations, and many others. Visit `http://docs.spring.io/spring/docs/current/spring-framework-reference/html/jdbc.html#jdbc-core` for more information on `JdbcTemplate`.

Before we write any data access code, we will create a **Data Transfer Object** (**DTO**), `CourseDTO`, which will just contain members that describe one `Course` and the setters and getters for them. Create `CourseDTO` in the `packt.jee.course_management.dto` package. Instances of this class will be used to transfer data between different tiers of our application.

```
public class CourseDTO {
  private int id;
  private int credits;
  private String name;

  //skipped setters and getters to save space
}
```

We will now create a simple DAO that will use the `JdbcTemplate` class to execute a query to get all courses. Create the `CourseDAO` class in the `packt.jee.course_management.dao` package. Annotate the `CourseDAO` class with `@Repository`. Just like `@Component`, the `@Repository` annotation marks the class as a Spring DI container managed class.

As per the Spring documentation (`http://docs.spring.io/spring/docs/current/spring-framework-reference/html/beans.html#beans-stereotype-annotations`), `@Component` is a generic annotation to mark a Spring container managed class and `@Repository` and `@Controller` are more specific ones. More specific annotations help to identify classes for specific treatments. It is recommended to use the `@Repository` annotations for DAOs.

`CourseDAO` needs to have an instance of the `JdbcTemplate` class to execute queries and other SQL statements. `JdbcTemplate` needs a DataSource object before it can be used. We will have DataSource injected in a method in `CourseDAO`.

```
@Repository
public class CourseDAO {

  private JdbcTemplate jdbcTemplate;

  @Autowired
```

```
    public void setDatasource (DataSource dataSource) {
      jdbcTemplate = new JdbcTemplate(dataSource);
    }
  }
```

The datasource that we have configured in `servlet-context.xml` will be injected by Spring when the `CourseDAO` object is created.

We will now write the method to get all courses. The `JdbcTemplate` class query method allows you to specify `RowMapper`, where you can map each row in the query to a Java object.

```
public List<CourseDTO> getCourses() {
  List<CourseDTO> courses = jdbcTemplate.query("select * from
  course",
    new CourseRowMapper());

  return courses;
}

public static final class CourseRowMapper implements
RowMapper<CourseDTO> {
  @Override
  public CourseDTO mapRow(ResultSet rs, int rowNum) throws
  SQLException {
    CourseDTO course = new CourseDTO();
    course.setId(rs.getInt("id"));
    course.setName(rs.getString("name"));
    course.setCredits(rs.getInt("credits"));
    return course;
  }
}
```

In the `getCourses` method, we will execute a static query. Later, we will see how to execute parameterized queries too. The second argument to the `query` method of `JDBCTemplate` is an instance of the `RowMapper` interface. We have created a static inner class `CourseRowMapper` that implements the `RowMapper` interface. We override the `mapRow` method, which is called for each row in `ResultSet`, and then, we create/map the `CourseDTO` object from `ResultSet` passed in the arguments. The method returns the `CourseDTO` object. The result of `JdbcTemplate.query` is a list of `CourseDTO` objects. Note that the query method can also return other Java collection objects, such as `Map`.

Now, let's write a method to add a course to the table.

```
public void addCourse (final CourseDTO course) {
  KeyHolder keyHolder = new GeneratedKeyHolder();
  jdbcTemplate.update(new PreparedStatementCreator() {

    @Override
    public PreparedStatement createPreparedStatement(Connection
    con)
        throws SQLException {
      String sql = "insert into Course (name, credits) values
      (?,?)";
      PreparedStatement stmt = con.prepareStatement(sql, new
      String[] {"id"});
      stmt.setString(1, course.getName());
      stmt.setInt(2, course.getCredits());
      return stmt;
    }
  }, keyHolder);

  course.setId(keyHolder.getKey().intValue());
}
```

When we add or insert a new course, we want to get the ID of the new record, which is auto-generated. Further, we would like to use the prepared statement to execute SQL. Therefore, first, we create `KeyHolder` for the auto-generated field. The update method of `JdbcTemplate` has many overloaded versions. We use the one that takes `PreparedStatementCreator` and `KeyHolder`. We create an instance of `PreparedStatementCreator` and override the `createPreparedStatement` method. In this method, we create JDBC `PreparedStatement` and return it. Once the update method is successfully executed, we retrieve the auto-generated value by calling the `getKey` method of `KeyHolder`.

The methods to update or delete a course are similar.

```
public void updateCourse (final CourseDTO course) {
  jdbcTemplate.update(new PreparedStatementCreator() {
    @Override
    public PreparedStatement createPreparedStatement(Connection
    con)
        throws SQLException {
      String sql = "update Course set name = ?, credits = ? where
      id = ?";
      PreparedStatement stmt = con.prepareStatement(sql);
```

```
            stmt.setString(1, course.getName());
            stmt.setInt(2, course.getCredits());
            stmt.setInt(3, course.getId());
            return stmt;
        }
    });
}

public void deleteCourse(final int id) {
    jdbcTemplate.update(new PreparedStatementCreator() {
        @Override
        public PreparedStatement createPreparedStatement(Connection
        con)
            throws SQLException {
            String sql = "delete from Course where id = ?";
            PreparedStatement stmt = con.prepareStatement(sql);
            stmt.setInt(1, id);
            return stmt;
        }
    });
}
```

We need to add one more method to `CourseDAO`, to get the details of a course, given the ID.

```
public CourseDTO getCourse (int id) {
    String sql = "select * from course where id = ?";
    CourseDTO course = jdbcTemplate.queryForObject(sql, new
    CourseRowMapper(), id);
    return course;
}
```

`queryForObject` returns a single object for a given query. We use a parameterized query here and the parameter is passed as the last argument to the `queryForObject` method. Further, we use `CourseRowMapper` to map the single row returned by this query to `CourseDTO`. Note that you can pass a variable number of parameters to the `queryForObject` method, although in this case, we pass a single value, that is, of ID.

We now have all the methods in the `CourseDAO` class to access data for `Course`. For a detailed discussion on data access using JDBC in Spring, refer to `http://docs.spring.io/spring/docs/current/spring-framework-reference/html/jdbc.html`.

Creating the Spring MVC Controller

We will now create the controller class. In Spring MVC, the controller is mapped to the request URL and handles requests matching this URL pattern. The request URL for matching an incoming request is specified at the method level in a controller. However, more generic request mapping can be specified at the `Controller` class level and a specific URL, with respect to the URL at the class level, can be specified at the method level.

Create a class called `CourseController` in the `packt.jee.course_management.controller` package. Annotate it with the `@Controller`. `@Controller` annotation is of type `@Component`, and allows Spring framework to identify class specifically as controller. Add a method to get courses in `CourseController`.

```
@Controller
public class CourseController {
  @Autowired
  CourseDAO courseDAO;

  @RequestMapping("/courses")
  public String getCourses (Model model) {
    model.addAttribute("courses", courseDAO.getCourses());
    return "courses";
  }
}
```

The `CourseDAO` instance is autowired; that is, it will be injected by Spring. We have added a `getCourses` method that takes a Spring Model object. Data can be shared between View and Controller by using this Model object. Therefore, we add an attribute to Model, named `courses`, and assign the list of courses that we get by calling `courseDAO.getCourses`. This list could be used in the view JSP as the `courses` variable. We have annotated this method with `@RequestMapping`. This annotation maps an incoming request URL to a controller method. In this case, we are saying that any request (relative to the root) that starts with `/courses` should be handled by the `getCourses` method in this controller. We will add more methods to `CourseController` later and discuss some of the parameters that we can pass to the `@RequestMapping` annotation, but first, let's create a view to display the list of courses.

Calling Spring MVC Controller

We have created data access objects for `Course` and Controller. Let's see how we can call them from a view. Views in Spring are typically JSPs. Create a JSP (name it `courses.jsp`) in the `src/main/webapp/WEB-INF/views` folder. This is the folder that we configured in `servlet-context.xml` to hold the Spring view files.

Add the JSTL tag library in `courses.jsp`:

```
<%@ taglib prefix="c" uri="http://java.sun.com/jsp/jstl/core" %>
```

The markup code to display courses is very simple; we make use of the `courses` variable that is made available in the Model from the `CourseController.getCourses` method and displays values using JSTL expressions.

```
<table>
  <tr>
    <th>Id</th>
    <th>Name</th>
    <th>Credits</th>
    <th></th>
  </tr>
  <c:forEach items="${courses}" var="course">
    <tr>
      <td>${course.id}</td>
      <td>${course.name}</td>
      <td>${course.credits}</td>
    </tr>
  </c:forEach>
</table>
```

Recall that courses is a list of objects of the `CourseDTO` type. Members of `CourseDTO` are accessed in the `forEach` tag to display the actual values.

Unfortunately, we can't run this page from Eclipse the way that we have so far in this book, that is, by right-clicking on the project or page and selecting **Run As | Run on Server**. If you try to run the project (right-click on the project and select the **Run** menu), then Eclipse will try to open the `http://localhost:8080/course_management/` URL, and because we do not have any start page (`index.html` or `index.jsp`), we will get **HTTP 404 error**. The reason that we can't run the page by right-clicking and selecting the run option is that Eclipse tries to open `http://localhost:8080/course_management/WEB-INF/views/courses.jsp`, and this fails because files in `WEB-INF` are not accessible from outside the server. Another reason, or rather the primary reason, that this URL will not work is that in `web.xml`, we have mapped all requests to be handled by `DispatcherServlet` of the Spring framework and it does not find suitable mapping for the request URL.

Mapping data using @ModelAttribute

In this section, we will implement a feature to insert a new course. In the process, we will learn more about mapping requests to methods and mapping request parameters to method arguments.

In a previous section, we implemented `CourseController` with one method, `getCourses`. We will now add methods to insert new courses. To add a course, we first need to display a view with a form that accepts a user input. When a user actually submits the course, the form should post data to a URL that handles the insertion of new course data in the database. Therefore, there are two requests involved here: the first is to display the added course form and the second is to handle the data posted from the form. We will call the first request `addCourse` and the second request `doAddCourse`. Let's first create the user interface. Create a new JSP and name it `addCourse.jsp`. Add the following markup to the body of the page (JSTL and other header declarations are skipped to save space):

```
<h2>Add Course</h2>
<c:if test="${not empty error}">
  <span style="color:red;">
    ${error}<br>
  </span>
</c:if>

<c:set var="actionPath"
value="${pageContext.request.contextPath}/doAddCourse"/>
<form method="post" action="${actionPath}">
  <table>
    <tr>
      <td>Course Name:</td>
      <td><input type="text" name="name" value="${course.name}">
      </td>
    </tr>
    <tr>
      <td>Credits:</td>
      <td><input type="text" name="credits"
      value="${course.credits}"> </td>
    </tr>
    <tr>
      <td colspan="2">
      <button type="submit">Submit</button>
      </td>
    </tr>
  </table>
  <input type="hidden" name="id" value="${course.id}">
</form>
```

The page expects the course variable to be made available by the controller. In the form body, it assigns values of the course to appropriate input fields; for example, the `${course.name}` value is assigned to the text input for `Course Name`. The form posts data to the `"${pageContext.request.contextPath}/doAddCourse"` URL. Note that since our application is not deployed in the root context, we need to include the context name in the URL.

Let's now add controller methods to handle two requests for add: `addCourse` and `doAddCourse`. When an `addCourse` request is made, we want to serve the abovementioned page that displays the input form. When a user clicks the **Submit** button, we want form data to be sent using the `doAddCourse` request. Open the `CourseController` class and add the following method:

```
@RequestMapping("/addCourse")
public String addCourse (@ModelAttribute("course") CourseDTO
course, Model model) {
  if (course == null)
    course = new CourseDTO();
  model.addAttribute("course", course);
  return "addCourse";
}
```

The `addCourse` method is configured, using the `@RequestMapping` annotation, to handle a request URL starting (relative to context root) with `"/addCourse"`. If previously, a `course` attribute was added to Model, then we want this object to be passed as an argument to this function. By using `@ModelAttribute`, we tell the Spring framework to inject the model attribute called `course` if it is present and assign it to the argument named `course`; else, null is passed. In case of the first request, Model would not have a `course` attribute, so it would be null. In the subsequent requests, for example, when the user-entered data in the form (to add a course) is not valid and we want to redisplay the page, Model will have the `course` attribute.

We will now create a handler method for the `'/doAddCourse'` request. This is a `POST` request sent when the user submits the form in `addCourse.jsp` (see the form and its `POST` attribute discussed earlier).

```
@RequestMapping("/doAddCourse")
public String doAddCourse (@ModelAttribute("course") CourseDTO
course,  Model model) {
  try {
    coursesDAO.addCourse(course);
```

```
    } catch (Throwable th) {
      model.addAttribute("error", th.getLocalizedMessage());
      return "addCourse";
    }
    return "redirect:courses";
  }
```

The `doAddCourse` method also asks Spring to inject the model attribute called `course` as the first argument. It then adds a course in the database by using `CourseDAO`. In case of any error, it returns the `addCourse` string, and Spring MVC displays `addCourse.jsp` again. If a course is successfully added, then the request is redirected to `courses`, which tell Spring to process and display `course.jsp`. Recall that in `servlet-context.xml` (the Spring context configuration file in the `src/main/webapp/WEB-INF/spring/appServlet` folder), we had configured a bean with the `org.springframework.web.servlet.view.InternalResourceViewResolver` class. This class is extended from `UrlBasedViewResolver`, which understands how to handle URLs with the `redirect` and `forward` prefixes. So, in `doAddCourse`, we save the data in the database, and if successful, we redirect the request to `courses`, which displays (after processing `courses.jsp`) the list of courses.

At this point, if you want to test the application, browse to `http://localhost:8080/course_management/addCourse`. Enter the course name and credits and click **Submit**. This should take you to the courses page and display the list of courses, with the newly added course also in the list.

Note that Spring MVC looks at the form field names and properties of the object in Model (in this case, `CourseDTO`) when mapping forms values to the object. For example, the form field `name` is mapped to the `CourseDTO.name` property. So, make sure that the names of the form fields and the property names in the class (objects of which are added to Model) are the same.

Using parameters in @RequestMapping

We have seen how to use the `@RequestMapping` annotation to map an incoming request to a controller method. So far, we have mapped static URL patterns in `@RequestMapping`. However, it is possible to map a parameterized URL (line ones used in REST – see `https://spring.io/understanding/REST`) by using `@RequestMapping`. The parameters are specified inside `{}`.

Let's add a feature to update an existing course. Here, we will only discuss how to code the controller method for this feature. The complete code is available when you download the samples for this chapter.

Let's add the following method in `CourseController`.

```
@RequestMapping("/course/update/{id}")
public String updateCourse (@PathVariable int id, Model model) {
  //TODO: Error handling
  CourseDTO course = coursesDAO.getCourse(id);
  model.addAttribute("course", course);
  model.addAttribute("title", "Update Course");
  return "updateCourse";
}
```

Here, we map the `updateCourse` method to handle a request with the following URL pattern: `/course/update/{id}`, where `{id}` could be replaced with the ID (number) of any existing course, or for that matter, any integer. To access the value of this parameter, we used the `@PathVariable` annotation in the arguments.

Using the Spring interceptor

Spring interceptors can be used to process any request before it reaches the controller. These could be used, for example, to implement security features (authentication and authorization). Like request mappers, interceptors can also be declared for specific URL patterns. We will add a login page to our application, which should be displayed before any other page in the application, if the user is not already logged in.

We will first create UserDTO in the packt.jee.course_management.dto package. This class contains the user name, password, and any message to be displayed on the login page, for example, authentication errors.

```
public class UserDTO {
  private String userName;
  private String password;
  private String message;

  public boolean messageExists() {
    return message != null && message.trim().length() > 0;
  }

  //skipped setters and getters follow
}
```

Now, let's create `UserController` that will process the login request. Once a user is logged in successfully, we would like to keep this information in the session. The presence of this object in the session can be used to check whether the user is already logged in. Create the `UserController` class in the `packt.jee.course_management.controller` package.

```
@Controller
public class UserController {
}
```

Add a handler method for the `GET` request for the login page.

```
@RequestMapping (value="/login", method=RequestMethod.GET)
public String login (Model model) {

  UserDTO  user = new UserDTO();
  model.addAttribute("user", user);
  return "login";
}
```

Note that we have specified the method attribute in the `@RequestMapping` annotation. When the request URL is `/login` and the HTTP request type is `GET`, only then will the `login` method be called. This method would not be called if the `POST` request is sent from the client. In the login method, we create an instance of `UserDTO` and add it to Model so that it is accessible to view.

We will add a method to handle the `POST` request from the login page. We will keep the same URL, that is, `/login`.

```
@RequestMapping (value="/login", method=RequestMethod.POST)
public String doLogin (@ModelAttribute ("user") UserDTO user,
Model model) {

  //Hard-coded validation of user name and
//password to keep this example simple
  //But validation could be done against database or
//any other means here.
  if (user.getUserName().equals("admin") &&
       user.getPassword().equals("admin"))
    return "redirect:courses";

  user.setMessage("Invalid user name or password. Please try
  again");
  return "login";
}
```

We now have two methods in `UserController` handling the request URL `/login`. However, the login method handles the `GET` request and `doLogin` handles the `POST` request. If authentication is successful in the `doLogin` method, then we redirect to the courses (list) page. Else, we set an error message and return to the login page.

We want to save the user object created in the login method in the HTTP session. This can be done with a simple `@SessionAttributes` annotation. You can specify the list of attributes in Model that need to be saved in the session too. Further, we want to save the `user` attribute of Model in the session. Therefore, we will add the following annotation to the `UserController` class:

```
@Controller
@SessionAttributes("user")

public class UserController {

}
```

Now, let's create the login page. Create `login.jsp` in the `views` folder and add the following code in the HTML `<body>`:

```
<c:if test="${user.messageExists()}">
  <span style="color:red;">
    ${user.message}<br>
  </span>
</c:if>

<form id="loginForm" method="POST">
  User Id : <input type="text" name="userName" required="required"
  value="${user.userName}"><br>
  Password : <input type="password" name="password"><br>
  <button type="submit">Submit</button>
</form>
```

The page expects `user` (instance of `UserDTO`) to be available. This is made available by `UserController` through Model.

We now have a login page and `UserController` to handle the authentication, but how do we make sure this page is displayed for every request when the user is not already logged in? This is where we can use a Spring interceptor. We will configure the interceptor in the Spring context configuration file: `servlet-context.xml`. Add the following code to `servlet-context.xml`:

```
<interceptors>
  <interceptor>
```

```
    <mapping path="/**"/>
      <beans:bean
class="packt.jee.course_management.interceptor.LoginInterceptor"/>
  </interceptor>
</interceptors>
```

In the above configuration, we are telling Spring to call `LoginInterceptor` before executing any request (indicated by `mapping path = "/**"`).

We will now implement `LoginInterceptor`. Interceptors must implement `HandlerInterceptor`. We will make `LoginInterceptor` extend `HandlerInterceptorAdapter`, which implements `HandlerInterceptor`.

Create `LoginInterceptor` in the `packt.jee.course_management.interceptor` package.

```
@Component
public class LoginInterceptor extends HandlerInterceptorAdapter {

  public boolean preHandle(HttpServletRequest request,
  HttpServletResponse response, Object handler)
        throws Exception {

    //get session from request
    HttpSession session = request.getSession();
    UserDTO user = (UserDTO) session.getAttribute("user");

    //Check if the current request is for /login. In that case
    //do nothing, else we will execute the request in loop
    //Intercept only if request is not /login
    String context = request.getContextPath();
    if (!request.getRequestURI().equals(context + "/login") &&
      (user == null || user.getUserName() == null)) {
      //User is not logged in. Redirect to /login
      response.sendRedirect(request.getContextPath() + "/login");
      //do not process this request further
      return false;
    }

    return true;
  }

}
```

The `preHandle` method of the interceptor is called before Spring executes any request. If we return `true` from the method, then the request is handled further; else, it is aborted. In `preHandle`, we first check whether the `user` object is present in the session. The presence of the `user` object means that the user is already logged in. In such a case, we don't do anything more in this interceptor and return `true`. If the user is not logged in, then we redirect to the login page and return false so that Spring does not process this request further.

Spring MVC application using JPA

In the previous section, we saw how to create a web application by using Spring and JDBC. In this section, we will take a quick look at how to use Spring with JPA (which stands for Java persistence API). We have already learnt how to use JPA in *Chapter 4, Creating a JEE Database Application*, and in *Chapter 7, Creating JEE Application using EJB*, so we won't get into detail of how to set up an Eclipse project for JPA. However, we will discuss how to use JPA along with Spring in detail in this section.

We will create a separate project for this example. Create a Spring MVC project as described in the *Creating a Spring project* section. On the second page of the project wizard, where you are asked to enter a top-level package name, enter `packt.jee.course_management_jpa`. Recall that the last part of this package name is also used to create the web application context.

Configuring JPA

We are going to use the EclipseLink JPA provider and the MySQL database driver in this project. So, add the Maven dependencies for them in the `pom.xml` file of the project.

```
<!-- JPA -->
<dependency>
      <groupId>org.eclipse.persistence</groupId>
      <artifactId>eclipselink</artifactId>
      <version>2.5.2</version>
    </dependency>
    <dependency>
      <groupId>mysql</groupId>
      <artifactId>mysql-connector-java</artifactId>
      <version>5.1.34</version>
    </dependency>
```

We will now configure the project for JPA. Right-click on the project and select **Configure | Convert to JPA Project**. This opens the **Project Facets** page, with JPA selected as one of the facets.

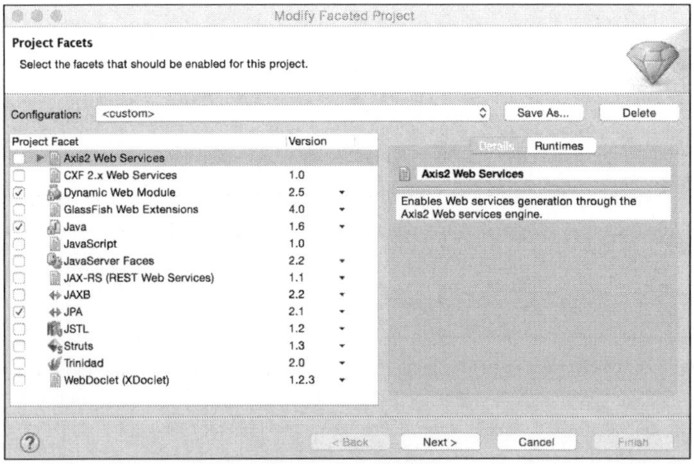

Figure 8.5 Project Facets

Click the **Next** button to configure the JPA facet.

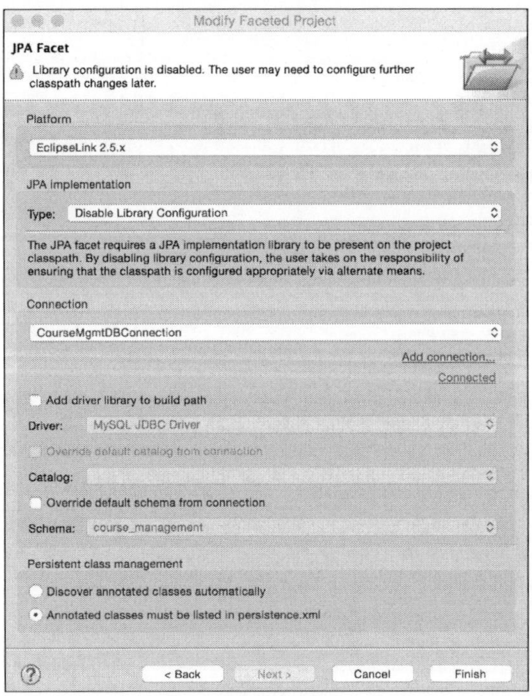

Figure 8.6 Project facets

Select the `EclipseLink` platform in the preceding page. We will also disable the library configuration (select from the drop-down for the **Type** field). Configure the MySQL **Connection** (named `CourseMgmtDBConnection`), as described in the *Configuring JPA* section of *Chapter 7, Creating JEE Applications with EJB*.

Click **Finish**. `Persistence.xml` is created under the **JPA Content** group in **Project Explorer** (the actual location of this file is `src/main/resources/META-INF/persistence.xml`). We will configure the properties for the MySQL JDBC connection in this. Open the file, and click the **Connection** tab.

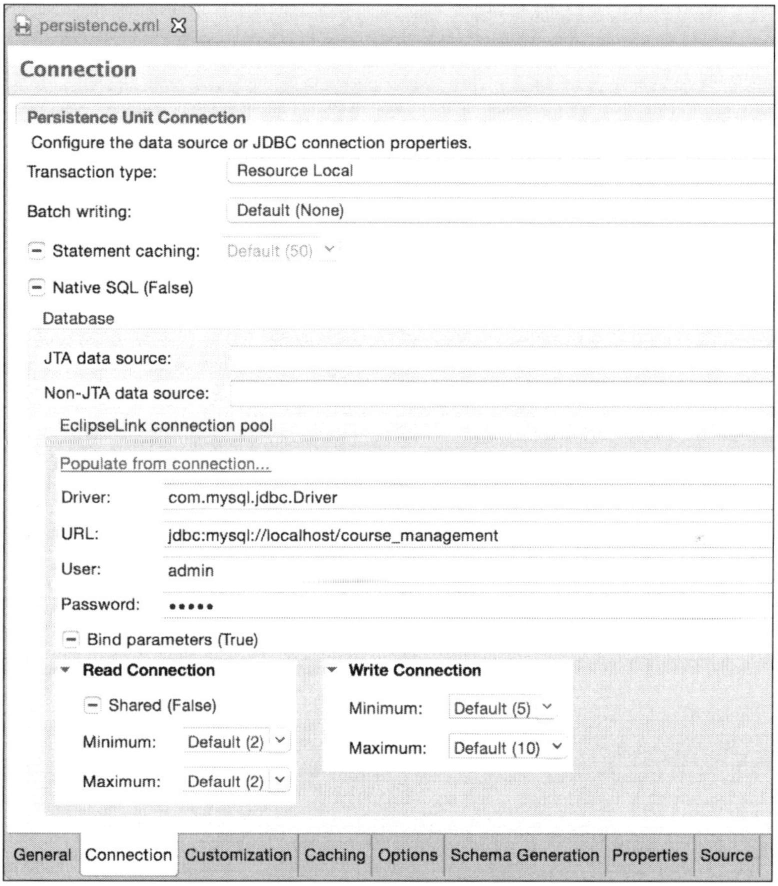

Figure 8.7 Configure connection in persistence.xml

Select **Transaction type** as `Resource Local`. Then, enter the JDBC driver details. Save the file.

Creating the Course entity

Right-click on the project and select the **JPA Tools** | **Generate Tables from Entities** menu.

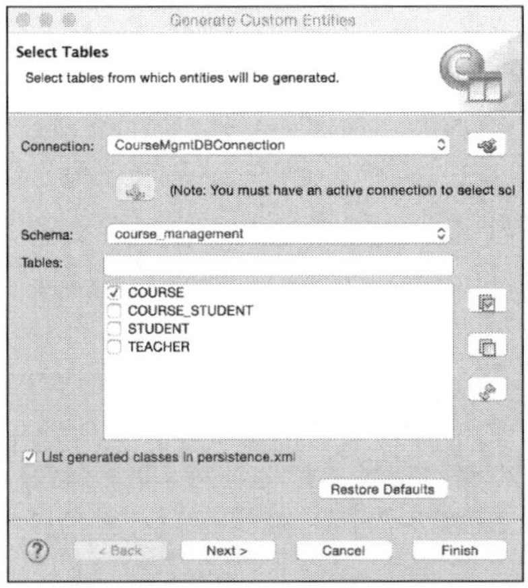

Figure 8.8 Generate Course entity

Make sure that `CourseMgmtDBConnection` is selected (refer to the *Configuring JPA* section of *Chapter 7, Creating JEE Applications with EJB*, for configuring the MySQL database connection in Eclipse) and that **List generated classes in persistence.xml** is selected. Click **Next** on this and the next page. In the **Customize Defaults** page, select `identity` **Key generator** and set the package name as `packt.jee.course_management_jpa.entity`.

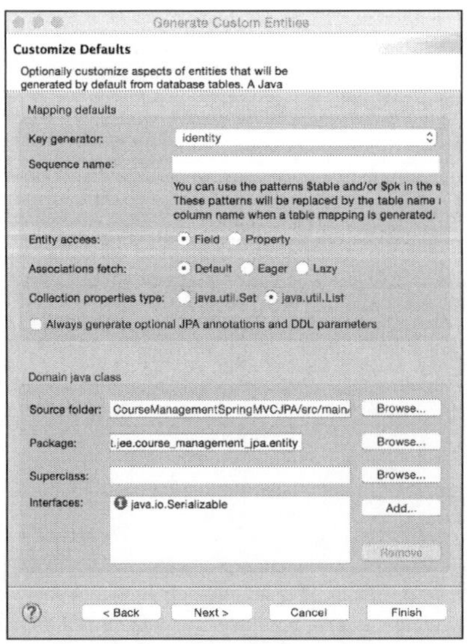

Figure 8.9 Customize JPA entity defaults

Click **Next**. Verify the entity class name and the other details.

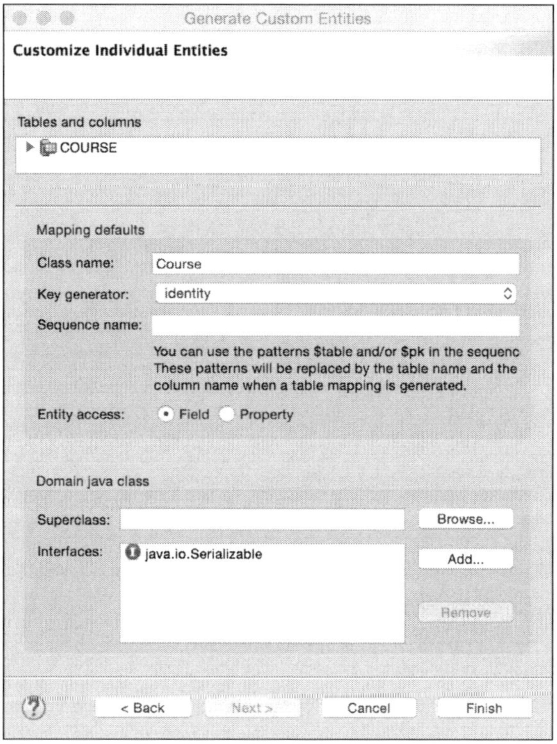

Figure 8.10 Customize JPA entity details

Click **Finish**. A course entity class would be created in the package selected in *Figure 8.9 Customize JPA entity defaults*.

```
//skipped imports
@Entity
@Table(name="COURSE")
@NamedQuery(name="Course.findAll", query="SELECT c FROM Course c")
public class Course implements Serializable {
  private static final long serialVersionUID = 1L;

  @Id
  @GeneratedValue(strategy=GenerationType.IDENTITY)
  private int id;

  private int credits;

  private String name;
```

```
    @Column(name="teacher_id")
    private int teacherId;

    //skipped setter and getters
  }
```

Note that the wizard has created a named query to get all the courses from the table.

We now need to create `EntityManagerFactory` so that `EntityManager` could be created from it (refer to the *JPA concepts* section in *Chapter 4, Creating a JEE Database Application*). We will create a Spring bean/component to create and store `EntityManagerFactory`. Further, we will inject (autowire) this component in the DAO class.

Create the `JPAEntityFactoryBean` class in the `packt.jee.course_management_jpa.entity` package.

```
  //skipped imports

  @Component
  public class JPAEntityFactoryBean {

    EntityManagerFactory entityManagerFactory;

    @PostConstruct
    public void init() {
      entityManagerFactory =
  Persistence.createEntityManagerFactory("CourseManagementSpringMVCJ
  PA");
    }

    public EntityManagerFactory getEntityManagerFactory() {
      return entityManagerFactory;
    }
  }
```

In the constructor of the preceding class, we create `EntityManagerFactory`. The argument to `createEntityManagerFactory` is the name of the persistence unit, as specified in `persistence.xml`.

Creating Course DAO and Controller

Let's first create the `CourseDAO` class. We will have an instance of `JPAEntityFactoryBean` injected (autowired) in this class. Create the `packt.jee.course_management_jpa.dao` package and the `CourseDAO` class in it.

```
@Component
public class CourseDAO {

  @Autowired
  JPAEntityFactoryBean entityFactoryBean;

  public List<Course> getCourses() {
    //Get entity manager
    EntityManagerFactory emf =
    entityFactoryBean.getEntityManagerFactory();
    EntityManager em = emf.createEntityManager();

    //Execute Query
    TypedQuery<Course> courseQuery =
    em.createNamedQuery("Course.findAll", Course.class);
      List<Course> courses = courseQuery.getResultList();
      em.close();

      return courses;
  }
}
```

In the `getCourses` method, we first create `EntityManager` (from `JPAEntityFactoryBean`) and execute the named query. Once we get results, we close `EntityManager`.

The controller class for `Course` will have `CourseDAO` autoinjected (autowired). Create `CourseController` in the `packt.jee.course_management_jpa.controller` package.

```
//skipped imports
@Controller
public class CourseController {
  @Autowired
  CourseDAO courseDAO;

  @RequestMapping("/courses")
```

```
    public String getCourses(Model model) {
      model.addAttribute("courses", courseDAO.getCourses());
      return "courses";
    }
  }
```

As we saw in `CourseController` created for the JDBC application earlier, we get courses from the database and add the list of courses to Model under the key name `courses`. This variable would be available to the view page that displays the list of courses.

Creating the Course list view

We have all the classes to get courses. We will now create a JSP to display the list of courses. Create `courses.jsp` in the `src/main/webapp/WEB-INF/views` folder. Add the following content in the HTML body of the page.

```
<h2>Courses:</h2>

<table>
  <tr>
    <th>Id</th>
    <th>Name</th>
    <th>Credits</th>
    <th></th>
  </tr>
  <c:forEach items="${courses}" var="course">
    <tr>
      <td>${course.id}</td>
      <td>${course.name}</td>
      <td>${course.credits}</td>
    </tr>
  </c:forEach>
</table>
```

The view page makes use of the JSTL tags to iterate over courses (by using the variable that was made available in Model by the controller) and display them.

We are not going to build the entire application here. The idea was to understand how to use JPA with Spring MVC, which we have learnt in this section.

Summary

In this chapter, we learnt how to use Spring MVC to create web applications. As the name indicates, Spring MVC implements an MVC design pattern, which enables a clear separation of the user interface code and the business logic code.

Using the dependency injection feature of the Spring framework, we can easily manage the dependencies of different objects in the application. We also learnt how to use JDBC and JPA along with Spring MVC to create data-driven web applications.

In the next chapter, we will see how to create and consume web services in JEE applications. We will look at both SOAP-based and RESTful web services.

9
Creating Web Services

As we learnt in *Chapter 7, Creating JEE Applications with EJB*, EJBs can be used to create distributed applications. This helps in the communication between different JEE applications in enterprises. However, what if an enterprise wants to let its partners or customers make use of some of the application functionality? For example, an airline might want to let its partners make online reservations. One option is for the partner to redirect its customer to the airline website, but this does not provide a unified experience to the end users. A better way to handle this is for the airline to expose its reservation APIs to partners who can integrate these APIs in their own applications, providing a unified user experience. This is the case of a distributed application, and EJBs can be used in such cases. However, for EJBs to work in such scenarios, where API calls cross enterprise boundaries, the client of APIs also need to be implemented in Java. As we know this is not practical. Some of the airline partners, in the above example, may have their applications implemented using different programming platforms, such as .NET and PHP.

Web services are useful in situations such as the abovementioned one. Web services are self-contained APIs that are based on open standards and are platform independent. They are widely used for communication between disparate systems. There are mainly two types of web service implementations:

- Simple Object Access Protocol (SOAP) based
- Representational State Transfer (RESTful) services

For many years, SOAP-based web services were quite popular, but recently, RESTful services are gaining ground because of the simplicity in its implementation and consumption.

Web services are a common integration form that offer **Service-Oriented Architecture** (**SOA**) in which certain components expose services for consumption by other components or applications. The consumer of such services can create an entire application by assembling a number of such loosely coupled services, possibly from different sources.

In this chapter, we will see how to develop and consume both SOAP and RESTful services by using JEE and Eclipse. However, before this, it will be useful to have a quick look at **Java Architecture for XML Binding** (**JAXB**), because it is used in the implementations of both REST and SOAP web services.

JAXB

JAXB provides an easy way to convert an XML or JSON representation of data into a Java object and vice versa. Using simple annotations, you can have a JAXB implementation create XML or JSON data from a Java object or create a Java object from XML or JSON. Since the XML and JSON data formats are widely used in web services, it is useful to learn JAXB APIs. The process of generating XML and JSON from Java objects is known as marshalling, and creating Java objects from XML or JSON is called unmarshalling. To understand how Java data types are mapped to XML schema types, refer to `https://docs.oracle.com/javase/tutorial/jaxb/intro/bind.html`.

The following are a few important JAXB annotations:

- `@XmlRootElement`: This annotation specifies the root element of the XML document and is typically used at the class level.
- `@XmlElement`: This annotation specifies an XML element that is not a root element. Java class members can be marked as `XMLElement` when the class is annotated with `@XmlRootElement`.
- `@XmlAttribute`: This annotation marks a field of the Java class as an attribute of the parent XML element.
- `@XmlAccessorType`: This annotation is specified at the class level. It lets you control how class fields are serialized to XML or JSON. Valid values are `XmlAccessType.FIELD` (every non-static and non-`@XmlTransient` field is serialized), `XmlAccessType.PROPERTY` (every pair of getter/setter that is not annotated with `@XmlTransient` is serialized), `XmlAccessType.NONE` (no fields are serialized, unless specific fields are annotated for serialization), and `XmlAccessType.PUBLIC_MEMBER` (all public getter/setter pairs are serialized, unless annotated with `@XmlTransient`).

- `@XMLTransient`: This annotation specifies the field or getter/setter pair that is not to be serialized.

For a complete list of JAXB annotations, refer to `https://jaxb.java.net/tutorial/section_6_1-JAXB-Annotations.html#JAXB Annotations`.

JAXB example

Let's create a Maven project to try out JAXB APIs. Select the **File | Maven Project** menu.

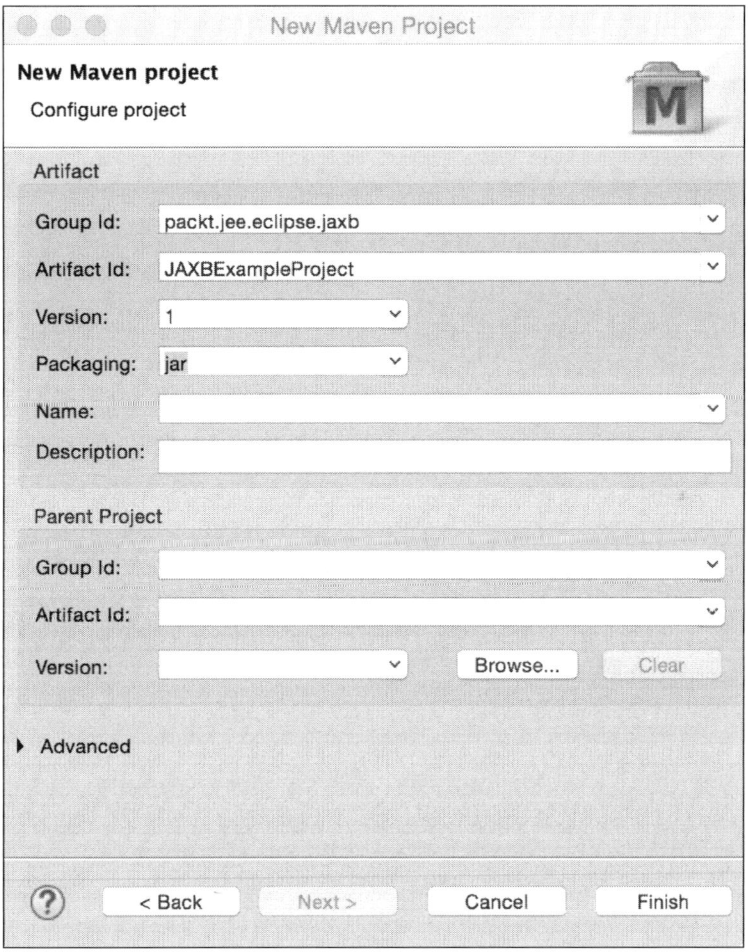

Figure 9.1 Create Maven project for JAXB example

Make sure that the project is configured to use JRE 1.7 or later. Let's now create two classes - `Course` and `Teacher`. We would want to serialize instances of these classes to XML and back. Create these classes in the `packt.jee.eclipse.jaxb.example` package.

```
package packt.jee.eclipse.jaxb.example;
//Skipped imports

@XmlRootElement
@XmlAccessorType(XmlAccessType.FIELD)
public class Course {
  @XmlAttribute
  private int id;
  @XmlElement(namespace="http://packt.jee.eclipse.jaxb.example")
  private String name;
  private int credits;
  @XmlElement(name="course_teacher")
  private Teacher teacher;

  public Course() {}

  public Course (int id, String name, int credits) {
    this.id = id;
    this.name = name;
    this.credits = credits;
  }

  //Getters and setters follow
}
```

When a `Course` is marshalled to an XML document, we want the `course` element to be the root. Therefore, the class is annotated with `@XmlRootElement`. You can specify a different name for the root element (other than the class name) by specifying the `name` attribute, for example:

```
@XmlRootElement(name="school_course")
```

The `id` field is marked as an attribute of the root element. You don't have to mark fields specifically as elements if there are public getters/setters for them. However, if you want to set additional attributes, then you need to annotate them with `@XmlElement`. For example, we have specified namespace for the `name` element/field. The `credits` field is not annotated, but it will still be marshalled as an XML element.

```
package packt.jee.eclipse.jaxb.example;

public class Teacher {
  private int id;
```

```
    private String name;

    public Teacher() {}

    public Teacher (int id, String name) {
      this.id = id;
      this.name = name;
    }

    //Getters and setters follow
  }
```

We are not annotating the `Teacher` class with JAXB because we are not going to marshal it directly. It will be marshalled by JAXB when an instance of `Course` is marshalled.

Let's create a class with the `main` method.

Create the `JAXBExample` class.

```
  package packt.jee.eclipse.jaxb.example;

  //Skipped imports

  public class JAXBExample {

    public static void main(String[] args) throws Exception {
      doJAXBXml();

    }

    //Create XML from Java object and then vice versa
    public static void doJAXBXml() throws Exception {
      Course course = new Course(1,"Course-1", 5);
      course.setTeacher(new Teacher(1, "Teacher-1"));

      JAXBContext context = JAXBContext.newInstance(Course.class);

      //Marshall Java object to XML
      Marshaller marshaller = context.createMarshaller();
      //Set option to format generated XML
      marshaller.setProperty(Marshaller.JAXB_FORMATTED_OUTPUT,
      true);
      StringWriter stringWriter = new StringWriter();
```

```
        //Marshal Course object and write to the StringWriter
        marshaller.marshal(course, stringWriter);
        //Get String from the StringWriter
        String courseXml = stringWriter.getBuffer().toString();
        stringWriter.close();
        //Print course XML
        System.out.println(courseXml);

        //Now unmarshall courseXML to create Course object
        Unmarshaller unmarshaller = context.createUnmarshaller();
        //Create StringReader from courseXml
        StringReader stringReader = new StringReader(courseXml);
        //Create StreamSource which will be used by JAXB unmarshaller
        StreamSource streamSource = new StreamSource(stringReader);
        Course unmarshalledCourse =
        unmarshaller.unmarshal(streamSource, Course.class).getValue();
        System.out.println("-----------------\nUnmarshalled course
        name -
        "
            + unmarshalledCourse.getName());
        stringReader.close();
        }
    }
```

To marshal or unmarshal using JAXB, we first create `JAXBContext`, passing it a Java class that needs to be worked on. Then, we create the marshaller or unmarshaller, set the relevant properties, and perform the operation. The code is quite simple. We first marshal the `Course` instance to XML and then, use the same XML output to unmarshal it back to a `Course` instance. Right-click on the class and select **Run As | Java Application**. You should see the following output in the console.

```
<?xml version="1.0" encoding="UTF-8" standalone="yes"?>
<course id="1" xmlns:ns2="http://packt.jee.eclipse.jaxb.example">
    <ns2:name>Course-1</ns2:name>
    <credits>5</credits>
    <course_teacher>
        <id>1</id>
        <name>Teacher-1</name>
    </course_teacher>
</course>

-----------------
Unmarshalled course name - Course-1
```

Let's now see how to marshal a Java object to JSON and back. JSON support in JAXB is not available out of the box in JDK. We will have to use an external library that supports JAXB APIs with JSON. One such library is EclipseLink MOXy (`https://eclipse.org/eclipselink/#moxy`). We will use this library to marshal the `Course` object to JSON.

Open `pom.xml` and add a dependency on EclipseLink.

```
<dependencies>
  <dependency>
    <groupId>org.eclipse.persistence</groupId>
    <artifactId>eclipselink</artifactId>
    <version>2.6.1-RC1</version>
  </dependency>
</dependencies>
```

We also need to set the `javax.xml.bind.context.factory` property to make the JAXB implementation use EclipseLink's `JAXBContextFactory`. Create the `jaxb.properties` file in the same package as the classes whose instances are to be marshalled. In this case, create the file in the `packt.jee.eclipse.jaxb.example` package. Set the following property in this file:

```
javax.xml.bind.context.factory=org.eclipse.persistence.jaxb.
JAXBContextFactory
```

This is very important. If you do not set this property, then the example won't work.

Open `JAXBExample.java` and add the following method:

```
//Create JSON from Java object and then vice versa
public static void doJAXBJson() throws Exception {

  Course course = new Course(1,"Course-1", 5);
  course.setTeacher(new Teacher(1, "Teacher-1"));

  JAXBContext context = JAXBContext.newInstance(Course.class);

  //Marshal Java object to JSON
  Marshaller marshaller = context.createMarshaller();
  //Set option to format generated JSON
  marshaller.setProperty(Marshaller.JAXB_FORMATTED_OUTPUT,
  true);
  marshaller.setProperty(MarshallerProperties.MEDIA_TYPE,
  "application/json");
```

```
    marshaller.setProperty(MarshallerProperties.JSON_INCLUDE_ROOT,
    true);

    StringWriter stringWriter = new StringWriter();
    //Marshal Course object and write to the StringWriter
    marshaller.marshal(course, stringWriter);
    //Get String from the StringWriter
    String courseJson = stringWriter.getBuffer().toString();
    stringWriter.close();
    //Print course JSON
    System.out.println(courseJson);

    //Now, unmarshall courseJson to create Course object
    Unmarshaller unmarshler = context.createUnmarshaller();
    unmarshler.setProperty(MarshallerProperties.MEDIA_TYPE,
    "application/json");
    unmarshler.setProperty(MarshallerProperties.JSON_INCLUDE_ROOT,
    true);

    //Create StringReader from courseJson
    StringReader stringReader = new StringReader(courseJson);
    //Create StreamSource which will be used by JAXB unmarshaller
    StreamSource streamSource = new StreamSource(stringReader);
    Course unmarshalledCourse = unmarshler.unmarshal(streamSource,
    Course.class).getValue();
    System.out.println("----------------\nUnmarshalled course
    name - " + unmarshalledCourse.getName());
    stringReader.close();
}
```

Much of the code is the same as in the method `doJAXBXml` method. Specific changes are as follows:

- We set the `marshaller` property for generating the JSON output (`application/json`)
- We set another `marshaller` property to include the JSON root in the output.
- We set the corresponding properties on `unmarshaller`

Modify the main method to call `doJAXBJson`, instead of `doJAXBXml`. When you run the application, you should see the following output:

```
{
   "course" : {
      "id" : 1,
```

```
        "name" : "Course-1",
        "credits" : 5,
        "course_teacher" : {
            "id" : 1,
            "name" : "Teacher-1"
        }
    }
}
-----------------
Unmarshalled course name - Course-1
```

We have covered the basics of JAXB in this chapter. For a detailed tutorial on JAXB, refer to `https://docs.oracle.com/javase/tutorial/jaxb/intro/index.html`.

REST web services

We will first start with REST web services because they are widely used and are easy to implement. REST is not necessarily a protocol but an architectural style, and is typically based on HTTP. REST web services act on the resources on the server side, and the actions are based on the HTTP method (`Get`, `Post`, `Put`, and `Delete`). The state of resources is transferred over HTTP in either the XML or the JSON format, although JSON is more popular. The resources on the server side are identified by URLs. For example, to get details of a course with ID `10`, you could use the HTTP `GET` method with the following URL: `http://<server_address>:<port>/course/10`. Notice that the parameter is a part of the base URL. To add a new `Course` or modify a `Course`, you could use either the `POST` or the `PUT` method. Further, the `DELETE` method could be used to delete a `Course` by using the same URL as that used for getting the course, that is, `http://<server_address>:<port>/course/10`.

Resource URLs in REST web services can be nested too; for example, to get all courses in a particular department (with ID, say `20`), the REST URL could be as follows: `http://<server_address>:<port>/department/20/courses`.

Refer to `https://en.wikipedia.org/wiki/Representational_state_transfer` for more details on the properties of REST web services and HTTP methods used for acting on the REST resources on the server side.

The Java specification for working with RESTful web services is called JAX-RS, a Java API for RESTful services (`https://jax-rs-spec.java.net/`). Project Jersey (`https://jersey.java.net/`) is the reference implementation of this specification. We will use this reference implementation to implement REST web services in this chapter.

Creating RESTful web services using Jersey

We will create a web service for the Course Management example that we have been developing in this book. The web service will have methods to get all courses and create a new course. To keep the example simple, we will not write the data access code (you could use the JDBC or JDO APIs that we have learnt in the previous chapters), but will hardcode the data.

First, create a Maven web project. Select **File** | **New** | **Maven Project**. Check the **Create a Simple Project** checkbox on the first page of the wizard and click **Next**.

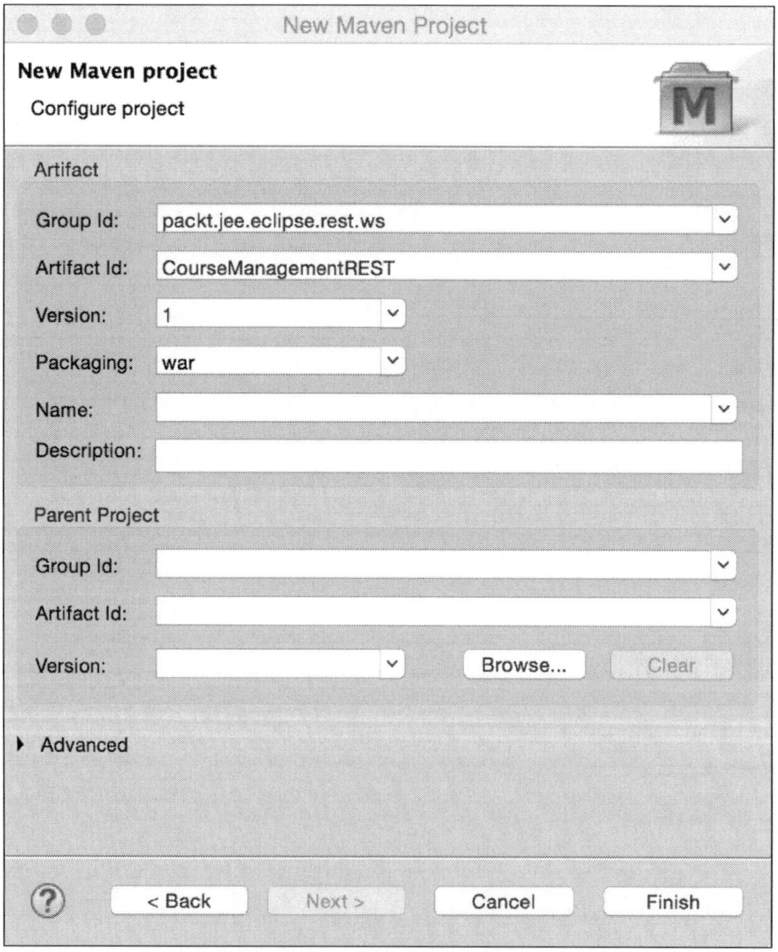

Figure 9.2 Create Maven project for REST web service

Enter the **Artifact** details and click **Finish**. Make sure that the packaging is `war`.

Since we are going to use the Jersey library for the JAX-RS implementation, we will add its Maven dependency into the project. Open `pom.xml` and add the following dependency:

```
<dependencies>
  <dependency>
    <groupId>org.glassfish.jersey.containers</groupId>
    <artifactId>jersey-container-servlet</artifactId>
    <version>2.18</version>
  </dependency>
</dependencies>
```

Using the JAX-RS `@Path` annotation, we can convert any Java class into a REST resource. Values passed to the `@Path` annotation are the relative URIs of the resource. Methods in the implementation class to be executed for different HTTP methods are annotated with one of the following annotations: `@GET`, `@PUT`, `@POST`, or `@DELETE`. The `@Path` annotation can also be used at the method level for a sub-resource path (the main resource or the root resource path is at the class level, again using the `@Path` annotation). We can also specify the mime type that these methods produce or consume by using the `@Produces` or `@Consumes` annotation, respectively.

Before we create a web service implementation class, let's create utility classes, more specifically in this case, DTO.

Create the `Course` and `Teacher` classes in the `packt.jee.eclipse.rest.ws.dto` package. We will also annotate them with the JAXB annotations.

Here is the `Teacher` class:

```
package packt.jee.eclipse.rest.ws.dto;

import javax.xml.bind.annotation.XmlAccessType;
import javax.xml.bind.annotation.XmlAccessorType;
import javax.xml.bind.annotation.XmlAttribute;
import javax.xml.bind.annotation.XmlElement;
import javax.xml.bind.annotation.XmlRootElement;

@XmlRootElement
@XmlAccessorType(XmlAccessType.FIELD)
public class Teacher {

  @XmlAttribute
  private int id;

  @XmlElement(name="teacher_name")
```

```
    private String name;

    //constructors
    public Course() {}

    public Course (int id, String name, int credits, Teacher
    teacher) {
      this.id = id;
      this.name = name;
      this.credits = credits;
      this.teacher = teacher;
    }

    //Getters and setters follow
  }
```

Further, here is the Course class:

```
package packt.jee.eclipse.rest.ws.dto;

import javax.xml.bind.annotation.XmlAccessType;
import javax.xml.bind.annotation.XmlAccessorType;
import javax.xml.bind.annotation.XmlAttribute;
import javax.xml.bind.annotation.XmlElement;
import javax.xml.bind.annotation.XmlRootElement;

@XmlRootElement
@XmlAccessorType(XmlAccessType.FIELD)
public class Course {

  @XmlAttribute
  private int id;

  @XmlElement(name="course_name")
  private String name;

  private int credits;

  private Teacher teacher;

  //constructors
  public Teacher() {}

  public Teacher (int id, String name) {
    this.id = id;
```

```
        this.name = name;
    }

    //Getters and setters follow
}
```

We have annotated the `id` fields in both classes as `@XMLAttribute`. If objects of these classes are marshalled (converted from Java objects) to XML, `Course id` and `Teacher id` would be the attributes (instead of elements) of the root element (`Course` and `Teacher`, respectively). If no filed annotation is specified and if public getters/setters for an attribute are present, then it is considered an XML element with the same name.

We have specifically used the `@XMLElement` annotation for name fields because we want to rename them as `course_name` or `teacher_name` when marshalled to XML.

Implementing the REST GET request

Let's now create a REST web service implementation class. Create the `CourseService` class in the `packt.jee.eclipse.rest.ws.services` package.

```
package packt.jee.eclipse.rest.ws.services;

import javax.ws.rs.GET;
import javax.ws.rs.Path;
import javax.ws.rs.PathParam;
import javax.ws.rs.Produces;
import javax.ws.rs.core.MediaType;

import packt.jee.eclipse.rest.ws.dto.Course;
import packt.jee.eclipse.rest.ws.dto.Teacher;

@Path("/course")
public class CourseService {

  @GET
  @Produces (MediaType.APPLICATION_XML)
  @Path("get/{courseId}")
  public Course getCourse (@PathParam("courseId") int id) {

    //To keep the example simple, we will return
    //hardcoded values here. However, you could get
```

```
        //data from database using, for example, JDO or JDBC

        return new Course(id,"Course-" + id, 5, new Teacher(2,
        "Teacher1"));
    }
}
```

The `@Path` annotation specifies that resources made available by this class will be accessible by the relative URI `"/course"`.

The `getCourse` method has many annotations. Let's discuss them one at a time.

The `@GET` annotation specifies that when the relative URI (as specified by `@Path` on the `CourseService` class) `"/course"` is called using the HTTP `GET` method, then this method will be invoked.

`@Produces (MediaType.APPLICATION_JSON)` specifies that this method generates a JSON output. If the client specifies the accepted mime types, then this annotation would be used to resolve the method to be called, if more than one method is annotated with `@GET` (or, for that matter, any of the other HTTP method annotations). For example, if we have another method called `getCourseJSON` annotated with `@GET` but producing data with different mime types (as specified by `@Produces`), then an appropriate method will be selected on the basis of the mime type requested by the client. The mime type in the `@Produces` annotation also tells the JAX-RS implementation the mime type of the response when marshalling the Java object that is returned from the method. For example, in the `getCourse` method, we return an instance of `Course`, and the mime type specified in `@Produces` tells Jersey to generate an XML representation of this instance.

The `@Path` annotation can also be used at the method level to specify sub-resources. The value specified in `@Path` at the method level is relative to the path value specified at the class level. The resource (in this case, `Course`) with ID `20` can be accessed as `/course/get/20`. The complete URL can be `http://<server-address>:<port>/<app-name>/course/get/10`. Parameter names in the path value are enclosed in `{}`.

Path parameters need to be identified in method arguments by using the `@PathParam` annotation and the name of the parameter as its value. The JAX-RS implementation framework matches the path parameters with arguments matching the `@PathParam` annotation and appropriately passes the parameter values to the method.

To keep the example simple and keep focus on the implementation of REST web services, we are not going to implement any business logic in this method. We could get data from the database by using, for example, the JDO or JDBC APIs (and we have seen examples of how to use these APIs in the earlier chapters), but we are just going to return hardcoded data. The method returns an instance of the `Course` class. The JAX-RS implementation would convert this object into an XML representation by using JAXB when the data is finally returned to the client.

We need to tell the Jersey framework what packages it needs to scan to look for REST resources. There are two ways to do this:

- One is by configuring the Jersey Servlet in `web.xml` (see `https://jersey.java.net/nonav/documentation/latest/user-guide.html#deployment.servlet`).
- For Servlet 3.x containers, we could create a subclass of `javax.ws.rs.core.Application`. Tomcat 8.0 that we have been using in this book is a Servlet 3.x container.

We will use the second option to create a subclass of `Application`. However, instead of directly subclassing `Application`, we will subclass the `ResourceConfig` class of Jersey, which in turn extends `Application`.

Create the `CourseMgmtRESTApplication` class in the `packt.jee.eclipse.rest.ws` package.

```
package packt.jee.eclipse.rest.ws;

import javax.ws.rs.ApplicationPath;

import org.glassfish.jersey.server.ResourceConfig;

@ApplicationPath("services")
public class CourseMgmtRESTApplication extends ResourceConfig {

  public CourseMgmtRESTApplication () {
    packages("packt.jee.eclipse.rest.ws.services");
  }

}
```

We have used the `@ApplicationPath` annotation to specify the URL mapping for the REST services implemented using JAX-RS. All `@Path` URIs on the resource implementation classes will be relative to this path. For example, the `"/course"` URI that we specified for the `CourseService` class would be relative to `"services"`, specified in the `@ApplicationPath` annotation.

Before we deploy the application and test our service, we need to generate `web.xml`. Right-click on the project in **Project Explorer** and select **Java EE Tools | Generate Deployment Descriptor Stub**. This will create `web.xml` in the `WEB-INF` folder. We don't need to modify it for this example.

Configure Tomcat in Eclipse as described in the *Installing Tomcat* section of *Chapter 1, Introducing JEE and Eclipse*, and in the *Configuring Tomcat in Eclipse* section of *Chapter 2, Creating a Simple JEE Web Application*). To deploy our web application, right-click on the configured Tomcat server in the **Servers** view and select the **Add and Remove** option. Add the current project.

Start the Tomcat server by right-clicking on the configured server in the `Servers` view and selecting **Start**.

Testing the REST GET request in browser

To test the web service, browse to `http://localhost:8080/CourseManagementREST/services/course/get/10`.

You should see the following XML displayed in the browser:

```
<?xml version="1.0" encoding="UTF-8" standalone="yes"?>
<course id="10">
  <course_name>Course-10</course_name>
  <credits>5</credits>
  <teacher id="2">
    <teacher_name>Teacher1</teacher_name>
  </teacher>
</course>
```

Instead of generating an XML response, let's say we want to create a JSON response, because it would be much easier to consume a JSON response from JavaScript in a web page than an XML response. To add support for creating a JSON response, we will have to change the value of the `@Produces` annotation in the `CourseService` class. Currently, it is set to `MediaType.APPLICATION_XML` and we want to set it to `MediaType.APPLICATION_JSON`.

```
public class CourseService {

  @GET
  @Produces (MediaType.APPLICATION_JSON)
  @Path("get/{courseId}")
  public Course getCourse (@PathParam("courseId") int id) {
...
}
}
```

We also need to add libraries to handle the JSON response. The Jersey library does support the creation of a JSON response, but we need to add a dependency on the module that handles this. Open `pom.xml` of the project and add the following dependency:

```
<dependency>
  <groupId>org.glassfish.jersey.media</groupId>
  <artifactId>jersey-media-json-jackson</artifactId>
  <version>2.18</version>
</dependency>
```

Restart the Tomcat server and browse to the `http://localhost:8080/CourseManagementREST/services/course/get/10` URL again. This time, you should see a JSON response:

```
{
    id: 10,
    credits: 5,
    teacher: {
        id: 2,
        teacher_name: "Teacher1"
    },
    course_name: "Course-10"
}
```

Let's create two versions of the `getCourse` methods, one that produces XML and the other that produces JSON. Replace the `getCourse` function (and annotation) with the following code:

```
@GET
@Produces (MediaType.APPLICATION_JSON)
@Path("get/{courseId}")
public Course getCourseJSON (@PathParam("courseId") int id) {

  return createDummyCourse(id);

}

@GET
@Produces (MediaType.APPLICATION_XML)
@Path("get/{courseId}")
public Course getCourseXML (@PathParam("courseId") int id) {

  return createDummyCourse(id);

}

private Course createDummyCourse (int id) {
  //To keep the example simple, we will return
```

```
        //hardcoded value here. However, you could get
        //data from database using, for example, JDO or JDBC

        return new Course(id,"Course-" + id, 5, new Teacher(2,
        "Teacher1"));
    }
```

We have refactored the code. We added the `createDummyCourse` method, which has the same code that we had earlier in the `getCourse` method. We now have two versions of `getCourse` methods: `getCourseXML` and `getCourseJSON`, producing the XML and JSON responses, respectively.

Creating a Java client for the REST GET web service

Let's now create a Java client application for our REST web service. Create a simple Maven project, call it `CourseManagementRESTClient`.

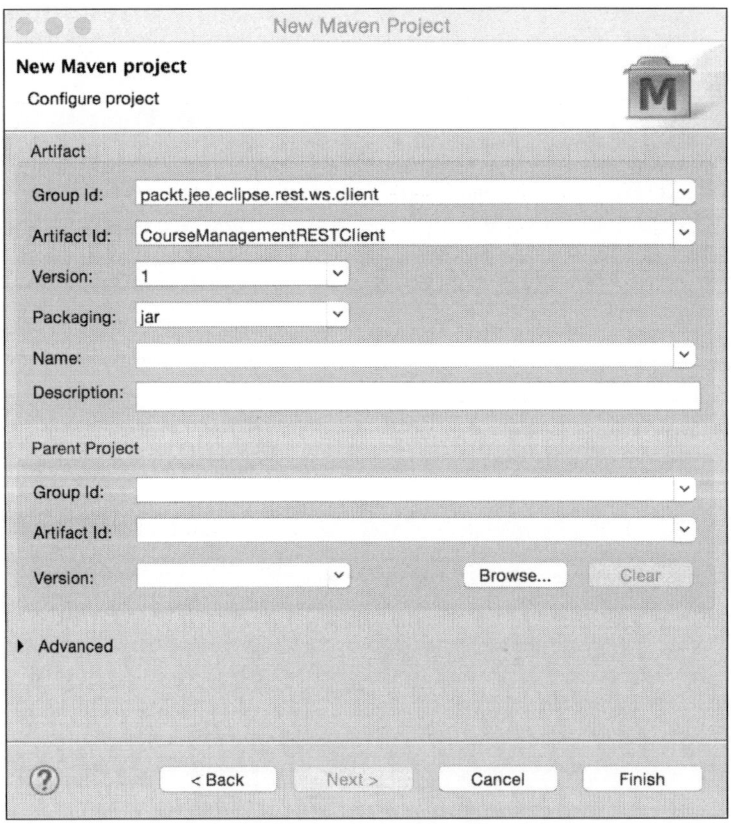

Figure 9.3 Create JAX-RS client project

Open `pom.xml` and add a dependency for the Jersey client module.

```
<dependencies>
  <dependency>
    <groupId>org.glassfish.jersey.core</groupId>
    <artifactId>jersey-client</artifactId>
    <version>2.18</version>
  </dependency>
</dependencies>
```

Create the Java class called `CourseManagementRESTClient` in the `packt.jee.eclipse.rest.ws.client` package.

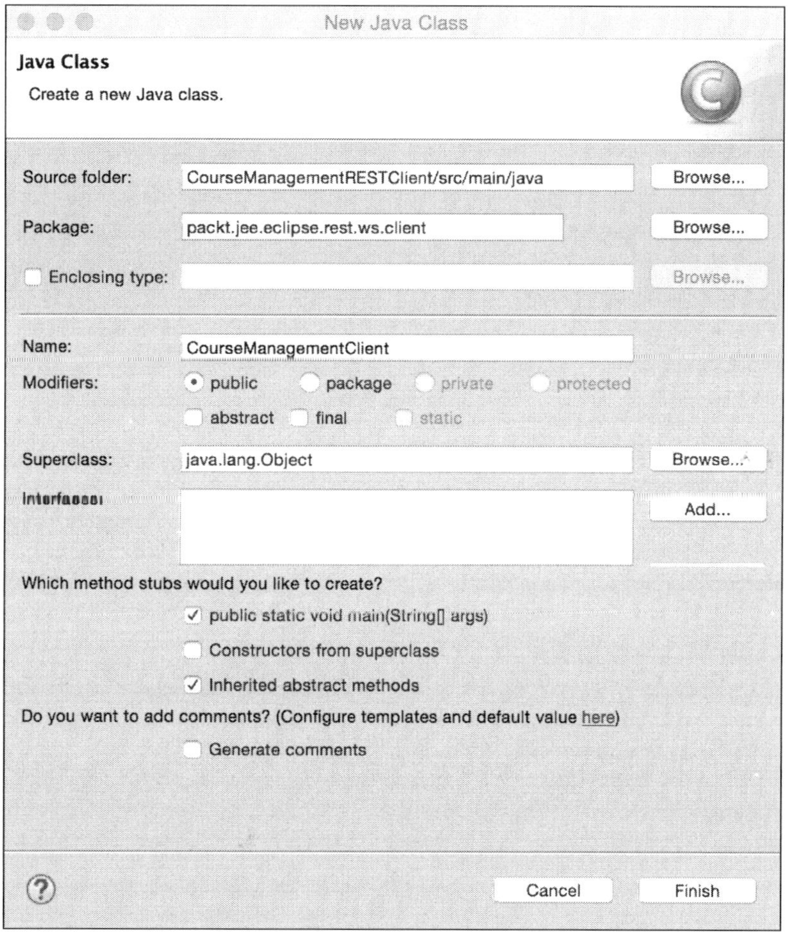

Figure 9.4 Create REST client main class

You could invoke a REST web service by using `java.net.HttpURLConnection` or other external HTTP client libraries, but the JAX-RS client APIs makes this task a lot easier, as you will see in the following code:

```
package packt.jee.eclipse.rest.ws.client;

import javax.ws.rs.client.Client;
import javax.ws.rs.client.ClientBuilder;
import javax.ws.rs.client.WebTarget;
import javax.ws.rs.core.MediaType;
import javax.ws.rs.core.Response;

/**
 * This is a simple test class for invoking REST web service
 * using JAX-RS client APIs
 */
public class CourseManagementClient {

  public static void main(String[] args) {

testGetCoursesJSON();

  }

  //Test getCourse method (XML or JSON) of CourseService
  public static void testGetCoursesJSON() {
    //Create JAX-RS client
    Client client = ClientBuilder.newClient();
    //Get WebTarget for a URL
    WebTarget webTarget =
client.target("http://localhost:8080/CourseManagementREST/services/
course");
    //Add paths to URL
    webTarget = webTarget.path("get").path("10");

    //We could also have create webTarget in one call with the full
URL -
    //WebTarget webTarget =
client.target("http://localhost:8080/CourseManagementREST/services/
course/get/10");


    //Execute HTTP get method
    Response response =
    webTarget.request(MediaType.APPLICATION_JSON).get();

    //Check response code. 200 is OK
```

```
        if (response.getStatus() != 200) {
          System.out.println("Error invoking REST Web Service - " +
          response.getStatusInfo().getReasonPhrase());
          return;
        }

        //REST call was successful. Print the response
        System.out.println(response.readEntity(String.class));
      }
    }
```

For a detailed description of how to use the JAX-RS client APIs, refer to `https://jersey.java.net/documentation/latest/client.html`.

Implementing the REST POST request

We saw an example of how to implement an HTTP `GET` request by using JAX-RS. Let's now implement a `POST` request. We will implement a method to add a course in the `CourseService` class, which is our web service implementation class in the `CourseManagementREST` project.

As in the case of the `getCourse` method, we won't actually access the database but will simply write a dummy method to save the data. Again, the idea is to keep the example simple and focus only on the JAX-RS APIs and implementation. Open `CourseService.java` and add following methods:

```
@POST
@Consumes (MediaType.APPLICATION_JSON)
@Produces (MediaType.APPLICATION_JSON)
@Path("add")
public Course addCourse (Course course) {

  int courseId = dummyAddCourse(course.getName(),
  course.getCredits());

  course.setId(courseId);

  return course;
}

private int dummyAddCourse (String courseName, int credits) {

  //To keep the example simple, we will just print
  //parameters we received in this method to console and not
```

```
        //actually save data to database.
        System.out.println("Adding course " + courseName + ", credits
    = " + credits);

        //TODO: Add course to database table

        //return hard-coded id
        return 10;
    }
```

The `addCourse` method produces and consumes JSON data. It is invoked when the resource path (web service endpoint URL) has the following relative path: `"/course/add"`. Recall that the `CourseService` class is annotated with the following path: `"/course"`. So, the relative path for the `addCourse` method becomes the path specified at the class level and at the method level (which in this case is `"add"`). We are returning a new instance of `Course` from `addCourse`. Jersey creates an appropriate JSON representation of this class on the basis of the JAXB annotation that we have added to the `Course` class. We have already added a dependency in the project on the Jersey module that handles the JSON format (in `pom.xml`, we added a dependency on `jersey-media-json-jackson`).

Restart the Tomcat server for these changes to take effect.

Writing a Java client for the REST POST web service

We will now add a test method in the `CourseManagementClient` (in the `CourseManagementRESTClient` project) class.

```
    //Test addCourse method (JSON version) of CourseService
    public static void testAddCourseJSON() {

        //Create JAX-RS client
        Client client = ClientBuilder.newClient();

        //Get WebTarget for a URL
        WebTarget webTarget =
    client.target("http://localhost:8600/CourseManagementREST/services/
    course/add");

        //Create JSON representation of Course,
        //with course_name and credits fields. Instead of creating
        //JSON manually, you could also use JAXB to create JSON from
```

```
        //Java object.
        String courseJSON = "{\"course_name\":\"Course-4\",
        \"credits\":5}";

        //Execute HTTP post method
        Response response = webTarget.request().
            post(Entity.entity(courseJSON,
            MediaType.APPLICATION_JSON_TYPE));

        //Check response code. 200 is OK
        if (response.getStatus() != 200) {
          //Print error message
          System.out.println("Error invoking REST Web Service - " +
          response.getStatusInfo().getReasonPhrase() +
              ", Error Code : " + response.getStatus());
          //Also dump content of response message
          System.out.println(response.readEntity(String.class));
          return;
        }

        //REST call was successful. Print the response
        System.out.println(response.readEntity(String.class));
    }
```

We need to send input data (the `Course` information) in the JSON format. Although we have hardcoded JSON in our example, you could use JAXB or any other library that converts a Java object into JSON.

Note that we have used the post method (`webTarget.request().post(...)`). We have also set the content type of the request to `"application/JSON"` (because our web service to add `Course` consumes the JSON format). This is done by creating an entity and setting its content type to `JSON`:

```
//Execute HTTP post method
Response response =
webTarget.request().post(Entity.entity(courseJSON,
       MediaType.APPLICATION_JSON_TYPE));
```

Modify the main method of the `CourseManagementClient` class to call the `testAddCourseJSON` method. Right-click on the class and select **Run As | Java Application**. You should see the `Course` information in the JSON format printed in the console. Also, check the Tomcat console in Eclipse. You should see the console message that we printed in the `CourseService`. dummyAddCourse method.

Invoking the POST REST web service from JavaScript

Here is a simple example of how to invoke our REST web service to add a course from JavaScript.

```
<!DOCTYPE html>
<html>
<head>
<meta charset="UTF-8">
<title>Add Course - JSON</title>

<script type="text/javascript">

  function testAddCourseJSON() {

    //Hardcoded course information to keep example simple.
    //This could be passed as arguments to this function
    //We could also use HTML form to get this information from
    users
    var courseName = "Course-4";
    var credits = 4;

    //Create XMLHttpRequest
    var req = new XMLHttpRequest();

    //Set callback function, because we will have XMLHttpRequest
    //make asynchronous call to our web service
    req.onreadystatechange = function () {
      if (req.readyState == 4 && req.status == 200) {
        //HTTP call was successful. Display response
        document.getElementById("responseSpan").innerHTML =
        req.responseText;
      }
    };

    //Open request to our REST service. Call is going to be asyc
    req.open("POST",
"http://localhost:8080/CourseManagementREST/services/course/add",
true);
    //Set request content type as JSON
    req.setRequestHeader("Content-type", "application/JSON");

    //Create Course object and then stringify it to create JSON
    string
```

```
      var course = {
        "course_name": courseName,
        "credits" : credits
      };

      //Send request.
      req.send(JSON.stringify(course));
    }
  </script>

  </head>
  <body>
    <button type="submit" onclick="return testAddCourseJSON();">Add
    Course using JSON</button>
    <p/>
    <span id="responseSpan"></span>
  </body>
  </html>
```

If you want to test this code, create an HTML file, say `addCourseJSON.html`, in the `src/main/webapp` folder of the `CourseManagementREST` project. Then, browse to `http://localhost:8080/CourseManagementREST/addCourseJSON.html`. Click the **Add Course using JSON** button. The response is displayed in the same page.

Creating the REST web service with Form POST

We have created the REST web services so far with HTTP `GET` and `POST`. The web service with the `POST` method took input in the JSON format. We can also have the `POST` method in the web service take input as HTML form elements. Let's create a method that handles the data posted from the HTTP form. Open `CourseService.java` from the `CourseManagementREST` project. Add the following method:

```
@POST
@Consumes (MediaType.APPLICATION_FORM_URLENCODED)
@Path("add")
public Response addCourseFromForm (@FormParam("name") String
courseName,
    @FormParam("credits") int credits) throws URISyntaxException {

  dummyAddCourse(courseName, credits);

  return Response.seeOther(new
URI("../addCourseSuccess.html")).build();
}
```

The method is marked to handle form data by specifying the `@Consume` annotation with the following value: `"application/x-www-form-urlencoded"`. Just as we mapped parameters in the path in the `getCourse` method with `@PathParam`, we map the form fields to method arguments by using the `@FormParam` annotation. Finally, once we successfully save course, we want the client to be redirected to `addCourseSuccess.html`. We do this by calling the `Response.seeOther` method. The `addCourseFromForm` method returns the `Response` object. Refer to `https://jersey.java.net/documentation/latest/representations.html` for more information on how to configure `Response` from the web service method.

We need to create `addCourseSuccess.html`. Create this file in the `src/main/webapp` folder of the `CourseManagementREST` project. The file contains just a simple message:

```
<h3>Course added successfully</h3>
```

Creating a Java client for the form-encoded REST web service

Let's now create a test method for calling the above web service that consumes form-encoded data. Open `CourseManagementClient.java` from the `CourseManagementRESTClient` project and the following method:

```
  //Test addCourse method (Form-Encoded version) of CourseService
  public static void testAddCourseForm() {

    //create JAX-RS client
    Client client = ClientBuilder.newClient();

    //Get WebTarget for a URL
    WebTarget webTarget =
client.target("http://localhost:8600/CourseManagementREST/services/
course/add");

    //Create Form object and populate fields
    Form form = new Form();
    form.param("name", "Course-5");
    form.param("credits", "5");

    //Execute HTTP post method
    Response response = webTarget.request().
        post(Entity.entity(form,
        MediaType.APPLICATION_FORM_URLENCODED));

    //check response code. 200 is OK
```

```
        if (response.getStatus() != 200) {
          //Print error message
          System.out.println("Error invoking REST Web Service - " +
          response.getStatusInfo().getReasonPhrase() +
              ", Error Code : " + response.getStatus());
          //Also dump content of response message
          System.out.println(response.readEntity(String.class));
          return;
        }

        //REST call was successful. Print the response
        System.out.println(response.readEntity(String.class));
      }
```

Notice that the form data is created by creating an instance of the `Form` object and setting its parameters. The POST request is encoded with `MediaType.APPLICATION_FORM_URLENCODED`, which has the following value: `"application/x-www-form-urlencoded"`.

Modify the `main` method to call `testAddCourseForm`. Right-click on the class and select **Run As** | **Java Application**. You should see the success message (from `addCourseSuccess.html`) printed in the console.

SOAP web services

Simple Object Access Protocol (**SOAP**) is a specification from **World Wide Web Consortium** (**W3C**) (`http://www.w3.org/TR/2007/REC-soap12-part0-20070427/`). Although we are referring to SOAP-based web services here, SOAP is one of the specifications used to implement XML-based web services. There are a few other specifications required to implement SOAP web services, which we will see later. One of the premises of SOAP web services was the dynamic discovery and invocation of services. For example, an application can look for a service from the central directory and invoke it dynamically. However, in practice, very few enterprises would be willing to invoke services dynamically without testing them, so this aspect of SOAP web services is less utilized.

W3C has defined many specifications for SOAP web services, for example, specifications for messages, auto discovery, security, and service orchestration. However, at the minimum, we need to understand the following specification before we develop SOAP web services.

SOAP

SOAP defines the format of message exchanges between a web service provider and a consumer.

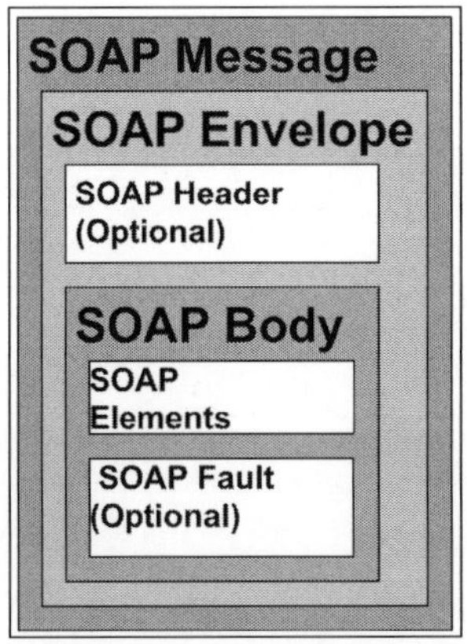

Figure 9.5 SOAP message structure

The top element in a **SOAP Message** is **SOAP Envelope**. It contains a **SOAP Header (Optional)** and a **SOAP Body**. **SOAP Body** actually contains the message payload (for processing by the consumer) and optionally **SOAP Fault**, if there is any error.

The SOAP header provides extensibility to a SOAP message. It can contain information such as user credentials, transaction management, and message routing.

WSDL

As the name suggests, **Web Service Description Language** (**WSDL**) describes web services; in particular, it describes the data types used (schemas), input and output messages, operations (methods), and binding and service endpoints.

```
<definitions>
 <import>*
 <types>
  <schema></schema>*
 </types>
 <message>*
  <part></part>*
 </message>
 <PortType>
  <operation>*
   <input></input>
   <output></output>
   <fault></fault>
  </operation>
 </PortType>
 <binding>*
  <operation>*
   <input></input>
   <output></output>
  </operation>
 </binding>
 <service>*
  <port></port>*
 </service>
</definitions>
```

Figure 9.6 WSDL structure

Although you don't necessarily need to understand the details of WSDL when creating web services in Java, it is good to know the basic structure of WSDL. WSDLs are typically meant to be produced and processed by programs instead of the developer hardcoding them.

- `definitions` is the root element of WSDL.
- The `Import` element allows you to import elements from an external file. This way, you can make the WSDL file modular.
- The `Types` element defines the schema for different data types used in WSDL.
- The `Messages` element defines the format of the input and output messages exchanged between web services and clients.
- `PortType` defines the methods or operations supported by web services. Each operation in `PortType` can declare the request and response messages. Operations in `PortType` refer to messages defined in a message element.

Although in the preceding figure, the `binding` element looks the same as `PortType`, it actually specifies the transport protocol bound to the operations and message type (*Remote Procedure Call* or *Document Type*) and encoding (encoded or literal) for messages of each operation declared in `PortType`. The typical transport protocol is HTTP, but it could be other protocols such as JMS and SMTP. The difference between RPC and Document type is that the RPC message type contains the name of the remote method in the message, whereas Document type does not contain the method name. The name of the method to process the payload in a Document-type message is either derived from the endpoint URL or from the information in the header. However, there is another type called Document Wrapped, which does contain the name of the method as the enclosing element for an actual message payload.

The service element contains the actual location of each web service endpoint.

UDDI

Universal Description, Discovery and Integration (**UDDI**) is a directory of web services where you can publish your own web services or search for existing web services. The directory could be global or could be local to enterprises. UDDI is also a web service with operations supported for publishing and searching contents.

We will not be focusing on UDDI in this book, but you can visit `http://docs.oracle.com/cd/E14571_01/web.1111/e13734/uddi.htm#WSADV226`.

Developing web services in Java

There have been many frameworks around for developing web services in Java. New frameworks have evolved as specifications changed. Some of the popular frameworks for developing web services in Java over the years are Apache Axis (`https://axis.apache.org/axis/`), Apache Axis2 (`http://axis.apache.org/axis2/java/core/`), Apache CFX (`http://cxf.apache.org/`), and GlassFish Metro (`https://metro.java.net/`).

Earlier implementations of web service frameworks were based on the **JAX-RPC (Java API for XML - Remote Procedure Call)** specification (`http://www.oracle.com/technetwork/java/docs-142876.html`). JAX-RPC was replaced with **Java API for XML - Web Services (JAX-WS)** in JEE 5. JAX-WS makes the development of web services easier by supporting annotations. In this chapter, we will learn how to create and consume web services using JAX-WS. Continuing with the example (Course Management) that we have been following in this book, we will create web services to get all courses and add a new course.

First, we will create a Maven web project. Select **File** | **New** | **Maven Project**. Check the **Create a simple project** option.

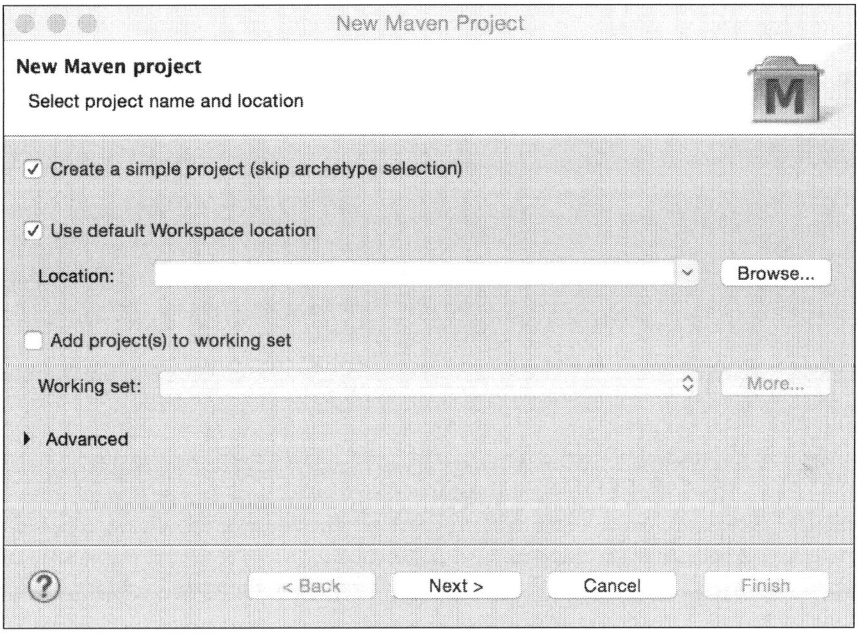

Figure 9.7 New Maven project

Click **Next**. Enter **Group Id**, **Artefact id**, and **Version** in the next page. Select the `war` packaging.

Figure 9.8 Enter artifact details

Click **Finish** to complete the wizard.

Creating a web service implementation class

JAX-WS annotations were added in Java EE 5.0. Using these annotations, we can turn any Java class (including POJO) into a web service. Use the `@Webservice` annotation to make any Java class a web service. This annotation can be used either on an interface or on a Java class. If a Java class is annotated with `@Webservice`, then all public methods in the class are exposed in the web service. If a Java interface is annotated with `@Webservice`, then the implementation class still needs to be annotated with `@Webservice` with the `endpointInterface` attribute and its value as the interface name.

Before we create the web service implementation class, let's create a few helper classes. The first one is the `Course` data transfer object. This is the same class that we created in the previous chapters. Create the `Course` class in the `packt.jee.eclipse.ws.soap` package.

```
package packt.jee.eclipse.ws.soap;

public class Course {
  private int id;
  private String name;
  private int credits;

  //Setters and getters follow here
}
```

Let's now create the web service implementation class. Create the class `CourseManagementService` in the `packt.jee.eclipse.ws.soap` package.

```
package packt.jee.eclipse.ws.soap;

import java.util.ArrayList;
import java.util.List;

import javax.jws.WebService;

@WebService
public class CourseManagementService {

  public List<Course> getCourses() {
    //Here courses could be fetched from database using,
    //for example, JDBC or JDO. However, to keep this example
    //simple, we will return hardcoded list of courses

    List<Course> courses = new ArrayList<Course>();

    courses.add(new Course(1, "Course-1", 4));
    courses.add(new Course(2, "Course-2", 3));

    return courses;
  }

  public Course getCourse(int courseId) {
    //Here again, we could get course details from database using
    //JDBC or JDO. However, to keep this example
```

```
        //simple, we will return hardcoded course

        return new Course(1,"Course-1",4);
    }
}
```

`CourseManagementService` has the following two methods: `getCourses` and `getCourse`. To keep the example simple, we have hardcoded the values, but you can very well fetch data from a database by using the JDBC or JDO APIs that we have discussed earlier in this book. The class is annotated with `@WebService`, which tells the JAX-WS implementation to treat this class as a web service. All methods in this class would be exposed as web service operations. If you want a specific method to be exposed, you could use `@WebMethod`.

Using the JAX-WS reference implementation (GlassFish Metro)

Annotating a class with `@WebService` is not enough to implement web services. We need an implementation of the JAX-WS specification that would process classes annotated with the JAX-WS annotations. There are a number of JAX-WS frameworks available, for example, Axis2, Apache CFX, and GlassFish Metro. In this chapter, we will use the GlassFish Metro implementation, which is also a reference implementation (`https://jax-ws.java.net/`) of JAX-WS from Oracle.

Let's add the Maven dependency for the JAX-WS framework. Open `pom.xml` and add the following dependency:

```
<dependencies>
  <dependency>
    <groupId>com.sun.xml.ws</groupId>
    <artifactId>jaxws-rt</artifactId>
    <version>2.2.10</version>
  </dependency>
</dependencies>
```

Replace the version number with the latest version above. The Metro framework also requires you to declare web service endpoints in a configuration file called `sun-jaxws.xml`. Create the `sun-jaxws.xml` file in the `src/main/webapp/WEB-INF` folder and add the endpoint as follows:

```
<?xml version="1.0" encoding="UTF-8"?>
<endpoints xmlns="http://java.sun.com/xml/ns/jax-ws/ri/runtime"
version="2.0">
  <endpoint name="CourseService" implementation="packt.jee.eclipse.
ws.soap.CourseManagementService"
```

```
        url-pattern="/courseService" />
</endpoints>
```

Endpoint implementation is the fully qualified name of our web service implementation class. `url-pattern` is just like the Servlet mapping that you specify in `web.xml`. In this case, any relative URL starting with `/courseService` would result in the invocation of our web service.

Inspecting WSDL

We are done with implementing our web service. As you can see, JAX-WS really makes it very easy to develop web services. Let's now inspect WSDL for our web service. Configure Tomcat in Eclipse as described in the *Installing Tomcat* section of *Chapter 1, Introducing JEE and Eclipse* and in the *Configuring Tomcat in Eclipse* section of *Chapter 2, Creating a Simple JEE Web Application*). To deploy our web application, right-click on the configured Tomcat server in the **Servers** view and select the **Add and Remove** option.

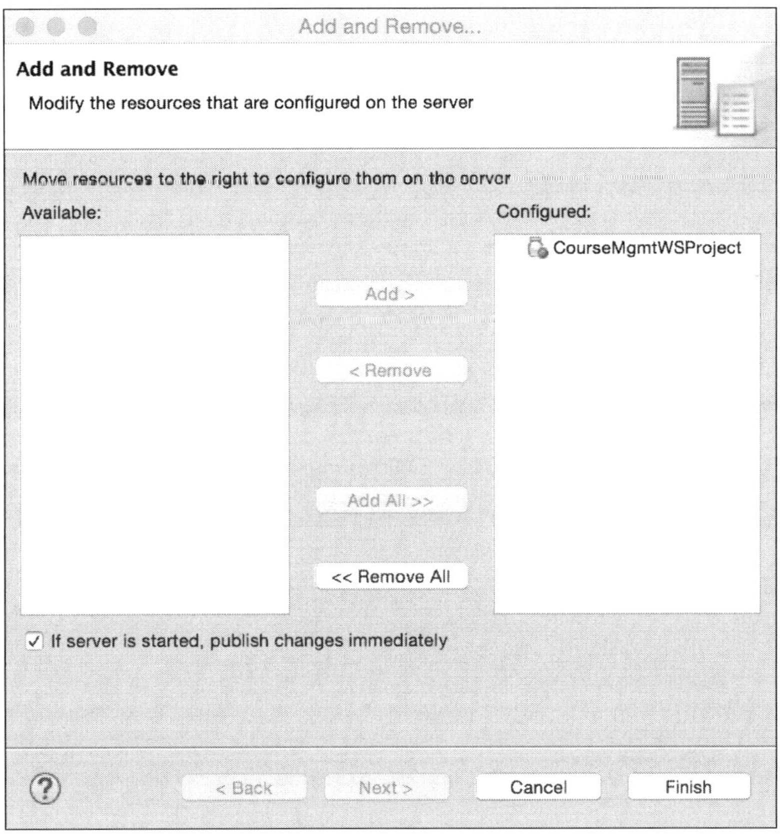

Figure 9.9 Add a project to Tomcat

Add the project and click **Finish**.

Start the Tomcat server by right-clicking on the configured server in the **Servers** view and selecting **Start**.

To inspect the WSDL of our web service, browse to `http://localhost:8080/CourseMgmtWSProject/courseService?wsdl` (assuming that Tomcat is running on port `8080`). The following WSDL is generated:

```
<definitions
  xmlns:wsu="http://docs.oasis-open.org/wss/2004/01/oasis-200401-wss-
wssecurity-utility-1.0.xsd"
  xmlns:wsp="http://www.w3.org/ns/ws-policy"
xmlns:wsp1_2="http://schemas.xmlsoap.org/ws/2004/09/policy"
  xmlns:wsam="http://www.w3.org/2007/05/addressing/metadata"
xmlns:soap="http://schemas.xmlsoap.org/wsdl/soap/"
  xmlns:tns="http://soap.ws.eclipse.jee.packt/"
xmlns:xsd="http://www.w3.org/2001/XMLSchema"
  xmlns="http://schemas.xmlsoap.org/wsdl/"
targetNamespace="http://soap.ws.eclipse.jee.packt/"
  name="CourseManagementServiceService">
  <types>
    <xsd:schema>
      <xsd:import namespace="http://soap.ws.eclipse.jee.packt/"
schemaLocation="http://localhost:8080/CourseMgmtWSProject/
courseService?xsd=1" />
    </xsd:schema>
  </types>
  <message name="getCourses">
    <part name="parameters" element="tns:getCourses" />
  </message>
  <message name="getCoursesResponse">
    <part name="parameters" element="tns:getCoursesResponse" />
  </message>
  <message name="getCourse">
    <part name="parameters" element="tns:getCourse" />
  </message>
  <message name="getCourseResponse">
    <part name="parameters" element="tns:getCourseResponse" />
  </message>
  <portType name="CourseManagementService">
    <operation name="getCourses">
      <input
wsam:Action="http://soap.ws.eclipse.jee.packt/CourseManagementService/
getCoursesRequest"
        message="tns:getCourses" />
      <output
```

```
wsam:Action="http://soap.ws.eclipse.jee.packt/CourseManagementService/
getCoursesResponse"
        message="tns:getCoursesResponse" />
    </operation>
    <operation name="getCourse">
      <input
wsam:Action="http://soap.ws.eclipse.jee.packt/CourseManagementService/
getCourseRequest"
        message="tns:getCourse" />
      <output
wsam:Action="http://soap.ws.eclipse.jee.packt/CourseManagementService/
getCourseResponse"
        message="tns:getCourseResponse" />
    </operation>
  </portType>
  <binding name="CourseManagementServicePortBinding"
  type="tns:CourseManagementService">
    <soap:binding transport="http://schemas.xmlsoap.org/soap/http"
      style="document" />
    <operation name="getCourses">
      <soap:operation soapAction="" />
      <input>
        <soap:body use="literal" />
      </input>
      <output>
        <soap:body use="literal" />
      </output>
    </operation>
    <operation name="getCourse">
      <soap:operation soapAction="" />
      <input>
        <soap:body use="literal" />
      </input>
      <output>
        <soap:body use="literal" />
      </output>
    </operation>
  </binding>
  <service name="CourseManagementServiceService">
    <port name="CourseManagementServicePort"
    binding="tns:CourseManagementServicePortBinding">
      <soap:address
location="http://localhost:8080/CourseMgmtWSProject/courseService"
/>
    </port>
  </service>
</definitions>
```

Notice that the schema (see the definitions of the `/types/xsd:schemas` element) for this web service is imported in the above WSDL. You can see the schema generated at `http://localhost:8080/CourseMgmtWSProject/courseService?xsd=1`.

```
<xs:schema xmlns:tns="http://soap.ws.eclipse.jee.packt/"
  xmlns:xs="http://www.w3.org/2001/XMLSchema" version="1.0"
  targetNamespace="http://soap.ws.eclipse.jee.packt/">

  <xs:element name="getCourse" type="tns:getCourse" />
  <xs:element name="getCourseResponse"
  type="tns:getCourseResponse" />
  <xs:element name="getCourses" type="tns:getCourses" />
  <xs:element name="getCoursesResponse"
type="tns:getCoursesResponse" />

  <xs:complexType name="getCourses">
    <xs:sequence />
  </xs:complexType>
  <xs:complexType name="getCoursesResponse">
    <xs:sequence>
      <xs:element name="return" type="tns:course" minOccurs="0"
        maxOccurs="unbounded" />
    </xs:sequence>
  </xs:complexType>
  <xs:complexType name="course">
    <xs:sequence>
      <xs:element name="credits" type="xs:int" />
      <xs:element name="id" type="xs:int" />
      <xs:element name="name" type="xs:string" minOccurs="0" />
    </xs:sequence>
  </xs:complexType>
  <xs:complexType name="getCourse">
    <xs:sequence>
      <xs:element name="arg0" type="xs:int" />
    </xs:sequence>
  </xs:complexType>
  <xs:complexType name="getCourseResponse">
    <xs:sequence>
      <xs:element name="return" type="tns:course" minOccurs="0" />
    </xs:sequence>
  </xs:complexType>
</xs:schema>
```

The schema document defines the data types for the `getCourse` and `getCourses` methods and their responses (`getCoursesResponse` and `getCourseResponse`) and also for the `Course` class. It also declares the members of the `Course` data type (`id`, `credits`, and `name`). Notice that the `getCourse` data type has one child element (which is an argument to the `getCourse` method in the `CourseManagementService` method) called `arg0`, which is actually the course ID of the `int` type. Further, notice the definition of `getCoursesResponse`. In our implementation class, `getCourses` returns `List<Course>`, which is translated in WSDL (or types in WSDL) as a sequence of course types.

In WSDL, the following four messages are defined: `getCourses`, `getCoursesResponse`, `getCourse`, and `getCourseResponse`. Each message contains a part element that refers to the data types declared in types (or schema).

The `PortType` name is the same as the web service implementation class called `CourseManagementService` and the operations of the port are the same as the public methods of the class. The input and output of each operation refer to the messages already defined in WSDL.

Binding defines the network transport type, which in this case is HTTP, and the style of message in the SOAP body, which is of the document type. We have not defined any message type in our web service implementation, but the JAX-WS reference implementation (GlassFish Metro) has set a default message type to `document`. Binding also defines the message encoding type for the input and output messages of each operation.

Finally, the `Service` element specifies the location of the port, which is the URL that we access to invoke the web service.

Implementing a web service using an interface

All methods declared in our web service implementation class, `CourseManagementService`, are exposed as web service operations. However, if you want to expose only a limited set of methods from the web service implementation class, then you can use the Java interface to declare the web service. For example, if we want to expose only the `getCourses` method as the web service operation, then we can create an interface, let's say `ICourseManagementService`.

```
package packt.jee.eclipse.ws.soap;

import java.util.List;

import javax.jws.WebService;

@WebService
```

```
public interface ICourseManagementService {
  public List<Course> getCourses();
}
```

The implementation class also needs to be annotated with `@WebService`, with the `endpointInterface` attribute.

```
package packt.jee.eclipse.ws.soap;

import java.util.ArrayList;
import java.util.List;

import javax.jws.WebService;

@WebService
(endpointInterface="packt.jee.eclipse.ws.soap.
ICourseManagementService")
public class CourseManagementService implements
ICourseManagementService {

  //getCourses and getCourse methods follow here
}
```

Now, restart Tomcat and inspect WSDL. You will notice that only the `getCourses` operation is defined in WSDL.

Consuming a web service using JAX-WS

We will create a simple Java console app to consume the web service that we created earlier. Select **File | New | Maven Project**. Check the **Create a simple project** option on the first page and click **Next**. Enter the following **Artifact** details:

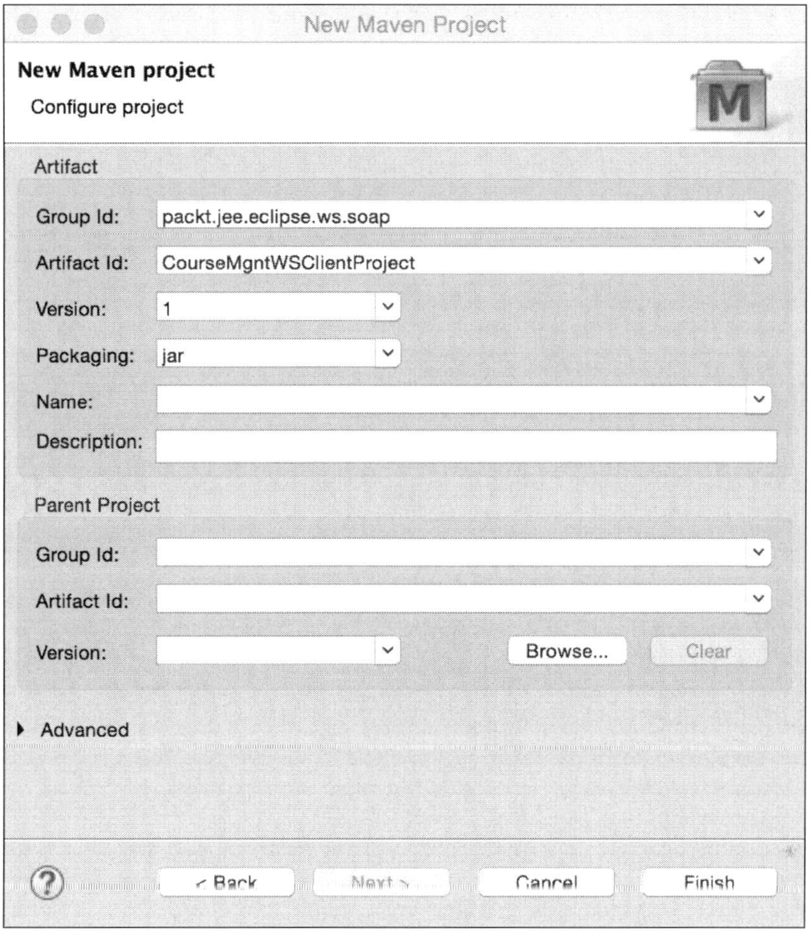

Figure 9.10 Create a Maven project for the web service client

Make sure that the **Packaging** type is `jar`. Click **Finish**.

We will now generate a stub and a supporting class on the client side for invoking our web service. We will use the **wsimport** tool to generate client classes. We will specify the package for the generated classes by using the `-p` option and the WSDL location to generate the client classes. The wsimport tool is a part of JDK and should be available in the `<JDK_HOME>/bin` folder, if you are using JDK 1.7 or later.

We will now run `wsimport` from the Command Prompt. Change the folder to `<project_home>/src//main/java` and run the following command:

```
wsimport -keep -p packt.jee.eclipse.ws.soap.client http://localhost:8080/
CourseMgmtWSProject/courseService?wsdl
```

The `-keep` flag instructs `wsimport` to keep the generated file.

The `-p` option specifies the package name for the generated classes.

The last argument is the WSDL location for our web service. In **Package Explorer** or **Project Explorer** of Eclipse, refresh the client project to see the generated files. The files will be in the `packt.jee.eclipse.ws.soap.client` package.

`wsimport` generates a client-side class for each type defined in the schema (in the types element of WSDL). Therefore, you will find the `Course`, `GetCourse`, `GetCourseResponse`, `GetCourses`, and `GetCoursesResponse` classes. Further, it generates classes for `portType` (`CourseManagementService`) and the service (`CourseManagementServiceService`) elements of WSDL. Additionally, it creates the `ObjectFactory` class that creates Java objects from XML by using JAXB.

Let's now write the code to actually call the web service. Create the `CourseMgmtWSClient` class in the `packt.jee.eclipse.ws.soap.client.test` package.

```
package packt.jee.eclipse.ws.soap.client.test;

import packt.jee.eclipse.ws.soap.client.Course;
import packt.jee.eclipse.ws.soap.client.CourseManagementService;
import packt.jee.eclipse.ws.soap.client.
CourseManagementServiceService;

public class CourseMgmtWSClient {

  public static void main(String[] args) {
    CourseManagementServiceService service = new
CourseManagementServiceService();

    CourseManagementService port =
    service.getCourseManagementServicePort();

    Course course = port.getCourse(1);
    System.out.println("Course name = " + course.getName());
  }

}
```

We first create the `Service` object and then get the port from it. The port object has operations defined for the web service. We then call the actual web service method on the port object. Right-click on the class and select **Run As | Java Application**. The output should be the name of the course that we hardcoded in the web service, that is, `Course-1`.

Specifying an argument name in a web service operation

As mentioned earlier, when WSDL was created for our `Course` web service, the argument for the `getCourse` operation name was created as `arg0`. You can verify this by browsing to `http://localhost:8080/CourseMgmtWSProject/courseService?xsd=1` and checking the `getCourse` type.

```
<xs:complexType name="getCourse">
    <xs:sequence>
        <xs:element name="arg0" type="xs:int"/>
    </xs:sequence>
</xs:complexType>
```

Thus, the client-side generated code (by `wsimport`) in `CourseManagementService.getCourse` also names the argument as `arg0`. It would be nice to give a meaningful name to arguments. This could be done easily be adding the `@WSParam` annotation in our web service implementation class, `CourseManagementService`.

```
public Course getCourse(@WebParam(name="courseId") int courseId)
{…}
```

Restart Tomcat after this change and browse to the WSDL schema URL (`http://localhost:8080/CourseMgmtWSProject/courseService?xsd=1`) again. You should now see a proper argument name in the `getCourse` type.

```
<xs:complexType name="getCourse">
    <xs:sequence>
        <xs:element name="courseId" type="xs:int"/>
    </xs:sequence>
</xs:complexType>
```

Generate the client-side code again by using `wsimport`, and you will see that the argument of the `getCourse` method is named `courseId`.

Inspecting SOAP messages

Although you don't necessarily need to understand the SOAP messages passed between the web service and the client, sometimes, looking at the SOAP messages exchanged between the two could help debug some of the issues.

You can print the request and response SOAP messages when running the client quite easily by setting the following system property:

```
com.sun.xml.internal.ws.transport.http.client.HttpTransportPipe.
dump=true
```

In Eclipse, right-click on the `CourseMgmtWSClient` class that we created in the previous section and select **Run As | Run Configurations**. Click on the **Arguments** tab and specify the following VM argument: `Dcom.sun.xml.internal.ws.transport.http.client.HttpTransportPipe.dump=true`

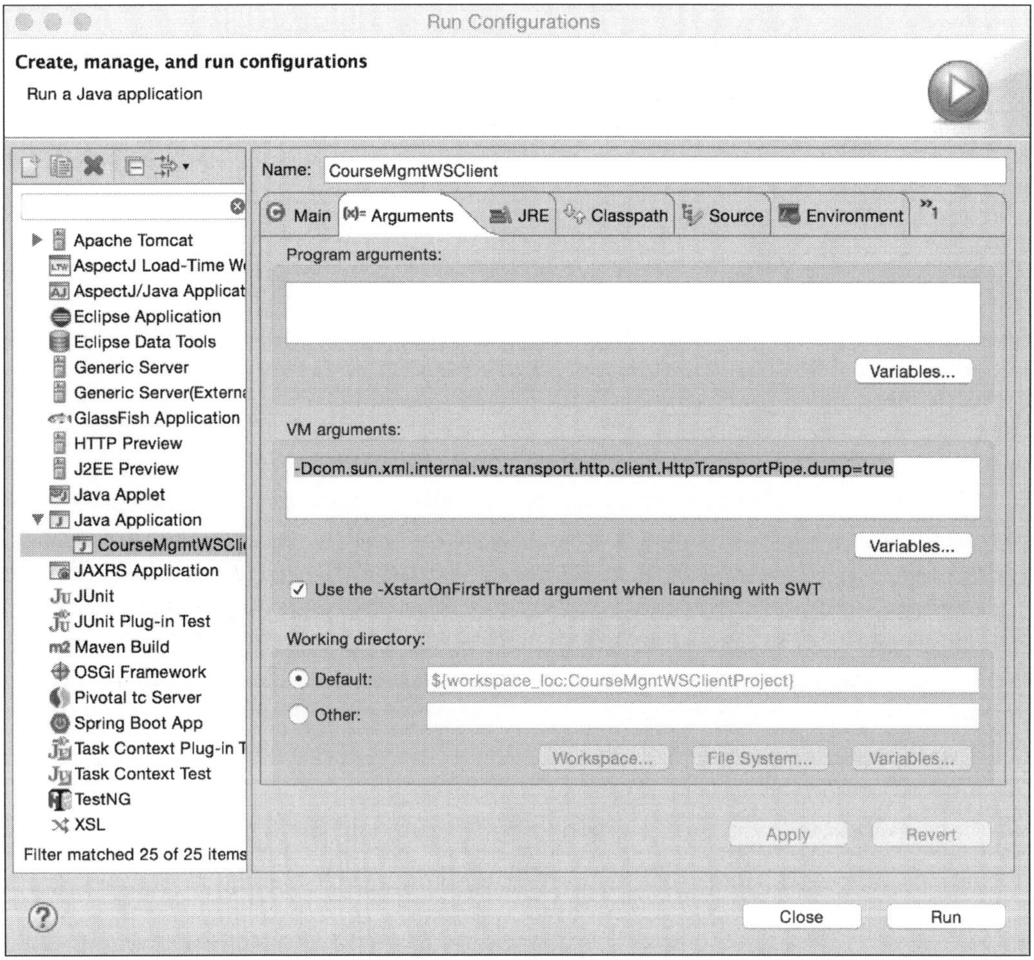

Figure 9.11 Set VM arguments

Click **Run**. You will see the request and response SOAP messages printed in the **Console** window in Eclipse. After formatting the request message, this is what the request SOAP message looks like:

```
<?xml version="1.0" ?>
<S:Envelope xmlns:S="http://schemas.xmlsoap.org/soap/envelope/">
  <S:Body>
```

```
        <ns2:getCourse xmlns:ns2="http://soap.ws.eclipse.jee.packt/">
          <courseId>1</courseId>
        </ns2:getCourse>
      </S:Body>
    </S:Envelope>
```

Further, the response is as follows:

```
    <?xml version='1.0' encoding='UTF-8'?>
    <S:Envelope xmlns:S="http://schemas.xmlsoap.org/soap/envelope/">
      <S:Body>
        <ns2:getCourseResponse
        xmlns:ns2="http://soap.ws.eclipse.jee.packt/">
          <return>
            <credits>4</credits>
            <id>1</id>
            <name>Course-1</name>
          </return>
        </ns2:getCourseResponse>
      </S:Body>
    </S:Envelope>
```

Handling interfaces in an RPC-style web service

Recall that the message style for our web service implementation class is `Document` and the encoding is `literal`. Let's change the style to RPC. Open `CourseManagementService.java` and change the style of the SOAP binding from `Style.DOCUMENT` to `Style.RPC`.

```
@WebService
@SOAPBinding(style=Style.RPC, use=Use.LITERAL)
public class CourseManagementService {…}
```

Restart Tomcat. In the Tomcat console, you might see the following error:

```
Caused by: com.sun.xml.bind.v2.runtime.IllegalAnnotationsException: 1
counts of IllegalAnnotationExceptions

java.util.List is an interface, and JAXB can't handle interfaces.

  this problem is related to the following location:

    at java.util.List
```

This problem is caused by this method definition in the `CourseManagementService` class:

```
public List<Course> getCourses() {…}
```

In RPC-style SOAP binding, JAX-WS uses JAXB, and JAXB cannot marshal interfaces very well. A blog entry at `https://weblogs.java.net/blog/kohsuke/archive/2006/06/jaxb_and_interf.html` tries to explain the reason for this. The workaround is to create a wrapper for `List` and annotate it with `@XMLElement`. So, create a new class called `Courses` in the same package.

```
package packt.jee.eclipse.ws.soap;

import java.util.List;

import javax.xml.bind.annotation.XmlAnyElement;
import javax.xml.bind.annotation.XmlRootElement;

@XmlRootElement
public class Courses {
  @XmlAnyElement
  public List<Course> courseList;

  public Courses() {

  }

  public Courses (List<Course> courseList) {
    this.courseList = courseList;
  }
}
```

Then, modify the `getCourses` method of `CourseManagementService` to return the `Courses` object instead of `List<Course>`.

```
public Courses getCourses() {
  //Here, courses could be fetched from database using,
  //for example, JDBC or JDO. However, to keep this example
  //simple, we will return hardcoded list of courses

  List<Course> courses = new ArrayList<Course>();

  courses.add(new Course(1, "Course-1", 4));
  courses.add(new Course(2, "Course-2", 3));

  return new Courses(courses);
}
```

Restart Tomcat after the preceding changes. This time, the application should be deployed in Tomcat without any error. Re-generate the client classes by using `wsimport`, run the client application, and verify the results.

Handling exceptions

In JAX-WS, a Java exception thrown from a web service is mapped to SOAP Fault when the XML payload is sent to the client. On the client side, JAX-WS maps SOAP Fault to either `SOAPFaultException` or an application-specific exception. The client code could wrap the web service call in the *try-catch* block to handle exceptions thrown from the web service. For a good description of how SOAP exceptions are handled in JAX-WS, refer to `https://docs.oracle.com/cd/E24329_01/web.1211/e24965/faults.htm#WSADV624`.

Summary

Web services are a very useful technology for enterprise application integration. They allow disparate systems to communicate with each other. Web service APIs are typically self-contained and lightweight.

There are broadly two types of web services: SOAP-based and RESTful. SOAP-based web services are XML based and provide many features such as security, attachments, and transactions. RESTful web services can exchange data by using XML or JSON. RESTful JSON web services are quite popular because they can be easily consumed from the JavaScript code.

In this chapter, we learnt how to develop and consume RESTful and SOAP-based web services by using the latest Java specifications, namely JAX-RS and JAX-WS, respectively.

In the next chapter, we will take a look at another technology for application integration: asynchronous programming using JMS (which stands for Java messaging service).

10
Asynchronous Programming with JMS

Thus far, we have seen examples of clients making requests to the JEE server and waiting till the server sends a response back. This is a synchronous model of programming. This model of programming may not be suitable when the server takes a long time to process requests. In such cases, a client might want to send a request to the server and return it immediately without waiting for the response. The server would process the request and somehow make the result available to the client. Requests and responses in such scenarios are sent through messages. Further, there is a message broker that makes sure that messages are sent to the appropriate recipients. This is also known as message-oriented architecture. The following are some of the advantages of adopting the message-oriented architecture:

- It can greatly improve the scalability of an application. Requests are put in a queue at one end, and at the other end, there could be many handlers listening to the queue and processing the requests. As the load increases, more handlers can be added, and when the load reduces, some of the handlers can be taken off.
- Messaging systems can act as the glue between disparate software applications. An application developed using PHP can put a JSON or XML message in a messaging system, which can be processed by a JEE application.
- It can be used to implement an event-driven program. Events can be put as messages in a messaging system, and any number of listeners can process events at the other end.
- It can reduce the impact of system outages in your application because messages are persisted till they are processed.

There are many enterprise messaging systems, such as Apache ActiveMQ (`http://activemq.apache.org/`), RabbitMQ (`https://www.rabbitmq.com/`), and MSMQ (`https://msdn.microsoft.com/en-us/library/ms711472(v=vs.85).aspx`). Further, the **JMS** (which stands for **Java messaging service**) specification provides a uniform interface to work with many different messaging systems. JMS is also a part of the overall Java EE specifications. Refer to `http://docs.oracle.com/javaee/7/tutorial/jms-concepts.htm#BNCDQ` for an overview of JMS APIs.

There are two types of message containers in messaging systems:

- **Queue**: This is used for point-to-point messaging. One message producer puts a message in a queue, and only one message consumer receives the message. There can be multiple listeners for a queue, but only one listener receives the message. However, it is not necessary that the same listener gets all the messages.
- **Topic**: This is used in a publish–subscribe type of scenario. One message producer puts messages in a topic, and many subscribers receive the message. Topics are useful for broadcasting messages.

In this chapter, we will see how to use JMS APIs for sending and receiving messages. We will use a GlassFish server, which also has a built-in JMS provider. We will use JMS APIs to implement a use case in the Course Management application, the same application that we have been building in the other chapters of this book.

Steps to send and receive messages using JMS

However, before we start using JMS APIs, let's take a look at the generic steps involved in using them. The following steps show how to send a message to a queue and receive it; however, the steps for topic are similar but with appropriate topic-related classes.

1. Look up `ConnectionFactory` using JNDI:

```
InitialContext ctx = new InitialContext();
QueueConnectionFactory connectionFactory =
(QueueConnectionFactory)initCtx.lookup("jndi_name_of_connection_
factory");
```

2. Create JMS connection and start it:

   ```
   QueueConnection con =
   connectionFactory.createQueueConnection();
   con.start();
   ```

3. Create JMS session:

   ```
   QueueSession session = con.createQueueSession(false,
   Session.AUTO_ACKNOWLEDGE);
   ```

4. Look up JMS `Queue`/`Topic`:

   ```
   Queue queue = (Queue)initCtx.lookup("jndi_queue_name");
   ```

5. For sending messages:
   - Create a sender:

     ```
     QueueSender sender = session.createSender(queue);
     ```

   - Create a message. The message could be of any of the following types: `TextMessage`/`ObjectMessage`/`MapMessage`/`BytesMessage`/`StreamMessage`:

     ```
     TextMessage textMessage = session.createTextMessage("Test
     Message");
     ```

   - Send the message:

     ```
     sender.send(textMessage);
     ```

   - Close the connection when no longer needed:

     ```
     con.close();
     ```

6. For receiving messages:
   - Create a receiver:

     ```
     //create a new session before creating the receiver.
     QueueReceiver receiver = session.createReceiver(queue);
     ```

   - Register a message listener or call a `receive` method:

     ```
     receiver.setMessageListener(new MessageListener() {
         @Override
         public void onMessage(Message message) {
             try {
                 String messageTxt =
                 ((TextMessage)message).getText();
     ```

```
                //process message
            } catch (JMSException e) {
                //handle exception
            }
        }
    });
```

    - Alternatively, you can use any variation of the receive method:

      ```
      Message message = receiver.receive(); //this blocks the
      thread till message is received
      ```

      Or:

      ```
      Message message = receiver.receive(timeout);
      ```

      Or:

      ```
      Message message = receiver.receiveNoWait(); //returns null
      if no message is available.
      ```

    - In a JEE application that uses EJB, it is recommended to use MDBs (which stands for message-driven beans). We will see an example of MDBs later in this chapter.

7. When done, close connection. This stops message listeners too:

   ```
   con.close();
   ```

Some of the steps can be skipped when JMS annotations are used or when MDBs are used to receive messages. We will see examples of these later.

Now, let's create a working example of sending and receiving messages using JMS. Make sure that you have installed the GlassFish application server (refer to the *Installing the GlassFish server* section in *Chapter 1, Introducing JEE and Eclipse*) and configured it in Eclipse JEE (refer to the *Configuring the GlassFish server in Eclipse* section in *Chapter 7, Creating JEE Applications with EJB*). The use case that we will implement in this example is adding a new course. Although this is not a strong use case for asynchronous processing, we will assume that this operation takes a long time and needs to be handled asynchronously.

Creating queues and topics in GlassFish

Let's create one queue and one topic in GlassFish. Make sure that the GlassFish server is running. Open the GlassFish admin console. You can right-click the GlassFish server instance configured in Eclipse (in the **Servers** view) and select **GlassFish | View Admin Console**. This opens the admin console in the built-in Eclipse browser. If you want to open it outside Eclipse in a browser, then browse to `http://localhost:4848/` (assuming a default GlassFish installation).

We will first create a JMS connection factory. In the admin console, go to the **Resources | JMS Resources | Connection Factories** page. Click the **New** button to create a new connection factory.

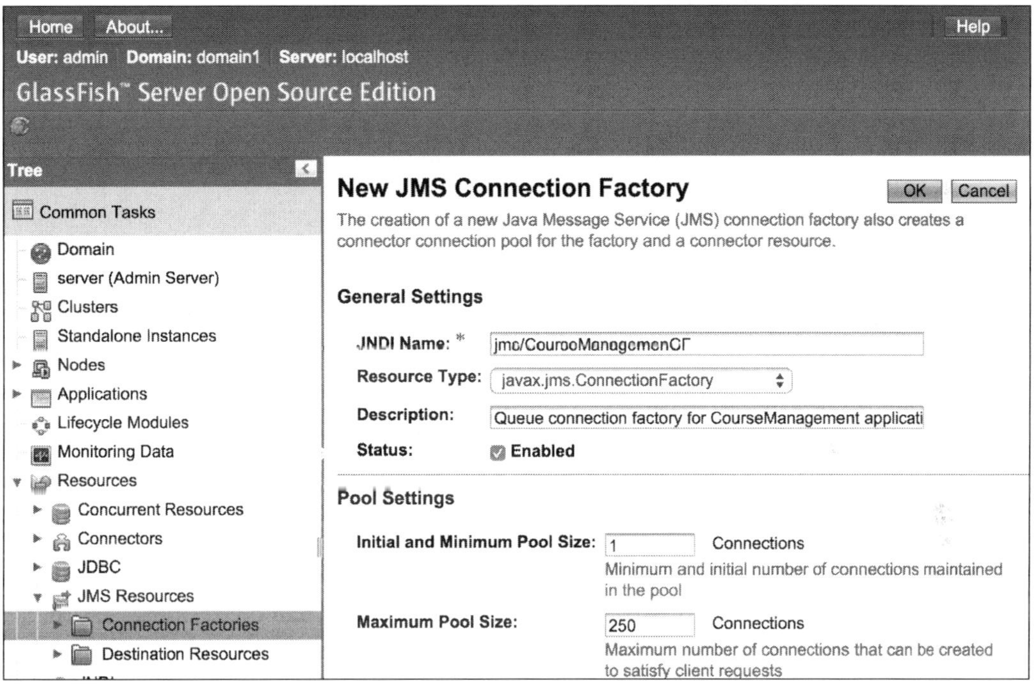

Figure 10.1 Create JMS Connection Factory

Enter **JNDI Name** of the factory as `jms/CourseManagementCF` and select `javax.jms.ConnectionFactory` as **Resource Type**. Leave the default values for **Pool Settings**. Click **OK**.

To create queues and topics, go to the **Resources** | **JMS Resources** | **Destination Resources** page. Click the **New** button.

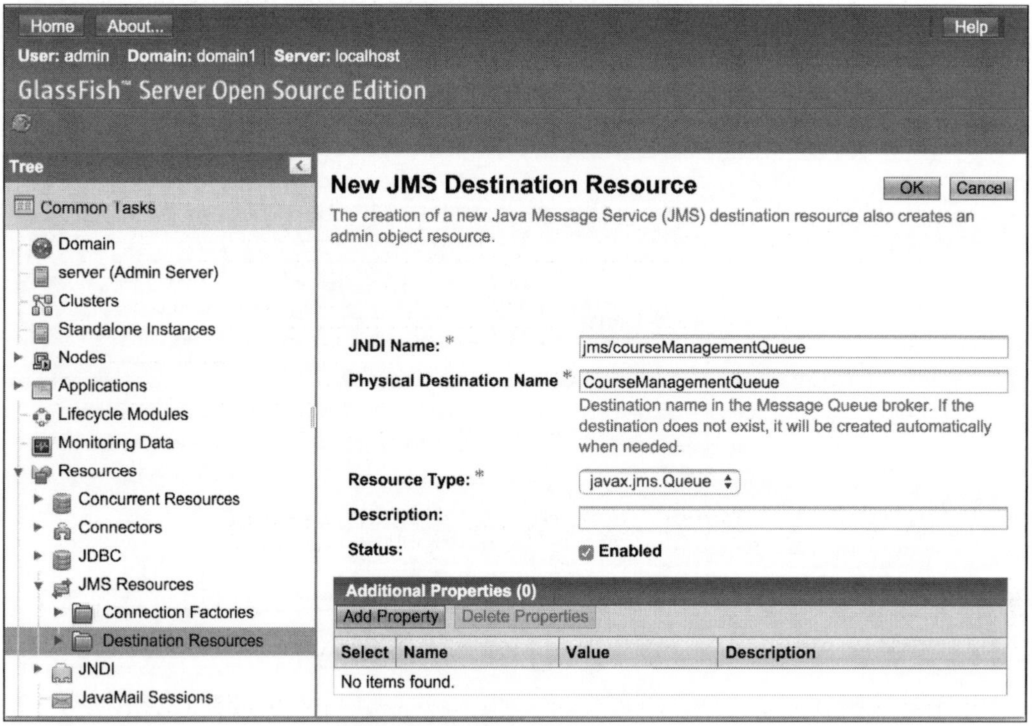

Figure 10.2 Create JMS queue

Enter **JNDI Name** of the queue as `jms/courseManagementQueue` and **Physical Destination Name** as `CourseManagementQueue`, and select `javax.jms.Queue` as **Resource Type**. Click **OK** to create the queue.

Similarly, create a topic by entering **JNDI Name** as `jms/courseManagementTopic` and **Physical Destination Name** as `CourseManagementTopic`, and select `javax.jms.Topic` as **Resource Type**.

You should now have one queue and one topic configured in the **Destination Resources** page.

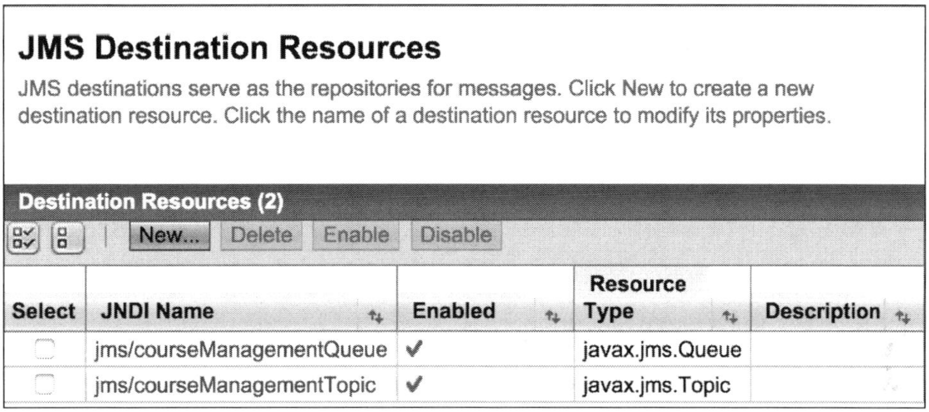

Figure 10.3 Queue and topic Created in GlassFish

Creating a JEE project for a JMS application

We will see examples of using JMS APIs in three different ways.

In the first example, we will create a simple `addCourse.jsp` page, one JSP bean, and one `Service` class that actually perform JMS tasks.

In the second example, we will use JSF and managed beans. We will use JMS APIs in the managed beans. We will also see how to use JMS annotations in JSF managed beans.

In the last example, we will use MDB to consume JMS messages.

Let's start with the first example that uses JSP, bean, and JMS APIs. Create a web project by selecting **File** | **New** | **Dynamic Web Project**.

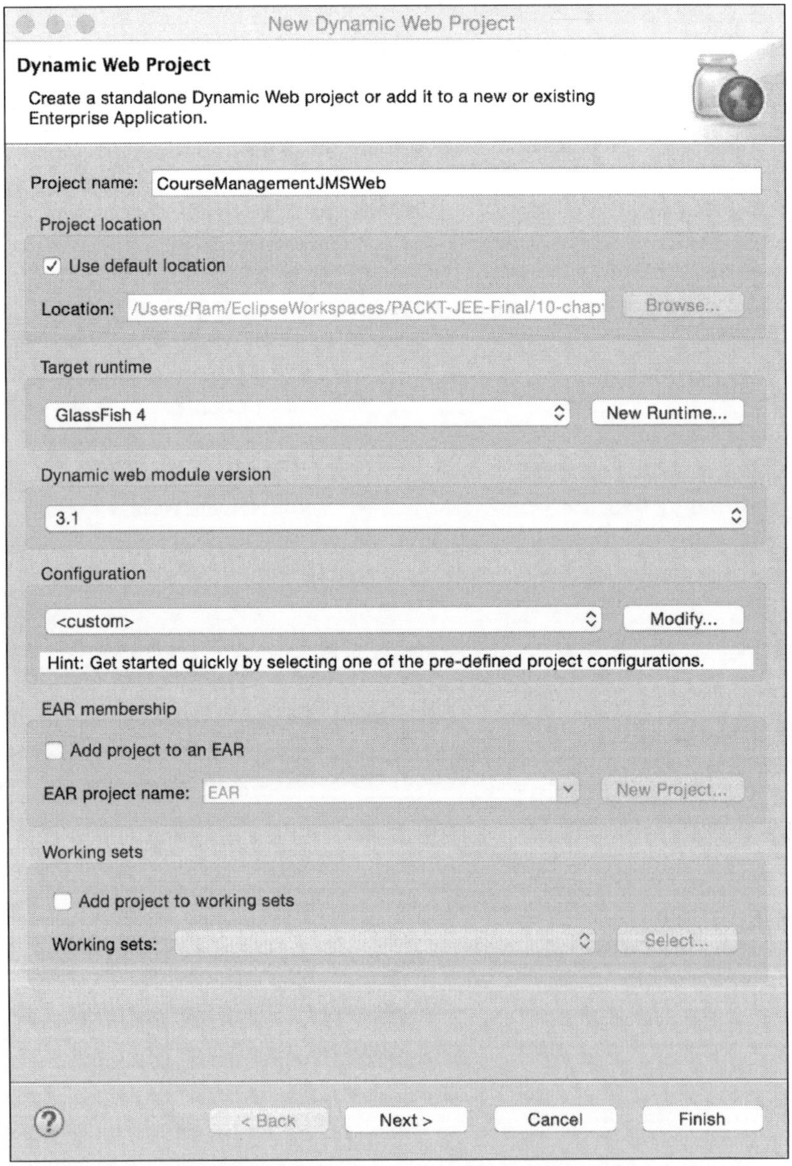

Figure 10.4 Create dynamic web project for JMS app

Enter **Project name** as `CourseManagementJMSWeb`. Make sure that **Target runtime** is `Glassfish 4`. Click **Next**, and accept all default options. Click **Finish** to create the project.

Creating a JMS application using JSP and JSP bean

Let's first create JSP that displays a form to enter course details and a **Submit** button. We will have a JSP bean to process the form data. Right-click on the `WebContent` folder under the project in the **Project Explorer** view and select **New | JSP File**. Create a JSP file named `addCourse.jsp`.

We will now create `CourseDTO` and JSP bean called `CourseJSPBean`. Create the `CourseDTO` class in the `packt.jee.eclipse.jms.dto` package. Add the `id`, `name`, and `credits` properties, and the getters and setters for them:

```
import java.io.Serializable;
public class CourseDTO implements Serializable {
  private static final long serialVersionUID = 1L;
  private int id;
  private String name;
  private int credits;

  //getters and setters follow
}
```

Create `CourseJSPBean` in the `packt.jee.eclipse.jms.jsp.beans` package:

```
import packt.jee.eclipse.jms.dto.CourseDTO;

public class CourseJSPBean {

  private CourseDTO course = new CourseDTO();

  public void setId(int id) {
    course.setId(id);
  }
  public String getName() {
    return course.getName();
  }
  public void setName(String name) {
    course.setName(name);
  }
  public int getCredits() {
    return course.getCredits();
  }
```

```
    public void setCredits(int credits) {
      course.setCredits(credits);
    }
    public void addCourse() {
      //TODO: send CourseDTO object to a JMS queue
    }
  }
```

We will implement the code to send the `CourseDTO` object to the JMS queue that we have configured in the `addCourse` method later. For now, add the following code to `addCourse.jsp`:

```
<%@ page language="java" contentType="text/html; charset=UTF-8"
    pageEncoding="UTF-8"%>
<%@ taglib uri="http://java.sun.com/jsp/jstl/core" prefix="c" %>
<!DOCTYPE html PUBLIC "-//W3C//DTD HTML 4.01 Transitional//EN"
"http://www.w3.org/TR/html4/loose.dtd">
<html>
<head>
<meta http-equiv="Content-Type" content="text/html; charset=UTF-
8">
<title>Add Course</title>
</head>
<body>
  <!-- Check if form is posted -->
  <c:if test="${\"POST\".equalsIgnoreCase(pageContext.request.method)
      && pageContext.request.getParameter(\"submit\") != null}">

    <!-- Create CourseJSPBean -->
    <jsp:useBean id="courseService" class="packt.jee.eclipse.jms.jsp_
beans.CourseJSPBean"
scope="page"></jsp:useBean>

    <!-- Set Bean properties with values from form submission -->
    <jsp:setProperty property="name" name="courseService"
    param="course_name"/>
    <jsp:setProperty property="credits" name="courseService"
    param="course_credits"/>

    <!-- Call addCourse method of the bean -->
```

```
    ${courseService.addCourse()}
    <b>Course detailed are sent to a JMS Queue. It will be
    processed later</b>
  </c:if>

  <h2>New Course:</h2>

  <!-- Course data input form -->
  <form method="post">
    <table>
      <tr>
        <td>Name:</td>
        <td>
          <input type="text" name="course_name">
        </td>
      </tr>
      <tr>
        <td>Credits:</td>
        <td>
          <input type="text" name="course_credits">
        </td>
      </tr>
      <tr>
        <td colspan="2">
          <button type="submit" name="submit">Add</button>
        </td>
      </tr>
    </table>
  </form>

</body>
</html>
```

At the top of the JSP file, we check whether the form is submitted. If yes, then we create an instance of `CourseJSPBean` and set its properties with values from the form submission. Then, we call the `addCourse` method of the bean.

Executing addCourse.jsp

We still haven't added any code to put the `Course` object in the JMS queue. However, if you want to test the JSP and bean, add the project to the GlassFish server configured in Eclipse. To do this, right-click on the configured server in the **Servers** view of Eclipse and select the **Add Remove ...** option. Select the web project that we created above and click **Finish**. Make sure that the server is started and the status is **[Started, Synchronized]**.

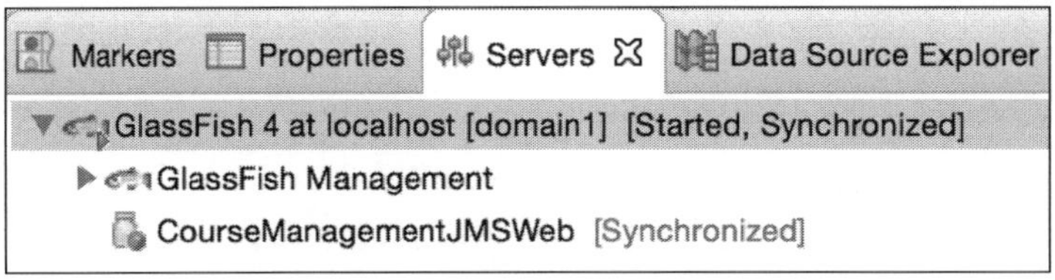

Figure 10.5 Status of GlassFish after adding web project

If the status is **Republish**, then right-click on the server and select the **Publish** option. If the status is **Restart**, right-click on the server and select the **Restart** option. You may not have to do this immediately after adding a project, but later when we make changes to the code, you may have to republish or restart the server or both. So, keep a watch on the server status before you execute the code in Eclipse.

To execute `addCourse.jsp`, right-click on the file in either **Project Explorer** or the editor, and select the **Run As | Run on Server** option. This will open the built-in Eclipse browser and open JSP in it. You should see the form for adding the course details. If you click the **Submit** button, you should see the message that we added in JSP when the form is submitted.

Let's now add a class to send the course details to the JMS queue.

Implementing a JMS queue sender class

Create the `CourseQueueSender` class in the `packt.jee.eclipse.jms` package.

```
package packt.jee.eclipse.jms;

//skipped imports

public class CourseQueueSender {
  private QueueConnection connection;
  private QueueSession session;
  private Queue queue;


  public CourseQueueSender() throws Exception {
```

```
        //Create JMS Connection, session, and queue objects
        InitialContext initCtx = new InitialContext();
        QueueConnectionFactory connectionFactory =
        (QueueConnectionFactory)initCtx.
              lookup("jms/CourseManagemenCF");
        connection = connectionFactory.createQueueConnection();
        connection.start();
        session = connection.createQueueSession(false,
        Session.AUTO_ACKNOWLEDGE);
        queue = (Queue)initCtx.lookup("jms/courseManagementQueue");

      }

      public void close() {
        if (connection != null) {
          try {
            connection.close();
          } catch (JMSException e) {
            e.printStackTrace();
          }
        }
      }
      @Override
      protected void finalize() throws Throwable {
        close(); //clean up
        super.finalize();
      }

      public void sendAddCourseMessage (CourseDTO course) throws
      Exception {
        //Send CourseDTO object to JMS Queue
        QueueSender sender = session.createSender(queue);
        ObjectMessage objMessage =
        session.createObjectMessage(course);
        sender.send(objMessage);
      }
    }
```

In the constructor, we look up the JMS connection factory and create the connection. We then create a JMS session and look up queue with the JNDI name that we used for creating the queue in a previous section.

Note that we did not specify any configuration properties when constructing `InitialContext`. This is because the code is executed in the same instance of the GlassFish server that hosts the JMS provider. If you are connecting to a JMS provider hosted in a different GlassFish server, then you will have to specify the configuration properties, particularly for the remote host. For example:

```
Properties jndiProperties = new Properties();
jndiProperties.setProperty("org.omg.CORBA.ORBInitialHost",
"<remote_host>");
//target ORB port. default is 3700 in Glassfish
jndiProperties.setProperty("org.omg.CORBA.ORBInitialPort",
"3700");

InitialContext ctx = new InitialContext(jndiProperties);
```

The `CourseQueueSender.sendAddcourseMessage` method creates a `QueueSender` object and `ObjectMessage`. Because the producer and the consumer of the message in this example are in Java, we use `ObjectMessage`. However, if you are to send a message to a messaging system where the message is going to be consumed by a non-Java consumer, then you could create JSON or XML from the Java object and send `TextMessage`. We have already seen how to serialize Java objects to JSON and XML by using JAXB in *Chapter 9, Creating Web Services*.

Now, let's modify `addCourse` in `CourseJSPBean` to use the preceding class to send JMS messages. Note that we could create an instance of `CourseQueueSender` in the bean class, `CouseJSPBean`, but the bean is created every time a page is requested. So, `CourseQueueSender` will be created frequently and the lookup for the JMS connection factory and the queue will also take place frequently, which is not necessary. Therefore, we will create an instance of `CourseQueueSender` and save it in the HTTP session. Then, we will modify the `addCourse` method to take `HttpServletRequest` as a parameter. We will also get the `HttpSession` object from the request.

```
public void addCourse(HttpServletRequest request) throws
Exception {
  //get HTTP session
  HttpSession session = request.getSession(true);

  //look for instance of CourseQueueSender in Session
  CourseQueueSender courseQueueSender =
  (CourseQueueSender)session
                    getAttribute("CourseQueueSender");
  if (courseQueueSender == null) {
    //Create instance of CourseQueueSender and save in Session
    courseQueueSender = new CourseQueueSender();
```

```
            session.setAttribute("CourseQueueSender",
            courseQueueSender);
        }

        //TODO: perform input validation
        if (courseQueueSender != null) {
          try {
            courseQueueSender.sendAddCourseMessage(course);
          } catch (Exception e) {
            e.printStackTrace();
            //TODO: log exception
          }
        }
      }
```

If we don't find the `CourseQueueSender` object in the session, then we will create one and save it in the session.

We need to modify the call to the `addCourse` method from `addcourse.jsp`. Currently, we do not pass any argument to the method. However, with the preceding changes to the `addCourse` method, we need to pass the `HttpServletRequest` object to it. JSP has a build-in property called `pageContext` that provides access to the `HttpServletRequest` object. So, modify the code in `addCourse.jsp` where `courseService.addCourse` is called as follows:

```
<!-- Call addCourse method of the bean -->
${courseService.addCourse(pageContext.request)}
```

We can test our code at this point, but although a message is sent to the queue, we haven't implemented any consumer to receive a message from the queue. So, let's implement a JMS queue consumer for our `Course` queue.

Implementing a JMS queue receiver class

Create the `CourseQueueReceiver` class in the `packt.jee.eclipse.jms` package.

```
public class CourseQueueReceiver {

  private QueueConnection connection;
  private QueueSession session;
  private Queue queue;

  private String receiverName;

  public CourseQueueReceiver(String name) throws Exception{

    //save receiver name
```

```
      this.receiverName = name;

      //look up JMS connection factory
      InitialContext initCtx = new InitialContext();
      QueueConnectionFactory connectionFactory =
  (QueueConnectionFactory)initCtx.lookup("jms/CourseManagemenCF");

      //create JMS connection
      connection = connectionFactory.createQueueConnection();
      connection.start();

      //create JMS session
      session = connection.createQueueSession(false,
      Session.AUTO_ACKNOWLEDGE);
      //look up queue
      queue = (Queue)initCtx.lookup("jms/courseManagementQueue");

      topicPublisher = new CourseTopicPublisher();

      QueueReceiver receiver = session.createReceiver(queue);
      //register message listener
      receiver.setMessageListener(new MessageListener() {

        @Override
        public void onMessage(Message message) {
          //we expect ObjectMessage here; of type CourseDTO
          //skipping validation
          try {
            CourseDTO course = (CourseDTO)
            ((ObjectMessage)message).getObject();
            //process addCourse action. For example, save it in the
            database

            System.out.println("Received addCourse message for Course
  name - " +
                course.getName() + " in Receiver " + receiverName);

          } catch (Exception e) {
            e.printStackTrace();
            //TODO: handle and log exception
          }
        }
      });
    }

    public void stop() {
      if (connection != null) {
```

```
            try {
              connection.close();
            } catch (JMSException e) {
              e.printStackTrace();
              //TODO: log exception
            }
          }
        }
      }
```

The code to look up the connection factory and the queue is similar to that in `CourseQueueSender`. Note that the constructor takes a name argument. We don't really need to use a JMS API, but we will use it as an identifier for instances of the `CourseQueueReceiver` class. We register a message listener in the constructor, and in the `onMessage` method of the listener class, we get the `CourseDTO` object from the message and print the message to the console. This message will appear in GlassFish console in Eclipse when we execute the code. To keep the example simple, we have not implemented the code to save the `Course` information to the database, but you can do so by using JDBC or JDO APIs that we have already learnt in *Chapter 4, Creating a JEE Database Application*.

We need to instantiate this class at the application startup so that it will start listening for messages. One way to implement this is in a Servlet that loads on startup.

Create the `JMSReceiverInitServlet` class in the `packt.jee.eclipse.jms.servlet` package. We will mark this Servlet to load at startup by using annotations and instantiate `CourseQueueReceiver` in the `init` method.

```
package packt.jee.eclipse.jms.servlet;

//skipped imports

@WebServlet(urlPatterns="/JMSReceiverInitServlet",
loadOnStartup=1)
public class JMSReceiverInitServlet extends HttpServlet {
  private static final long serialVersionUID = 1L;

  private CourseQueueReceiver courseQueueReceiver = null;

    public JMSReceiverInitServlet() {
        super();
    }

    @Override
    public void init(ServletConfig config) throws ServletException
{
```

```
        super.init(config);
        try {
        courseQueueReceiver = new CourseQueueReceiver("Receiver1");
      } catch (Exception e) {
        log("Error creating CourseQueueReceiver", e);
      }
      }

      @Override
      public void destroy() {
        if (courseQueueReceiver != null)
          courseQueueReceiver.stop();
        super.destroy();
      }
  }
```

Publish the project again in the server and execute `addCourse.jsp` (see the *Executing addCourse.jsp* section). Switch to the **Console** view in Eclipse. You should see the message that we printed in the `onMessage` method in `CourseQueueReceiver`.

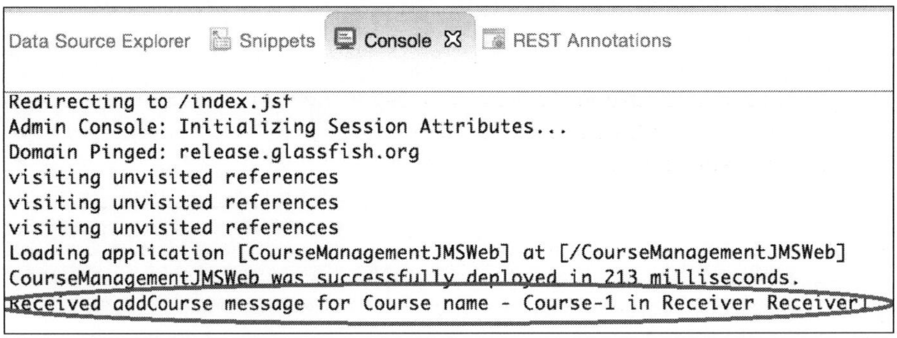

Figure 10.6 Example of console message from JMS receiver class

Adding multiple queue listeners

Queues are meant for point-to-point communication, but this does not mean that there can't be more than one listener for a queue. However, only one listener gets a message. Further, it is not guaranteed that the same listener will get the message every time. If you want to test this, add one more instance of `CourseQueueReceiver` in `JMSReceiverInitServlet`. Let's add the second instance with a different name, say `Receiver2`.

```
@WebServlet(urlPatterns="/JMSReceiverInitServlet",
loadOnStartup=1)
public class JMSReceiverInitServlet extends HttpServlet {
  private CourseQueueReceiver courseQueueReceiver = null;
```

```
    private CourseQueueReceiver courseQueueReceiver1 = null;

      @Override
      public void init(ServletConfig config) throws ServletException
  {
        super.init(config);
        try {
          //first instance of CourseQueueReceiver
        courseQueueReceiver = new CourseQueueReceiver("Receiver1");
        //create another instance of CourseQueueReceiver with a
        different name
        courseQueueReceiver1 = new CourseQueueReceiver("Receiver2");

      } catch (Exception e) {
        log("Error creating CourseQueueReceiver", e);
      }
      }

      @Override
      public void destroy() {
        if (courseQueueReceiver != null)
          courseQueueReceiver.stop();
        if (courseQueueReceiver1 != null)
          courseQueueReceiver1.stop();
        super.destroy();
      }

      //rest of the code remains the same
  }
```

Republish the project, execute `addCourse.jsp`, and add a few courses. Check the **Console** messages. You may see that some of the messages were received by `Receiver1` and the others by `Receiver2`.

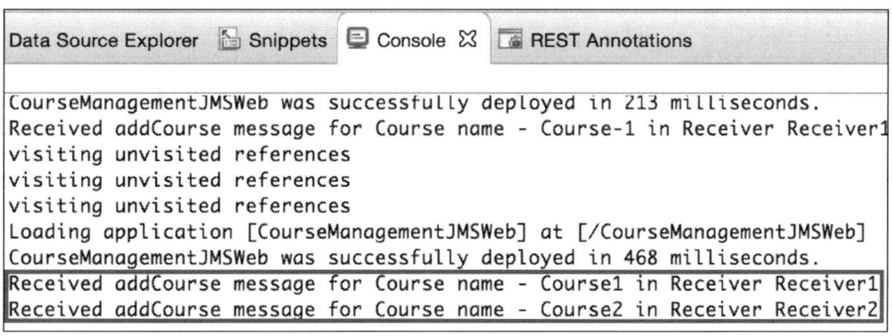

Figure 10.7 Console output showing multiple JMS receivers listening to a JMS queue

Implementing the JMS topic publisher

Let's say that we want to inform a bunch of applications when a new course is added. Such use cases can be best implemented by JMS topic. Topic can have many subscribers. When a message is added to a topic, all subscribers are sent the same message. This is unlike queue where only one queue listener gets a message.

Steps to publish messages to topic and subscribe for messages are very similar to those for queue, except for the different classes, and in some cases, different method names.

Let's implement a topic publisher, which we will use when a message for adding course is successfully handled in the `onMessage` method of the listener class implemented in `CourseQueueReceiver`.

Create `CourseTopicPublisher` in the `packt.jee.eclipse.jms` package.

```
package packt.jee.eclipse.jms;

//skipped imports

public class CourseTopicPublisher {
  private TopicConnection connection;
  private TopicSession session;
  private Topic topic;

  public CourseTopicPublisher() throws Exception {
    InitialContext initCtx = new InitialContext();
    TopicConnectionFactory connectionFactory =
    (TopicConnectionFactory)initCtx.
        lookup("jms/CourseManagemenCF");
    connection = connectionFactory.createTopicConnection();
    connection.start();
    session = connection.createTopicSession(false,
    Session.AUTO_ACKNOWLEDGE);
    topic = (Topic)initCtx.lookup("jms/courseManagementTopic");
  }

  public void close() {
    if (connection != null) {
      try {
        connection.close();
      } catch (JMSException e) {
        e.printStackTrace();.
```

```
        }
      }
    }

    public void publishAddCourseMessage (CourseDTO course) throws
    Exception {
      TopicPublisher sender = session.createPublisher(topic);
      ObjectMessage objMessage =
      session.createObjectMessage(course);
      sender.send(objMessage);
    }
  }
```

The code is quite simple and self-explanatory. Let's now modify the queue receiver class that we implemented, `CourseQueueReceiver`, to publish a message to the topic from the `onMessage` method, after the message from the queue is handled successfully.

```
  public class CourseQueueReceiver {

    private CourseTopicPublisher topicPublisher;

    public CourseQueueReceiver(String name) throws Exception{

      //code to lookup connection factory, create session,
      //and look up queue remains unchanged. Skipping this code

      //create topic publisher
      topicPublisher = new CourseTopicPublisher();

      QueueReceiver receiver = session.createReceiver(queue);
      //register message listener
      receiver.setMessageListener(new MessageListener() {

        @Override
        public void onMessage(Message message) {
          //we expect ObjectMessage here; of type CourseDTO
          //Skipping validation
          try {
            //code to process message is unchanged. Skipping it

            //publish message to topic
```

```
            if (topicPublisher != null)
              topicPublisher.publishAddCourseMessage(course);

          } catch (Exception e) {
            e.printStackTrace();
            //TODO: handle and log exception
          }
        }
      });
    }

    //remaining code is unchanged. Skipping it
  }
```

Implementing the JMS topic subscriber

We will now implement a topic subscriber class. Create the `CourseTopicSubscriber` class in the `packt.jee.eclipse.jms` package.

```
package packt.jee.eclipse.jms;
//skipping imports
public class CourseTopicSubscriber {

  private TopicConnection connection;
  private TopicSession session;
  private Topic topic;

  private String subscriberName;

  public CourseTopicSubscriber(String name) throws Exception{

    this.subscriberName = name;

    InitialContext initCtx = new InitialContext();
    TopicConnectionFactory connectionFactory =
(TopicConnectionFactory)initCtx.lookup("jms/CourseManagemenCF");
    connection = connectionFactory.createTopicConnection();
    connection.start();
    session = connection.createTopicSession(false,
    Session.AUTO_ACKNOWLEDGE);
    topic = (Topic)initCtx.lookup("jms/courseManagementTopic");

    TopicSubscriber subscriber = session.createSubscriber(topic);
```

```
    subscriber.setMessageListener(new MessageListener() {

      @Override
      public void onMessage(Message message) {
        //we expect ObjectMessage here; of type CourseDTO
        //skipping validation
        try {
          CourseDTO course = (CourseDTO)
          ((ObjectMessage)message).getObject();
          //process addCourse action. For example, save it in
          database
          System.out.println("Received addCourse notification for
          Course name - "
              + course.getName() + " in Subscriber " +
              subscriberName);

        } catch (JMSException e) {
          e.printStackTrace();
          //TODO: handle and log exception
        }
      }
    });
  }

  public void stop() {
    if (connection != null) {
      try {
        connection.close();
      } catch (JMSException e) {
        e.printStackTrace();
        //TODO: log exception
      }
    }
  }
}
```

Again, JMS APIs to subscribe to a topic are similar to those in `CourseQueueReceiver`, but with different class names and method names. We also identify subscribers with names so that we know which instance of the class receives the messages.

In the preceding example, we created the topic subscriber by calling `TopicSession.createSubscriber`. In this case, the subscriber will receive messages from the topic as long as the subscriber is active. If the subscriber becomes inactive and then active again, it loses messages published by the topic during that period. If you want to make sure that the subscriber receives all messages, you need to create a durable subscription using `TopicSession.createDurableSubscriber`. Along with the topic name, this method takes the subscriber name as the second argument. Refer to `https://docs.oracle.com/javaee/7/api/javax/jms/TopicSession.html#createDurableSubscriber-javax.jms.Topic-java.lang.String-` for more information.

We will create two instances of this class (so there would be two topic subscribers) in `JMSReceiverInitServlet`, so that subscribers start listening for messages on the application start (the Servlet is loaded on startup).

```
@WebServlet(urlPatterns="/JMSReceiverInitServlet",
loadOnStartup=1)
public class JMSReceiverInitServlet extends HttpServlet {
  private CourseQueueReceiver courseQueueReceiver = null;
  private CourseTopicSubscriber courseTopicSubscriber = null;
  private CourseQueueReceiver courseQueueReceiver1 = null;
  private CourseTopicSubscriber courseTopicSubscriber1 = null;

    @Override
    public void init(ServletConfig config) throws ServletException
{
      super.init(config);
      try {
      courseQueueReceiver = new CourseQueueReceiver("Receiver1");
      courseQueueReceiver1 = new CourseQueueReceiver("Receiver2");
      courseTopicSubscriber = new
      CourseTopicSubscriber("Subscriber1");
      courseTopicSubscriber1 = new
      CourseTopicSubscriber("Subscriber2");

    } catch (Exception e) {
      log("Error creating CourseQueueReceiver", e);
    }
    }

    //remaining code is unchanged. Skipping it
}
```

Therefore, now, we have two queue listeners and two topic listeners ready when the application starts. Republish the project, execute `addCourse.jsp`, and add a course. Check messages in the **Console** view of Eclipse. You will see that the message published in the topic is received by all subscribers, but the same message published in queue is received by only one receiver.

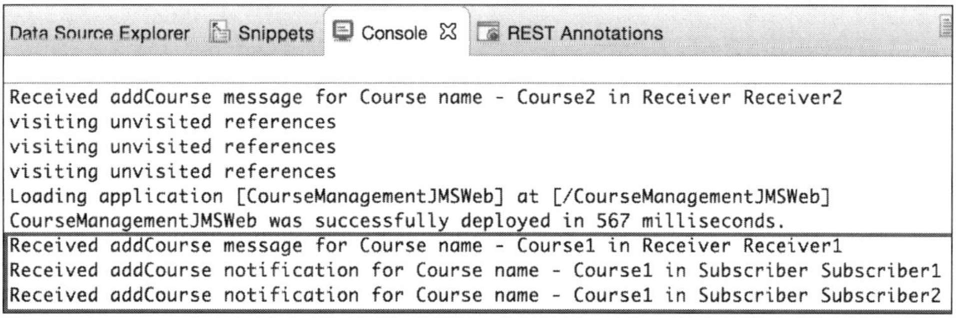

Figure 10.8 Console output showing multiple JMS receivers listening to JMS queue and topic

Creating a JMS application using JSF and managed beans

In this section, we will see how to create a JMS application by using JSF and managed beans. With managed beans, we can reduce the code that you write to using JMS APIs, because we can use annotations to inject objects such as the JMS connection factory, queue, and topic. Once we obtain reference to these objects, steps to send or receive data are the same as those discussed in the previous section. Therefore, our examples in this section do not list the entire code. For the complete source code, download the source code for this chapter.

To prepare our project for using JSF, we need to create web.xml and add the JSF Servlet definition and mapping in it. Right-click on the project and select the **Java EE Tools | Generate Deployment Descriptor Stub** option. This creates `web.xml` in the `WebContent/WEB-INF` folder. Add the following Servlet definition and mapping (within the `web-app` tag) in `web.xml`:

```
<servlet>
  <servlet-name>JSFServelt</servlet-name>
  <servlet-class>javax.faces.webapp.FacesServlet</servlet-class>
  <load-on-startup>1</load-on-startup>
</servlet>

<servlet-mapping>
```

```
    <servlet-name>JSFServelt</servlet-name>
    <url-pattern>*.xhtml</url-pattern>
  </servlet-mapping>
```

We will first create three managed beans for JSF. The first one is `CourseManagedMsgSenderBean`. The second one is `CourseManagedMsgReceiverBean`, and the last one is `CourseJSFBean`, which will be referenced from the JSF page.

Create the `CourseManagedMsgSenderBean` class in the `packt.jee.eclipse.jms.jsf_bean` package:

```
package packt.jee.eclipse.jms.jsf_bean;

//skipped imports

@ManagedBean(name="courseMessageSender")
@SessionScoped
public class CourseManagedMsgSenderBean {


  @Resource(name = "jms/CourseManagemenCF")
  private QueueConnectionFactory connectionFactory;
  @Resource(lookup = "jms/courseManagementQueue")
  private Queue queue;

  QueueConnection connection;
  QueueSession session;
  Exception initException = null;

  @PostConstruct
  public void init() {
    try {
      connection = connectionFactory.createQueueConnection();
      connection.start();
      session = connection.createQueueSession(false,
      Session.AUTO_ACKNOWLEDGE);
    } catch (Exception e) {
      initException = e;
    }
  }

  @PreDestroy
```

```
    public void cleanup() {
      if (connection != null) {
        try {
          connection.close();
        } catch (JMSException e) {
          e.printStackTrace();
          //TODO: log exception
        }
      }
    }

    public void addCourse(CourseDTO courseDTO) throws Exception {

      if (initException != null)
        throw initException;

      QueueSender sender = session.createSender(queue);
      ObjectMessage objMessage =
      session.createObjectMessage(courseDTO);
      sender.send(objMessage);
    }
  }
```

Notice that the JMS connection factory and queue objects are injected using the `@Resource` annotation. We have used the `@PostConstruct` annotation to create a JMS connection and session and the `@PreDestroy` annotation for a clean-up operation. The `addCourse` method is similar to the code that we have already implemented in the `CourseQueueSender` class in a previous section.

Now, create a JMS message receiver class. Create the `CourseManagedMsgReceiverBean` class in the `packt.jee.eclipse.jms.jsf_bean` package.

```
package packt.jee.eclipse.jms.jsf_bean;

//skipped imports

@ManagedBean(name="courseMessageReceiver")
@ApplicationScoped
public class CourseManagedMsgReceiverBean {

  @Resource(name = "jms/CourseManagemenCF")
  private QueueConnectionFactory connectionFactory;
```

```
@Resource(lookup = "jms/courseManagementQueue")
private Queue queue;

QueueConnection connection;
QueueSession session;
Throwable initException = null;

@PostConstruct
public void init() {
  try {
    connection = connectionFactory.createQueueConnection();
    connection.start();
    session = connection.createQueueSession(false,
    Session.AUTO_ACKNOWLEDGE);

    //skipped code to create receiver and add MessageListener
    //the code is same as in the constructor of
    CourseQueueReceiver
  } catch (Throwable e) {
    initException = e;
  }
}

//skipped @PreDestroy method to close connection
}
```

In this class also, JMS resources are injected using the `@Resource` tags. The `@PostConstruct` method creates a connection, session, and a receiver. It also registers `MessageListener`. The code is similar to what we wrote in the constructor of `CourseQueueReceiver`, so some of the code is skipped in the previous listing. Please download the source code for this chapter to see the complete source code.

We need to create an instance of this class on application startup. We have already created `JMSReceiverInitServlet` that loads on startup in a previous section. We also instantiated the course and topic listeners that we created earlier in the `init` method of this Servlet. So, now, let's create an instance of `CourseManagedMsgReceiverBean` in the `init` method.

```
@Override
public void init(ServletConfig config) throws ServletException {
  super.init(config);

//get JSF Managed bean for receiving Course messages
FacesContext context = FacesContext.getCurrentInstance();
//Evaluating #{courseMessageReceiver} expression will
```

```
//instantiate CourseManagedMsgReceiverBean and start
//message listener
context.getApplication().evaluateExpressionGet(context,
"#{courseMessageReceiver}",
    CourseManagedMsgReceiverBean.class);
    }
```

Note that if you want only CourseManagedMsgReceiverBean to receive messages from the course queue, then remove the previously added message receivers from the init method.

Now, let's create the CourseJSFBean class in the packt.jee.eclipse.jms.jsf_bean package.

```
package packt.jee.eclipse.jms.jsf_bean;

//skipped imports

@ManagedBean(name="course")
@RequestScoped
public class CourseJSFBean {
  private CourseDTO courseDTO = new CourseDTO();

  @ManagedProperty(value="#{courseMessageSender}")
  private CourseManagedMsgSenderBean courseMessageSender;

  //skipped getters and setters

  public void setCourseMessageSender(CourseManagedMsgSenderBean
  courseMessageSender) {
    this.courseMessageSender = courseMessageSender;
  }

  public void addCourse() throws Exception {
    //skipping validation
    //TODO: handle exception properly and show error message
    courseMessageSender.addCourse(courseDTO);
  }
}
```

CourseJSFBean obtains a reference to CourseManagedMsgSenderBean by using the @ManagedBean annotation. We need to provide the setter for CourseManagedMsgSenderBean so that the container can set its value. The addCourse method simply calls the same named method in CourseManagedMsgSenderBean.

Finally, create `addCourse.xhtml` in the `WebContents` folder.

```
<html xmlns="http://www.w3.org/1999/xhtml"
 xmlns:f="http://java.sun.com/jsf/core"
 xmlns:h="http://java.sun.com/jsf/html">

<head>
  <title>Add Course</title>
</head>

 <body>
  <h2>Course Details</h2>

  <h:form>
    <table>
      <tr>
        <td>Name:</td>
        <td>
          <h:inputText id="course_name" value="#{course.name}"/>
        </td>
      </tr>
      <tr>
        <td>Credits:</td>
        <td>
          <h:inputText id="course_credits"
          value="#{course.credits}"/>
        </td>
      </tr>
      <tr>
        <td colspan="2">
            <h:commandButton value="Submit"
            action="#{course.addCourse}"/>
        </td>
      </tr>
    </table>
  </h:form>

</body>

</html>
```

Form fields are bound to fields in `CourseJSFBean`. When the **Submit** button is clicked, the `addCourse` method of the same bean is called, which puts a message in the JMS queue.

Republish the project and execute `addCourse.xhtml` by right-clicking it and selecting **Run As | Run on Server**. Add a course and see the message printed (from `MessageListener` in `CourseManagedMsgReceiverBean`) in the GlassFish **Console** view of Eclipse.

Consuming JMS messages using MDB

Message-driven beans (**MDBs**) make consuming JMS messages a lot easier. With just a couple of annotations and implementing the `onMessage` method, you can make any Java object a consumer of the JMS messages. In this section, we will implement an MDB to consume messages from the `Course` queue. To implement MDB, we need to create an EJB project. Select **File** | **New** | **EJB Project** from the main menu.

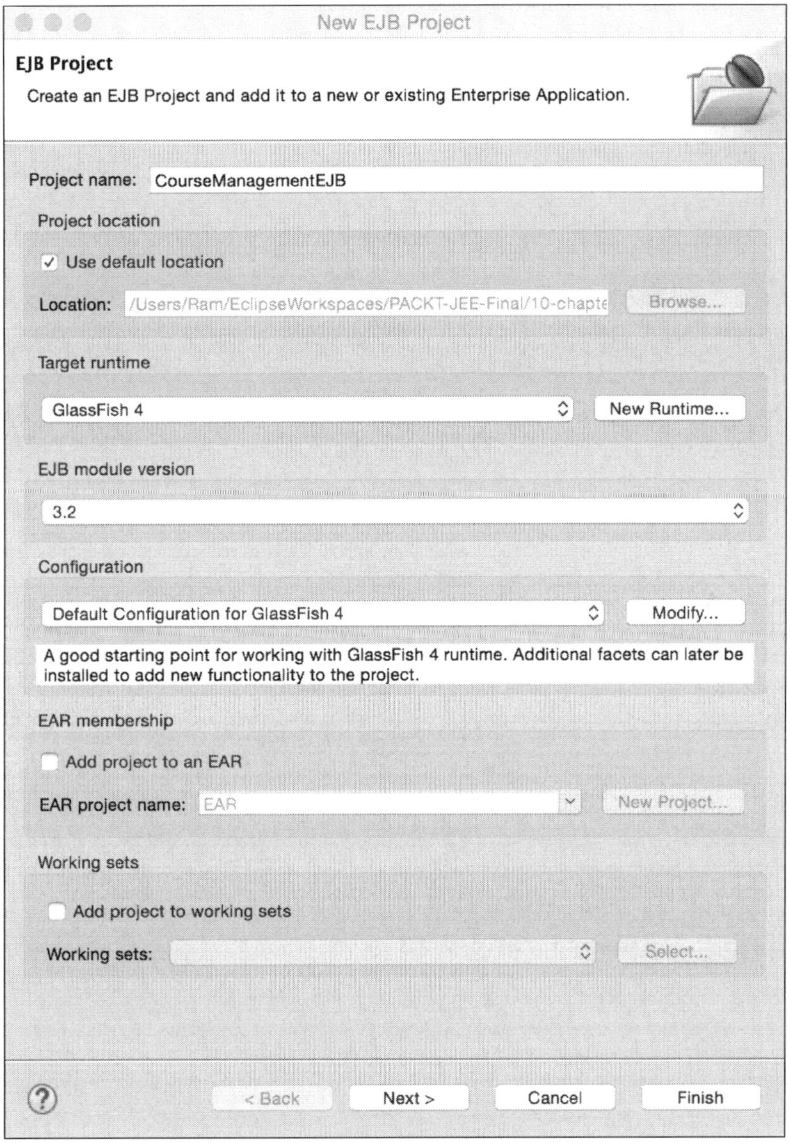

Figure 10.9 Create EJB project to implement MDB

Enter **Project name** as `CourseManagementEJB`. Click **Next**. Accept the default values on the subsequent pages, and click **Finish** on the last page.

Right-click on the project, and select the **New** | **Message-Driven Bean** option. This opens the MDB creation wizard.

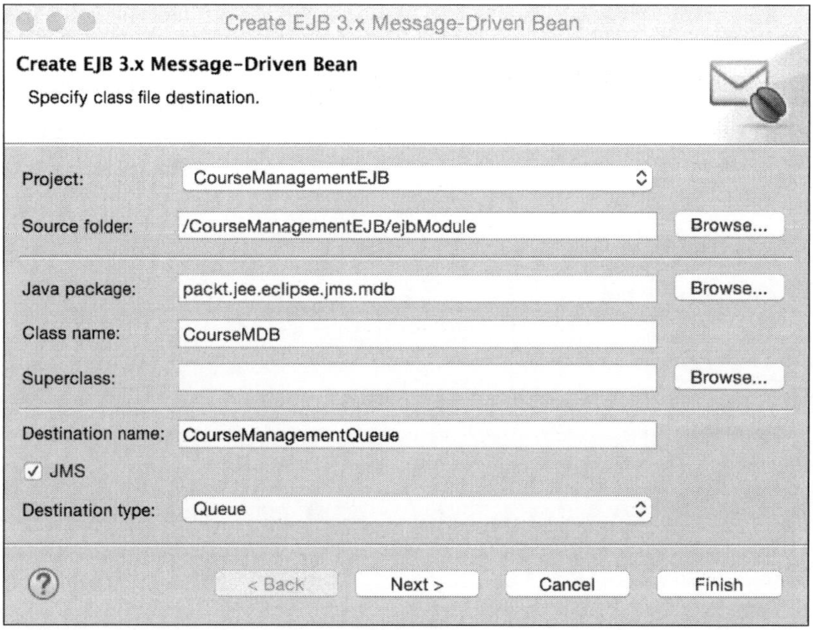

Figure 10.10 MDB creation wizard: class file information

Enter `packt.jee.eclipse.jms.mdb` as **Java package** and `CourseMDB` as **Class name**. Keep **Destination type** as `Queue`.

Destination name is the physical destination name that we specified when creating the queue and is not the JNDI name.

Figure 10.11 JMS queue physical destination name in GlassFish admin console

Enter `CourseManagementQueue` as **Destination type**. Click **Next**. Accept the default values on the second page and click **Finish**. The wizard creates the following code:

```
@MessageDriven(
    activationConfig = {
      @ActivationConfigProperty(propertyName = "destinationType",
            propertyValue = "javax.jms.Queue"),
      @ActivationConfigProperty(propertyName = "destination",
            propertyValue = "CourseManagementQueue")
    },
    mappedName = "jms/courseManagementQueue")
public class CourseMDB implements MessageListener {

    /**
     * Default constructor.
     */
    public CourseMDB() {
        // TODO Auto-generated constructor stub
    }

  /**
     * @see MessageListener#onMessage(Message)
     */
```

```
        public void onMessage(Message message) {
            System.out.println("addCourse message received in
            CourseMDB");

        }

    }
```

The class is annotated with `@MessageDriven` with `activationConfig` with the JMS destination parameters specified in the wizard. It also creates the `onMessage` method. In this method, we just print a message that the MDB received for adding a course. To process `ObjectMessage` in this class, we will have to refactor the `CourseDTO` class to a shared `.jar` between EJB and the web project. This is left to the readers as an exercise.

At runtime, the JEE container creates a pool of MDB objects for a single MDB class. An incoming message can be handled by any one of the instances of MDB in the pool. This can help in building a scalable message processing application.

Summary

Messaging systems can be powerful tools for integrating disparate applications. They provide an asynchronous model of programming. The client does not wait for the response from the server and the server does not necessarily process requests at the same time that the client sends them. Messaging systems can also be useful for building scalable applications and batch processing. JMS provides uniform APIs to access different messaging systems.

In this chapter, we discussed how to send and receive messages from queue and to publish and subscribe messages from topic. There are many different ways to use JMS APIs. We started with the basic JMS APIs and then, discussed how annotations can help reduce some of the code. We also discussed how to use MDBs to consume messages.

In the next chapter, we will see some of the techniques and tools used for profiling the CPU and memory usage in Java applications.

11
Java CPU Profiling and Memory Tracking

Enterprise applications tend to be quite complex and big. There could be situations when the application does not perform as per your requirements or expectations. For example, some of the operations performed in the application might be taking too long or consuming more memory that you expected. Further, debugging performance and memory issues could sometimes become very difficult.

Fortunately, there are tools available, both in JDK and Eclipse, to help us debug these issues. JDK 6 (update 7) and above are bundled with the **jVisualVM** application that can connect to remote or local applications. You can find this tool in the `<JDK_HOME>/bin` folder. jVisualVM can help to profile memory and CPU usage and jVisualVM can also be configured to launch from Eclipse when an application is run from Eclipse. We will discuss how to use VisualVM to profile Java applications in this chapter. You can find detailed information about jVisualVM/VisualVM at `http://docs.oracle.com/javase/7/docs/technotes/guides/visualvm/index.html` and `http://visualvm.java.net/`.

We will create a small standalone Java application to simulate performance and memory issues and will see how to use VisualVM for troubleshooting. Although the real application that you may want to troubleshoot would be a lot more complex, the techniques that we learn in this chapter can be used there too.

Creating a sample Java project for profiling

We will create a simple standalone Java application so that it is easy to learn by using VisualVM. Although it would be a standalone application, we will create similar classes as those that we created for the `CourseManagement` web application in some of the previous chapters, particularly `CourseDTO`, `CourseBean` (JSP bean), `CourseService` (service bean), and `CourseDAO` (for database access).

Create a standard Java project in Eclipse, named `CourseManagementStandalone`. Create `CourseDTO` in the `packt.jee.eclipse.profile.dto` package.

```
package packt.jee.eclipse.profile.dto;

public class CourseDTO {
  private int id;
  private String name;
  private int credits;

  //skipped Getters and Setters
}
```

Create the `CourseDAO` class in the `packt.jee.eclopse.profile.dao` package.

```
//skipped imports
public class CourseDAO {

  public List<CourseDTO> getCourses() {
    //No real database access takes place here
    //We will just simulate a long-running database operation

    try {
      Thread.sleep(2000); //wait 2 seconds
    } catch (InterruptedException e) {
      e.printStackTrace();
    }

    //return dummy/empty list
    return new ArrayList<>();
  }
}
```

We simulate a long-running database operation in the `getCourses` method by making the thread sleep for a few seconds.

Create the `CourseService` class in the `packt.jee.eclipse.profile.service` package.

```
//skipped imports
public class CourseService {

  private CourseDAO courseDAO = new CourseDAO();


  public List<CourseDTO> getCourses() {
    return courseDAO.getCourses();
  }
}
```

`CourseService.getCourses` delegates the call to `CourseDAO`.

Create `CourseBean` in the `packt.jee.eclipse.profile.bean` package.

```
//skipped imports
public class CourseBean {
  private CourseService courseService = new CourseService();

  public List<CourseDTO> getCourses() {
    return courseService.getCourses();
  }
}
```

`CourseBean.getcourses` delegates to `CourseService`.

Finally, create `CourseManagement` in the `packt.jee.eclipse.profile` package. This class contains the `main` method and starts the loop to call the `getCourses` method repeatedly after reading any character from the standard input.

```
//skipped imports
public class CourseManagement {

  public static void main(String[] args) throws IOException {

    CourseBean courseBean = new CourseBean();

    System.out.println("Type any character to get courses. Type q
    to quit.");

    int ch;
    while ((ch = System.in.read()) != -1) {
```

```
          if (ch != 10 && ch != 13) { //ignore new lines
            if (ch == 'q') //quit if user types q
              break;

            System.out.println("Getting courses");
            List<CourseDTO> courses = courseBean.getCourses();
            System.out.println("Got courses");

            System.out.println("Type any character to get courses.
            Type q to quit.");
          }
        }

        System.out.println("Quitting ...");
      }
    }
```

Run the application (right-click on the file and select **Run As | Java Application**). In the console window, type any character and press *Enter*. You should see the **Getting courses** and **Got courses** messages.

Profiling a Java application

Run jVisualVM from the `<JDK_HOME>/bin` folder.

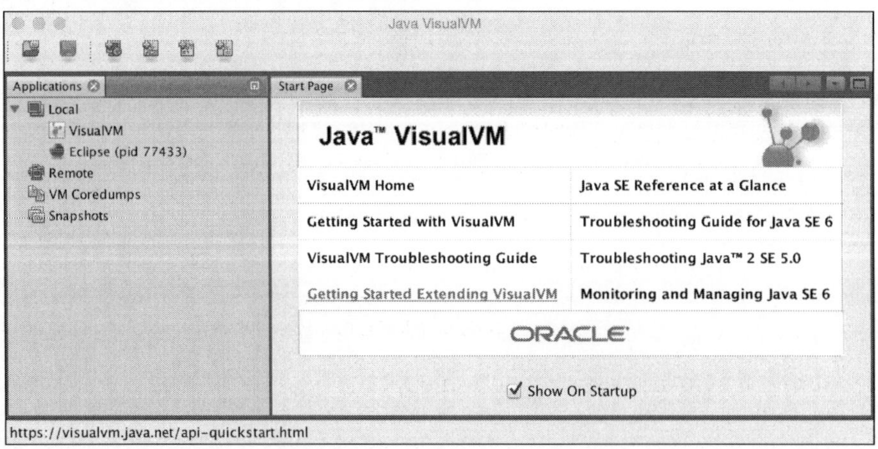

Figure 11.1 Java VisualVM profiler

VisualVM lists all Java processes that can be profiled by it on the local machine under the **Local** node. You can see VisualVM itself listed along with Eclipse. Once you run the `CourseManagement` application, the process should also show up under **Local**.

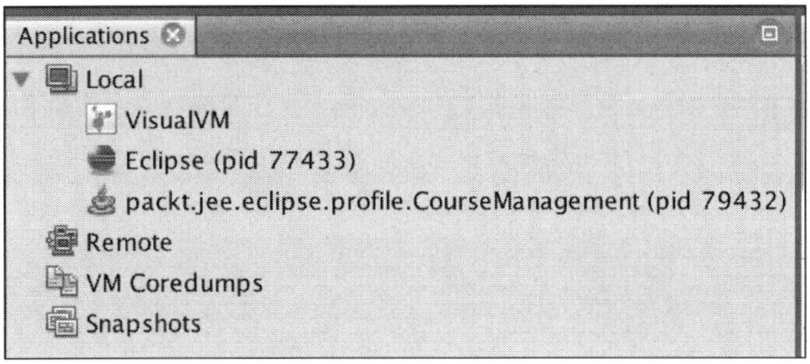

Figure 11.2 CourseManagement application available for profiling

Double-click on the process (or right-click and select **Open**). Go to the **Profile** tab. Then, click the **CPU** button.

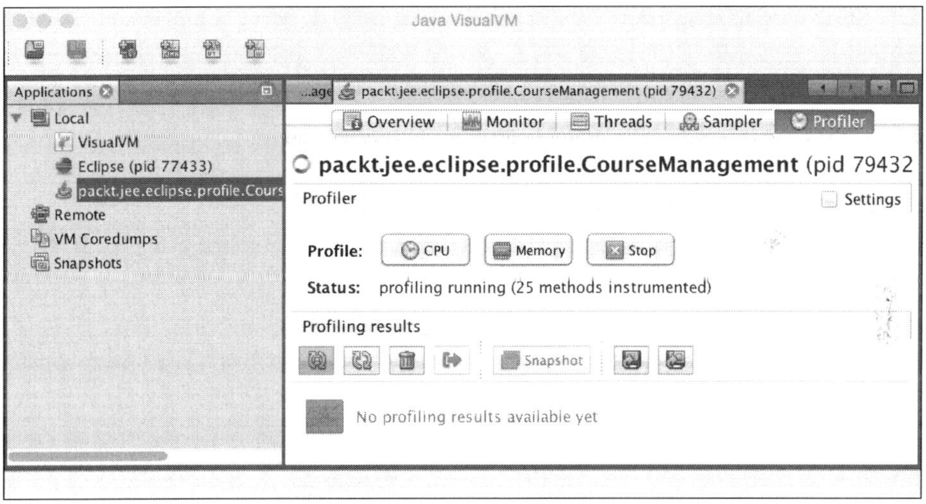

Figure 11.3 VisualVM Profiler tab

You should see the **profiling running** status.

After starting CPU profiling, if you get an error such as **Redefinition failed with error 62**, try running the application with the `-XVerify:none` parameter. In Eclipse, select the **Run | Run Configurations** menu and then, select the **CourseManagement** application under the **Java Application** group. Go to the **Arguments** tab, and add `-Xverify:none` to **VM arguments**. Run the application again.

In the VisualVM **Profiler** page, click on the **Settings** checkbox to see the packages included for profiling. Note that VisualVM selects these packages automatically.

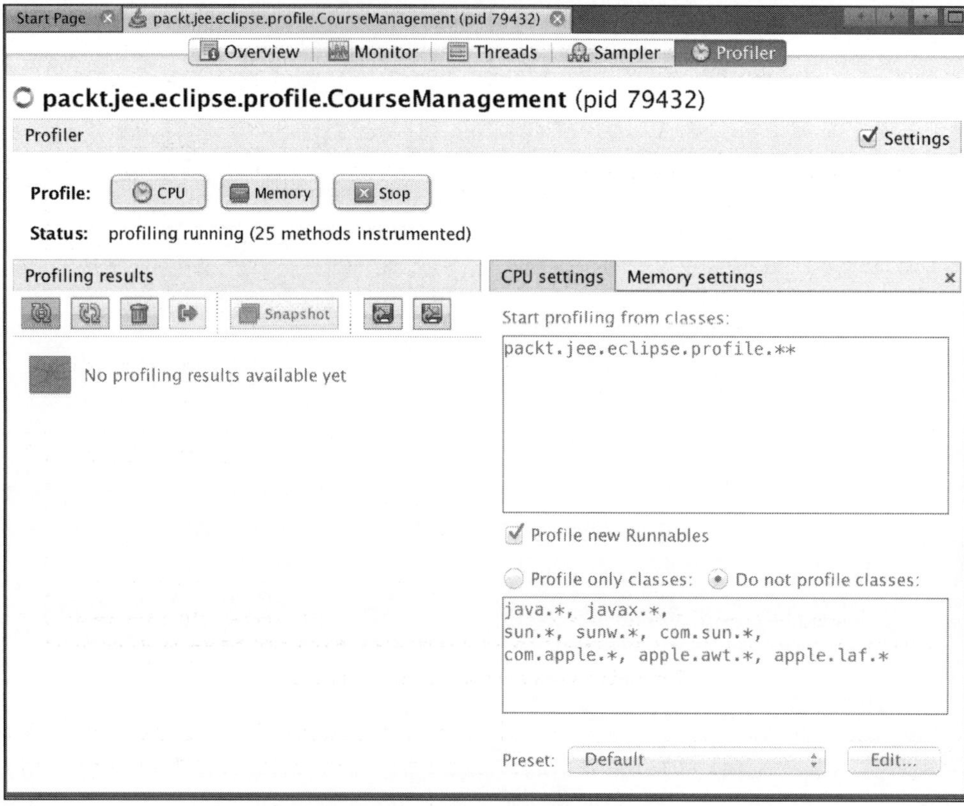

Figure 11.4 VisualVM Profiler settings

You must stop CPU profiling to edit settings. However, we will retain the default settings. Uncheck the **Settings** box to hide the settings.

Click on the **Monitor** table for the overview of profiling activities.

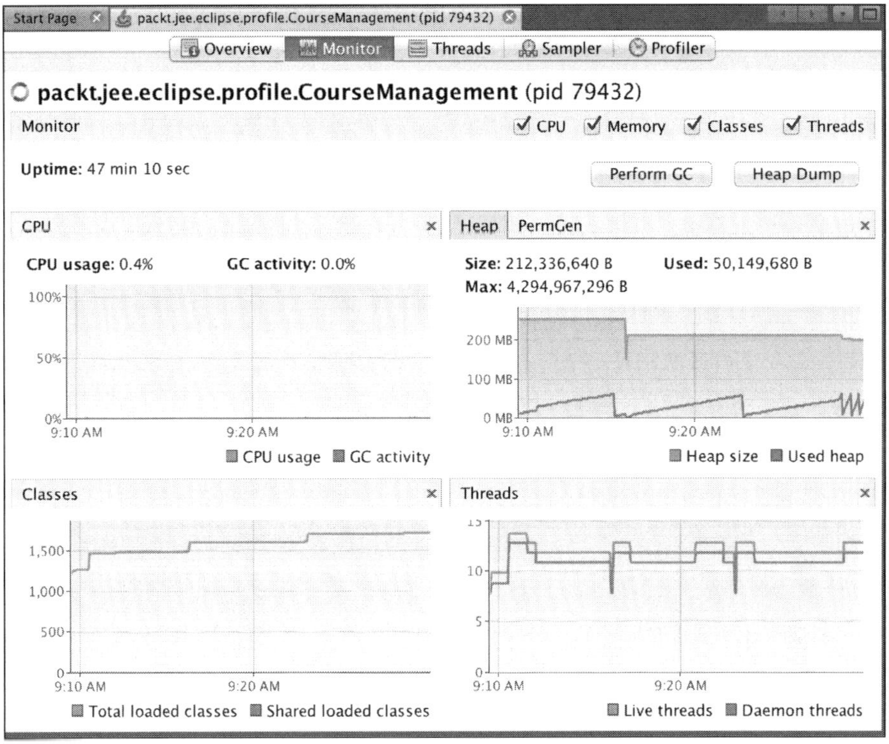

Figure 11.5 Overview of profiling activities

Now, let's execute the `getCourse` method in our application. Go to the console view of Eclipse in which our application is running, type a character (other than `q`), and hit *Enter*. Go to the **Profiler** tab of VisualVM to view the profiled data.

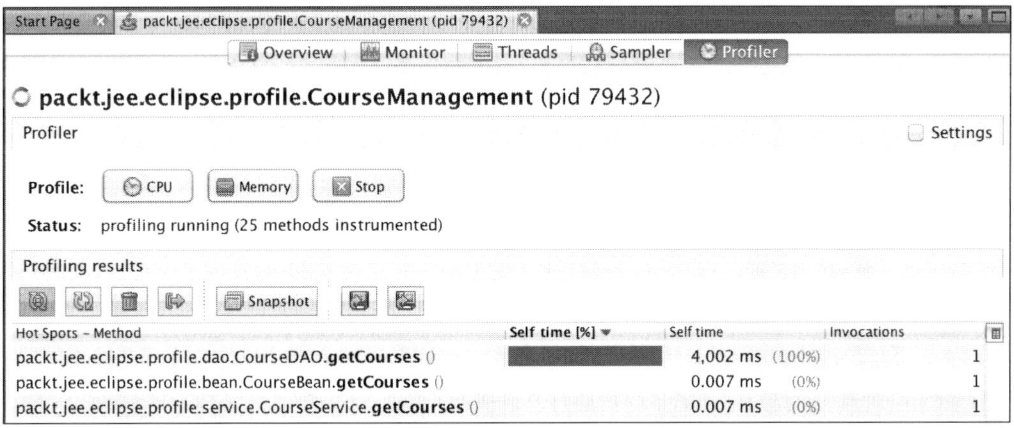

Figure 11.6 CPU profiling of CourseManagement

Observe the **Self time** column. This indicates the CPU time or the elapsed time required to execute the corresponding method, excluding the time required to execute methods called from this method. In our case, `CourseDAO.getCourses` took the maximum time, so it is at the top of the list. This report could help you identify the bottlenecks in your application.

Identifying resource contention

In a multithreaded application, it is typical for threads to lock or wait for a lock. The thread dump could be used for identifying resource contentions. Let's simulate this scenario in our application by modifying the main method of the `CourseManagement` class to call `courseBean.getCourses` in separate threads.

```
public class CourseManagement {

  public static void main(String[] args) throws IOException {

    final CourseBean courseBean = new CourseBean();

    System.out.println("Type any character to get courses. Type q
    to quit.");

    int ch, threadIndex = 0;
    while ((ch = System.in.read()) != -1) {
      if (ch != 10 && ch != 13) { //ignore new lines
        if (ch == 'q') //quit if user types q
          break;

        threadIndex++; //used for naming the thread
        Thread getCourseThread = new Thread("getCourseThread" +
        threadIndex)
{

          @Override
          public void run() {
            System.out.println("Getting courses");
            courseBean.getCourses();
            System.out.println("Got courses");
          }
        };

        //Set this thread as Daemon so that the application can exit
        //immediately when user enters 'q'
```

```
          getCourseThread.setDaemon(true);

          getCourseThread.start();

          System.out.println("Type any character to get courses.
          Type q to quit.");
        }
      }

      System.out.println("Quitting ...");
    }
  }
```

Note that we create a new Thread object in the while loop and call courseBean.getCourses in the run method of the thread. The while loop does not wait for getCourses to return results and can process the next user input immediately. This will allow us to simulate a resource contention.

To actually cause a resource contention, let's synchronize CourseService.getCourses.

```
public class CourseService {

  private CourseDAO courseDAO = new CourseDAO();

  public synchronized List<CourseDTO> getCourses() {
    return courseDAO.getCourses();
  }
 }
```

The synchronized getCourses method will result in only one thread executing this method in an instance of the CourseService class. We can now trigger multiple getCourses calls simultaneously by typing characters in the console without waiting for the previous call to the getCourse method to return. To give us more time to get the thread dump, let's increase the thread sleep time in CourseDAO.getCourses to say 30 s.

```
public class CourseDAO {

  public List<CourseDTO> getCourses() {
    //No real database access takes place here.
    //We will just simulate a long-running database operation

    try {
      Thread.sleep(30000); //wait 30 seconds
    } catch (InterruptedException e) {
```

```
            e.printStackTrace();
        }

        //return dummy/empty list
        return new ArrayList<>();
    }
}
```

Run the application and start monitoring this process in VisualVM. In the console window where the application is running in Eclipse, type a character and press *Enter*. Repeat this one more time. Now, two calls to `getCourses` would be triggered. In VisualVM, go to the **Threads** tab and click the **Thread Dump** button. A new thread dump is saved under the process node and is displayed in a new tab. Look for threads starting with the `getCourseThread` prefix. Here is a sample thread dump of two `getCourseThreads`:

```
"getCourseThread2" daemon prio=6 tid=0x000000001085b800 nid=0x34f8
waiting for monitor entry [0x0000000013aef000]
   java.lang.Thread.State: BLOCKED (on object monitor)
  at
packt.jee.eclipse.profile.service.CourseService.
getCourses(CourseService.java:13)
  - waiting to lock <0x00000007aaf57a80> (a
packt.jee.eclipse.profile.service.CourseService)
  at packt.jee.eclipse.profile.bean.CourseBean.getCourses(CourseBean.
java:12)
  at packt.jee.eclipse.profile.CourseManagement$1.
run(CourseManagement.java:27)

   Locked ownable synchronizers:
  - None

"getCourseThread1" daemon prio=6 tid=0x000000001085a800 nid=0x2738
waiting on condition [0x000000001398f000]
   java.lang.Thread.State: TIMED_WAITING (sleeping)
  at java.lang.Thread.sleep(Native Method)
  at packt.jee.eclipse.profile.dao.CourseDAO.getCourses(CourseDAO.
java:15)
  at packt.jee.eclipse.profile.service.CourseService.
getCourses(CourseService.java:13)
  - locked <0x00000007aaf57a80> (a packt.jee.eclipse.profile.service.
CourseService)
  at packt.jee.eclipse.profile.bean.CourseBean.getCourses(CourseBean.
java:12)
```

```
    at packt.jee.eclipse.profile.CourseManagement$1.
run(CourseManagement.java:27)

     Locked ownable synchronizers:
    - None
```

From the preceding thread dumps, it is clear that `getCourseThread2` is waiting (to lock <0x00000007aaf57a80>) and `getCourseThread1` is holding lock on the same object (locked <0x00000007aaf57a80>).

Using the same technique (of inspecting locks), you can also detect deadlocks in the application. In fact, VisualVM can detect deadlocks and explicitly point to threads that are deadlocked. Let's modify the `main` method in the `CourseManagement` class to cause a deadlock. We will create two threads and make them lock two objects in the reverse order.

> **WARNING**: The following code will cause the application to hang. You will have to kill the process to exist.

```
public static void main(String[] args) throws IOException {

  System.out.println("Type any character and Enter to cause
  deadlock - ");
  System.in.read();

  final Object obj1 = new Object(), obj2 = new Object();

  Thread th1 = new Thread("MyThread1") {
    public void run() {
      synchronized (obj1) {
        try {
          sleep(2000);
        } catch (InterruptedException e) {
          e.printStackTrace();
        }

        synchronized (obj2) {
          //do nothing
        }
      }
    }
  };

  Thread th2 = new Thread("MyThread2") {
    public void run() {
      synchronized (obj2) {
```

```
            try {
              sleep(2000);
            } catch (InterruptedException e) {
              e.printStackTrace();
            }

            synchronized (obj1) {

            }
          }
        }
      };


      th1.start();
      th2.start();
```

`MyThread1` first locks `obj1` and then it tries to lock `obj2`, whereas `MyThread2` locks `obj2` first and then tries to lock `obj1`. When you monitor this application by using VisualVM and switch to the **Threads** tab, you would see the **Deadlock detected!** message.

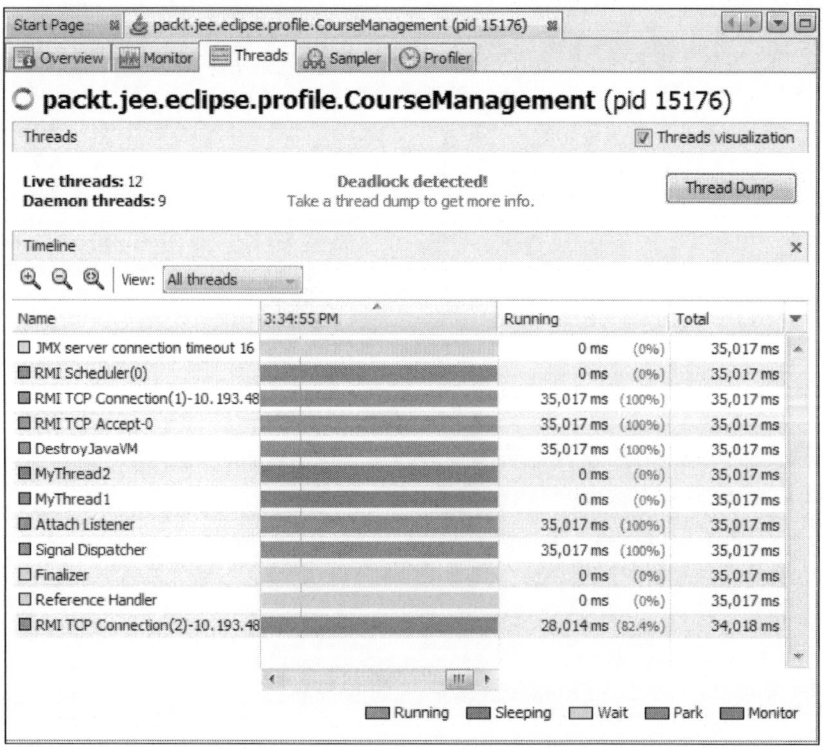

Figure 11.7 Detecting deadlock with VisualVM

If you take the thread dump, it will specifically show you where the deadlock is caused:

```
Found one Java-level deadlock:
=============================
"MyThread2":
  waiting to lock monitor 0x000000000f6f71a8 (object
0x00000007aaf56538, a java.lang.Object),
  which is held by "MyThread1"
"MyThread1":
  waiting to lock monitor 0x000000000f6f4a78 (object
0x00000007aaf56548, a java.lang.Object),
  which is held by "MyThread2"
```

Memory tracking

VisualVM can be used to monitor memory allocations and to detect the possible memory leaks. Let's modify our application to simulate a large memory allocation that is not released. We will modify the `CourseService` class.

```
public class CourseService {

  private CourseDAO courseDAO = new CourseDAO();

  //Dummy cached data used only to simulate large
  //memory allocation
  private byte[] cachedData = null;

  public synchronized List<CourseDTO> getCourses() {

    //To simulate large memory allocation,
    //let's assume we are reading serialized cached data
    //and storing it in the cachedData member
    try {
      this.cachedData = generateDummyCachedData();
    } catch (IOException e) {
      //ignore
    }

    return courseDAO.getCourses();
  }

  private byte[] generateDummyCachedData() throws IOException {
    ByteArrayOutputStream byteStream = new ByteArrayOutputStream();
```

```
        byte[] dummyData = "Dummy cached data".getBytes();

        //write 100000 times
        for (int i = 0; i < 100000; i++)
          byteStream.write(dummyData);

        byte[] result = byteStream.toByteArray();
        byteStream.close();
        return result;
      }
    }
```

In the `getCourses` method, we create a large byte array and store it in a member variable. The memory allocated to the array would not be released till an instance of `CourseService` is not garbage collected. Now, let's see how this memory allocation shows up in VisualVM. Start monitoring the process, and go to the **Profiler** tab. Click the **Memory** button to start monitoring memory. Now, go back to the console window in Eclipse and enter a character to trigger the `getCourses` method. Go back to VisualVM to inspect the memory profiling report.

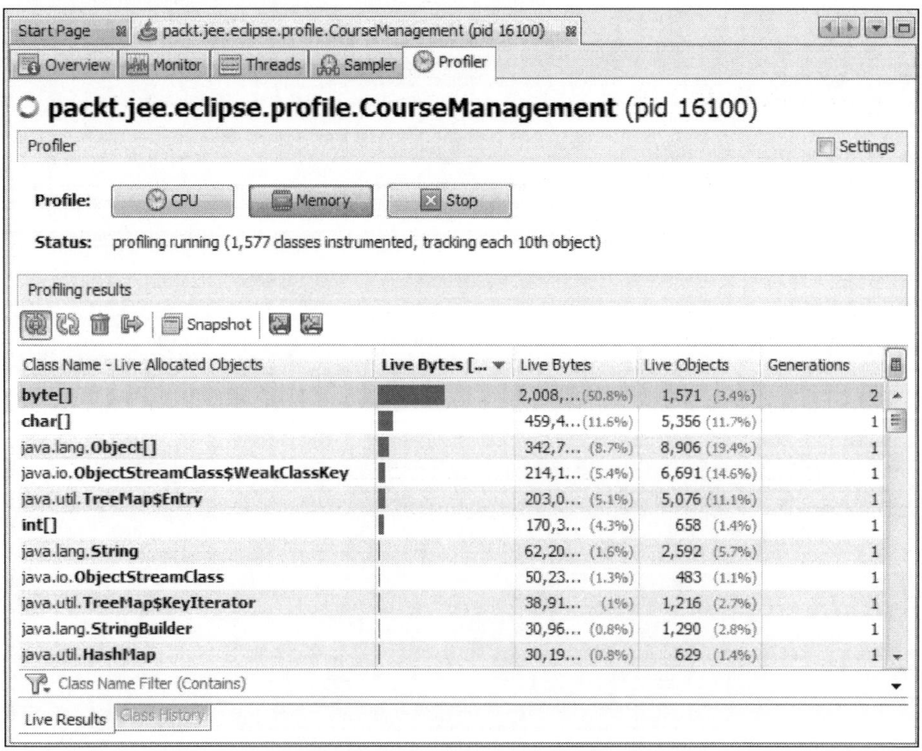

Figure 11.8 Memory monitoring with VisualVM

This report is useful for seeing the live status of the memory consumed by different objects in the application. However, if you want to analyze and find where exactly the allocation is made, then take a heap dump. Go to the **Monitor** tab, and click the **Heap Dump** button. A heap dump report is saved under the process node. Click on the **Classes** button in the heap dump report and then, on the **Size** column to sort objects in the descending order of the amount of memory consumed.

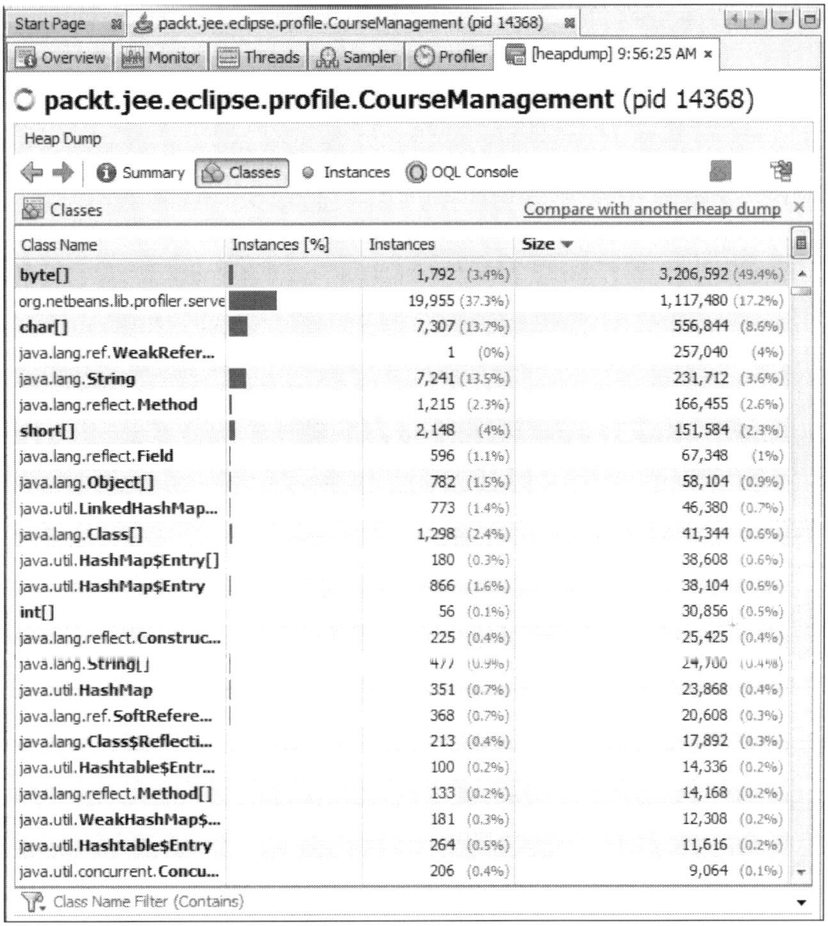

Figure 11.9 Classes in heap dump report

According to the report, `byte[]` takes up the maximum memory in our application. To find where the memory is allocated, double-click on the row containing `byte[]`.

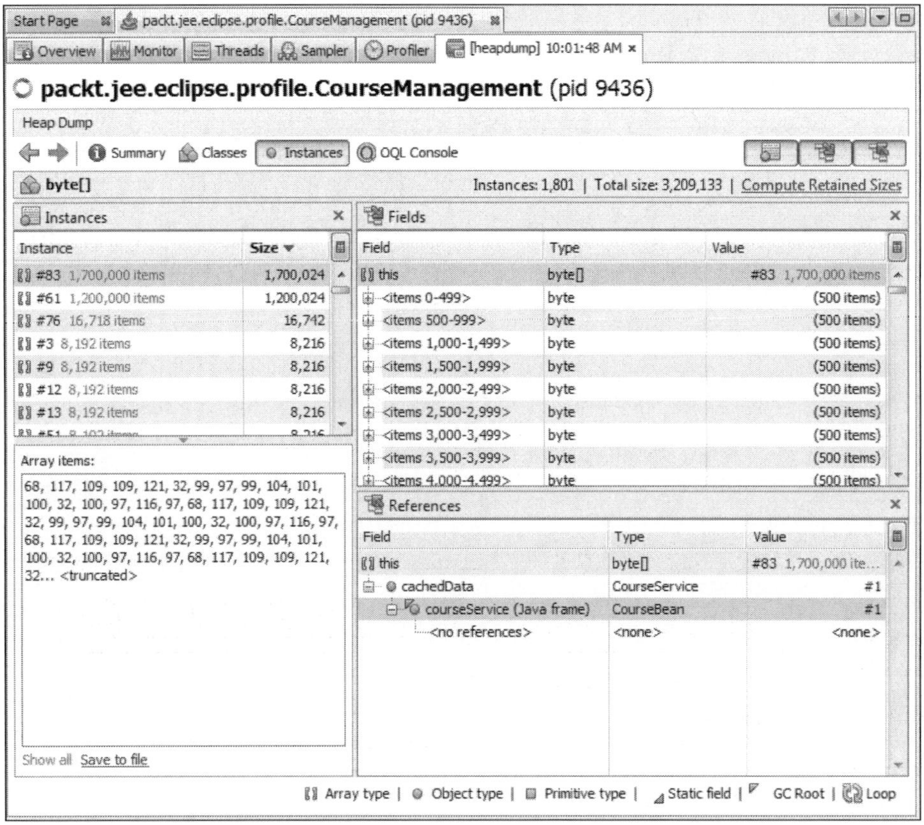

Figure 11.10 Object instance report in heap dump

The references window at the bottom-right shows objects holding a reference to the selected instance in the top-left window. As you can see, a reference to `byte[]` is held by the `cachedData` field of `CourseServe`. Further, a reference to `CourseService` is held by `CourseBean`.

Large memory allocation does not necessarily mean a memory leak. You may want to keep a reference to a large object in your applications. However, the heap dump can help you find where the memory was allocated and if that instance is intended to be in the memory. If not, you could find where the memory was allocated and release it at the appropriate place.

The heap dump that we have taken will be lost if we restart VisualVM. Therefore, save it to the disk; to do so, right-click on the **Heap Dump** node and select **Save As**. We will use this heap dump in Eclipse Memory Analyzer in the next section.

Eclipse plugins for profiling memory

Eclipse Memory Analyzer (`https://eclipse.org/mat/`) can be used to analyze a heap dump created by VisualVM. It provides additional features such as auto memory leak detection. Further, by using it as an Eclipse plugin, you can quickly jump to the source code from the heap dump reports. You can use this tool either as a standalone application or as an Eclipse plugin. We will see how to use it as an Eclipse plugin in this section.

To install the Memory Analyzer plugin, open **Eclipse Marketplace** (select the **Help | Eclipse Marketplace** menu). Search for `Memory Analyzer` and install the plugin.

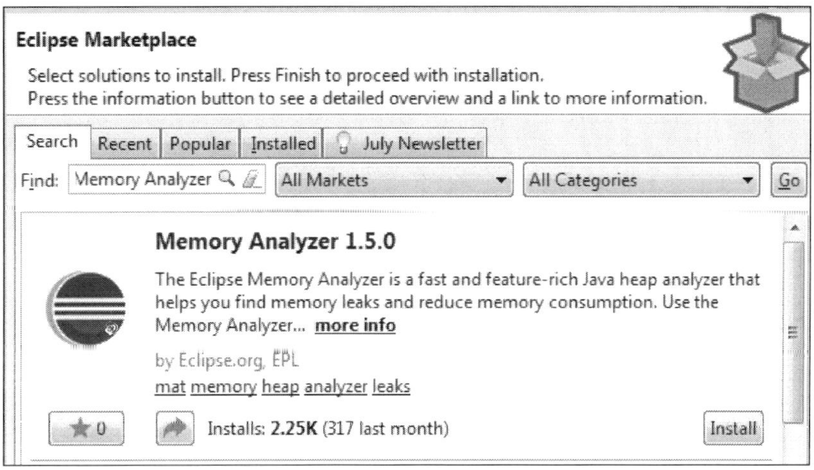

Figure 11.11 Search Memory Analyzer plugin in Eclipse Marketplace

Once you install the plugin, open the heap dump that you saved in the previous section by using VisualVM. Select the **File** | **Open File** menu and select the `.hprof` file saved by VisualVM. Memory Analyzer will prompt you to select a report type:

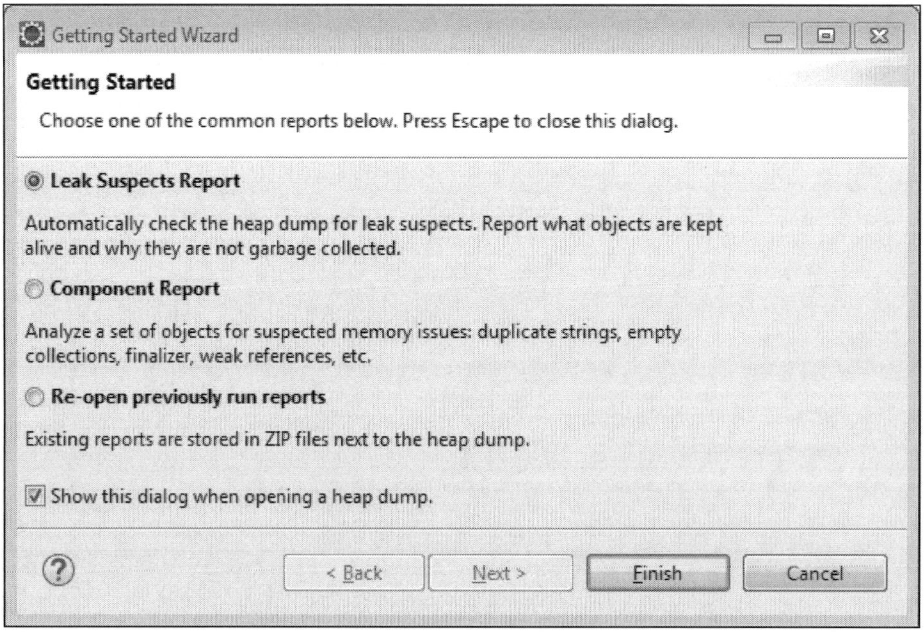

Figure 11.12 Eclipse Memory Analyzer: Getting Started Wizard

Select **Leak Suspects Report** and click **Finish**. Eclipse Memory Analyzer creates the **Leak Suspects** report with a couple of **Problem Suspects**.

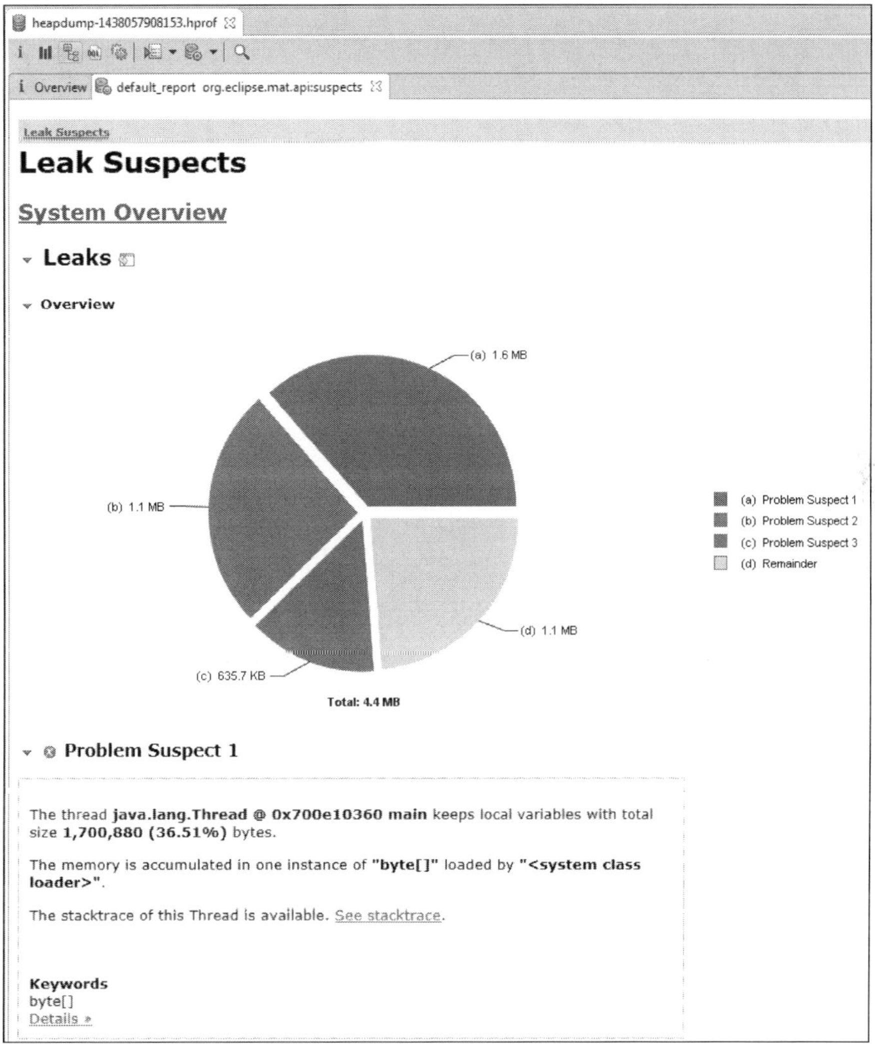

Figure 11.13 Eclipse Memory Analyzer: Leak Suspect report

Click on the **Details** link in the first **Problem Suspect**.

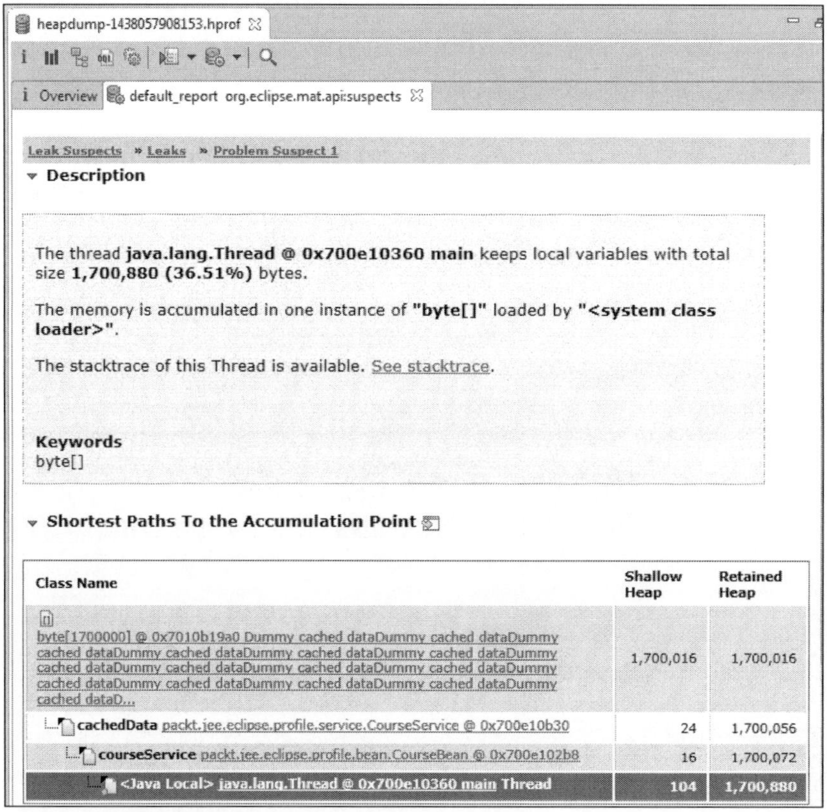

Figure 11.14 Eclipse Memory Analyzer: Details of Problem Suspect

The report clearly identifies `cachedData` in `CourseService` as a leak suspect. To open the source file, click on a node and select the **Open Source File** option.

Memory Analyzer also provides many other useful reports. Refer to `http://help.eclipse.org/mars/index.jsp?topic=/org.eclipse.mat.ui.help/welcome.html` for details.

Summary

The VisualVM tool shipped with JDK 6 and above is useful for detecting performance bottlenecks and memory leaks.

In this chapter, we discussed how to use this tool in a simple Java application. However, the technique could be used in large applications too. Eclipse Memory Analyzer can be used to quickly detect memory leaks from a heap dump.

Index

D

E

F

G

H

I

J

L

M

O

P

Q

R

S

T

U

[PACKT] open source
community experience distilled
PUBLISHING

Thank you for buying

Java EE Development with Eclipse

Second Edition

About Packt Publishing

Packt, pronounced 'packed', published its first book, *Mastering phpMyAdmin for Effective MySQL Management*, in April 2004, and subsequently continued to specialize in publishing highly focused books on specific technologies and solutions.

Our books and publications share the experiences of your fellow IT professionals in adapting and customizing today's systems, applications, and frameworks. Our solution-based books give you the knowledge and power to customize the software and technologies you're using to get the job done. Packt books are more specific and less general than the IT books you have seen in the past. Our unique business model allows us to bring you more focused information, giving you more of what you need to know, and less of what you don't.

Packt is a modern yet unique publishing company that focuses on producing quality, cutting-edge books for communities of developers, administrators, and newbies alike. For more information, please visit our website at `www.packtpub.com`.

About Packt Open Source

In 2010, Packt launched two new brands, Packt Open Source and Packt Enterprise, in order to continue its focus on specialization. This book is part of the Packt Open Source brand, home to books published on software built around open source licenses, and offering information to anybody from advanced developers to budding web designers. The Open Source brand also runs Packt's Open Source Royalty Scheme, by which Packt gives a royalty to each open source project about whose software a book is sold.

Writing for Packt

We welcome all inquiries from people who are interested in authoring. Book proposals should be sent to `author@packtpub.com`. If your book idea is still at an early stage and you would like to discuss it first before writing a formal book proposal, then please contact us; one of our commissioning editors will get in touch with you.

We're not just looking for published authors; if you have strong technical skills but no writing experience, our experienced editors can help you develop a writing career, or simply get some additional reward for your expertise.

[PACKT] open source
community experience distilled
PUBLISHING

Java EE 7 Development with WildFly

ISBN: 978-1-78217-198-0 Paperback: 434 pages

Leverage the power of the WildFly application server from JBoss to develop modern Java EE 7 applications

1. Develop Java EE 7 applications using the WildFly platform.
2. Discover how to manage your WildFly production environment.
3. A step-by-step tutorial guide to help you get a firm grip on WildFly to create engaging applications.

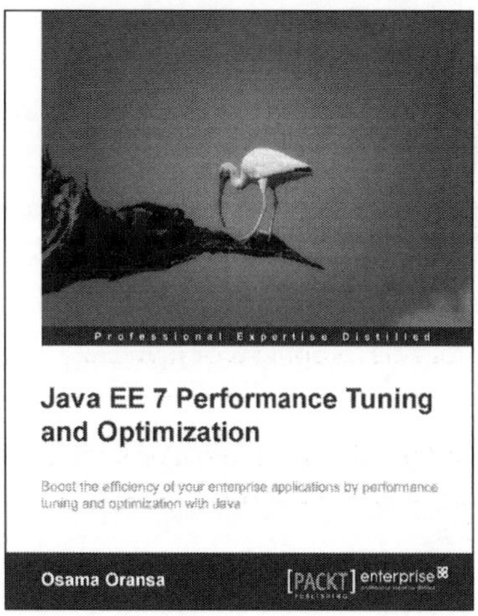

Java EE 7 Performance Tuning and Optimization

ISBN: 978-1-78217-642-8 Paperback: 478 pages

Boost the efficiency of your enterprise applications by performance tuning and optimization with Java

1. Learn to plan a performance investigation in enterprise applications.
2. Build a performance troubleshooting strategy.
3. Design and implement high performing Java enterprise applications.

Please check **www.PacktPub.com** for information on our titles

[PACKT] open source
community experience distilled
PUBLISHING

Advanced Java® EE Development with WildFly®

ISBN: 978-1-78328-890-8 Paperback: 416 pages

Your one-stop guide to developing Java® EE applications with the Eclipse IDE, Maven, and WildFly® 8.1

1. Develop Java EE 7 applications using the WildFly platform.
2. Discover how to use EJB 3.x, JSF 2.x, Ajax, JAX-RS, JAX-WS, and Spring with WildFly 8.1.
3. A practical guide filled with easy-to-understand programming examples to help you gain hands-on experience with Java EE development using WildFly.

Java EE 7 Development with NetBeans 8

ISBN: 978-1-78398-352-0 Paperback: 364 pages

Develop professional enterprise Java EE applications quickly and easily with this popular IDE

1. Use the features of the popular NetBeans IDE to accelerate your development of Java EE applications.
2. Covers the latest versions of the major Java EE APIs such as JSF 2.2, EJB 3.2, JPA 2.1, CDI 1.1, and JAX-RS 2.0.
3. Walks you through the development of applications utilizing popular JSF component libraries such as PrimeFaces, RichFaces, and ICEfaces.

Please check **www.PacktPub.com** for information on our titles